'Nick Spencer ranges stylis[...] Augustine's landing in Kent t[...] [...] documenting how this realm [...] England was a biblically based [...] even before the realm of England was invented. Clarity [...] rning lightly worn make this book stand out from the herd [...] year celebrating King James's contribution to biblical [...] tion.'

[...] aid MacCulloch, Professor of the History of the Church, [...] sity of Oxford.

[...] nyone freshly curious to understand that jagged and some- [...] bloodstained terrain between religion and politics, Church [...] tate in these islands, this is the book for you. Nick Spencer is [...] e historical cartographer of that landscape; a guide of fluency and judgement for those who wish to cross it from the seventh co [...] iry to the present day.'

Lor[d] Peter Hennessy, Attlee Professor of Contemporary British H[ist]ory, Queen Mary, University of London.

'In [...] book that somehow manages to be both sweeping and concise, Ni[ck] Spencer demonstrates just how much the political culture of Br[ita]in owes to that massive seedbed of ideas – the Bible.'

To[m] Holland, historian and author of *Rubicon*.

Freedom and Order

History, Politics and the English Bible

NICK SPENCER

HODDER

First published in Great Britain in 2011 by Hodder & Stoughton
An Hachette UK company
This paperback edition first published in 2012

1

Copyright © Nick Spencer, 2011

A CIP catalogue record for this title is available from the British Library

ISBN 978 0 340 99624 9
eBook ISBN 978 1 444 70301 6

Typeset in Sabon by Hewer Text UK Ltd, Edinburgh

Printed and bound in the UK by CPI Group (UK) Ltd, Croydon CR0 4YY

Hodder & Stoughton policy is to use papers that are natural, renewable
and recyclable products and made from wood grown in sustainable
forests. The logging and manufacturing processes are expected to
conform to the environmental regulations of the country of origin.

Hodder & Stoughton Ltd
338 Euston Road
London NW1 3BH

www.hodderfaith.com

For KT, El and Jon

Contents

List of illustrations

Acknowledgements

Writing about the influence of the Bible on British politics is a kind of iceberg history. You are left constantly, if only vaguely, aware of the size and range of material left beneath the surface. I can only crave the readers' indulgence and ask them to judge me on what they see rather than what they do not. What they see has been immeasurably strengthened by the critical eyes applied to the text by friends, colleagues and academics. In particular I would like to thank David Bebbington, Nigel Biggar, Andrew Bradstock, Malcolm Brown, James Campbell, Jonathan Chaplin, John Coffey, Dominic Erdozain, Ann Holt, David Landrum, Brian Stanley, Stephen Tomkins and Graham Tomlin for reading through and commenting on selected chapters. I would also like to thank Andrew Atherstone, Sue Coyne, Peter Hennessy, Boyd Hilton, Richard Kershaw, Diarmaid MacCulloch, Charles Moore, Richard Roberts and Andrew Rumsey for their advice and time.

I am deeply grateful to my colleagues at Theos – Paul Bickley, Jennie Pollock and Paul Woolley – for their comments, company and friendship, and particularly thankful, as ever, to Toby Hole for yet again heroically reading through and critiquing another complete manuscript of mine and for having the courage to tell me when early drafts were really not very good.

I would like to thank Katherine Venn at Hodder & Stoughton for being so enthusiastic about the idea of a book on the Bible and politics, and for persuading me to cut when the book needed it, and Ian Metcalfe for giving me a subtitle when I was struggling with permutations.

In a book of this size and breadth there are bound to be errors. I can only hope they are few, insignificant and that the reader is willing to forgive the author for them.

Nick Spencer
London, September 2010

He that travels the roads now, applauds his own strength and legs that have carried him so far in such a scantling of time; and ascribes all to his own vigour; little considering how much he owes to their pains, who cleared the woods, drained the bogs, built the bridges, and made the ways possible.

The Reasonableness of Christianity
John Locke

Economy and politics . . . must have ground beneath themselves.
F.D. Maurice to John Ludlow, 24 September 1852

Introduction: The political Bible

Even those who hate it most are willing to praise the English Bible. 'Not to know the King James Bible is to be in some small way barbarian,' Professor Richard Dawkins remarked in 2010.[1] Dawkins was speaking for many. The English Bible, which for most people means the King James Version, cannot be praised too highly.

Richard Dawkins was also speaking for many when he explained *why* we should know and celebrate the Bible. 'You can't appreciate English literature unless you are steeped to some extent in the King James Bible,' he told the King James Bible Trust.[2] The significance of the Bible lies in its impact on our language, our literature, our culture. Not to know it – it being the King James translation – is not to know the origins and in some instances meaning of many everyday phrases such as 'my brother's keeper', 'give up the ghost', 'the skin of my teeth', 'the writing on the wall', 'the salt of the earth', 'eat, drink and be merry'.[3]

Its relevance extends beyond eloquent phrases. Not to know the Bible is to obscure large tracts of English literature. How can you hope to understand *The Canterbury Tales*, *The Pilgrim's Progress*, *The Mill on the Floss*, *The Lord of the Flies*, *The Handmaid's Tale*, much of Shakespeare, most of Eliot and pretty much of all of Donne, Herbert, Milton and Hopkins without knowing the plot, characters, language and mental landscape of the Bible?[4]

The same goes for music. You may delight in the offerings of Tallis, Byrd, Bach, Fauré, Pärt or Tavener to name just some of the most obviously 'Christian' of composers, but you may delight in it more with some understanding of why and what they wrote. It's a similar story with the visual arts. Without knowing the Bible much of the work of Giotto, Donatello, Michelangelo, El Greco, Caravaggio, Jan Brueghel the Elder and Stanley Spencer will be a blank canvas as, on a humbler scale, will the architecture and art of your local parish church. All in all, not to know the Bible is to close down innumerable avenues of cultural enrichment.

Few today disagree. Yet, the story goes oddly quiet when we move from language, literature, music and art to politics. The Bible may have leavened the lump of English literature but it appears to have had little impact on our political life. After all, does it not itself say that we should 'render . . . unto Caesar the things which are Caesar's; and unto God the things that are God's'?[5] Politics and the Bible do not mix; hence the deafening silence.

Coronation and parliament

And yet it is beyond serious doubt that the Bible has been central to our national politics since the earliest days. Mediated through missionaries, bishops, abbots, monks, pastors, theologians, translators, kings, councillors, peers, philosophers, politicians, campaigners, factory workers and farmhands, the Bible has been the single most influential text in British political history.

If we seek the origins of the belief that rulers should face judgement for the extent to which they served, or failed to serve, the common good – keeping the peace, judging justly, protecting the weak – then we will find ourselves digging around among biblical roots. If we want to understand the supposedly self-evident truth that the king should be subject to the same laws as his subjects, or to trace the development of the idea that it is legitimate for the people to resist, even to overthrow, their ruler, we will need to do the same. If we hope to understand where the doctrine of toleration came from and how it was justified, or our conviction that all humans are of equal worth and its political consequences, or even how 'England' and 'Britain' came to be political identities in the first place, we need to look to the Bible.

Such apparently ambitious claims may be supported by two concrete examples that could hardly be more central to our political tradition, the coronation and the Houses of Parliament. The coronation has its origins in a service first used in 973.[6] Although modified greatly since then, it retains the same basic structure, being located in a Christian church, presided over by a Christian minister and based on the service of the Eucharist.

According to the most recent precedent, from 2 June 1953, the service, which is held in Westminster Abbey, begins with the choir singing an anthem based on Psalm 122.[7] Once seated, the monarch promises, among other things, to 'maintain the Laws of God and the true profession of the Gospel' and to uphold the cause of law, justice and mercy.[8] She is presented with a copy of the Bible ('the most valuable thing that this world affords') by the Moderator of the Church of Scotland, who says to her, 'Here is Wisdom; this is Royal Law; these are the lively Oracles of God.'

The Communion Service then begins with the words of Psalm 84.[9] It proceeds along familiar lines (prayer, readings, creed) but is interrupted by the anointing, at which the hymn 'Veni, Creator Spiritus' is sung. The queen is anointed with oil just as 'Zadok the Priest, and Nathan the Prophet anointed Solomon [the] King,' in the words of Handel's anthem 'Zadok the Priest', which has been sung at every coronation since 1727.[10] She is presented with the orb, with the words, 'Remember that the whole world is subject to the Power and Empire of Christ our Redeemer.' She is invested with the coronation ring, with the words, 'Receive the ring of kingly dignity, and the seal of Catholic Faith . . . may you continue steadfastly as the Defender of Christ's Religion.' She receives the sceptre with the cross, 'the ensign of kingly power and justice'. And she is given the rod 'of equity and mercy', marked by the dove, the symbol of the Holy Spirit.

At the coronation itself the Archbishop of Canterbury says, 'God crown you with a crown of glory and righteousness, that having a right faith and manifold fruit of good works, you may obtain the crown of an everlasting kingdom by the gift of him whose kingdom endureth forever.' Following this, there is the Benediction, Enthroning and Homage, after which the ceremony returns to the Communion Service, with the queen receiving the bread and wine, the archbishop pronouncing a blessing and the choir singing 'Gloria in Excelsis' and finally, *Te Deum*. Whatever one might think of all this, it would be difficult to understand it without reference to the Bible.

The second example comes from just over the road. The House of Commons is steeped in Christian symbolism. The Central Lobby hosts mosaics of the patron saints of the four constituent parts of the United Kingdom. On its tiled floor there is the Latin text of Psalm

127:1, 'Except the Lord build the house, they labour in vain that build it.' The Latin text of Proverbs 21:1, 'The king's heart is in the hand of the Lord,' is in the floor tiles of the Royal Gallery. The text of 1 Peter 2:17 – 'Fear God. Honour the King' – is in the floor of the Commons Lobby, as is that of Proverbs 11:14, 'Where no counsel is, the people fall: but in the multitude of counsellors there is safety.' Understanding the Houses of Parliament without knowing the Bible would hardly be easier than understanding the coronation.

It is important to acknowledge at the outset that none of this is to claim that the Bible has been the *only* influence on our political system, or that British politics is shaped by Christianity alone. Nor is it to claim that the contribution of the Bible to national politics has always been a positive one. Rather, the central claim of this book is that just as it is impossible to appreciate or understand English literature fully without recourse to the Bible, so it is impossible to understand the nation's politics.

A political story

The reasons for our modern theo-political deafness are far from clear and we shall return to them at the end of the book. What can be said for sure is that they are not because of the Bible itself.

In 2009 the *Sunday Times* published a review of two books by the distinguished Jewish New Testament historian Geza Vermes. At one point in the article the reviewer wrote: 'Jesus' main concern was healing the sick, comforting the poor and preaching about the coming of the Kingdom of God. He had no interest in politics, revolution or theology.' It is a remarkable statement. The idea that 'Kingdom' is not a political term, 'God' is not a theological term, and preaching about the 'coming' of both is not a revolutionary act (however we understand that phrase) is somewhat strange, to say the least.

The truth is that the Bible is a thoroughly, uncompromisingly, almost obsessively political book. 'When you read the Bible or hear it read in churches or chapels attend to its politics!' exhorted early nine-teenth-century Christian radicals.[11] The problem is that its politics are complex and unpredictable in a way that helps to explain our contemporary deafness to its political nature and also the sheer range of political meanings that have been drawn from it throughout our history.

The Old Testament comprises thirty-nine accepted or 'canonical' books and tells the story of the people of Israel, formed, rescued, delivered, warned, protected, punished and restored by God.[12] Israel traced its origins back to a single, wealthy pastoralist Abram, subsequently renamed Abraham,[13] and traced its name to his grandson, Jacob, who was renamed Israel, meaning 'he struggles with God', after an all-night wrestling match with a mysterious stranger.[14] The nation was properly formed, however, many centuries later, from a position of political powerlessness when God saw and rescued his people from slavery in Egypt. Their escape was accompanied by the giving of the law ('torah'), an extensive and often highly detailed account of how the nation should live, both individually and corporately, how it should worship God and, in one highly significant passage for our story, what limits should be placed on royal power. God jealously guarded his liberated people, insisting they be kept 'holy' or separate from other nations, in order that they might be a 'light' to them. The Bible's first five books – Genesis, Exodus, Leviticus, Numbers and Deuteronomy – tell this story of origin, call, rescue and law but begin with a series of stories that deal with events on a bigger canvas, such as the creation of the world and the human condition, which would also have massive political consequences.

The following two books, Joshua and Judges, outline the first 200 or so years of the nation's life. They detail the brutal, but only partial, conquest of Canaan and the attempt to establish a stable tribal confederacy, ruled by non-hereditary, charismatic leaders or 'judges' chosen by God. Around 1000 BC (not that the Bible itself offers any such clear timeframe) one of these leaders, Saul, was chosen to be king. The 'elders of Israel' had petitioned the prophet Samuel for a monarch, against Saul's wishes, Samuel's and God's.[15] The reign was not a success, at least according to the author of 1 Samuel in which it is recorded. His successor, David, became the nation's pre-eminent monarch, a king after God's own heart, in spite of his adultery with Bathsheba and murder of her husband Uriah.[16] During his reign, the nation was unified and attained unprecedented wealth and power, an achievement that continued into the time of his son, Solomon, who succeeded where David had failed and built the national temple to God. This part of Israel's story is recounted primarily in the history books 1 and 2 Samuel and 1 Chronicles and was looked back on as a golden age, in which kingship was united with godliness, security and wealth.

Following Solomon's death the nation split into two, Israel in the north and Judah in the south. Both kingdoms were marked by a more or less constant stream of venal or backsliding monarchs, with only a few, such as Hezekiah or Josiah, earning the Bible's praise. In 722 BC, the northern kingdom, Israel, was conquered by the Assyrian Empire and 130 years later the southern one, Judah, suffered the same fate, this time at the hands of the Babylonians. The woeful history of wicked rulers, national apostasy, prophetic judgement and apparent abandonment by God is recounted in 1 and 2 Kings and 2 Chronicles, and also in the many books of prophecy that were included in the Old Testament canon. It was to leave behind it a tradition of political criticism and confrontation that would prove as significant as the more positive royal history of David and Solomon. The northern kingdom was never to be resurrected but within seventy or so years the exiles from Judah returned home. Return did not, however, entail a return to political autonomy and, with the exception of a century-long interlude after a revolt in 167 BC,[17] the people of Israel were ruled by a succession of Persian, Greek, Syrian and then Roman overlords. The time of God's reign was apparently past.

Except that most Jews did not think so and numerous prophets promised otherwise. Jesus Christ was born at a time of political fervour, in which many Jewish sects expected a delivering saviour or 'messiah', and some actively plotted to overthrow their political masters, usually with gruesome consequences when they invariably failed. It was into this political maelstrom that Jesus, aged around thirty according to Luke's gospel, came, preaching that the kingdom of God was at hand. A more incendiary political or revolutionary message it would be hard to imagine. In keeping with this form, he spoke and acted as if he were the messiah who was about to herald the kingdom. He forgave sins on his own authority. He taught without reference to the requisite rabbis and texts, and seemingly corrected the scriptures ('. . . but I tell you . . .'). He healed and exorcised without calling on the use of prayers or amulets. He gathered round him twelve disciples (the allusion to the original twelve tribes of Israel would have been obvious). He rode into Jerusalem in the way that the messiah was expected to. And he threatened to replace the Temple, the centre of national life and resistance. In spite of all this, it became clear that Jesus had no plans to fulfil the expected messianic role of ousting the occupiers by force. Instead, he allowed himself to be submitted to an excruciating and humiliating death that he appeared to expect and to see as consistent with God's plans. Just as announcing the kingdom of God under Roman noses could not have been much more politically antagonistic, behaving as Jesus did could not have been more religiously provocative.

Jesus' followers were devastated by his death and transformed by his resurrection. They preached in Jerusalem and then beyond, once the capital had become too dangerous a place to remain. Their message, delivered first to Jews and then to Gentiles, was the problematic idea that the crucified and risen Jesus was indeed God's promised messiah. Not surprisingly, they earned as many friends among the political authorities as Jesus had. And yet despite this, the earliest Christians were not political revolutionaries, at least in the narrow sense that we would understand the word. Indeed, they were generally respectful of the ruling authorities and the earliest extant Christian documents adopt a tone of political obedience. In certain coded contexts, such as the prophetic book of Revelation with which the Bible ends, they could be venomously critical of Rome, but for the most part they deferred to 'the powers that be'.

What should be clear from this rather brief tour of the biblical story is not only the range of documents that comprise the Christian Bible – law, historical narrative, biography and apocalypse, not to mention songs, sayings, prophecy and letters – but also the range of political situations in which the people of God found themselves. They lived as oppressed slaves;[18] as a federation of semi-independent tribes whose leaders were chosen by God's will rather than human lineage; as a united kingdom, into which they stumbled for the wrong reasons before flourishing in a blaze of power and splendour; as a disunited kingdom that endured centuries of division, disorder and defeat; as an exiled and disenfranchised people; and then as subjugated and largely disenfranchised people. Even the New Testament, far shorter than the Old and concentrated into a much briefer time-frame, offers various models of political engagement, from deference to disobedience. It is not surprising that those who looked to the Bible for political answers were to come up with more or less anything they wanted.

Freedom and order

Is there anything that might give shape to the way in which the Bible has been used politically in British history, or was it (and is it) genu-inely a free-for-all?

In one regard, it could not but be a free-for-all. It is, in effect, impossible to stop people plundering a text the size and significance of the Christian Bible for their own political ends and without refer-ence to its original meaning or legitimate interpretation. Put less cynically, how we read any text is always influenced by the context in which we read it, and the Bible is certainly no exception. When the Anglo-Saxons read it through the lens of a warrior culture and found examples of heroic bravery, they were not being any more cynical than when socially marginal Baptists read it in the seventeenth century and found ideas of toleration. Everyone reads the Bible from somewhere.

This should not be taken to mean that the reader is the author of the book, or that context is everything and content is nothing. On the contrary, there is a definite political content to the Bible. It is just that it is not straightforward. The argument of this book – beyond the contention that the Bible pervades British political history in a way that is rarely recognised – is that the Bible contains two powerful, distinct and apparently conflicting political impulses.

The first is to freedom, both the negative freedom *from* political constraints and the positive freedom *to* enable the fulfilment of inher-ent human potential. Ideas of negative freedom were derived from the story of the Exodus, the supreme icon of political liberation. They were drawn from the conditions placed upon kings in the torah. They were drawn from the origins of Israelite kingship in all its ambi-guity. They were read from the various tales of wicked Old Testament kings who angered God and were (sometimes) punished for their sins. And they were drawn from the subservience of all kings before the King of Kings, who would one day judge them for the way in which they discharged the divinely set obligations of their office. If the biblical thrust towards negative freedom has a proof text it is Acts 5:29, on which Reformers eager to find a biblical warrant for resistance seized: 'we ought to obey God rather than men.'

Ideas of positive freedom were closely linked to those of negative freedom. Thus the divine judgement that implicitly limited royal authority, also presented kings with the duty to secure the safety, peace, justice and common wealth of their people. The frequent injunctions in the Old Testament to care for society's weakest were repeatedly used as a yardstick against which rulers were measured. When Christ told his audience in Matthew 25 that whatever they did 'unto one of the least of these my brethren' – the hungry, the thirsty, the stranger, the naked, the prisoner – they did for him, he emphasised in the strongest possible terms the imperative of caring for the weak. Perhaps most influentially, the creation story of Genesis 1 told how 'God created man in his own image', an idea that did more than any other to underline human equality and dignity. The duty to secure that dignity did not rest with the king alone, of course, but he bore much of its responsibility.

The impulse to freedom, then, was a major theme and contribution of the Bible to British political thought. However, it cannot be divorced from a second, rather different impulse, the impulse towards political order. This was an idea that underpinned the sanctity of the king, his divine right and the unforgivable wickedness of rebellion. It was an idea that, when combined with the hierarchical universe of the medieval mind, underlined that everyone and everything had its rightful place in the order of creation and that to challenge it was to detune the entire cosmic order, to question God and to invite his punishment. It was an idea that was deeply antipathetic to calls for political or social freedom.

This emphasis on order was drawn from the respectful way in which both Old and New Testaments spoke about royal power. It was drawn from the way in which Old Testament kings were anointed, thereby sanctifying them with the very authority of God. It was drawn from the way in which David, even when hunted down by a tyrannical Saul and presented with the opportunity to kill him, declined, saying he could never lay his hand on God's anointed. It was drawn from the fact that Israel's glory days were synonymous with kingship. It was drawn from Christ's recognition that Caesar had a right to what he was due. And it was drawn from the exceptionally high level of respect that the earliest Christians had towards political authority. If this biblical thrust towards political order has a proof text it is Romans 13:1: 'Everyone must submit himself to the governing authorities, for there is no authority except that which God has established.'

There is no doubt that, intertwined as these two impulses have been throughout British political history, it is the latter one, towards order, that has had the upper hand. There is also no doubt that it is this impulse to order that our liberated age is most liable to see as unforgivably authoritarian. There is no denying that authoritarianism, but modern readers would do well at least to try to understand it rather than condemning it out of hand. We would do well to remember that at the time when the impulse to political order was at its most authoritarian, the majority of people lived in highly flammable timber and thatched houses that were lit and heated only by fire. They subsisted one or two harvests away from starvation and a family death, or even injury, away from complete ruin. They had no police, no insurance and no meaningful medical services. They were frequently worried about the threat of invasion, attack and fifth columnists. And they believed that social or political disobedience could actually undermine the foundations of creation. It is only by entering this mental world that we can begin to understand why people placed such a premium on public order.

This kind of empathy should make the biblical impulse towards political order that was so central to former generations more understandable. But it does not make it any easier to reconcile with the impulse towards political freedom. Is it possible to square 'we ought to obey God rather than men' with 'everyone must submit himself to the governing authorities'?

The simple answer is no – at least, not fully and not here. The tension between these two impulses is profound rather than cosmetic. According to this conception of human politics, there is no endpoint, no polity, and no earthly system in which both impulses are satisfactorily served. Search for it as we might, there is no place where peace and security, justice and righteousness, freedom and order perfectly co-exist; no Utopia; no heaven on earth.

The reason for this lies in that fundamental Christian conviction of inherent human fallibility. Perfect freedom and perfect order are unrealisable because our very nature makes them unrealisable. Put another way, because humans are sinful, we are apt to abuse our freedom in a way that harms others. Although we should use our freedom for the common good, we tend not to, preferring instead, even if unconsciously, to deploy it for our own ends, even when those ends damage others. We need political order to keep us in check.

But what applies to political freedom applies also to political order. We are as liable to abuse political authority as we are freedom with even more deleterious effects. Political order, structure and authority are necessary but they too demand limitation. Thus a ruler's reign is always under law, his authority is under judgement and his power is limited, in particular by the need to respect and honour the relationship between the individual (or the Church) and God himself. It is this freedom that, historically, formed the basis of wider, political freedoms. Thus, just as political order necessarily constrains our freedom, religious and political freedom must undermine our order.

The result is a dynamic rather than a static situation. Politics never achieves a still point in the turning world because human nature will not let it. Our struggles for freedom will always need to be restrained by political order. Our emphasis on order will always need to be challenged by freedom. Only when humans themselves are transformed, in the final kingdom of God, can there possibly be a resolution to this. In the meantime we are stuck with a situation in which our twin impulses towards freedom and order struggle together.

The argument

Freedom and order, then, are the keys with which to unlock the biblical influence on British political history. This is not for a moment to say that an agonistic message of balance and tension has been the dominant one of Christian politics through the ages. It has not. Most individual Christian political thinkers have leant strongly towards one end or the other of the spectrum (mostly towards the end of political order). But the *cumulative* effect of the tradition has been agonistic, a perpetual and irreconcilable tussle between freedom and order.

This book uses the ideas of freedom and order to try to bring some pattern to that tradition. Part 1 explores the political influence of the Bible in the millennium or so before the printing of the first English Bibles. Covering such an expanse of time, when there was little to divide religious from political affairs, has necessitated an episodic approach. Chapter 1 outlines the political foundations laid in the pre-Conquest era and Chapter 2 proceeds to some of the more significant events, which in effect means conflicts, of the post-Conquest one.

Part 2 looks at what it calls the age of biblical politics and the shadow it cast. Beginning with William Tyndale translating the New Testament in the 1520s, it charts the initial, powerful movement towards authoritarianism, followed by the struggles relating to the need and justification for disobedience in the later sixteenth century. Chapter 5 follows the differing opinions as they grew more pronounced in the first half of the seventeenth century, reaching a climax in the Civil Wars and the chaos of the Interregnum, a chaos that threw up a range of seminal political ideas and, in the process, cast a long shadow over national politics, which is explored in Chapter 6.

Part 3 looks at the reassertion of the Bible in national politics from the mid-eighteenth century onwards, powered by the evangelical revival that began in the 1730s, but chastised and changed by the experience of preceding centuries. Chapter 7 examines the evangelical revival and the massive impact it had on politics from the 1780s, and in particular the way it was shaped and channelled by the French Revolution, the Napoleonic Wars and the emerging discipline of political economy. Chapter 8 follows the story through the later nineteenth century, encompassing the domestic efforts of the Seventh Earl of Shaftesbury, the impact on the British Empire and the late climax of nonconformist politics, before charting the reasons for the decline of political evangelicalism. Chapters 9 and 10 look at the tradition of Christian radicalism and socialism which, although still peripheral in the early nineteenth century, had assumed centre-stage by the early twentieth. Chapter 11 brings the story up to date, charting the slow decline of biblically informed politics in the first three-quarters of the twentieth century and then the equally slow, but rather less expected, rise in the final decades of the millennium.

Freedom and Order focuses disproportionately on English politics, a fact that demands a word of explanation. The book began as a study on British politics but it soon became clear that my focus was largely south of the border. For reasons of space, it was decided to maintain that focus rather than risk doing an injustice to Scottish, Welsh or Irish politics by dealing with them cursorily. For that reason, the 'history' and 'politics' of the subtitle refer primarily to English history and English politics. That said, 'English' remains a limited and inadequate term for all the obvious reasons. As a result, there were times, before 1707, where it was impossible to adhere rigidly to these self-imposed geographical limitations, just as there were times after it when to use the word 'English' rather than 'British' sounded arch and incorrect. Thus, while parts 1 and 2 use 'English' more or less exclusively, part 3 uses both terms. I hope confusion has been avoided and the relevant terms have been deployed accurately and appropriately throughout.

A short Postscript at the end of the book looks forward to what we might expect from the twenty-first century and asks what lessons Christians, and others, might learn from history. As mentioned above, it is a paradox of the role of the Bible in British political history that so many utterly self-confident and determined pronouncements on the imperative of either political order or political freedom should result in a cumulative tradition that is agonistic and hesitant: freedom *and* order, both necessary and irreconcilable. It is this cumulative, agonistic understanding of human politics that is perhaps the Bible's greatest gift to our national political tradition. In an age of conspicuous political scepticism born in no small measure from political hubris, it is a message we could do well to recapture.

PART I

Before the English Bible

I

'Whether you will or not, you will have him as a judge': Laying foundations

On the sixth day of rye harvest in the autumn of AD 695, Wihtred, most gracious king of the people of Kent, assembled the leading men of his kingdom at Bearsted, near Maidstone. The company was led by Brihtwold, Archbishop of Canterbury and the only primate in the country, and included 'every order of the Church [which] spoke in unanimity with the loyal people'. There, 'with the consent of all', the kingdom's leading men devised twenty-eight decrees that were to be added to the existing laws of the Kentish people. The first one ran as follows: 'The Church [is to be] free from taxation. And the king is to be prayed for, and they are to honour him of their own free-will without compulsion.'[1]

It would be hard to frame more succinctly the intimate and symbiotic relationship between Christianity and political power that would dominate national life for the next 1,300 years. Spiritual and temporal power worked together. Each reinforced the other's authority. Each legitimised the other's rule. Church and state, archbishop and king, God and Caesar were partners, of equal significance in the government of the realm.

Wihtred's laws do not quote the Bible but are self-evidently indebted to it. 'Men living in illicit cohabitation are to turn to a right life with repentance of sins, or to be excluded from the fellowship of the Church,' Clause 3 commands.[2] 'If a servant, by his lord's command, do servile work between sunset on Saturday evening and sunset on Sunday evening, his lord is to pay 80 shillings,' says Clause 9.[3] Sexual morality, Sabbath observance, fasting, the rule of law over lord and servant alike – all were rooted, ultimately, in biblical teaching.

Much the same can be said of the only surviving laws from any other contemporary English kingdom, the West Saxons.[4] These begin with the significant prologue, 'Ine, by the grace of God, King of the West Saxons . . .', and declare in their opening clause, 'First we enjoin that the servants of God observe their proper rule.' They proceed to deal with baptism, observing the Sabbath and rights of sanctuary.[5] King Ine, like his contemporary Wihtred, was advised by 'a great assembly of the servants of God' and was just as concerned to legislate according to his kingdom's new Christian faith.

Two centuries later, King Alfred's laws are explicit about their biblical debt.[6] Alfred was determined to invigorate the ecclesiastical, educational and moral life of his kingdom. The Viking invasions that dominated his reign were seen as a sign of divine judgement. God's help was essential for victory and although nothing could force the Almighty's hand, he would surely be more likely to look favourably on a nation that knew and obeyed his laws.[7] Alfred personally contributed to this task. His biographer, Asser, describes how the king 'listen[ed] eagerly and attentively to Holy Scripture being read out by his own countrymen', and never ceased from 'personally giving . . . instruction in all virtuous behaviour and tutelage in literacy'.[8] He translated a number of classic Christian texts and scoured the country for learned men to edify the West Saxon court. He helped establish a court school that would educate his children, those of other noblemen 'and a good many of lesser birth as well'.[9] In his preface to Gregory's *Pastoral Rule* he even proclaimed his intention to translate into the vernacular 'certain books' that all men should know, 'so that all free-born young men now in England who have the means to apply themselves to it, may be set to learning . . . until the time that they can read English writings properly'.[10] The scheme for universal education of free men in the vernacular was abortive but there is no reason to doubt its seriousness. Gregory's *Pastoral Rule* emphasised how a bishop needed to be learned if he were to teach his flock and Alfred believed this applied to temporal authorities too.

It was in this context that Alfred's law code, issued towards the end of his reign, should be understood. The code itself is long and without any obvious structure. In an introduction that takes up about a fifth of the entire work, Alfred writes how he 'collected these [earlier law codes] together and ordered to be written many of them which our forefathers observed, which I liked'. The code illustrates an explicit and repeated biblical basis.[11] The introduction begins with the Ten Commandments from Exodus 20 and sixty-six verses of Mosaic law from the following three chapters of Exodus.[12] It then moves from the Old Testament to the New by means of Christ's words from Matthew's gospel: 'think not that I am come to destroy the law.'[13] It explains that Christ 'had come not to shatter or annul the commandments but to fulfill them; and he taught mercy and meekness' and then quotes the golden rule, as given in Matthew 7:12, 'What you wish that other men may not do to you, do not to other men,' of which it remarks, 'A man can think on this one sentence alone, that he judges each one rightly: he has need of no other law-books.' The introduction then quotes the apostolic letter of Acts 15, the fruit of what was in effect the first church council, held at Jerusalem around the year AD 50, which advised Gentile believers to 'abstain from food sacrificed to idols, from blood, from the meat of strangled animals and from sexual immorality.'[14] The law code itself, which comprises provisions protecting the weaker members of society against oppression, limiting the ancient custom of blood-feud and emphasising the duty of a man to his lord, is less explicitly biblical but is divided in 120 chapters, 120 being the age at which Moses died,[15] the number of believers in the earliest church[16] and standing for law in the number symbolism of early medieval biblical exegetes.[17]

Historians have observed that Alfred's law code, at least as existing manuscripts preserve it, would have been of little use to a judge in court, disordered and full of contradictions as it was. It was not intended, however, to provide a comprehensive law code for English society any more than the Old Testament law on which it drew was intended to present early Israel with a constitution. Rather, Alfred's law code, like Wihtred's and Ine's before it, was intended to be powerfully symbolic, placing the king's legislative activity on a historical stage that stretched back through the early Church and Christ to Moses and the divine law itself.

Moreover, by explicitly acknowledging and integrating earlier law codes from different English kingdoms, such as Aethelbert of Kent and Offa of Mercia, this king of the West Saxons was consciously integrating the historically warring English kingdoms into a whole.[18] And he was doing so by inviting all the people to see themselves as a, even *the*, people of God. Alfred helped forge the identity of a Christian people that was defending itself against a violent, irreligious menace, in much the same way as Old Testament Israel had done. He was, in effect, forming the idea of the English people by means of biblical law and narrative, and placing them firmly within God's protection and his purposes for the world.[19]

'There are two things by which this world is ruled': the structure of power

Alfred's laws, like those of the Kentish and Mercian kings on which he drew, assumed a relationship between temporal and spiritual authority that was based on, and delineated by, Christian theology. Anglo-Saxon political thought was part of a broader tradition already over 500 years old by Alfred's time.

By the time of Alfred that tradition had divided into two distinct streams, relating to what had been the Eastern and Western Roman Empire. When the Emperor Constantine adopted Christianity in the early years of the fourth century he transformed its status. From having been a growing but marginal and sometimes persecuted minority religion, Christianity became officially recognised and protected. Constantine became a hero of the Church, with some Christians lauding him as a second Christ. The historian Eusebius articulated an extreme but not unrepresentative opinion in seeing Constantine's conversion as a turning point in world history, a fulfilment of God's promises to Abraham. Roman history, according to Eusebius, was being determined by divine providence. The empire had been founded under Augustus, in whose reign Christ had been born. Its hidden purpose had, all along, been to enable the spread of Christianity, the culmination of which came with Constantine. Accordingly, the emperor was seen as God's vicegerent on earth, ruling over an empire that reflected the very kingdom of heaven. Just as monotheism was the basis of the cosmic order, with God the single, supreme ruler of the universe, so the world was to be ruled by only one emperor, who could legitimately claim jurisdiction over all matters, including ecclesiastical ones.

Constantine had legalised Christianity but it was not until the 380s that it became the official religion of the empire. Thereafter

Church and empire formed a (theoretically) harmonious whole, the emperor deriving his authority directly from God and exercising jurisdiction over all affairs within the unified entity of Church and empire. The emperor's will constituted law. 'Let the imperial rank be exempted from all our provisions, because God has subjected the laws themselves to the emperor, by sending him as a living law to men.'[20]

This was the source from which all medieval conceptions of political power flowed. The currents of history, however, took Eastern and Western empires and ideas in different directions. Although under constant pressure from, and losing considerable territory to Islam, the Byzantine East survived. The Byzantines remained self-consciously 'Roman' and maintained the earlier Roman idea in which Church and state were indissolubly linked.[21] As a result, the Orthodox Church preserved a theo-political proximity, a tight and mutually edifying relationship between Church and state that was never again achieved in the West.

The Western empire subsided under barbarian invasions between the fourth and seventh centuries, during which period the papacy emerged as a governmental institution. Western Christendom was shaped by this disaster and, in particular, by St Augustine's *The City of God against the Pagans*, which was his response to the situation.[22] This was written in the wake of Rome's destruction in 410, although the idea of two cities, one earthly, the other eternal, predated this event in Augustine's mind by at least two decades. *The City of God* relocated the Christian's home and hopes from the earthly to heavenly realm. In doing so, it helped explain recent, seemingly calamitous events and directed political expectations away from empire and emperor, and towards a remote deliverance that was the gift of God alone.

Deflating earthly political ambitions as Augustine did, he did not do away with them altogether. The city of God co-existed with that of the people, albeit tarnished by the sins of the world, in the form of the Church, which, uniquely, emerged standing from the ruins of the Roman West. During these centuries, the Pope's role as pastor and teacher was supplemented by a jurisdictional one, whereby he governed a Church that was understood not just as a communion of believers but as an organised, effective and distinct corporate body within society. This was where the city of God assumed its earthly presence.

Two biblical texts were central to this process, both of which would exert a massive influence on medieval political thought. The first was Matthew 16:18–19, in which Christ tells Peter: 'thou art Peter, and upon this rock I will build my church; and the gates of hell shall not prevail against it. And I will give unto thee the keys of the kingdom of heaven: and whatsoever thou shalt bind on earth shall be bound in heaven: and whatsoever thou shalt loose on earth shall be loosed in heaven."

This was read as referring to the papacy specifically and interpreted in a jurisdictional rather than simply spiritual manner. It was combined with another passage from John 21 in which Christ asks Peter three times whether he truly loves him and tells him, when he answers in the affirmative, to 'feed my lambs', 'feed my sheep' and 'feed my sheep'.[23] Taken together these texts provided the biblical foundation for the papacy's spiritual, pastoral, jurisdictional and political claims.

The idea that the papacy was a separate jurisdictional power was to be of immense importance in the later Middle Ages, providing an alternative source of authority that limited temporal power and in the process created a great deal of tension with it. In the early Middle Ages, however, the relationship was less strained and more harmonious. This relationship was most clearly and influentially articulated in a letter written by Pope Gelasius to Emperor Anastasius I in 494, in which he declared that 'there are two things . . . by which this world is ruled: the consecrated authority of priests and the royal power.'[24] These two powers worked together to bring security, order and welfare to society. The Church was in control of religious matters, as the emperor 'though first of the human race in dignity' must 'submit devoutly to those who are preeminent in God's work . . . so learning . . . to be subordinate in religious matters'. The emperor, in turn, was supreme in the temporal sphere, as priests 'conscious that divine providence has conferred the empire upon you, obey your laws as public discipline requires'. Gelasius admitted that, of the two powers, 'priests have the greater responsibility, in that they will have to give account before God's judgment seat for those who have been kings of men,' a responsibility that implied that of a superior answerable for the actions of an inferior.

This was the source of the 'two swords' analogy – government divided between temporal and spiritual powers – that was to dominate the Christian West for a millennium. It meant that there were two parallel jurisdictions within Christendom, two sources of legitimate authority, two claims on public loyalty. It meant that the claims of temporal authorities within their own territory would never be unchallenged or supreme, as they were always frustrated by another, spiritual, authority. Work together as these two authorities usually did, the idea of the 'two swords' meant that there was always the potential for a seismic conflict of interests within Western Christendom.

At the time of its inception, Gelasius' ambitious vision did not have much of an impact, partly because the imperial court never accepted its validity and partly because Gelasius' successors did not always adopt such a severe attitude to temporal power. Gregory I, for example, the Pope who sent missionaries to Kent in the late sixth century, took a rather less antagonistic stance. If, as the Anglo-Saxon scholar Alcuin of York wrote in 793, it was true that 'we are fellow-citizens by a two-fold relationship: sons of one city in Christ, that is, of Mother Church, and natives of one country,' it was also true that this dual nationality could be harmonious and constructive.[25]

'Let us all kneel, and jointly beseech the true and living God Almighty': the partnership of Church and state

As the empire in the West lost its authority, it was overrun and replaced by various smaller kingdoms. The Vulgate translation of the Bible, completed by St Jerome around the end of the fourth century and destined to be the medieval West's only official version, contained around 520 references to 'kingdom' in general, 70 to the 'kingdom of God' and 30 to the 'kingdom of heaven'. These played an important role in legitimising and sustaining the innumerable local kings whose power now spread across Western Europe.

A number of specific texts were used to justify royal power. Some were obvious. Romans 13, a passage of unparalleled significance in European history, began: 'Let every soul be subject unto the higher powers. For there is no power but of God: the powers that be are ordained of God.' John 19:11 read: 'Jesus answered [Pilate], "Thou couldest have no power at all against me, except it were given thee from above."' Such verses had obvious implications for the legitimacy of royal power, the importance of political order and the duty of obedience owed by subjects, and they were widely deployed to that effect. The Old Testament, with its extensive history of kings and kingship, was also drawn upon to demonstrate the divine origins of royal power. The manner in which the prophet Samuel anointed Saul, Israel's first king, or the way in which the young David refused to kill Saul when relations between them soured, provided a powerful basis for the sacred authority of kingship. The fact that the Old Testament was also profoundly ambivalent about kingship was largely ignored. The king was God's vicegerent on earth, often described as his vicar. Political authority in the newly Christian kingdoms was legitimised by the Church by drawing on biblical concepts.

This was a two-way process. The (re-)conversion of Western Europe was predominantly a top-down affair, with England being no exception. In Book II of his *Ecclesiastical History of the English People* Bede describes how, when King Edwin of Northumbria received the faith, Bishop Paulinus of York spent thirty-six days 'fully occupied in catechising and baptizing' the locals.[26] Elsewhere, in his *Life of St Cuthbert*, Bede describes peasants mocking a handful of monks, swept out to sea by the mouth of the River Tyne. They shouted at them, 'May God spare none of them, for they have taken away from men the ancient rites and customs, and how the new ones are to be attended to, nobody knows.'[27] Christianity was not, it appears, a popular creed, at least in the early years of its reintroduction, and its success resided entirely on its appeal to the royal and noble classes within society.

Thus from its earliest days, English Christianity was bound up, indeed often synonymous, with political authority. Bishops frequently lived and acted like noblemen, which is what many were. The monasteries that dominated the Anglo-Saxon landscape were commonly owned and run by members of royal households. It was not uncommon for Churches to become thoroughly mired in the circle of violence that accompanied the factional politics of the time.[28]

The Church was accordingly quick to secure political and financial advantage. Wihtred's law code began, as we saw, with an exemption from taxation. Aethelberht gave the Church a heavier compensation for theft than he did himself. Ine's laws commanded the payment of church-scot, a forerunner of tithe, by Martinmas (11 November) and threatened a 60 shilling fine, the law's largest, 'if anyone does not discharge it'.[29] Charters show how rapidly royal land was donated, inalienably, to the Church, to the consternation of many rulers. The *Penitential* of the seventh-century reforming Archbishop of Canterbury, Theodore of Tarsus, stipulated that, although clerics could not fight, the Church should receive one-third of war booty. Theodore also insisted that tithe should be voluntary for the poor, rather than a burden on them, although over the following centuries it was to become a legal obligation, enforced by the state, and directed to general Church use rather than for pilgrims and the poor as it had been.[30]

The effect of this was not simply to identify the Church with aristocratic status or to present it with immediate access to political and financial power, but also to shape the way in which Christianity was understood and exercised. Association with the noble classes meant immersion in noble virtues, specifically the warrior culture that dominated Anglo-Saxon England. Bede describes how King Oswald of Northumbria 'erected the sign of the holy cross' before fighting the pagan army of Cadwalla in 635. Oswald 'cried to his army, "Let us all kneel, and jointly beseech the true and living God Almighty, in his mercy, to defend us from the haughty and fierce enemy; for He knows that we have undertaken a just war for the safety of our nation."'[31] The Christian God was a frightening and apparently unbeatable warrior to have on one's side.

Another example of the way in which, in the early years, Anglo-Saxon warrior culture moulded Christianity, rather than the other way round, was unearthed in July 2009, when a vast hoard of gold was discovered in Staffordshire. Among the 1,500 or so objects, most with some military connection, was a strip of gold bearing an inscription from Numbers 10:35: 'Rise up, O Lord, and may thy enemies be dispersed and those who hate thee be driven from thy face.'[32] Although it is not clear whether the strip would have been attached to a military or ecclesiastical object – the text was also used in the liturgy for the consecration of churches – the way the object was interred in such a martial hoard is highly suggestive. In the words of historian Patrick Wormald, 'Christianity had been assimilated by a warrior nobility which had no intention of abandoning its culture, or seriously changing its traditions, customs, tastes, and loyalties into the articulation of the new faith.'[33]

And not only the warrior nobility; the clergy too were affected by the culture in which they operated. Although the evidence of clerics bearing arms, in contravention of Church law, is limited, it clearly did happen, not only because some sources describe it but because some ecclesiastics spoke out against it. In the process of doing so, they revealed that some defended the practice on biblical grounds. In a pastoral letter of the late tenth century, Aelfric wrote how 'some priests say that Peter had a sword when he cut off the ear of the wicked man, the Jewish servant . . . but we say in truth that the right-eous Saviour, and those who followed him, did not go armed or with any warfare . . . if Peter had been allowed to kill the man, Christ would not have commanded him to hide the sword.'[34]

All this naturally shaped the engagement with the Christian scrip-tures, which were read and sometimes reinterpreted within the framework of the prevailing culture. The Old Testament was, as we shall note below, an obvious source for newly Christianised Anglo-Saxon England. Its stories of battles and conquest, kings and warriors, enemies and invasion had a clear appeal. Even those that were more subversive of such martial virtues could be re-worked.[35] It could present other, more pervasive problems, however. Aelfic complained about how his contemporaries liked to cite Old Testament support for their own predilection for taking concubines or exacting revenge. Such practices were not Christian and pointed to the dangers, of which the Western Church would grow steadily more aware, of allowing the laity to engage with the scriptures directly, either through a vernacular translation or without the protective guidance of the clergy.

The New Testament itself presented a different challenge. Here there was no martial culture to legitimise Saxon warrior ethics. Indeed, the problem was the very opposite. Christ's teaching and self-sacrifice were antipathetic to a culture that celebrated violence and vengeance. It seems, therefore, to be no accident that Anglo-Saxon poets appear to have largely ignored much of the gospels – the nativity, the baptism of Christ, his teachings, his healings – in favour of the great culminating events of salvation history – incarnation, crucifixion, the harrowing of hell, the ascension and the Last Judgement – which they interpreted again through the only matrix they knew. Thus Christ is described as a triumphant prince. The apostles are a band of thegns. The harrowing of hell is, in effect, a military attack from which the triumphant Lord returns with booty, the souls he has rescued, to celebrate his glorious victory like any good king by giving gifts to his followers.

It would be misleading to see only one-way cultural traffic in the relationship between temporal and spiritual authorities in Anglo-Saxon England. As we shall shortly see, Church and Bible had considerable opportunity and ability, and some success, in shaping the exercise of political power. Nor would it be fair to see the relationship as simply self-serving – the Church legitimising and sanctifying political claims in return for military protection, and financial and political privilege. Clerics were sometimes willing to challenge the exercise of political power, for which they believed they would in part be accountable on Judgement Day. Nevertheless, it is clear that, for all that it was an independent body within society, the Church was an independent body with ties so close to royalty that its ability, and inclination, to think and act outside the culture of the age was blunted. The very process of conversion to, and establishment of, Christianity bestowed upon the Church the same stature that enabled it to – and dissuaded it from – shape the exercise of political power.

'Whether you will or not, you will have him as a judge': the limits of kingship

Both the nature of the relationship between spiritual and temporal authorities and the theological foundations that justified it, meant that the protection of God's Holy Church was the king's foremost duty. When papal legates visited the country in 786, they attended the Mercian and Northumbrian courts and presented to the assembled lords and bishops twenty papal canons.[36] Chapters 11–14 of these canons comprise a brief treatise on political theory, heavily biblical in its language and logic, which offers as complete, if theoretical, a picture of the biblical parameters of kingship in mid-Anglo-Saxon England as exists anywhere.

The first of this group, canon eleven, deals with the duties of the king and, in particular, the nature of his relationship with the Church. Kings and leaders should govern with prudence and discipline, and judge justly. That meant, among other things, dealing with the Church in the appropriate manner. Leaders should consider how they wished their own wives to be treated and then care for the Church, the bride of Christ, in the same way. They should not be arrogant in their exercise of power, not oppress others and not exact unjust tribute.

Particular emphasis was placed on the importance of heeding episcopal teaching, and recognising not only ecclesiastical independence but also supremacy. A series of biblical texts showed how bishops had authority over secular rulers. They were the key-bearers of heaven. They were answerable for the souls of the laity on the Day of Judgement. They were messengers of God and spoke in his place. Only God could judge them.[37] Such high esteem demanded considerable respect and Anglo-Saxon kings took their duties to the Church very seriously. Bede tells us that as soon as King Edwin was baptised, he built 'a larger and nobler church of stone, which was to enclose the little oratory he had built before'.[38] A little later in his narrative he records how King Oswiu, newly victorious over the powerful pagan King Penda, immediately fulfilled his vow of giving his daughter Elfieda, 'who was scarce a year old', to be consecrated to God 'in perpetual virginity'.[39]

The royal responsibility to God's Church went beyond building churches and consecrating virgins. One of the consequences of the closeness of the relationship between Church and king was that the latter was charged with duties that, at least as far as the New Testament conceived them, were entirely those of the Church. The Anglo-Saxon abbot Eanwulf wrote to Charlemagne in 773, advising him to 'hasten to spread the Christian faith among the peoples subject to you, increase your righteous zeal for their conversion, suppress the worship of idols, [and] cast down the buildings of their temples.'[40] A true, godly king was one who not only enabled the gospel to be preached but zealously suppressed other religions in the process. In return, he would receive the prayers and honour of the faithful, 'without compulsion' – as Ine's laws put it entirely without irony – and, ultimately, the rewards of heaven. Thus the two swords worked together, the king using one to spread the gospel, the Church the other to legitimise his rule.

In legitimising the king's rule, however, the Church also began the process of limiting it, not just by existing as a separate authority in itself, a fact that only began to shape European politics significantly in the eleventh century, but also by articulating what the king needed to do in order to maintain his earthly legitimacy. This was where the traffic started flowing in the other direction.

The principal way in which Church and Bible shaped kingship as it was exercised in England was to place it under judgement. Kings were kings by grace not merit. '[It was] not your own merit but the abundant goodness of God [that] appointed king and rule over many,' wrote St Boniface to Aethelbert, King of Mercia in 747.[41] Kings would have to give account of their actions before the King of Kings. 'Whether you will or not, you will have him as a judge,' Alcuin warned Ethelred.[42]

Recognising royal accountability to God was not, at this stage, the same thing as recognising royal accountability to the Pope. In the early Middle Ages, the accountability of the king before God meant that kings were regularly reminded of their duties by the clergy who preached, wrote to them or drafted their legislation. 'Ponder . . . within yourself how diligently to establish God's law over the people of God,' Cathwulf urged Charlemagne.[43] 'Above all, have the love of God in your hearts, and show that love by keeping his commandments,' Alcuin reminded Ethelred.[44]

The choice of the word 'commandments' was not an accident. The duties incumbent upon kings and the judgement they faced were derived ultimately from the scriptures. In the first instance this meant obedience to the law. Fundamental to Old Testament Israel was the idea that the law was supreme over all, including the king. 'When [the king] sitteth upon the throne of his kingdom, that he shall write him a copy of this law . . . it shall be with him, and he shall read therein all the days of his life . . . that he turn not aside from the commandment.' The king was as subject to the law as were his subjects.[45]

This meant that just as kings were subject to the law, their subjects could theoretically avail themselves of it. Towards the end of the Anglo-Saxon period, King Ethelred's law code began: 'it is the decree of our Lord and his councillors that just practices be established and all illegal practices abolished, and that every man is to be permitted the benefit of law.'[46] This placed on the king the responsibility for justice, a responsibility that was central to Old Testament law and closely linked to royal accountability to God. It was a repeated feature of Anglo-Saxon law-making. 'Judge thou very fairly: Do not judge one judgment for the rich and another for the poor,' commanded Clause 43 of Alfred's laws, quoting Exodus 23:6.[47]

In addition to the duty of justice, the king was responsible for peace. This was a live issue throughout the Anglo-Saxon period, no more so than when Pope Gregory had sent his missionaries to an 'England' that comprised numerous separate, militaristic kingdoms that lived in a state of more or less constant conflict. Of the six East Anglian kings who assumed the throne in the first half of the seventh century, for example, five died violently and the fate of the sixth is unknown. Peace was a priority. Accordingly, the duty to work for and secure peace across the nation was among the highest laid upon Anglo-Saxon kings by the Church. Bede says that after King Egfrith's brother was killed at the Battle of the Trent in 679, there would have been a prolonged feud had Archbishop Theodore not intervened and ensured that compensation for the prince was paid instead.

Alfred remarked in the introduction to his law code that 'when it came about that many people had received the faith of Christ . . . throughout the English people . . . they established, for that mercy which Christ taught, that secular lords might with their permission receive without sin compensation in money for almost every misdeed at the first offence.'[48] This was part of the carefully choreographed history that marked Alfred's laws in which the severity of the Mosaic law was attenuated by the mercy of Christ before informing Saxon legislation. Thus it was that Anglo-Saxon law codes listed, often in considerable detail, what limbs, eyes and lives were 'worth'. Some, like Ine's, outlined the various fines to be imposed on those found fighting in the king's house, in a minster church or in an ealdorman's house. Others, like King Ethelred's code of 1008, commanded that 'at these holy seasons ... there is to be peace and unity among all Christian men, and every suit is to be laid aside,' and exhorted all people to be zealous about the improvement of peace.[49] It was all part of the slow and dangerous transition from a blood-feud culture, in which killing not only merited but demanded revenge, to what might be termed a compensation culture.

The antagonism to bloodshed also manifested itself in the right to sanctuary, which reflected the Old Testament's setting aside 'cities of refuge' to which perpetrators of manslaughter could flee.[50] Ine's laws offered sanctuary not only to those facing the death penalty but to those 'liable to be flogged'.[51] To be a king over a Christian people meant mitigating justice with mercy. 'Christian men are not to be condemned to death for ... too small offences.'[52] It also meant adopting an attitude to life which saw it as a gift of God that should not be disposed of, either by death or by surrendering people into slavery, a genuine problem in the age of Viking raids. 'No Christian and innocent men are to be sold out of the country, and especially not among the heathen people, but care is earnestly to be taken that those souls be not destroyed which God bought with his own life,' proclaimed Clause 2 of King Ethelred's 1008 code.[53]

After the responsibilities of justice and of peace came those towards the weak. Canon 13 of the 786 legatine council advised the rich and powerful to make just and impartial judgements, refuse bribes and protect the widows, orphans and poor, and ended with the promise of Matthew 25:34.[54] When a group of missionary bishops wrote to King Aethelbald of Mercia to admonish him for his personal behaviour in 747, they also praised him for his charity in such a way as to link it to the judgement he would one day face. 'We have heard that you give very many alms,' they said, 'and we rejoice greatly in this; because those who bestow alms on the least and needy brethren will, according to the evangelical truth, hear from the Lord on the day of Judgement the Merciful sentence which says, "As long as you did it to one of these my least brethren, you did it to me."'[55] Bede tells approvingly of how King Oswald was 'once sitting at dinner, on the holy day of Easter, with ... a silver dish full of dainties before him', when a servant, 'whom he had appointed to relieve the poor', approached and told him 'that a great multitude of needy persons from all parts were sitting in the streets begging some alms of the king. Immediately, [Oswald] ordered the meat set before him to be carried to the poor, and the dish to be cut in pieces and divided among them.'[56]

This concern for the needs of the weak and poor would increase as Viking raids traumatised the country, and people tried to work out why a nation that had settled into relative peace after years of internal strife was suddenly thrown back into conflict. Taking its cue from the Old Testament prophets who asked themselves a similar question as Israel and Judah were conquered by the Assyrians and then the Babylonians, the Anglo-Saxon response often emphasised a disregard for the poor and the needy. Thus, when the Viking 'Great Army' came to England in 1009 King Ethelred commanded, among other things, a fast, of which he wrote: 'the food also, which each would have consumed if the fast had not been ordained for him, is all to be willingly distributed for God's sake after the fast to needy men and bedridden persons and men so afflicted that they are unable to fast thus.'[57]

Biblical teaching also placed upon Anglo-Saxon kings the responsibilities of personal virtue. The same letter in which the missionary bishops praised Aethelbald for his charity concentrated, in some detail, on the king's sexual misdemeanours. The bishops could accept that the king had 'never taken in matrimony a lawful wife', but only if he had also chosen to 'maintain . . . chaste abstinence for God's sake'. Aethelbald, however, had not. Instead he preferred a life of 'lasciviousness and adultery . . . committed in the monasteries with holy nuns and virgins consecrated to God'.[58] The bishops were indignant. 'To what punishment is a servant liable from his master if he violates his master's wife in adultery?' they reasoned. 'How much more he who defiles with the filth of lust the bride of Christ, the Creator of heaven and earth; as the blessed Apostle Paul says. "Know you not that your members are the temple of the Holy Ghost?"'[59]

Interestingly, it is in the bishops' admonition of Aethelbald's sexual licentiousness that we come across the earliest reference to 'the image of God' in English political writing. 'It is proved to be indecent,' they warned, 'that you should transform the image of God, which is created in you, into the image and likeness of the malignant devil through wanton living.' Genesis 1:26–7 – 'And God said, Let us

make man in our image, after our likeness: and let them have dominion over the fish of the sea, and over the fowl of the air, and over the
cattle, and over all the earth, and over every creeping thing that creep-
eth upon the earth. So God created man in his own image, in the
image of God created he him; male and female created he them.'– is
not an obviously political text in the same way as, say, Romans 13.
But it had enormous political implications and was to be used repeatedly throughout the nation's political history. The bishops' use of it
to correct the king's sexual crimes seems trivial compared to some of
the battles in which it would subsequently be deployed, but it is notable nonetheless. If all people were made in the image of God, how
much more important was it, in a rigidly stratified society like that of
the early Middle Ages, that a *king* should not mar God's image in
him.

Altogether, the responsibilities that Christianity placed upon the
king – justice, peace, care for the weak, personal morality – gesture in
the direction of a monarch who, while in no way contracted with his
people, was placed in a political order that intimated that the legitimacy of his position was somehow dependent on the discharge of
those duties. It was kingship *under God*, oriented, however hopefully,
to the common good of the people.

This was recognised by the Anglo-Saxons themselves. It was not
unusual for law codes to begin with an affirmation that laws were
determined, with the advice of the king's counsellors, 'for the praise
of God and for [the king's] own royal dignity and for the benefit of
all his people'.[60] This was rhetoric, of course, but it wasn't just rhetoric. In his *Treatise on the Old and New Testament*, Aelfric outlined
the classic division of medieval society, quoting St Paul in the
process:

Labourers are they who provide us with sustenance, ploughmen
and husbandmen devoted to that alone. Beadsmen [men of prayer]
are they who intercede for us to God and promote Christianity
among Christian peoples in the service of God, as spiritual toil,
devoted to that alone for the benefit of us all. Soldiers are they who
guard our boroughs and also our land, fighting with weapons
against the oncoming army; as St Paul, the teacher of the nations,

said in his teaching: 'The soldier beareth not the sword without cause. He is God's minister to thy profit, appointed for vengeance on him that doth evil.'[61]

His point was not simply to outline the contours of Anglo-Saxon society but to emphasise that the health of the king and his kingdom depended on the health of each of these roles. 'On these three supports the throne stands, and if one is broken down, it falls at once, certainly to the detriment of the other supports.'

Kings (and soldiers and beadsmen) may have needed labourers to feed them, but it was rather hopeful to imagine that the throne rested on them. Nevertheless, it was an idea that ran deep within the Anglo-Saxon imagination. In the soul-searching following the Viking raids, there were many attempts to understand why God had abandoned the English or, more precisely, which national sins had displeased him. Was it, as Alcuin informed the King of Northumbria, a corrupt sense of fashion?[62] Or was it injustice and inequality, as Alcuin went on to argue, drawing on both Old and New Testaments to make his case:

Such customs once injured the people of God, and made it a reproach to the pagan races, as the prophet says 'Woe to you, who have sold the poor for a pair of shoes' [Amos 2:6] . . . Some labour under an enormity of clothes, others perish with cold; some are inundated with delicacies and feasting like Dives clothed in purple, and Lazarus dies of hunger at the gate [Luke 16:19–31]. Where is brotherly love? Where the pity which we are admonished to have for the wretched? The satiety of the rich is the hunger of the poor. That saying of the Lord is to be feared: 'For judgement without mercy to him that hath not done mercy' [Jas. 2:13].

'Be rulers of people, not robbers; shepherds not plunderers,' Alcuin concluded.[63]

The apparent dependence of a kingdom's health on the extent to which its king served the good of the people would point, in the fullness of time, towards the need for the people themselves to agree to a particular monarch. Such an idea was hardly in the mind of those

Anglo-Saxon ecclesiastics who wrote about the king being judged by God for his sins, but very occasionally they hinted at it. In a homily for Palm Sunday, delivered in the last years of the tenth century, Aelfric remarked that 'No man can make himself king, but the people has the choice to choose a king whom they please; but after he is consecrated as king, he then has dominion over the people, and they cannot shake his yoke from their necks.'[64] This was an extraordinary idea for the time, not so very far from the ideas of Thomas Hobbes or John Locke over six centuries later.

Aelfric would never have imagined that the people over which the king ruled were the *source* of his authority. Christian theology was clear that authority was God's alone. He granted it to kings. Kings ruled. The people obeyed. There is nothing in Aelfric's scheme to moderate the top-down hierarchy of Anglo-Saxon society. Yet, authority was *granted* by God to the king and that grant was connected to the king's performance, his ability and willingness to discharge the responsibilities of justice, peace, care of the weak, personal morality and, of course, loyalty to the Church. In the words of historian Joseph Canning, 'precisely because rulership was understood to have been instituted by God it was considered to exist for a divinely willed end . . . Kingship was viewed as an office existing within a Christian . . . structure: there was no place for the arbitrary exercise of the monarch's will. The king's role was that of Christian service for the common good of his people.'[65]

'God's law henceforth is to be eagerly loved by word and deed': a biblical people

If the Bible shaped the idea of kingship in early medieval England, it also helped shape the English themselves, forming the identity of the people over which kings ruled. This formation had a long history, dating back to before Pope Gregory's mission to when Gildas, a mid-sixth-century monk, wrote a history about 'the ruin and conquest of Britain' after the withdrawal of the Roman legions in 410, which was heavy with biblical allusion and imagery.[66] His impact on English self-identity was not significant, although his account of the way Romano-Christian Britain fell to pagan invaders in the fifth and sixth centuries did provide a model for Anglo-Saxon clerics later trying to explain the Viking invasions.[67]

Far more influential was Bede, the Northumbrian monk who had joined the monastery of Sts Peter and Paul of Monkwearmouth and Jarrow at the age of seven and died there fifty-five years later, in 735. Bede is remembered today primarily for his *Ecclesiastical History of the English People*, the most informative and readable account of early Anglo-Saxon history we have. He, however, considered himself to be primarily a biblical scholar and theologian, ending his *Ecclesiastical History* with a brief biographical sketch in which he describes how 'I wholly applied myself to the study of Scripture, and . . . always took delight in learning, teaching, and writing,' and then lists his various works, the majority of which are biblical commentaries.[68]

Not surprisingly the *Ecclesiastical History* is marked by Bede's biblical erudition and his desire to instruct his audience, formally King Ceolwulf of Northumbria but more broadly all devout readers, about good Christian practice. 'I warmly welcome the diligent zeal and sincerity with which you study the words of Holy Scripture,' he praised Ceolwulf in the book's dedicatory preface, before proceeding to outline its didactic intent: 'For if history records good things of good men, the thoughtful hearer is encouraged to imitate what is good: or if it records evil of wicked men, the devout religious listener or reader is encouraged to avoid all that is sinful and perverse and to follow what he knows to be good and pleasing to God.'[69]

The *Ecclesiastical History* is divided into five books, like the Old Testament law, a parallel to which Bede alludes in his opening chapter: 'this island at present, following the number of the books in which the Divine law was written, contains five nations.'[70] It begins with a geographical description of the British Isles which is thought to show deliberate resonances with the idea of Paradise before the Fall.[71] It is thought to be modelled on the Old Testament history book, 2 Samuel, which tells the story of David's kingship.[72] And it identifies an 'English people' who Bede models on, and associates with, Israel of the Old Testament.

Like Pope Gregory before him, Bede was alert to the *idea* of the English people before it was a reality. The fact that Gregory overlooked the violent division between regions and tribes, and conceived of his missionary Church as a single English entity was enormously significant. In the provocative words of historian John Barrow: 'the English owe their existence as a people, or at least the recognition of it, to the papacy.'[73] Bede followed Gregory in his frequent references to 'the English people', going so far as to see the invading Angles and Saxons as the instrument of God's justified wrath against the Britons and hence a chosen people.

Understanding one's own nation as a new people of God was far from unique. As the most powerful Catholic people of the time (most of the invaders who conquered the Western Roman Empire were Arian Christians),[74] the Franks had been encouraged by the papacy to see themselves as the new Israel, a vehicle for God's grace and mission in a heterodox, indeed heretical environment. That recognised, the association would have seemed especially natural to the Anglo-Saxons. The Old Testament history books told the story of a collection of tribes, invading and trying to establish themselves in a hostile, if promised, land. Once established, their security was a tenuous thing, and they were frequently attacked by unbelieving foreign forces, many coming from the sea. The parallels were too obvious to miss. The peculiar detail for the English was not that they associated themselves with the people of God in such a way as would help fashion their national identity, but that it was such a powerful and long-lived association, emerging with force at the Reformation, and remaining part of the national psyche even up to the Second World War.[75]

This sense of identity, founded on the model of biblical Israel, carried with it certain connotations. It meant there was a narrative, an order, to English history, a thread that could be followed through the vicissitudes of history and that could and (one day) would make sense of them. Not only was history linear, in the fashion of the biblical history, but it also made sense, even when it apparently did not.

This was the thinking that shaped the reaction to the Viking invasions, the automatic reaction to which was to reach through the nation's identity to the biblical narrative that lay beneath it and offered a precedent for, and helped made sense of, the trauma afflicting the English people. Old Testament Israel had been punished and apparently abandoned by God because, according the prophets, they had turned away from him. 'Foxes pillage the chosen vine, the heritage of the Lord has been given to a people not his own; and where there was praise of God, are now the games of the Gentiles; the holy festivity has been turned to mourning,' wrote Alcuin, quoting one such prophet.[76] The lesson was obvious. 'Whoever reads the Holy Scriptures and ponders ancient histories and considers the fortunes of the world will find that for sins of this kind kings lost kingdoms and peoples their country.' For the Anglo-Saxons the Old Testament was often simply a veiled way of talking about their own national problems.

Being God's chosen people loaded the English with responsibilities. If the model of biblical Israel provided a sense of identity, narrative and explanation, it also gave the nation a grave corporate moral burden. Like chosen kings, chosen people had duties. If these were discharged well, the people were assured of God's blessing. 'God's law henceforth is to be eagerly loved by word and deed, then God will at once become gracious to this nation,' read Clause 26 of King Ethelred's 1008 law code.[77] If they were not, the people risked defeat and conquest. Just as the king fell under the judgement of God according to whether he maintained justice, peace, morality and Christian truth, so did his people.

According to this way of thinking, the Viking calamity 'was merited by sins and by contempt of God's command, and especially by the withdrawing of the tribute which Christian men ought to render to God in their tithes'.[78] Rectifying this was straightforward: tithe more diligently and more joyfully. Only God could help defeat the pagan marauders and restore God's people to their land in peace, but how could he be expected to do that if the people ignored and exploited his Holy Church? The responsibility to pay tithes was not the end of the matter, however. 'Those servants of God who receive the dues which we pay to God, are to live a pure life, that through that purity they may intercede for us to God.' Each of the three pillars of society had its role to play, the clergy as much as king and commoners. Society needed to be properly ordered if it were to flourish or, indeed, even survive. All were under the judgement of God.

This sense of social order and collective moral identity carried with it at least the potential for exclusion and persecution. As already noted, this obviously meant the destruction of pagan armies and idols. Old Testament Israel had been conceived and defined against the idolatrous peoples and practices of the ancient Near East and if the people had often been remiss in keeping away from, and suppressing, those practices, their God remained implacably and violently opposed. Thus, Bede spoke highly of those kings who crushed paganism, remarking approvingly of Earconberht of Kent, that he was 'the first of the English kings to give orders for the complete abandonment and destruction of idols throughout his whole kingdom'.[79]

Being a chosen people of God did not simply mean dealing with external religious threats. Just as serious were internal ones, in particular, in the seventh century, the continued existence of British Christianity which, for all its piety and evangelistic vigour, lay theologically and administratively outside the true Catholic Church. Augustine met with the British bishops in 603 but when they stubbornly refused to comply with Roman practice, he replied ('in a threatening manner'): 'if they would not preach the way of life to the English nation, they should at their hands undergo the vengeance of death.' This, Bede happily comments, 'fell out exactly as he had predicted . . . through the dispensation of the Divine judgment'.[80]

Much the same could be said of internal moral threats. The behaviour proscribed by Anglo-Saxon law codes was not simply construed as immoral. Within the mental framework that generated such legislation, it was a fundamental threat to the nature and even the very existence of the people itself, just as it had been to Old Testament Israel. To work on a Sunday or force one's slave to work, to sacrifice to devils or to live 'in illicit cohabition' was not to behave badly.[81] It was to disobey God, risk his ill-favour and betray the very identity that promised the nation peace and security.

Ultimately, the manner in which the Bible helped form 'the English people' during the Anglo-Saxon period was of a piece with its impact on the idea of kingship. It created the idea of an English people, offering it a sense of identity, narrative and coherence that could, at its best, inspire mutual responsibility and accountability. And it placed it under judgement. Archbishop Wulfstan complained in his famous 'Sermon to the English':

Widows are wrongfully forced into marriage . . . too many are reduced to poverty and greatly humiliated . . . poor men are sorely deceived and cruelly defrauded and sold far and wide out of this country into the power of foreigners; and children in the cradle are enslaved for petty theft by cruel injustice widely throughout the people. The rights of freemen are withdrawn and the rights of slaves are restricted and charitable obligations are curtailed.[82]

The list of Wulfstan's concerns – widows, the poor, children, slaves – had a clear biblical ring. His warnings and exhortations only made sense in a society formed by specific moral presuppositions, a society in which his audience would have instantly understood that the state of widows, the poor, children and slaves mattered so much to God that the very existence of the nation was put under threat by their maltreatment.

But if the English envisaged themselves as God's people, formed and blessed by God, they needed to obey God's law. Failure to do so came at a cost, perhaps the cost of history repeating itself. 'There was a historian in the time of the Britons, called Gildas, who wrote about their misdeeds,' preached Wulfstan, 'how with their sins they infuriated God so excessively that He finally allowed the English army to conquer their land, and to destroy the host of the Britons entirely.' As with the Britons, so with the English: 'This nation . . . has become very corrupt . . . through murder and through evil deeds, through avarice and through greed, through stealing and through robbery, through man-selling and through heathen vices.' Ultimately, being a people of God, like being a Christian king, meant being under his judgement. That judgement may take the imminent form of invasion and conquest, or the ultimate one of 'the great Judgment to which we all shall go'. But it was an unavoidable part of Christian politics.

2

'No traitor to the king but a priest of God': Discord and conflict in the Middle Ages

In 1027 King Cnut travelled to Rome. He was there to attend the coronation of Emperor Conrad by Pope John XIX and also, as he subsequently told his subjects, 'to pray for the remission of my sins and for the safety of the kingdoms and of the people which are subjected to my rule'.[1] He had long planned to make the journey only to have been repeatedly hindered by affairs of state. Now, however, he gave thanks to Almighty God for his visit.

While there Cnut learned from 'wise men' that the holy Apostle Peter 'had received from the Lord great power to bind and to loose, and was the keeper of the keys of the kingdom of heaven'. He was impressed and wrote how 'therefore, I consider it very profitable diligently to seek his special favour before God.' This did not mean he would be supine in his dealings with the Bishop of Rome. While there he had complained to 'the lord pope' about the amounts that English archbishops were expected to pay when they came to the apostolic see to receive the pallium, the special vestment conferred by the Pope. It did indicate, however, that English kings, like others across Western Europe, were becoming aware of a slowly reforming papacy that would, over the next two centuries, aspire to the role of supreme monarch over Western Christendom. This aspiration was to have a profound impact on English and, indeed, all European politics over coming centuries, and to be the foremost way in which the Bible shaped English politics in the high and late Middle Ages.

'Every power in the world should be subject to the Pope': the balance of power

The Western Church had been undergoing a transformation for more than a century when Cnut visited Rome. New religious communities were being founded, older ones reformed. Many religious houses had become like family businesses, the position of abbot passing along family lines or, should no suitable relative be available, sold to the highest bidder. Members of communities saw little need to live in poverty, hold their property in common or even obey their abbot. Authority was often lax or non-existent.

Certain continental reformers, such as St Odo of Cluny, sought to address these problems and in doing so helped create a clerisy for whom ecclesiastical loyalties took precedence over family ones. Thus they gave oxygen to the long-standing idea that the clergy were different from, and superior to, the world in which they operated. Leading Church members gained self-confidence and became increasingly willing to assert the rights and privileges of clergy over royal power. The pre-eminent English reformers had all had some experience of reformed continental monasteries and, during the tenth century, they helped transform the English Church under a succession of sympathetic kings.

Although the storm had been gathering through much of the century, it broke with the papacy of Gregory VII which lasted from 1073 to 1085. Gregory was a leading reformer, whose implacable commitment to the papal cause was to redirect the history of Western Europe. He based his papacy on two familiar biblical texts that had been central to Rome's self-understanding for over half a millennium: Matthew 16:18–19 ('thou art Peter, and upon this rock I will build my church') and John 21:15–17 ('feed my lambs . . . feed my sheep . . . feed my sheep'.) These were the ultimate source of the 'great power' to which Cnut referred in his letter, now interpreted in a 'strong' governmental rather than 'weak' penitential sense. Here lay the justification for the universal scope of papal jurisdiction, for just as all were Christ's sheep, so all were in the Pope's flock. Unlike Pope Gelasius who, six centuries earlier, had considered temporal and spiritual power to exist in parallel, each within its own sphere, Gregory interpreted the texts to mean that temporal power was subject to spiritual.[2]

The consequence of this was not simply that it became unacceptable for kings to promote or demote bishops as they saw fit but that kings and emperors, being mere laymen, were to be judged by spiritual authorities for their capacity and right to rule. Early on in his papacy, Gregory produced a document entitled 'Dictates of the Pope' that listed twenty-seven propositions outlining papal prerogatives. Some of these were relatively uncontroversial. Others, such as the Pope's right to depose emperors and absolve subjects of their allegiance to wicked rulers, were unprecedented and struck at the heart of the contemporary understanding of monarchy. As one contemporary document put it: 'every power in the world should be subject to the pope . . . He can change kingdoms.'[3]

Papal claims were put to the test in the so-called Investiture Contest, which lasted, in one form or another, from 1075 to 1122. This had begun before Gregory's pontificate, with a battle between Pope Alexander II and Emperor Henry IV over an appointment to the archbishopric of Milan. Gregory's first actions in the affair had been emollient but the situation swiftly deteriorated, with incendiary letters, excommunication, suspension, deposition and the election of an antipope. Gregory ended up fleeing Rome and dying in exile but his cause outlived him. Lay investiture, the question of who should appoint to ecclesiastical offices, became a lightning rod for the wider storm of where sovereignty lay within the Church, what was the nature and extent of kingship and, more generally, what was the relationship between spiritual and temporal power. The Investiture Contest left a deep mark on European conceptions of political power and formulated an answer to the question that was left begging by many early medieval discussions of kingship, namely what was to be done if a king failed to exercise his duty. To whom was a king accountable? Who could possibly legitimately depose an errant monarch?

Gregory had an answer. It ended up turning the Church into a more centralised, legalistic, bureaucratic and coercive institution than it had previously been. It also helped establish a serious alternative political authority across Western Europe, one that was capable of infringing or openly challenging the power of kings and emperors.

In doing so, it enabled what has been called Europe's first political revolution, in which political power was limited and political loyalties were constantly being negotiated.

The papal reform movement and its implications touched England, as it did every province of Western Christendom, but slowly and in its own uniquely dramatic way. Duke William, before he became a conqueror, had actively supported the monastic reform movement in Normandy. He fought at Hastings with a papal banner and maintained close relations with Rome during his reign. However, when pressed to do fealty to the papacy for his kingdom, he simply refused and there was nothing Gregory could do about it.[4] William of Normandy was not one to surrender his political authority.

The tension carried over into the reigns of William Rufus and Henry I, during which Archbishop Anselm of Canterbury was twice exiled. Eventually differences were patched up and the immediate conflict abated but wider problems remained. Bishops and archbishops continued to fight with kings throughout the twelfth century, and the conflict in England reaching a dramatic climax in the decade-long fight between Henry II and his turbulent archbishop.

Thomas Becket was a difficult and widely disliked man, who did rather more for the Church's political authority in his death than he did in his life. Born in 1120 to a London merchant of relatively humble origins, he studied (although not, it seems, very hard) at the University of Paris before entering the household of a wealthy London merchant. He joined the household of Archbishop Theobold in 1145 and, a decade later, began work for the new king as his chancellor. In time Henry heeded Theobold's recommendation and chose Thomas as his successor in Canterbury. It may be that Henry had misjudged his chancellor. Biographers later wrote that beneath his worldly pose Thomas was deeply pious, and Thomas himself is reported to have remarked, 'if it should come about that I am promoted, I know the king so well, indeed inside out, that I would either have to lose his favour or, God forbid!, neglect my duty to the Almighty.'[5] Alternatively, it may be that Thomas's elevation to Canterbury changed him profoundly and unexpectedly. Either way, the appointment proved a disaster for everyone involved.

Henry was eager to recover many of the royal rights that had been lost in the chaos of King Stephen's reign and generally to withstand the claims of an ever mightier papacy. He resented Church courts hearing land cases and disliked the growing number of appeals to the papacy. These objections were aggravated by what he felt was Thomas's unwillingness to toe the royal line and his general ingratitude to him. The situation rapidly deteriorated, with Thomas angering his fellow bishops as much as his king before he fled to France where he spent the next six years in exile accompanied by a small, loyal but not uncritical band of followers, navigating a labyrinth of negotiations.

Eventually, king and archbishop were reconciled and Thomas made plans to return home, arriving to jubilant crowds on the road from Sandwich to Canterbury. The conflict was not, however, settled. Thomas reacted furiously to the coronation of Henry's young son by the Archbishop of York, while he had been in exile, provoking the elder Henry to lament the 'miserable drones and traitors have I nourished and promoted in my household, who let their lord be treated with such shameful contempt'.[6] The rest of the story is well known.

Thomas's death stunned all those present but was not immediately recognised as martyrdom. Indeed some onlookers were critical, saying that the archbishop had wanted to be a king. However, as the news spread across Europe, Thomas's cause gathered momentum. His words in response to the four knights who followed him into the cathedral – 'Here I am. No traitor to the king but a priest of God' – became emblematic of his saintly resistance to tyrannical authority. Henry was ordered to abolish all customs introduced in his time injurious to the Church's liberty, and was forbidden to impede lawful appeals to the Pope in ecclesiastical cases or to withdraw his obedience from Pope Alexander III or his successors. More dramatically, he did public penance in July 1174 when he walked barefoot through Canterbury to Thomas's tomb, lay prostrate, fasted overnight, publicly confessed his sins and allowed himself to be scourged, presumably quite gently. Thomas's murder grew in significance as reports of miracle cures began to be reported from the location of the murder and its gory remains. The martyr was canonised in 1173 and became medieval England's most popular saint, a healing cult with a barely concealed political message.

Thomas's time as archbishop was as futile as it was painful. The issues that caused the row could have been solved by more emollient characters, and the row itself was as much between Church members as it was between spiritual and temporal authorities. Nevertheless, its effect was to fortify the Church in the face of royal power, increasing the number of appeals to the papal curia, thereby bypassing royal authority and acting as a further spur to papal organisation. Less concretely, but no less importantly, it set the name of a precious martyr against the exercise of royal power. This may not have had the impact of, say, Magna Carta but it did create a popular cult around an individual who represented the Church's costly challenge to temporal power. Not without reason did Henry VIII systematically demolish Becket's enormous shrine in 1538.

'It is just for public tyrants to be killed': resisting tyranny

If the self-consciously political way in which the reforming papacy read certain key New Testament texts was the principal means by which the Bible shaped high medieval politics, it was not the only one. The eleventh and twelfth centuries saw a slow growth in biblical studies, primarily in cathedral schools and the early universities. This took two forms: *glossa*, in which masters glossed the meaning of the biblical texts in their margins or between lines, and continuous commentaries on entire books, of which there is less surviving material. At first commentaries favoured the Psalms (on account of their liturgical use) and the Pauline letters (on account of their theological depth), but they grew to encompass the other biblical books in the later years of the twelfth century. Scholars would also think through the implications of biblical teaching and examples on contemporary ideas of political authority, one of the most significant instances of which came from the pen of John of Salisbury.

Born around 1120, John was taught by, and friends with, the leading intellectual, ecclesiastical and political figures of his age. He was a companion of Thomas Becket, whom he followed into exile, and was present in the cathedral when the archbishop was murdered. John himself was not a political figure, certainly not in the way Becket was. Rather, he was a man of letters, writing long, self-consciously learned tomes, the most significant of which was *Policraticus: Of the Frivolities of Courtiers and the Footprints of Philosophers*. This vast, sprawling work (at 250,000 words there is still no complete English translation) was written in the 1150s and dedicated to Becket, when he was Henry's chancellor and still his friend. Although about politics (the title appears to have been made up by John, as were some of the examples he used in the book, in order to parade his learning), it is also a work of moral theology, satire, speculative philosophy, legal procedure, self-consolation, biblical commentary and personal meditation.[7]

It was the central part of the work (Books 4, 5 and 6: the so-called 'Statesman's Book') that was most contentious and had greatest influence on later writers. In it John used classical and Christian sources to exhort and warn kings about their roles and, most contentiously, to discuss the justification for tyrannicide. The difference between a tyrant and a prince, John reasoned, is that a prince 'is obedient to law, and rules his people by a will that places itself at their service'.[8] Princes 'are concerned with the burdens of the entire community'. They have a duty to 'love justice, cherish equity, procure the utility of the republic, and in all matters prefer the advantage of others to [their] private will'. They have a particular duty to the vulnerable. The prince's shield 'is a shield for the feeble . . . Those who are advanced most by [their] duties of office are those who can do least for themselves.'[9] Above all, the prince must obey the biblical law, which John enthusiastically describes as 'a gift of God, the likeness of equity, the norm of justice, the image of the divine will, the custodian of security, the unity and confirmation of a people, the standard of duties, the excluder and exterminator of vices, and the punishment of violence and all injuries'.[10]

John drew on a range of sources for his discussion of the duties of a prince, plundering the Old Testament for examples of good kings and of tyrants. He dwelt at length on the Mosaic law and quoted Deuteronomy 17:14–20, which outlines the duties and limitations of the king and the manner in which he should study and obey the law. Not surprisingly, given his own interests, John used this to exhort kings both to literacy and to a willingness to accept good advice from his courtiers. 'Need one ask whether anyone whom this law constrains is limited by law?' he asked rhetorically. 'Certainly this is divine and cannot be dismissed with impunity. Each word of this text is thunder in the ears of the prince if he is wise.'[11]

John quoted the New Testament less frequently, although no less insistently. In particular, he drew from the New Testament an emphasis on the need for princely humility. It is 'most difficult', he observed, for a prince 'to ascend through the ranks of honour without engendering imprudence in his soul'. Both the apostles James and Peter, quoting Proverbs, remark that 'God above all opposes the haughty and He gives grace to the humble.'[12] Thus, John concluded, quoting Luke's gospel, 'whoever . . . loves the eminence of his own rank should maintain with the greatest diligence the utmost humility of moral character . . . For it is perpetually maintained that "whoever humbles himself will be exalted and, reciprocally, whoever exalts himself is pressed down."'[13]

John's emphasis on the importance of princely righteousness presents him with a problem when he comes to the issue of succession. While clearly accepting the principle of hereditary succession, the fact that it is a prince's willingness and ability to rule humbly, mercifully and justly and to follow the law of God that marks him out as worthy of his rule, rather than the accident of his birth, means that there is inevitably a question mark hanging over the automatic legitimacy of any heir. Was a prince a prince by right of birth or by right of morality?

John cited examples from the Old Testament in which rulers and priests who put family loyalty above public duty were punished, and he quoted Psalms whose conditional tone is pregnant with meaning: 'If thy children will keep my covenant and my testimony that I shall teach them, their children shall also sit upon thy throne for evermore.'[14] In case these were not sufficiently clear, John spelt out the implications. Kingdoms may be 'translated from family to family', and those hereditary heirs 'who seem to be followers of the flesh' rather than of righteousness and justice may legitimately be 'eradicated', with 'the succession [being] transferred to those who are ascertained to be the inheritors of faith and justice'.[15] In the absence of any mechanism for 'transferring' kingship to more rightful hands, any threat behind John's words was a hollow one. Nevertheless, in taking the time to think through the responsibilities of kingship and the consequences of flouting them, John helped to provide the moral basis of a theory of limited monarchy, and to point forward to the doctrine of an accountable executive.[16]

The closest John got to working through the implications of his thought was in the last book of *Policraticus* in which he discussed the legitimacy of tyrannicide. This was a difficult subject, not just for the obvious reason, but for a major theological one. John, like all medieval thinkers, had a very high opinion of royal authority, which not only underpinned the entire structure of society but reflected the nature of God and his creation. 'The prince is the public power and a certain image on earth of divine majesty,' he recognised. 'Whatever the prince can do, therefore, is from God.'[17]

How then could a tyrant be removed if all power – including the tyrant's – was from God? 'I do not deny that tyrants are ministers of God,' he admitted.[18] Indeed, as Protestant reformers would later say, sometimes tyrants were actively used by God to punish a wicked people. Yet, even though 'the power of tyrants' can 'in a certain sense [be] good', John insisted that 'it is just for public tyrants to be killed and the people to be liberated for obedience to God.'[19] Just as the prince 'is to be loved, venerated and respected' because he is the 'image of the deity' (significantly it is the prince, not man, who is in the image of God), so 'the tyrant, as the image of depravity, is for the most part even to be killed.'[20]

John justified this extreme doctrine with an extended reference to the Apocryphal book of Judith, in which the eponymous Jewish heroine decapitates the Assyrian general, Holofernes, for his violent, oppressive blasphemy. Having retold the story of Judith's revenge in detail, John was careful to preach forbearance. Poison was forbidden, presumably because it was too secretive and denied any possibility of accountability. Tyrants, if removed, 'are to be removed without loss to religion and honour'. Moreover, great care should be taken 'lest anyone cause the death of a tyrant who is bound to him by the obligation of fealty of a sacred oath'. In general, it is better for those oppressed by tyrants to 'resort to the protection of God's clemency' and implore him to remove 'the scourge with which they are afflicted' – to which end John gives innumerable examples of how 'wickedness is always punished by the Lord.'[21]

John was thus not interested in setting out a detailed programme for removing tyrants, a theologically problematic and politically (indeed, literally) suicidal enterprise for his time. Rather, his discussion of tyrannicide was simply the logical extension of his earlier examination of the duties of and limitations on the prince. Sometimes God 'uses His own sword' and sometimes 'he uses a sort of human sword' to punish tyrants. But John's fundamental point was that whether they are killed in battle (like Ahab in 1 Kgs 22), thrown out of a window (like Jezebel in 2 Kgs 9), plagued by 'natural' disasters (like Pharaoh in Exod. 7), afflicted by disease (like Sennacherib in 2 Kgs 19), or lose their mind (like Nebuchadnezzar in Dan. 4) – all examples cited by John – or whether, like Holofernes, they are killed by an assassin, 'the end of tyrants is confusion.'[22]

'When a king errs, the people should resist him': the king under law

Policraticus was read and cited widely in the later Middle Ages and beyond, but it did not have a direct impact on the exercise of power in England at the time. Quite apart from its length and disorderly format deterring such application, its author was too engaged in the world of books to reshape the world of politics. The two worlds were hardly mutually exclusive, however, and it was quite possible for a biblically sophisticated ecclesiastic to make his mark on contemporary politics. Stephen Langton, born a generation after John, master at the University of Paris where he became one of the most prolific and respected biblical scholars, and subsequently Archbishop of Canterbury, constitutes perhaps the classic example of the two worlds meeting.

Langton's political thinking was of a piece with John's and, while at Paris, he wrote about two matters on which *Policraticus* had touched. The first was obedience to the law. In 1 Samuel 10:24–5 the Israelites, having demanded a king against God's wishes, witness the prophet Samuel choose Saul and Samuel then 'told the people the manner of the kingdom, and wrote it in a book, and laid it up before the Lord'. Langton interpreted this as meaning that kings should not demand anything beyond what had been written down, identifying the law of the realm with the book of Deuteronomy. Just as John of

Salisbury had done, he proposed that written law should control and contain the activities of kings.[23]

The second matter was the question of what to do when kings behaved tyrannously. Langton, like many of his peers, explored the implications of Paul's exhortation to obedience in Romans 13, asking whether and how one could legitimately resist the ordinance of God. He concluded that, 'if someone abuses the power that is given to him by God and if I know that this bad use would constitute a mortal sin for me, I ought not to obey him, lest I resist the ordinance of God.'[24] Elsewhere he remarked that 'when a king errs, the people should resist him as far as they can; if they do not, they sin.'

He explored the issue further through a series of medieval thought games. What should an executioner do if he knows that the convicted criminal is innocent? (His answer rested on Prov. 24:11–12: 'Rescue those who are being taken away to death.'[25]) Or, again, what should you do if the king calls you to perform service in an unjust war (a question of timeless relevance)? His answer was: '[I] arrive as summoned, but when it comes to taking up arms, either I retire, or I remain without taking up arms.'[26]

In principle, like John of Salisbury and every other medieval thinker of note, Langton was for submission to a prince even when his actions were unjust. The biblical teaching on authority was clear and, perhaps more persuasively, the spectre of anarchy was simply too frightening to the medieval mind. However, he acknowledged exceptions. If the injustice of a particular condemnation is common knowledge, the executioner may refuse to obey the prince's command. If the king commands a mortal sin, one has the right to resist. If a war is declared without the decision of a legitimate court, the people can resist and an individual knight can abstain from active service. And significantly, given Langton's future career, if someone has been condemned without a judicial sentence, the people are allowed to free the victim. Overall, Langton was willing to defend political authority even if unjust, just as long as it was legally adjudicated. The imperative of judgement by a legitimate court was his 'personal signature'.[27]

Stephen Langton was the man whom Pope Innocent III chose to assume the see of Canterbury when Hubert Walter died in 1205. This was not a popular choice, least of all with King John, and the ensuing dispute lasted eight years. When Langton was finally able to take up his post in 1213, he quoted a pastoral letter he had written to his flock on his consecration many years earlier. This cited the Paris School teaching of his earlier years and claimed that the sinful command of a king may legitimately be disregarded in favour of a higher power. 'By human law even a serf is not held to obey a lord in atrocities, much less should you who profess freedom of heart and condition . . . Whatever is imposed by a temporal king in prejudice of the eternal king produces, without doubt, sedition.'[28] These were fighting words and even though he soon absolved King John of the excommunication that had been laid upon him during his conflict with Innocent III, Langton soon became a focus for the baronial opposition to the king.

John had been unpopular with his leading noblemen for a number of years. Having lost most of his lands in northern France within a few of years of ascending to the throne, he spent much of the next decade trying to recover them. His campaigns in Normandy were unsuccessful and expensive, and the high-handed way he went about raising revenue for them managed to alienate many barons, particularly those from the north who had fewest links to the continent. In late August 1213 Langton met with various bishops, abbots and barons and told them that when absolving Henry the previous month, he had obliged the king to swear that he would abolish evil laws and establish good ones, precisely what the frustrated nobility wanted. Langton then produced a charter that had been drawn up in 1100 to elicit support for Henry I's weak claim to the throne. After the example of the prophet Samuel, Langton used this law to define the 'ancient liberties' that King John had flouted and presented it to the gathered bishops, abbots and barons to galvanise opposition.[29] This so-called 'Coronation Charter' of Henry became one of the sources for Magna Carta. Langton did not, of course, have any role in drafting it but it seems likely that he did influence a second source of the great charter, the so-called 'Unknown Charter'. This was not so much a formal agreement as a draft of the discussions that preceded Magna Carta.[30] Its first article reads: 'King John concedes that he will not accept anything for justice or commit injustice and that he will not take a man without judgment.' Although the first two clauses would have been familiar to contemporaries, the third was less so, and reflects Langton's earlier treatment of the question of obedience due to a political authority.

After Pope Innocent had rebuked him for his partisan role, Langton began to act as a mediator between the parties. Nevertheless, a number of his concerns found their way into Magna Carta itself. In the first place, just as Henry I's Coronation Charter had opened with a declaration of the liberty of the Church, so did Magna Carta. More substantively, Langton's concern for the necessity of legitimate judgement was also present, in the form of Article 39 ('No free man shall be taken or imprisoned or disseised [dispossessed] or outlawed or exiled or in any way ruined . . . except by the lawful judgment of his peers or by the law of the land'), Article 40 (' To no one will we sell, to no one will we deny or delay right or justice') and Article 52 ('If any one has been disseised or deprived by us without lawful judgment of his peers of lands, castles, liberties, or his rights, we will restore them to him at once').[31]

Runnymede was the beginning rather than the end of the story of Magna Carta. John rapidly disavowed the agreement and Pope Innocent, now thoroughly a king's man after John's fealty to him, annulled the charter and excommunicated the barons. Langton refused to publish the sentence and was suspended from his functions, leaving the country and only returning when Innocent and John were both dead. In the ensuing years, Langton defended the great charter and was instrumental in obtaining the reissues of 1223 and 1225.

Overall, Langton was 'a mediator and a moderator, rather than an originator'.[32] He was trained as a biblical scholar and theologian, not as a politician. Yet his training helped him shape and reinforce the baronial programme in its early stages. Although thoroughly influenced by the doctrine of submission to the authorities, Langton had thought carefully about when it was and was not legitimate to resist those authorities, and the result was a particular focus on legal procedure. If the prince proceeds without a legal judgement of his court, his action may be resisted. This principle of due process, which Langton forged in his disputations and which prefaced the Unknown Charter, was subsequently incorporated into Magna Carta and became a lasting contribution to English law. It is noteworthy that of the four articles of Magna Carta in 1215 that survive on the English Statute Book today, three (Article 1, freedom of the Church; Article 39, due process; and Article 40, sale of justice) were shaped by Stephen Langton's biblical studies in Paris.[33]

'From the beginning all men were created equal by nature': the threat of the Bible

Stephen Langton, like Becket and John of Salisbury before him, made a small but significant contribution to the idea of political freedom. That recognised, his contribution, again like Becket's and Salisbury's, was almost accidental. None of them fought for the cause of political liberty or championed anything remotely like democratic accountability. They may have derived arguments for political resistance from their biblical studies, but they would have been horrified at the thought that such biblically justified resistance might threaten the established order.

Yet it could, as both the most notorious popular rising of the medieval period and its most notorious heretic were to demonstrate. As contemporary sources for the Peasants' Revolt are all hostile it is not always clear what happened in the summer of 1381 and why. The Black Death, which had halved Europe's population thirty years earlier, had shaken the medieval economy by enabling those labourers left alive to charge higher wages for their services. This was resented by the authorities who passed the Statute of Labourers in 1351 which tried to fix wages. The law was unworkable (which did not stop landlords trying to work it) and widely resented, a resentment that was compounded by the financial mismanagement of an increasingly disastrous war with France, which precipitated a series of regressive and draconian taxes.

Tired of paying for an incompetent and unsuccessful campaign, the last parliament of Edward III's reign proposed a poll tax in which 4 pence, the equivalent of three days' labour according to prices set by the Statute of Labourers, would be taken from every man and woman over fourteen. The tax was taken but made little difference. Edward III's death in 1377 brought his nine-year-old grandson,

Richard, to the throne, together with his uncle, John of Gaunt, as regent. Two more universal taxes were raised in 1379 and 1380 and, although these were progressive rather than flat rate, both were resented and heavily evaded. Yet another tax, even blunter and heavier, was levied in late 1380 and when it too was widely evaded, royal commissioners were sent to investigate why. Their heavy-handed tactics, coming on the back of burdensome taxation, incompetent war management and the Statute of Labourers became too much. Labourers in Essex and Kent marched on London, led by Wat Tyler, Jack Straw and a rebel priest called John Ball.

The little that's known about Ball paints him as a long-standing radical and troublemaker. A preacher whose sermons had put him in conflict with the ecclesiastical authorities, Ball had been excommunicated, forbidden to preach and imprisoned on at least three occasions. At the time of the revolt he was in prison in Maidstone in Kent, but was quickly sprung and preached to the rebels camped at Blackheath. The French chronicler Jean Froissart, who called him 'a crack-brained priest', recorded how he had the habit on Sundays after Mass of going to the cloisters or graveyard, assembling the people round him and preaching a message of aggressive egalitarianism: 'Good people, things cannot go right in England and never will, until goods are held in common and there are no more villeins and gentlefolk, but we are all one and the same. In what way are those whom we call lords greater masters than ourselves? How have they deserved it? Why do they hold us in bondage?' [34] The rationale for his dangerous levelling was explicitly biblical. 'If we all spring from a single father and mother, Adam and Eve, how can they claim or prove that they are lords more than us, except by making us produce and grow the wealth which they spend?'

It is entirely possible that this sermon was simply made up by Froissart who was no eyewitness and who wanted to depict Ball in the most lurid political light. Nevertheless, the ideas accord well with other sources, not least the rhyming couplet for which Ball is best known: 'When Adam delved [dug] and Eve span,/ Who was then the gentleman?'

In the end neither Ball's biblically justified levelling nor Ball himself amounted to much. One fizzled out at Smithfield after three days of rioting and bloodshed, while the other was captured on the run and then hanged, beheaded, disembowelled and quartered a month later. The fact that Ball had based his egalitarianism and proto-communism on Genesis 1 was, however, significant. He understood the biblical creation story to emphasise a human equality which threatened to undermine the ordered hierarchy of the medieval universe. Unlike John of Salisbury in *Policraticus* or St Boniface four centuries before him, John Ball took 'the image of God' of Genesis 1 as applying to everyone, not simply or especially princes. In doing so, he attempted to level the ground beneath the existing political structures in such a way as threatened to topple them.

Ball's use of the Bible to challenge rather than simply sustain the existing social and political order showed how the scriptures could threaten as well as safeguard, a fact that was becoming particularly clear at the time in the 'perverse doctrines and opinions and crazy heresies' of the theologian of whom John Ball allegedly confessed he had been a disciple.[35] John Wyclif was from a very different stratum in society to Ball, and Ball's confession of his theological allegiance may simply have been made up in order to further blacken the rebel's name. Nevertheless, there is more of a link between the two men than just the casual association of all things threatening. Wyclif had an immensely productive and varied academic career, in which he wrote and lectured on philosophical, theological, biblical and political topics. Some of his works, notably *On Civil Dominion*, which was published a few years before the Peasants' Revolt and which argued (among other things) that 'all the goods of God should be common', sounded a similar, if more erudite, note to that of the rebels.[36] As one of Wyclif's modern interpreters has remarked, the revolutionaries 'would not have been doing violence to the text of *On Civil Dominion* if they had claimed its support for the expropriation of the wicked rich'.[37]

Perhaps the most astonishing thing about Wyclif's life was that it ended naturally. Born in the mid-1320s in North Yorkshire, he studied at Oxford where he was influenced by Franciscan ideals of poverty. His initial focus was philosophical but he became involved in politics from the 1370s. Dealings with the papacy hardened his attitude to ecclesiastical authority, and he subsequently attacked the traditional defence of papal authority, arguing that to believe the Pope exercises such a power was, in itself, heretical.

His political experience marked him and reshaped the multi-volume theological treatise he was writing. The first two books of this had been orthodox and narrowly academic; the ensuing ones were both topical and controversial. This was where, in *On Civil Dominion*, he explored when it was legitimate to resist a tyrant, how 'all things should be in common', and how, because 'by the law of Christ every man is bound to love his neighbour as himself . . . [so a civil lord] is bound not to impose slavery on any brother in Christ.'[38] He also argued for the disendowment of the Church, for whom Christ's advocacy of poverty remained a vocational necessity. Worse still, 'temporal lords', he wrote, were justified in 'confiscating the moveable and immoveable property of delinquent churchmen' when their abuse was 'habitual', with Wyclif offering a definition of abuse that was clearly intended to finger his contemporaries.

Most significant for the way in which the Bible was encountered in England for the next 150 years was the fact that Wyclif based many of his arguments, to use the title of one of his treatises, *On the Truth of Sacred Scripture*. This polemical work drew on his many years of biblical study at Oxford and did much to earn him the title of 'Evangelical Doctor' and 'Morning Star of the Reformation'. It had three main objectives.[39]

The first was to show that the Bible was free from error and that its authority derived from its divine authorship. This wasn't quite the kind of literalist fundamentalism of popular imagination, as Wyclif believed it was necessary to read scripture on different levels, mentioning 'five degrees' of sacred scripture. His view of the Bible was threatening not so much because it attributed inerrancy to it, but because he elevated the text above its interpreter, including ecclesiastical interpreters. He removed from the Church the right to be sole adjudicator of biblical meaning.

Second and closely linked to this, Wyclif claimed that truth resided in the Bible and not in any of the other examples of supposed divine revelation that had been made to, and passed down by, the Church through the ages. That meant that the Bible should be the yardstick by which to judge popes, bishops, theologians and philosophers, rather than the other way round. He did not hide the implications of this. 'Even the lord Pope . . . may be ignorant of the sense of Scripture and in a greedy quest for wealth interpret it in a sense contrary to Christ.'[40]

Finally, and again consequently, since the Bible contains truth and no one, even the Pope, has a monopoly on its interpretation, scripture should be placed at the disposal of all Christians, both lay and ordained. Wyclif recognised that this did not mean that readers would automatically arrive at the correct interpretation. Nevertheless, he argued, the *right* person would interpret scripture rightly, wherever they stood in the great chain of being. 'The faithful whom [Christ] calls in meekness and humility of heart, whether they be clergy or laity, male or female, bending the neck of their inner man to the logic and style of Scripture will find in it . . . the wisdom hidden from the proud.'[41] The implications of this were clear, as Wyclif himself noted in another work, *Mirror of Secular Lords*. 'Christ and his apostles converted a great multitude by unveiling sacred scripture to them, and that in the language which was most familiar to the people . . . Why then should not modern disciples of Christ [do likewise]?'[42] It is not clear whether Wyclif himself translated the Bible into the vernacular (it seems unlikely), but by the end of the 1380s there were at least 100 English manuscripts in circulation, twenty of which encompassed the entire Bible, an astonishing effort of production in pre-printing days. These were, in effect, the first English Bibles (a few texts had been glossed or translated from the standard, Vulgate Latin the later Anglo-Saxon period). Altogether over 250 manuscripts from the period survive, more than any other medieval text.[43]

The initial reaction against Wyclif, the Lollard movement (Lollard meant, contemptuously, 'mutterer' and was used to describe Wyclif's alleged followers) and the English Bible was muted. Wyclif himself was protected by John of Gaunt, who found in the theologian's teaching useful material for his on-going conflict with the ecclesiastical establishment. Those who came after him were not so fortunate. Lollardy boasted some aristocratic support at first, which helps explain why the authorities were slow to act against it. But act they eventually did. In 1401 Henry IV passed the law, *De heretico comburendo*, forbidding anyone from owning or reading a vernacular Bible on pain of being burned to death. Eight years later, Archbishop Thomas Arundel called a Provincial Council in Oxford, which passed a series of articles banning vernacular translations.[44] When, in 1414, a number of Lollards supported a rebellion headed by Sir John Oldcastle, the association of Wyclif, Lollardy and antisocial threat was sealed.

Ironically, this was *in spite* of what Wyclif and many Lollards actually believed about political authority itself. Like the early reformers the Lollards were generally quite conservative in their attitude to secular (as opposed to ecclesiastical) power. The fact that Wyclif saw the best hope for ecclesiastical reform in the king and secular nobility led him to stress not only the legitimacy of political authority, but also its rights over the Church. One Lollard text insisted that 'since there is no power but that ordained by God . . . he that withstands the just power of kings, withstands God to his own damnation,' as orthodox a position as one could imagine. As historian Anne Hudson has observed, although we do not know how Oldcastle justified his rebellion against the king, what is certain is that Wycliffite texts (or, at least those we still have) have him giving no encouragement to rebel.[45]

Lollard texts tended to be far more concerned with, and prepared to countenance resistance to, spiritual tyrants than temporal ones. It was not so much the *political* order that was directly threatened by Lollardy as the *ecclesiastical* order to which it was married. However, as many reformers were to find a century or so later, professions of political loyalty were to count for little when set against a challenge to the religious foundations on which political authority was founded. It was the Wycliffite determination to expose and redraw those foundations that made the movement a political threat.

So it was that for the duration of the fifteenth century the Bible became both the basis for political order and, in the vernacular at least, its greatest threat. On the one hand, it showed how monarchy was validated by God, how the king was his deputy on earth, how he was anointed with holy oil and appointed to rule in God's place, how rebellion against him was rebellion against God, how tyrants should be tolerated and how society was ordered in such a way as reflected the hierarchical and cosmic order. On the other, in the hands of disreputable rebels like John Ball or, worse, reputable scholars like John Wyclif, it could be used to show how all people were created equal, how none should lord his power over others and how all deserved unmediated access to God's Word.

The fact that Wyclif claimed to derive his teaching from the Bible was alarming. The fact that he had translated or enabled the translation of that Bible into English was worse. And the fact that he had advocated the distribution of those Bibles to ordinary people, whose interpretation he deemed legitimate, was inexcusable. 'The word of God', it appeared, was indeed 'quick, and powerful, and sharper than any two-edged sword'.[46]

PART 2

The Age of Biblical Politics and its Shadow

3

'The authority of princes may not be resisted': The weight of obedience

In late March 1532 two men met in a field outside Antwerp. One was Stephen Vaughan, a merchant and old friend of Henry VIII's chief adviser, Thomas Cromwell. The other was a heretic and fugitive.

Vaughan had been sent by Cromwell to make contact with the man whose support the king apparently wished to enlist in his increasingly acrimonious dispute with the papacy. Vaughan had written to him three times, with the offer of safe conduct to England. He had no success. Each time the fugitive had through an intermediary courteously refused the offer, believing it to be a trap.

Eventually and without warning, a messenger had approached Vaughan, inviting him to meet 'an unknown friend'. Vaughan was suspicious but acquiesced, following the messenger through the city gates and into a nearby field where the stranger was waiting. 'Do you not know me?' he asked abruptly. 'I do not well remember you,' Vaughan replied diplomatically. 'My name is Tyndale,' the stranger said.[1]

William Tyndale had been a refugee for nearly a decade. He was a scholar, a linguist of unsurpassed ability and responsible, more than any other man, for the shape of the English Bible and thereby the English language over the next 300 years.

'Nothing can be more poisonous than a rebel': Martin Luther and obedience

About twenty years before Tyndale and Vaughan met, Martin Luther had had an epiphany. Recently appointed to the Chair of Theology at Wittenberg University, he had been an observant but troubled monk for many years. Struggling through the reasons for his anxiety, he came to the conclusion that the way in which he had been trying to set himself right with God, as a good Augustinian monk, through prayer, fasting, pilgrimage, confession and other 'works', was not only inadequate but unnecessary. Instead, all that was needed was faith, the trust that God gave to sinful men, through no merit of their own, God's own righteousness. Salvation came through faith alone.

Luther worked through the meaning and implications of this in lectures on the Psalms, and the New Testament letters Romans, Galatians and Hebrews between 1513 and 1517, before going public with his renowned ninety-five theses protesting at the sale of indulgences, another form of 'works', in order to raise money to rebuild St Peter's in Rome.[2] The implications were wide-ranging, not least for the Church. If salvation came through faith alone, the entire purpose of the Church was transformed. In one move, it changed from being the visible presence of God's authoritative kingdom on earth to being a largely superfluous middleman, a kind of unnecessary broker in the deal between God and the human soul. This did not mean there was no longer any such thing as a Church, or that its work of administering the sacraments or preaching the Word was unimportant. Rather it meant that the true Church was an invisible body of believers scattered throughout society. The ramifications for the Church's ability to act as an alternative source of political authority, challenging and even deposing the tyrannous as necessary, were immense.

Luther rejected the idea that the Church possessed separate jurisdictional powers. He rejected the idea of canon law and a separate legal system. He rejected the idea that the Church held authority over any secular power. Because the Church was a congregation of the faithful it simply could not exercise jurisdictional powers. Luther continued to speak of two kingdoms but these were no longer public, secular government and the Church. Instead, the two kingdoms were now public government and the purely personal, inward, spiritual form of self-government, a government of the soul, which had no outward form, ecclesiastical or otherwise.

In his 1523 tract *Temporal Authority: to what extent it should be obeyed,* Luther argued that all Christians live simultaneously in two kingdoms, that of the world and that of Christ, but that while the former is ruled by the temporal authorities the latter is ruled not by the Pope or ecclesiastics, but directly by Christ, simply, spiritually and without coercion. Thus the Church, which had grown up over the last 500 years into the major curb on the exercise of political power, was cut down, its public authority, jurisdiction and legal system all removed.

If there was a resulting power vacuum in this vision, it was quickly and explicitly filled by temporal power. The governing authorities now had the monopoly on all use of coercive power, including over the visible Church. Kings did not become sacred, at least no more sacred than anointing already made them, nor did they have the authority to pronounce on matters of doctrine, although some tried. Rather they had the monopoly on all political power, which they derived directly from God and had a duty to use in securing religious uniformity and orthodoxy within their territories.

Luther derived much of this doctrine from Romans 13. As noted earlier, the first verse of Romans 13 reads: 'Let every soul be subject unto the higher powers. For there is no power but of God: the powers that be are ordained of God.' Luther followed this closely and saw in it no legitimate reason for disobedience. In some ways the history of political theology in the sixteenth century is the attempt by Christians, mainly but not exclusively Protestants,[3] to clamber out of the hole that Luther's reading of Romans 13 had dug them into.

In his defence, much of Luther's authoritarianism was derived, as it was for many of the Reformers, from the fear that his reforming programme would become mixed up with political radicalism and insurrection, thereby proving right the accusations against him and destabilising his reform. He had good reason to be concerned. The years 1524–25 witnessed a massive uprising across Europe which, although economic in origin, was exacerbated by Reformation politics and ideas.[4]

Luther was worried and incensed by the events. Although beginning in a conciliatory tone, with *An Admonition to Peace* which was published in April 1525, he rapidly moved to one of barely disguised hysteria, and republished *An Admonition* a month later, amid growing social disorder, this time with an appendix memorably entitled 'Against the Robbing and Murdering Hordes of Peasants'. This took its stand firmly on Romans 13:1, and advised, graphically, that 'everyone who can [should] smite, slay and stab, secretly or openly, remembering that nothing can be more poisonous, hurtful or devilish than a rebel.'[5]

In reality, Luther's reading of Paul, even at this most authoritarian stage of his life, was not as severe as might first appear. He wrote that the prince was not to use his powers arbitrarily. Rather, he was to use them in a godly way, to 'protect and maintain [his subjects] in peace and plenty', 'to bring about external peace', and to 'prevent evil deeds'. Perhaps most significantly, he was to avoid any attempt 'to, command or compel anyone by force to believe this or that', since the regulation of such a 'secret, spiritual, hidden matter' can never be said to lie within his competence.[6] The ruler who flouted these regulations and, in particular, the one who tried to compel his subjects into ungodly ways could not demand obedience. Luther's justification for this came in repeated references to Acts 5 when the apostles were hauled up before the Jewish assembly and told not to preach. 'We obey God (who desires the right) rather than men,' they replied. Luther summarised his point in the form of a catechism at the end of *Temporal Authority*. 'What if a prince is in the wrong? Are his people bound to follow him then too?' The answer was 'No, for it is no one's duty to do wrong.' It was these cracks in the doctrine of absolute obedience that would, in the fullness of time, widen to become liberty of conscience.

In spite of this recognition of the possibility of conscience, however, and the tension between the freedom of Acts 5 and the order of Romans 13, the latter always has the upper hand in Luther's thought. He instructed his readers that if the prince were to command them to do evil, they must refuse. Should the prince then 'seize your property on account of this and punish such disobedience', subjects must passively submit and 'thank God that you are worthy to suffer for the sake of the divine word'. Tyranny 'is not to be resisted but endured'. Luther held this uncompromising position throughout the 1520s, although he changed it in the early 1530s when the new reform movement came under severe threat. However, it was the Luther of the 1520s who influenced the most important early English Reformer, William Tyndale.

'The authority of princes may not be resisted': Tyndale and the English Bible

William Tyndale was heavily indebted to Luther. Born in 1494, Tyndale studied at Oxford where he encountered the new humanist learning that was making such an impact across Europe. This advocated, among other things, a return to the sources, to original, ancient documents, among them the Bible. In 1516 the greatest of European humanists, Desiderius Erasmus, published his *Novum Instrumentum* or New Instrument, which printed the New Testament in its original Greek and alongside it a new Latin translation, which made about 400 changes to the traditional Latin Vulgate translation, and then followed it up with over 300 pages of notes explaining these changes.

Elsewhere Erasmus had written: 'Christ wishes his mysteries to be published as widely as possible . . . I would wish they were translated into all languages.'[7] Tyndale clearly had the same vision. Living and working as a tutor in Gloucestershire in the early 1520s he is said to have remarked to a clergyman over dinner, 'If God spare my life ere many years I will cause a boy that drives the plough shall know more of the scripture than you do.'[8] He soon travelled to London to seek official sanction for his translation work, aware that the post-Wyclif legislation against any such work was still in place. He had hoped that Cuthbert Tunstall, the Bishop of London, who had helped Erasmus track down some of his Greek manuscripts, would provide the sponsorship. Tunstall refused to see him, however, and Tyndale swiftly realised that 'there was no place in all England' for his work.

He promptly left for Germany where he translated the New Testament from Greek and saw it through to the printers. It was an epochal publication. Tyndale was a brilliant linguist. The translation is simple, accurate, vivid and accessible to the common people. It was to form the basis of every major translation of the English Bible for the next century. The volume was published in an octavo or pocket-sized format, making it easier to conceal, a serious consideration given that no sooner were they arriving in England than they were banned and burned. Soon those caught with them faced the same fate.

Tyndale's New Testament was the most significant political text of the English Reformation, not so much because of what it said but simply because of its existence. It aimed to give everyone access to the foundation documents of their society. In doing so, it threatened to change everything. The translation itself scored some significant, Lutheran points that undermined the authority of the Church. Tyndale rendered the Greek noun *ecclesia* not as 'church' but 'congregation', while *presbyteros* was translated initially as 'senior' and, in later revisions, as 'elder' rather than 'priest'. The implications were clear. Not only was Tyndale placing society's founding document in the hands of every person, not only was he translating it so that the worker in the field might actually read and understand it, but he was translating it in such a way as radically reformed the authority of the very body that ordered and defined society. It was a profoundly, dangerously democratic thing to do, although Tyndale was anything but a democrat.

The authorities condemned the translation. Bishop Tunstall organised a bonfire of Bibles and the king ordered that those caught reading it should receive 'further sharp correction and punishment'.[9] Tyndale, Henry VIII contended, had produced 'pestiferous English books . . . to pervert . . . the people . . . to stir and incense them to sedition'.[10] This was an understandable opinion, if somewhat ironic given that Tyndale was convinced that princes were responsible for the religious beliefs of their people and that they should be obeyed without question. Two years after the first complete New Testament rolled off the presses, he published his most substantial work of political thought, *The Obedience of a Christian Man*. The context of the book, as with Luther's work on the same subject, was the accusation that Protestants were social revolutionaries. Tyndale set out to prove the opposite was true.[11]

He began by locating political order in the wider order of creation. Tyndale demonstrated that hierarchy was part of the social, indeed cosmic, order, and that this could be seen in scripture itself. Thus the command in Exodus 20 to 'honour thy father and mother' underpinned the obedience of children to their parents. The consequences of the Fall in Genesis 3, coupled with Peter's words in 1 Peter 3[12] and Paul's in Ephesians 5[13] underpinned the 'obedience of wives unto their husbands'. The same texts, supplemented by Paul's short letter to Philemon, in which the apostle 'sent home Onesimus unto his master' justified the obedience of servants to their masters. The obedience of subjects 'unto kings, princes, and rulers' fitted into this structure, as the classic texts of 1 Peter 2[14] and Romans 13 showed.

Following Luther, Tyndale reasoned that this picture of a divinely ordained social order meant not only that subjects have a duty to obey their political masters but also that they must not actively resist tyranny. 'Neither may the inferior person avenge himself upon the superior, or violently resist him, for whatsoever wrong it be,' he stated, before going on to explain that in doing so he 'takes upon him that which belongs to God only, which says, "Vengeance is mine, and I will reward."'[15]

There was another side to the coin, however, relating to the duty that rulers have to their people. The lead here was Romans 13, in which Tyndale struck a slightly different note to Luther, combining the authoritarianism of verse 1 (and 2) with the more attenuated tone of verse 3 (and 4). Shortly after Paul insisted, in verse 2, that 'whosoever therefore resisteth the power, resisteth the ordinance of God,' he introduced what appears – and was understood to be – a caveat: 'For he is the minister of God to thee for good.' In other words, the godly prince has a duty to serve the welfare of his people.

Thus, having outlined the obedience due of children to parents, wives to husbands, servants to masters and subjects to rulers, Tyndale wrote about the 'duties' of each of these 'offices'. In doing so he drew on precisely the same biblical sources as he did in outlining his teaching on obedience. Thus a father should 'move not your children unto wrath, but bring them up in the nurture and information'.[16] 'Husbands [ought to] love [their] wives as Christ loved the congregation, and gave himself for it.'[17] Masters should 'give [their] servants kind words, food, raiment, and learning [and] be not bitter unto them'.[18] And, adding another office, Christian landlords ought to 'be content with their rent and old customs; not raising the rent or fines, and bringing up new customs to oppress their tenants'.[19]

The duties of the king fitted into this context. Christian kings ought to 'give themselves altogether to the wealth [welfare] of their realms after the ensample of Christ'.[20] They should 'remember . . . that the people are God's, and not theirs', and that 'the king is but a servant, to execute the law of God, and not to rule after his own imagination.' Tyndale even, on occasion, slips into the kind of rhetoric of radical equality that was in danger of confirming the accusations made against him and his fellow Reformers. 'The most despised person in his realm is the king's brother, and fellow-member with him, and equal with him in the kingdom of God and of Christ.'[21] If there are the seeds of egalitarianism and future resistance theories in Tyndale's reading of politics, Tyndale does little more than gesture vaguely in the direction of a limited monarchy, preferring admonition and exhortation over anything more substantive. Overall, there is little doubt where Tyndale himself stands. As with Luther, he can envisage passive resistance. If a wicked prince 'command[s] to do evil, we must then disobey, and say, "We are otherwise commanded of God."' But that does not legitimise rebellion. 'The authority of princes . . . may not be resisted: do they never so evil.'[22]

Tyndale was the most important although not the only early English Lutheran. Robert Barnes, an exact contemporary, was educated at the more radical Cambridge where he preached what is said to have been the first openly evangelical sermon of the English Reformation in 1526. He wrote several short political tracts, exploring the nature of the Church and the extent and legitimacy of political obedience that were pure Luther in their logic. He did, however, diverge from the strict Lutheran template in his recognition that there is a second limitation on a ruler's power, beyond the universally acknowledged imperative not to legislate against God's law. This related to the enormously influential concept of *adiaphora* or 'indifferent things'. Here the argument went that while there are some (divine) laws that are essential for salvation, there are other (human) laws that are not. God apparently intended a number of activities to be neither prescribed nor proscribed, and that 'an erroneous situation' will be created 'by enacting them into laws'.[23] Barnes argued that a godly prince is limited not only by the need not to legislate against God's laws but also the need not to 'command certain indifferent things as if they must be done of necessity'.[24] It is from this tiny and seemingly insignificant seed that the doctrine of tolerance would grow. It would, however, first be fed by much blood and charred flesh, including that of both Tyndale and Barnes.

'If a man marries his brother's wife, it is an act
of impurity': Reformation and the 1530s

The way in which Tyndale, Barnes and the other early Reformers
deconstructed the Church's temporal power, denied its historical
claim to judge and depose tyrannical rulers, and sank the theological
foundations on which a doctrine of near-absolute monarchy could be
built, should have made them perfect allies for the Henrician reforms
of the 1530s.

There is some evidence, how reliable it is not clear, that Anne
Boleyn managed to place a copy of Tyndale's *Obedience* into Henry
VIII's hands. The king is supposed to have enjoyed it, remarking that
this was a book 'for me and all kings to read'.[25] It would be wrong,
however, to read from this story (assuming its authenticity) that
Tyndale's thinking exerted a direct influence on the king's programme
of reform in the 1530s. Although Henry would undoubtedly have
appreciated the Lutheran position on obedience, he admired little
else in the new movement. Henry had been among the first European
princes to denounce the heresy, publishing a tract against it in 1521,
for which Pope Leo named him 'Defender of the Faith', and calling
Luther a pig and a drunkard. Even after the break with Rome and his
use of Lutheran political theology, Henry never had much inclination
to become a Lutheran, showing particular hostility to the fundamental doctrine of justification by faith, which he saw as a licence to sin
without fear.

Lutheranism was a tiny and largely foreign problem for England in
the 1520s. Its growth towards the end of the decade led to a more
aggressive policy through which at least thirteen people were burned
between 1530 and 1533. Ironically this was also the time during
which the king's 'Great Matter' opened the door to (aspects of)
Lutheran thinking. Henry's divorce was, in itself, as profoundly biblical an issue as it was political and sexual. His all-consuming desire to
be rid of Catherine of Aragon and to wed Anne Boleyn, which
informed his personal conviction that his first marriage was unlawful
and displeasing to God, hinged on a single verse from Leviticus: 'If a
man shall take his brother's wife, it is an unclean thing: he hath uncovered his brother's nakedness; they shall be childless.' (Lev. 20:21)

That this originally referred to marrying the wife of a living brother is strongly suggested by another command in the book of Deuteronomy.[26] According to Old Testament law, a brother had a positive duty to marry, impregnate and support his deceased brother's spouse, and even though Christian theologians had viewed this law as being part of the ceremonial corpus that was abrogated by Christ, there was little in the scriptures to suggest that Henry had committed as ghastly a sin as he seemed to think. With his enviable ability to convince himself utterly, Henry ignored the Deuteronomy text and wilfully interpreted the Leviticus one as referring to the special dispensation he had obtained from Pope Julius II in 1503 in order marry Catherine, then his older brother Arthur's widow.

Henry's scriptural exegesis failed to persuade the relevant authorities. The Leviticus passage declared that such illicit unions would remain "childless", which pliant biblical scholars interpreted as meaning "without a son", and as this was precisely the source of Henry's frustration with Catherine, it served to confirm in his mind the rightness of his cause. Catherine, however, insisted that her marriage to Henry's older brother had never been consummated, which rendered the Leviticus verse redundant and so undermined Henry's case. Moreover, the fact that Henry was seeking a divorce from his deceased brother's wife so that he could marry the sister of his former mistress, Mary Boleyn, rather weakened the moral force of his case. In any event, Pope Clement VII was unmoved. Not only was Henry's rationale not as strong as he imagined, either biblically or in terms of canon law, but the Pope was acutely conscious that Catherine's nephew was Charles V, the Holy Roman Emperor. Clement had, in effect, been Charles' prisoner since the latter's troops had sacked Rome in 1527. As if this weren't enough, the Pope badly needed the Emperor's support in combating the spread of Lutheranism. As Charles was resolutely opposed to the divorce for theological, personal and political reasons, there was no chance that Clement VII would grant Henry's wishes.

After several years of fruitless legal manoeuvrings, the tone of Henry's cause began to shift, with pressure on the Church, both at home and in Rome, giving way to explicit attacks. The English bishops were instructed to submit the Church's laws to royal and parliamentary authority, and the Pope's authority and jurisdiction in England were effectively abolished. It was into this increasingly tense situation that Tyndale's political theology spoke. The logic and rhetoric of Tyndale's theology of obedience was co-opted into a programme with which it shared only limited objectives. Both Henry and Tyndale may have shared similar attitudes to papal and princely authority, but they did so for very different reasons. For Tyndale the theology drove the politics; for Henry the politics necessitated the theology.

The consequence of all this for the role of the Bible in English politics was enormous, spreading an official position on authority that was Tyndale's in all but name, but carried with it little of Tyndale's evangelical logic. As part of his campaign to defend the Henrician reforms, Cromwell drew on the services of numerous propagandists who outlined the legitimacy of the break with Rome and the theological necessity of complete obedience to temporal powers. Some of these were able to speak with a measure of authenticity. Edward Foxe, one of Henry's most Lutheran bishops, published *The True Difference between the Regal Power and the Ecclesiastical Power* in 1534, in which he wrote, with genuine conviction, that the Church is nothing more than 'the multitude of faithful people' and that the Pope has no legitimate political jurisdiction.[27] He proceeded to cite a number of examples from the Old Testament in order to prove that 'God did give with His own mouth kings to be rulers of His people'.[28] He then backed this up with reference to Romans, from which he concluded that Paul makes three crucial points: 'all men to be obedient'; this 'excepts no man at all'; and there is damnation to any man who disobeys his ruler in any respect.[29]

Not all could speak so authentically. Stephen Gardiner was one of the king's most conservative, anti-Lutheran bishops who ended his career as Queen Mary's Lord Chancellor, from which position he re-enacted Archbishop Arundel's anti-heresy statute of 1401 and began the persecution of the English Protestants. In 1535, however, he wrote *On True Obedience*, which stated that the only proper source for understanding of political authority is the scriptures.[30] Like Foxe, he drew on the Old Testament doctrine that 'princes reign by his [God's] authority' and on a whole range of New Testament texts much favoured by the Reformers.[31] He also deployed another argument that anticipated the principle of the 1555 Treaty of Augsburg: *cuius regio eius religio*: 'Whose realm, his religion'. Since the Church, Gardiner argued, 'is nothing else but the congregation of men and women of the clergy and of the laity united in Christ's profession', it is thus also simply part of the temporal realm.[32] And since the king is head of his realm, it is 'absurd and foolish' to imagine that he is not, also, head of the Church within his realm.

Over and above these apologists, the most significant statement of Henrician faith was the *King's Book*, published in 1543. This was fully authorised by both king and parliament and dwelt, in loving detail, on the obedience owed to the king. In particular, it spent inordinate time explaining how the fifth commandment referred not only to parents but also to temporal powers. 'In this commandment, by these words father and mother, is understood not only the natural father and mother which did carnally beget us, and brought us up, but also princes and all other governors, rulers, and pastors, under whom we be nourished and brought up, ordered and guided.'[33]

It is here that we see a conflation of parental power and royal authority that was to prove so important to the doctrine of the divine right of kings in the seventeenth century. More broadly, it is also here that we see the doctrine of obedience being transformed from one (important) element of the wider Protestant Reformation, whose main focus was on the nature of salvation and the authority of scripture, to being the single most distinctive element within the Henrician Reformation. In essence, we see the emphasis on political order that was so important to the early Reformers being divorced from the equally – indeed *more* – important emphasis on the freedom for everyone to read the scriptures in their own language, wherever and whenever they please.

It was by means of propagandists like Foxe and Gardiner, and official statements like the *King's Book*, that Lutheran ideas of political obedience came to dominate England in the 1530s and for many years after. Protestants, ever insecure under a mercurial and often hostile monarch, welcomed and tried to exploit the phenomenon. At first, their success was limited but in the longer run they proved profoundly influential.

*'Admonish every man to read the very word
of God': 'Authorised' versions*

Partly because he was convinced that the book of Leviticus allowed
him to annul his marriage with Catherine; partly because he was
persuaded by the doctrine of royal supremacy that the Protestants
had derived from scripture; partly because by the mid-1530s some
were beginning to think that it was simply impossible to prevent
unauthorised translations reaching England; and partly because by
that time there were also signs of serious resistance to his reform,
Henry (and Cromwell) began to use the Bible.

Thomas Cranmer, the new, evangelical Archbishop of Canterbury,
had already tried for a vernacular translation. There was serious
resistance to the project from certain bishops, such as Stephen
Gardiner, who (later) described the idea of having a Bible in English
as a way of making 'each one man to be a church alone'. Cranmer
was not successful. [34] In 1535 Miles Coverdale, a Cambridge scholar
who had been influenced by Robert Barnes and was also working in
exile, completed a full English translation. As part of the new turn in
the king's campaign, this was permitted to 'go forth under the king's
privilege'. [35] At the same time, Cromwell passed injunctions instructing parish priests to provide a Bible in their churches, and telling
them to 'admonish every man to read the same as the very word of
God . . . whereby they may the better know their duties to God, to
their sovereign lord the king, and their neighbour.' [36] Thus, in a
remarkably rapid *volte face*, the vernacular Bible turned from being a
threat to the established political order to being a bulwark.

This can be seen in the title pages of the Bible translations that
were published in the 1530s. Coverdale's is by Hans Holbein the
Younger, and tells the full Bible story, from Adam to Christ (Fig. 1).
The focus is clearly on the Word of God. The central title is garnished
with New Testament quotations, celebrating the Word and encouraging attention: 'Let the word of Christ dwell in you plenteously in
all wisdom . . . Let not the book of this law depart out of thy mouth.'
The pictorial panels surrounding it support the message. Moses
receives the law, and Ezra preaches it. Christ sends out the apostles to
preach the gospel, which they do in a picture depicting Pentecost. At

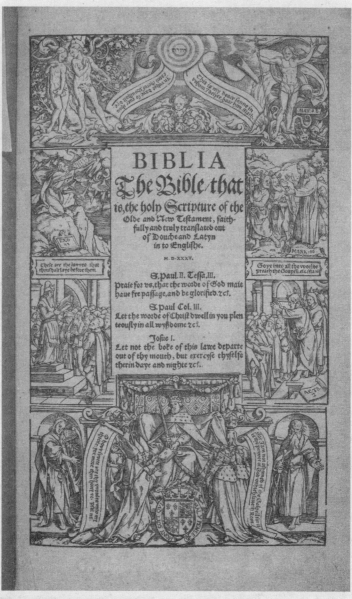

Fig. 1: Title page of Coverdale Bible (1535)

Fig. 2: Title page of Great Bible (1539)

the bottom, sitting grandly on his throne, is King Henry himself, dispensing the Bible to grateful prelates, surrounded by unfurled banners which proclaim how 'sweet are thy words' (from Ps. 119) and how 'I am not ashamed of the gospel' (Rom. 1:16). Coverdale dedicated his translation to the king with suitable bowing and scraping, but the focus was nevertheless clearly on the Word.

The following year John Rogers, chaplain to the English merchants in Antwerp, compiled a new translation, drawing on Tyndale and Coverdale's work. Cranmer reckoned it the best translation available and urged Cromwell to obtain from the king 'a license that the same may be sold and read of every person'.[37] It was this version that formed the basis for the 'Great Bible' that, in 1538, Cromwell ordered to be set up in every parish church in the country. This translation boasted a frontispiece (Fig. 2) that was markedly different from Coverdale's. Gone are the scriptural quotations in the centred title box. The page is busy and confusing, although there is no mistaking the dominant figure. King Henry is, again, on his throne, although now seated at the head of the page rather than its foot. Above him God is squeezed rather uncomfortably into a tiny heaven, from where he blesses the king and unfurls scrolls with words from the prophet Isaiah and the book of Acts.[38] The king then passes the Word of God to Archbishop Cranmer and Thomas Cromwell, both with heads uncovered in obedience. Cranmer receives the Word and is addressed by a scroll with words from 1 Timothy 4:11 ('these things command and preach'), while Cromwell is told by another scroll (from Deut. 1:16) to 'judge righteously between every man'. Yet another scroll announces (from Dan. 6:26), 'I make a decree that in all the dominion of my kingdom, men tremble and fear before the God of Daniel.'

Beneath this dominant scene, Cranmer and Cromwell distribute the Word to the clergy and the laity respectively: Cranmer to a tonsured priest kneeling before him who is advised to 'feed the flock of Christ' (1 Pet. 5:2); and Cromwell to a nobleman, who is told to 'eschew evil and do good' (Ps. 34:14). Finally, in the bottom third of the page, innumerable common folk listen to a preacher hold forth on the impeccably respectable 1 Timothy 2:1–2[39] which has the desired effect, as members of the congregation obediently proclaim VIVAT REX and GOD SAVE THE KING. In the very bottom right, we glimpse Newgate Prison, where those traitorous few who refuse to honour the king are incarcerated. The entire, ordered yet bewilderingly busy woodcut displays society as it should be ordered: the king, supreme, blessed by God, distributing the scriptures, which structure, order and guarantee society.

The difference between this and the Coverdale front page is striking and is exacerbated by one other notable difference. Unlike the Coverdale front page, every biblical text on the front page of the Great Bible is in Latin, despite it being a vernacular Bible. This is compounded by the fact that none of the commoners on the front page actually touches the Bible. The 'people' only ever *hear* the Word of God. This underlines the fact that by 1540 there was already considerable nervousness about the wisdom of placing the Bible into the hands of the common man (let alone woman). It was too radical a book to be read by the common people.

Cranmer had optimistically written in his preface to the second edition of the Great Bible that scripture would be available to 'all manner of persons, men, women, young, old, learned, unlearned, rich, poor, priests, laymen, Lords, Ladies, officers, tenants, and mean [poor] men, virgins, wives, widows, lawyers, merchants, artificers, husbandmen, and all manner of persons of what estate or condition so ever they be'. It was a thoroughly egalitarian sentiment, justified by the simple reason that 'it is convenient and good [that] the scripture be read of all sorts and kinds of people, and in the vulgar tongue.'[40]

The idea of widespread biblical reading and engagement soon soured, however. It was simply too dangerous. Almost as soon as parishes were ordered to keep a Bible for the people to read, Henry started passing restrictions on Bible reading. A 1541 proclamation ordering the Great Bible to be placed in churches also commanded that 'lay subjects' should not 'presume to take upon them any common disputation, argument, or exposition of the mysteries therein contained'.[41] It was a case of shutting the stable door too late. Two years later the Act for the Advancement of True Religion forbade subjects 'of the lower sort' from reading the Bible, declaring 'no women [though some noblewomen were exempted] nor artificers, prentices, journeymen, serving men of the degrees of yeoman or under, husbandmen, nor labourers shall read the Bible or New Testament to himself or any other, privately or openly.' In the same year *The King's Book*, which had dwelt so long on the necessity of obedience, argued that 'the having, reading, and studying of holy scripture' is 'necessary' only for that part of the Church 'whose office is to teach other'. The ideals on the frontispiece of the Great Bible were being legislated into life.

This disappointed Protestants who had expected so much from the 1530s. The truth was, however, that to Henry and his more conservative bishops, the vernacular Bible was still far too much of a risk to the political order. In spite of all the Henrician propaganda, from tame bishops, official publications and elaborate woodcut frontispieces, the fact remained that unrestricted access to the Bible threatened to 'beguile the people into the refusal of obedience'.[42]

'When the king heard the words of the Book of the Law, he tore his robes': King Edward and King Josiah

From the very earliest days of English history, the Bible had offered a conceptual scheme, a coherent, moral narrative complete with identifiable characters, into which contemporary history might be fitted, and through which contemporary rulers might be praised (or warned). Nowhere was this more pronounced for English politics than in the middle years of the sixteenth century.

English monarchs had been compared with kings of Israel and Judah for centuries in a way that both flattered them and reminded them of their duties. There was much straightforward sycophancy in these analogies but also sometimes something else, never more so than with Henry's only legitimate son and immediate successor. Edward VI was nine when he came to the throne in 1547. His surviving schoolwork indicates that he had serious evangelical leanings, which helped his short reign become the brief evangelical summer of sixteenth-century England.[43]

Edward was compared to numerous biblical kings, including Solomon, Hezekiah, Jehoshaphat and Jehu,[44] but there was one comparison that dominated all others. King Josiah ruled Judah between 640 and 601 BC. He had come to the throne at the age of eight and ruled wisely, purging the land of idols, renewing the nation's covenant with God and instituting major religious reforms that were all based on the rediscovery of ancient scripture. The similarities between the youthful, reforming, scripture-inspired Josiah and young King Edward were too powerful to ignore. Biblical history provided English evangelicals with a compelling model that legitimised their programme of reform.

At times that programme seemed to beckon the social and political anarchy that Protestants had long been desperate to avoid. Outbursts of iconoclasm in which reforming mobs destroyed images, tore down rood screens and defaced saints became common. Official censorship of printing was all but abandoned, and the early years of Edward's reign saw a significant increase in publishing, including all manner of controversial religious tracts. Fringe groups like Anabaptists, Unitarians and Free-willers, rejecting predestination and proclaiming possible salvation for all, emerged in a hint of the chaos that Protestantism threatened and, a century later, delivered.[45]

A threat to the established social and political order, as some may have viewed them, the reality was that at no point during Edward's reign did the English Protestants waver in the doctrine of political obedience that had been theirs for nearly thirty years. On Edward's accession in 1547 preaching licences were suspended, under the pretext that sermons had been stirring up civil disorder. Only those explicitly authorised by the new regime were allowed to preach. Where this left empty pulpits, an official *Book of Homilies*, containing twelve sermons, many by Archbishop Thomas Cranmer, was published to fill the gap. Royal injunctions required clergy to read these aloud to their flocks on appointed days.[46]

The *Homilies* spoon-fed their congregations official evangelical teaching, on such subjects as holy scripture, the misery and salvation of humanity, the role of good works and the obedience owed to princes. Homily 10, 'An exhortation to obedience', offers an admirably clear statement of political submission, true to Reformed teaching and intended to counter fears that evangelical freedom entailed political insubordination and social unrest. 'Almighty God hath created and appointed all things, in heaven, earth, and waters, in a most excellent and perfect order,' it began. This was how 'the goodly order of God' operated, 'without the which no house, no city, no common-wealth can continue and endure'. The implications of detuning this cosmic and political harmony were then put on full display. 'Take away kings, princes, rulers, magistrates, judges, and such estates of God's order, no man shall ride or go by the highway unrobbed; no man shall sleep in his own house or bed unkilled.' Although the homily offers some gestures towards the responsibilities of kingship, they are perfunctory in comparison to the overwhelming emphasis on political obedience. 'St. Paul threatens no less pain than everlasting damnation to all disobedient persons . . . it is an intolerable igno-rance, madness, and wickedness for subjects to make any murmuring, rebellion, resistance, commotion, or insurrection against their most dear and most dread Sovereign Lord and King, ordained and appointed of God's goodness for their commodity, peace, and quietness.'

The 'Homily on Obedience' was entirely of a piece with Luther's, Tyndale's and the Henricians' theology but it was also a product of its time – uncertain, nervous, opportunistic. A new evangelically inclined and malleable king, with broadly sympathetic advisers, offered a unique opportunity for well-placed Reformers to reshape the nation's religious landscape in a way that had been looking increasingly unlikely in Henry's final years. With such elements in place, Protestants had nothing to lose and everything to gain from stressing obedience, a fact that was reinforced by the perpetual need to deny that Protestantism elevated personal freedom at the expense of collective order. Within a few years, however, circumstances were very different and it was the need to explore the legitimacy of resist-ance – *active* resistance – that became most urgent.

4

'God at this point gives the sword into the people's hand':
Struggling with disobedience

The European political landscape changed in the 1540s and for a while it appeared as if the Reform movement might be exterminated. Luther died in 1546 and in the following year Charles V, the Holy Roman Emperor, won a decisive battle against the so-called Schmalkaldic League, an alliance of Lutheran princes that sought to defend its religious and political independence against Pope and Empire. Although some Reformers were willing to accept the religious settlement, known as the Augsburg Interim, imposed by the emperor, many others fled the Continent. Their destination was England, under the new Edwardian regime. For the next six years the country became a refuge for a number of the leading European Reformers and was seen by many to be the Reformation's last best hope, an idea that further justified all the comparisons with Old Testament Israel.

Protestant hope came to an abrupt halt in 1553 when Edward died and was succeeded by his Catholic half-sister, Mary, only daughter of Henry VIII's first marriage. The entire religious climate changed. Edward's Protestant legislation was repealed. Over 2,000 clergy were dispossessed and 300 Protestants were arrested and publicly burned. A similar crisis hit Scotland, which had been making its own strides towards a Reformation. Those strides had been made under English influence but when, in the late 1540s, the English occupied much of southern and eastern Scotland with more than usual brutality, the Scots sought help from their old ally, France, which helped them impose a humiliating peace on England and pledged the dauphin, the Crown Prince of France, in marriage to Mary, the five-year-old Queen of Scots.

Catholic thought had, by the mid-sixteenth century, developed theories of political resistance and constitutionalism that were considerably more sophisticated than those of the Reformers. That, however, was little solace to English Protestants who could not easily draw on them and were, in any case, forced to go underground or flee abroad to avoid persecution. Just as England had been a beacon of evangelical freedom in the late 1540s, so Frankfurt, Strasburg, Zurich and Geneva became cities of refuge in the 1550s. It was there that a number of Reformers were compelled by circumstances to rethink the doctrine of political obedience that had been a cornerstone of their theology since the 1520s.

'A prince or judge is not always ordained by God': resistance in the 1550s

In taking this radical step, the English were, in reality, doing no more than catching up with continental Reformers who had been thinking through the legitimacy of active resistance, again compelled by circumstances, for over twenty years. Early Lutheran ideas on obedience had been changing ever since 1529 when Charles V withdrew all the concessions he had previously made to the Lutherans. (The Lutherans issued a formal protest to this change in policy, hence earning the name Protestants.) Philip I of Hesse, an early Lutheran prince, argued that 'the powers that be' that Paul talks about in Romans 13 were 'ordained to perform a particular office', a stipulation which included 'the duty of observing a number of legal obligations . . . [including] ensuring the well-being and salvation of their own immediate subjects'. The conclusion followed that 'if the Emperor oversteps the bounds of his office by persecuting the gospel or offering violence to any of the princes, he must be in breach of the obligations imposed on him at his election, and can thus be lawfully opposed.'[1] Luther himself was initially lukewarm towards this reasoning but he, along with other leading Reformers, changed his mind by the end of 1530 and was prepared to recognise and even advocate active resistance to 'tyrannical' rulers, drawing on reasons from a number of sources, by no means all of them biblical.

John Calvin, the French Reformer who was to assume Luther's mantle as Europe's leading Reformer after his death, and in whose city many English Protestants took refuge in the 1550s, began his theological career in a similar position. Writing in the wake of the rebellions of the 1520s, Calvin strongly advocated obedience to the governing authorities in his chapter on civil government in the first edition of his *Institutes of the Christian Religion*. Even he, however, admitted cracks in this doctrine. In one respect, these were the cracks that existed in every Reformer's teaching on political obedience, relating to the need to obey God rather than man when the two were directly in conflict. But Calvin also explored the possibility of popular magistrates resisting in the name of the people and by the time of the final, definitive Latin edition of the *Institutes*, in 1559, he was willing at least to countenance active resistance to the governing authorities.

The English Reformers were not, therefore, completely alone in their exploration of political resistance in the 1550s. Nevertheless their position marked a crossing of the Rubicon in English political thought. Up until this point in English history, there had been much discussion of the limits and accountability placed on political power and even some reputable discussion on what action was permissible when faced with a tyrant. Before the Reformation all such discussions had ended up pointing towards the Church as the only body in society with the authority to challenge and, if necessary, depose tyrannous rulers. After the Reformation, however, the Church in England could no longer lay claim to such powers.

At first, this did not appear to present any problems. Henry may not have been the ideal Protestant monarch but his rule offered enough to keep the Reformers happy. Edward VI's minority offered still more. England became a light unto the darkening Continent. English Reformers had no need to rethink the doctrine of political obedience in the way that the Lutherans had in the 1530s. With the arrival of Queen Mary, however, the need for a convincing and coherent doctrine of political resistance suddenly became overwhelming. Moreover, for the first time in English history, there was no institutional Church to turn to for help. Those Reformers who took refuge on the Continent during Mary's reign had to find some rationale for resistance that did not rely on the intervention of an external supra-authority (i.e. the Pope). Resistance, if there was to be any, had to be internal, coming from those who lived within the country and under the governing authorities they sought to resist.

Two exiles were particularly important in the way in which they worked through these arguments. John Ponet was Bishop of Winchester before he fled to Frankfurt on Mary's accession. Educated at Cambridge and a respected classical scholar, he drew on a wide range of sources – embarrassingly wide for a leading Protestant – for his radical (and anonymously published) *A Shorte Treatise of Politike Power*. Like Reformers before him, Ponet recognised that 'princes are ordained to do good, not to do evil' but, unlike them, he thought through in some detail what should actually be done if a prince fails to discharge those duties and instead attempts 'to spoil and destroy the people'.[2]

Drawing on examples from civil and canon law and biblical history, Ponet argued that the 'crimes of a ruler who exceeds the bounds of his office are in fact no different – and ought to be treated no differently – from the same crimes when committed by any ordinary citizen.' He then outlined situations in which such resistance was justifiable, including among them when a ruler 'goes about to betray and make away his country to foreigners'. The example was carefully chosen, as Mary had married Prince Philip of Spain two years earlier. Ultimately the magistrate who grossly abused his office could no longer demand the obedience of their subjects, who now had a duty to resist and even 'depose and remove [them] out of their places and offices'.

Ponet's device of identifying the ruler as an 'ordinary citizen', although not original, was deeply threatening, demystifying authority and threatening to loosen the joints of the entire political order. What was original was his willingness to take the duties incumbent on a magistrate one step forward and reach the conclusion that there was a difference between the *office* and the *person* of a magistrate. The person who found himself magistrate may have been granted (a measure of) God's authority for government, but if that authority were contingent on discharging his godly duties, it was perfectly possible for him to lose the divine authority of his position. 'A prince or judge is not always ordained by God,' Ponet concluded. This was a revolutionary claim for a Protestant thinker and it is telling that

Ponet had to draw on the ideas of Catholic thinkers to justify it.[3]

Ponet could do this, albeit in a slightly embarrassed and apologetic manner, partly because he had the necessary learning and partly because he was willing to draw on a wider range of sources than were many English Protestants. His fellow exile, Christopher Goodman, was more narrowly biblical in his thinking, although he managed to reach a similar conclusion. Goodman had been Lady Margaret Professor of Divinity at Oxford before exile. His 1558 publication *How Superior Powers Ought to be Obeyed of their Subjects* had begun life as a sermon and was more explicitly biblical than Ponet's work, but shared much common ground. Goodman's starting point was the orthodox Pauline, Protestant view that the governing authorities are ordained by God. However, Goodman insisted, rulers are not *merely* ordained, but 'ordained to see justice administered to all sorts of men'.[4] Rulers had duties, many of which are outlined in the New Testament: 'to punish the evil and to defend the good', 'to obtain peace and quietness', to maintain 'the preservation of the people' and 'to see justice administered to all sorts of men'. They were, in effect, ordained 'for our profit'. Consequently, when they 'transgress God's laws themselves, and command others to do the like, then have they lost that honour and obedience which otherwise their subjects did owe to them, and ought no more to be taken for magistrates'. In effect, they relinquished their status as 'public persons' who bear God's authority and instead became 'private persons and no longer as genuine magistrates'. This was Ponet's distinction between the office and the person of the magistrate, hardened into the idea of private and public persons.

Goodman is clear that the magistrate's offences had to be grave in order for subjects to reach for this line of reasoning. Resistance was unjustified if rulers were merely 'rough' or if their wickedness was not 'manifestly against God and his laws'. When, however, 'without fear they transgress God's laws', resistance is not only permissible but necessary. As if this were not threatening enough, Goodman (like Ponet) also suggested that private citizens – and not simply other ordained magistrates – had the right to resist tyrannical rulers. 'When the magistrates and other officers cease to do their duty,' he reasoned, the people 'are, as it were, without officers, yea, worse than if they had none at all'. In such extreme circumstances, and given that the magistrate's actions have reduced him to nothing more than a common criminal, the people themselves may resist him. 'God at this point gives the sword into the people's hand.'

Ponet and Goodman were radical in the way they engaged with the Bible. Ponet took a philological approach to the text, examining what words and phrases like 'power' and 'every soul' actually meant in context. Goodman took a historical approach, arguing that Paul only placed such emphasis on obedience because the Roman Christians to whom he wrote, newly freed from the burdens of the law, were prone to rejecting all authority. And both read the relevant texts in their wider biblical context, balancing the rights of political authority of Romans 13:1 with other texts and examples that stressed its responsibilities. In this way, they were able to free Protestant theology from its straitjacket of complete submission into which it had worked itself earlier in the century.

Ponet and Goodman's rebalancing of political order with political freedom and their versatile engagement with the Bible marked a watershed in the influence of the Bible on national politics. It released the Bible's latent capacity for political radicalism that had formerly been denied or minimised by English Protestants. It was not their tracts, however, that were to provide the main source for English political radicalism over the next fifty years. That would come from the most important product of the Marian exiles, the Geneva Bible.

'Brief annotations upon all the hard places': the Geneva Bible

When the exiles left for the Continent in 1553, *the* English Bible was the Great Bible of 1539, large, authorised and authoritarian in intent. Four years later Geneva saw the publication of an English New Testament. Unattributed but probably translated by William Whittington, who had written the preface to Goodman's book, the Geneva New Testament was heavily dependent on Tyndale's work. Pocket-sized, in readable Roman rather than heavy Gothic type, it was the first English Bible to divide chapters into numbered verses, each of which it printed on a new line. It contained 'arguments' for every chapter of every book, used italics to indicate which words

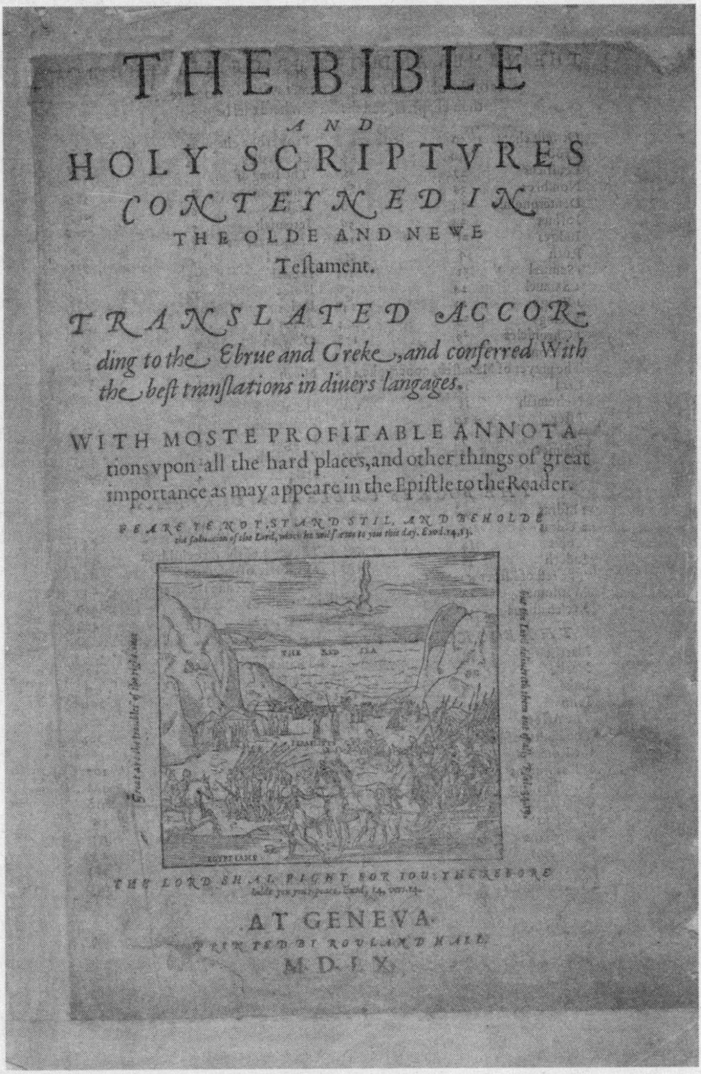

THE BIBLE

AND

HOLY SCRIPTVRES

CONTEYNED IN

THE OLDE AND NEWE Testament.

TRANSLATED ACCOR-

ding to the Ebrue and Greke, and conferred with the best translations in diuers langages.

WITH MOSTE PROFITABLE ANNOTA-
tions vpon all the hard places, and other things of great importance as may appeare in the Epistle to the Reader.

FEARE YE NOT, STAND STIL, AND BEHOLDE
the saluation of the Lord, which he wil shewe to you this day. Exod. 14.13.

THE RED SEA.

EGYPTIANS.

THE LORD SHAL FIGHT FOR YOU: THEREFORE
holde you your peace. Exod. 14. vers. 14.

AT GENEVA

PRINTED BY ROVLAND HALL

M. D. L X.

Fig. 3: Title page of Geneva Bible (1560)

were added to satisfy English idiom and even signalled variant Greek readings with footnotes. Three years later, in 1560, a complete Bible was brought out from the same source. This maintained the style and innovations of the 1557 New Testament but added maps, woodcut illustrations, tables of proper names, an index and a calculation of the period of time from the creation of the world to the current day, of huge importance to those energised by millenarian promises. The Geneva Bible was to be the most influential English Bible of the next 100 years. Small and cheap (by contemporary standards), it was published to be owned, read and understood by anyone. It was, in effect, what Tyndale had been hoping for when he vowed to teach the ploughboy scripture. It put into every person's hand the Word of God and helped them understand it.

The front cover spoke of liberation (Fig. 3). The dominant image depicted a key moment from Exodus. The people of God have left Egypt and arrived at the Red Sea. They are surrounded by mountains and the Egyptian Army is approaching fast. The situation looks hopeless but a pillar of cloud has appeared on the horizon and every reader knows what is about to happen. In itself, this was not an immediate political threat. The very point of the Exodus was that it was God who rescued the Israelites, not they themselves, a point that was underlined by the two scriptural quotations that surrounded the picture: 'The Lord shall fight for you, therefore hold your peace' (Exod. 14:14) and 'Great are the troubles of the righteous but the Lord delivers them out of all' (Ps. 34:19). The godly English faced great woes but they could be assured that God would deliver them.

Far more contentious was the way in which the Geneva version helped readers to understand the text. The Geneva Bible came with notes. Its outer margins bore literally hundreds of comments of many varieties. Some gave variant translations, some cross-references, some definitions. Some identified quotations in the New Testament from pagan authors. And some were 'brief annotations upon all the hard places', based on the recognition that the Bible needed explanation.[5]

Many of these points outlined the basic tenets of Reformed Protestant theology. Many others, however, particularly in the Old Testament, alighted on those political questions that sorely vexed Whittington's fellow exiles: when is it right to resist a tyrannous ruler and who may do so legitimately? Thus, commenting on the Hebrew midwives disobeying Pharaoh's order to kill all male babies in Exodus 1, the Geneva notes stated, 'Their disobedience herein was lawful, but their dissembling evil.' On God threatening to abandon Israel 'because of the sins of Jeroboam' in 1 Kings 14:16 the Geneva notes remarked, 'The people shall not be excused, when they do evil at [the] commandment of their governors.' Of Jehu's murder of Jezebel in 2 Kings 9, the notes said that Jehu did this 'by the motion of the Spirit of God' and that Jezebel's death is an 'example of God's judgements to all tyrants'. In a note pertaining to Israel's worship of the Golden Calf in Exodus 32, the editors said that 'in revenging God's glory we must have no respect to person, but put off all carnal affection.' It was notes such as these, which amounted to leading theologians whispering about the legitimacy of political revolt in the ears of the masses, that were to provoke so much controversy over the next century.

Yet, the Geneva Bible was not simply a cover for political radicalism. Not only were notes of this kind vastly outnumbered by the less politically contentious ones, but there were also other 'political' annotations that were more conservative. Indeed, the predominant advice regarding idolatrous tyrants was that the people should pray for forgiveness and await God's intervention. Thus, the note to Psalm 37:12 remarked, 'the godly are assured [that] the power and craft of the wicked shall not prevail against them, but fall on their own necks, and therefore ought patiently to abide Gods time.'

There is, therefore, an ambiguity in the political notes to the Geneva Bible that reflects the political ambiguity of the Bible as a whole. On the one hand, the editorial preface to Deuteronomy emphasises the divine origin of rulers. On the other, the notes to Chapters 16 and 17 of that book take care to indicate that political power in Israel originally had an elective element, commenting on how Moses 'gave authority to that people for a time to choose them selves magistrates'. In the words of one scholar, 'the translators' faithfulness to the Bible's intrinsic indeterminacy generates a set of notes whose overall political message is irreducibly complex and undecidable ... [the] oscillation between recommending prayer, passive resistance and revolutionary action simply reflects

oscillations and contradictions that are internal to the text of the
Bible itself.'[6]

If the Geneva Bible was not straightforwardly revolutionary,
however, it was still dangerous. The fact that it put the Word of God
into people's hands was bad enough. The fact that it did so in such a
way as to make the text readable, engaging, relevant and comprehen-
sible was worse. The fact that it unapologetically discussed the many
occasions in the Old Testament (and it was the Old: the New proved
much less politically contentious) in which the people or their leaders
had legitimately resisted or even overthrown tyrants was worse still.
Superficially this was no different to what John of Salisbury had done
four centuries earlier, but his discussion of tyrants was in a massive,
handwritten, erudite, Latin treatise that was never going to get
anywhere near the masses. The Geneva Bible was written to be read
and inwardly digested. Ultimately, it was not so much its content that
was revolutionary as the fact that its notes enabled readers to use the
Bible to interpret contemporary events for themselves. 'By demon-
strating how biblical texts could be applied generally – to any idolater
or tyrant – the Geneva translators were training their readers as readers, empowering them to make the specific application to their own
particular circumstances.'[7]

'Rebellion is the very root of all other sins': threats from both sides

Much of the Geneva Bible was translated while Mary was England's
monarch but the book was actually published after England's new
queen, Elizabeth I, to whom it was dedicated, had come to the throne.
The dedicatory epistle was addressed to 'the most virtuous and noble
Queen Elizabeth' from her 'humble subjects of the English Church at
Geneva', who expected much of her.

Elizabeth would both satisfy and disappoint. The queen herself
was a sincere Protestant but not in the Genevan mould. Unwilling to
abolish the liturgical style of the Church in which she had grown up,
and equally unwilling to risk civil strife by imposing the exiles' agenda
on her subjects, she was practical and realistic in her aspirations.
Thus, despite the Geneva Bible's dedication, the volume made little
early impression on its intended audience. Instead, in the first decade

of the queen's reign, Matthew Parker, the Archbishop of Canterbury, launched, steered and completed a new translation. Working with 'mete', i.e. suitably orthodox scholars, most of whom were bishops, the new translation would update the now inadequate Great Bible of 1539, while avoiding the more militant phrases and notes of the Geneva version.

The resulting Bishops' Bible, printed in 1568, was a lavish volume. Although not dedicated to Elizabeth, the queen dominated its title page in a portrait that surmounted an impeccable Reformation text – Romans 1:16: 'I am not ashamed of the gospel of Christ: for it is the power of God unto salvation to everyone that believeth' – but one that, like the Great Bible's frontispiece, was in Latin (Fig. 4). There was a similar message on the title page of a quarto edition published the following year, which showed the queen on her throne, surrounded and crowned by justice, mercy, fortitude and prudence, and above a small illustration of a minister in his pulpit preaching to a large, rapt congregation (Fig. 5). The message was clear. The pendulum had shifted from its Genevan position and the Bible was once again understood as a bulwark of social order.

This was also the message of a second *Book of Homilies* that was published in 1571 after licences to preach were once again suspended, in the wake of the 'Northern Rebellion', when Catholic noblemen tried to depose the queen, and of the papal bull, *Regnans in Excelsis*, in which Pope Pius V declared Elizabeth a heretic and absolved subjects of any allegiance to her.[8] The second book contained twenty-one sermons, the last of which was a homily 'against disobedience and wilful rebellion', which sounded exactly the same note as the earlier 'exhortation to obedience'. Thus, congregations were told how, as Lucifer was the first rebel, 'rebellion . . . [is] both the first and greatest and the very root of all other sins,' and consequently 'the first and principal cause both of all worldly and bodily miseries, sorrows, diseases, sicknesses, and deaths; and, which is infinitely worse than all these, as is said, the very cause of death and damnation eternal also'. The second *Book of Homilies*, like the first, was the product of a nervous moment of a generally nervous reign and needs to be read in that context. Nevertheless, it remains a significant reminder that ideas of resistance, such as were to be read in the

Fig. 4: Title page of Bishops' Bible (1568)

Fig. 5: Title page of Bishops' Bible, Quarto edition (1569)

publications of the Genevan exiles, remained on the fringes of English society.

It was a different story in Scotland. One of Ponet and Goodman's fellow exiles was John Knox, a pugnacious Scottish clergyman who had first been exiled to England in 1549, following nineteenth months as a French galley slave, and then again from England on the accession of Queen Mary. While in exile, Knox had pondered some of the issues that worried his fellow English exiles. Should a minor be regarded as a lawful magistrate and be obeyed as of divine right? Could a woman legitimately rule and transfer rights to her husband? Should magistrates who enforced idolatry be obeyed? Might Christians support the nobility if it actively resisted an idolatrous ruler? Given the fact that England was currently under the sceptre of a Catholic woman married to a Spanish prince, and Scotland was ruled by a twelve-year-old girl whose Catholic mother was now regent, these were clearly not theoretical questions. Neither Calvin nor Bullinger was willing to give Knox the clear answers he wanted. Their reservations did not, however, prevent him from publishing a series of tracts over the next few years that moved slowly towards the political radicalism of Ponet and Goodman.

At first, Knox warned against rebellion and advocated co-operation with the governing authorities in order to achieve his all-consuming goal of completing a godly Reformation in Scotland. As his more moderate interventions failed to make an impact, he began to argue that the nobility, as subordinate magistrates, had a duty to see that true Christian instruction was provided in the country and that, if it was not forthcoming, the Old Testament clearly showed that loyalty to the covenant with God allowed, even required, disobedience to the monarch, up to and including resistance by force of arms.[9]

Although his notoriously named *First Blast of the Trumpet Against the Monstrous Regiment of Women*, a none-too-subtle attack on England's queen and Scotland's regent, was Knox's best known tract, it was its unfinished successor that outlined his most radical political thinking. A summary of this *Proposed Second Blast of the Trumpet* promised to show that 'it is not birth only . . . that makes a king lawfully to reign above a people professing Christ Jesus,' but the fact that his 'election [observes] the ordinance, which God has established in the election of inferior judges'. It aimed to demonstrate that 'no manifest idolater . . . ought to be promoted to any public regiment.' It argued that 'neither can oath nor promise bind any such people to obey and maintain tyrants against God.' And it maintained that 'if either rashly they have promoted any manifestly wicked person . . . most justly may the same men depose and punish him.'[10]

This was as serious a departure from the Protestant doctrine of obedience as had yet been voiced. Yet its long-term significance was less in its inclination towards civil disobedience than in the covenantal thinking that underpinned it. The manner in which numerous Protestant thinkers, Knox among them, found in the story of Old Testament Israel a narrative by means of which they could understand their Reformation, made the idea of a covenant, the voluntary but binding agreement between God and his people, an obvious model for their politics. A reformed nation, such as Knox sought in Scotland, would also be a covenanted nation in which 'all' people had sworn their loyalty and allegiance to God. As such, each participated in, and was responsible for, the common religious life. It was an idea whose potential for political equality and political chaos was huge, and that would, in the long run, influence much political thought, from its role in catalysing the English Civil War eighty years later to shaping the American political settlement and beyond.[11]

In the immediate term, there was a sudden and momentous turnaround in Scottish politics. Leading Protestant nobles made demands of the regent, such as the right to host evangelical sermons on their estates and it looked at first as if the Scottish Reformation might be a tolerant, conciliatory and piecemeal affair. It wasn't to be. Attempts at compromise failed and the Reformation rapidly descended into a complete and often violent religious rebellion during which the regent died, reformed Christianity came to dominate the country and Knox attained a position of supreme influence. Perhaps not entirely surprisingly, in the wake of the revolution Knox adopted a more conciliatory tone towards political authority, writing of civil magistrates in the new Kirk's Confession of Faith 'that such persons as are placed in authority are to be loved, honoured, feared, and held in most reverent estimation because they are the lieutenants of God, in whose sessions God himself does sit and judge.'[12]

The radicalism he had articulated in *Second Blast* was not only circumstance and expediency, however. When the Catholic Mary, Queen of Scots returned home in 1561 she had several long and difficult interviews with her virulently anti-Catholic subject, during which he told her that she merited her subjects' obedience just so long as she remained within her proper limits. Queen Elizabeth herself was not notably better disposed towards Mary Stuart than Knox, but that was about all she and Knox had in common. Quite apart from the fact that Elizabeth was unlikely to be well disposed to someone who had publicly proclaimed her reign 'monstrous', Knox's defiant and destabilising zeal and his open political rebelliousness, albeit to a Catholic monarch, epitomised what Elizabeth distrusted most in Puritan thinking.[13]

Such sedition was not limited to Scotland. Puritans were constantly pressing for further Reformation of the English Church, attacking the bishops with particular gusto in a series of anonymous tracts that went under the pen-name of Martin Mar-Prelate. Angrily suppressed by the authorities, the small, separatist groups which they formed, often named 'Brownists' after Robert Browne, a prominent separatist of the 1580s, were never a significant threat to public order, not least because at this stage most Puritans had not given up hope of reforming the Church from within. However, they remained a significant feature of the theo-political landscape, if only as bogeymen deployed by the authorities to demonstrate how the nation would be fragmented if the queen were to accede to the wider Puritan agenda.

The Elizabethan emphasis on the doctrine of obedience was a response to such separatist Puritanism, but not to it alone. At the other end of the theological spectrum from Knox, Browne and the separatists, Elizabethan Catholics found themselves having to wrestle with questions of political obedience now that they lived under a monarch whom Pope Pius V had excommunicated and proclaimed deposed. In the 1560s a number of English Catholics fled abroad, in particular to Louvain and Rheims, which became the Catholic equivalent of Protestant Frankfurt and Geneva in the previous decade. At Rheims, the exiles produced their own translation of the New

Testament, which was taken from the Latin Vulgate and published in 1582. This had arguments and annotations, in the fashion of the Geneva Bible, and was intended to put a more acceptable version in English Catholic hands, although in contrast with the Geneva version it placed its emphasis on readers being *taught* the meaning of the text rather than discovering it for themselves.

A number of the notes outlined the Catholic critique of the Protestant doctrine of the godly prince, emphasising how all temporal power was under the judgement of God, which meant, of course, the Pope. Thus the note to Mark 12:17 ('Render to Caesar the things that are Caesar's, and to God the things that are God's') informed readers:

> Heretics, to flatter temporal Princes . . . do not only inculcate men's duty to the Prince . . . But also give to the Prince more than due, and take from God his right and duty. But Christ allowing Caesar his right, warns them also of their duty toward God. And that is what Catholics inculcate, obey God, do as he commands, serve him first and then the Prince.[14]

Although this remained the basis of the Catholic attitude to political power, there was a variety of ways in which it worked itself out among the English Catholic community during Elizabeth's reign. At times of greater tension, such as the early 1570s, in the wake of the Northern Rising of Catholics, *Regnans in Excelsis* and the Ridolfi Plot to depose the queen, English Catholics became the natural scapegoats for the realm's political insecurity and resistance theory was readily discussed, particularly among the exiles. At other times, Catholic apologists emphasised how they were entirely loyal to the crown, drawing on the classic texts of Romans 13 and 1 Peter 2 to explain their allegiance, and comparing themselves with the apostles who had refused to accept Roman paganism but were not disloyal to the state. The Catholic Church required believers to offer 'true obedience to their Princes, for conscience sake, even as unto God himself'.[15]

That noted, English Catholics also made a great deal of Hebrews 13:17, which was translated in the Rheims New Testament as 'Obey your prelates, and be subject to them. For they watch as being to render an account of your souls; that they may do this with joy, and not with grief.' The translation of the word 'prelate' – the Geneva version has the more ambiguous 'them that have the oversight of you' – was significant in that it gave a scriptural justification for disobeying temporal princes in favour of spiritual prelates. Thus even when, during periods of obedience, English Catholics cited Romans 13 to prove they were not traitors, there were always texts and arguments on which they could and did draw in order to show that St Paul commanded political rather than religious obedience. In an age when political and religious loyalties were often largely coterminous, this could be seen to weaken the value of English Catholic pledges of political loyalty. Although the actual threat to Elizabeth from Catholic kingdoms waxed and waned over the forty-five years of her reign, the Catholic understanding of political power remained as much of a constant, background hazard as did the Puritan one.

'The harmony of the world': law and the middle way

It was between the twin ideas of Puritan and Catholic political resistance that Elizabethan political theory picked its way. Those ideas differed in many ways but they shared the belief that God's law was above human law (as all Christians did) and, more importantly, that someone *other* than the earthly prince had the final call on its interpretation. For the Catholic, that someone was the Pope. For the Puritan, it was the individual believer, inspired and guided by the Holy Spirit and, if necessary (and it usually was) the godly preacher. Whichever way it was dressed up, however, such views constituted a threat to the political order.

The 'official' Elizabethan response was driven by a variety of factors. There was simple pragmatism. Governing a people that was religiously plural or, more precisely, whose religious plurality was, for the first time, publicly acknowledged, demanded a degree of intelligence and sensitivity if the monarch was to avoid open anarchy. There was also a great deal of principle, much of it based on the Protestant doctrine of absolute obedience to the godly prince, as the 1570 homily made admirably clear. The principle went beyond blunt authoritarianism, however. Elizabethan political thought took account of *adiaphora*, 'things indifferent'. It was possible for subjects to differ in (some) matters of religious doctrine without that constituting a threat to public order. The official position was not to 'sift' people's consciences, nor to persecute religious opinions except in so far as they constituted a threat to national security. The laws demanded outward conformity to the new religious settlement, including attendance at Anglican services (or the payment of a fine for absence) and an allegiance to the crown. This, it could be argued, was pretty much impossible for English Catholics and therefore amounted to *de facto* persecution. But the fact remained that, at least in theory, the official emphasis on obedience was tempered by an openness to other commitments that was absent under Edward VI or Henry VIII.

There was also open discussion on the limitations of political power. John Aylmer, another exile, wrote a response to Knox's *First Blast* which was published as *An Harborowe for Faithful and True Subjects* in 1559 and which became the first defence of the Elizabethan settlement. It criticised resistance theories but also insisted England was not a mere monarchy but a mixture of monarchy, aristocracy and democracy, and contended that the monarch was bound by the laws of the land. In a similar vein, John Bridges, a Fellow of Pembroke Hall, Cambridge, wrote *The Supremacie of Christian Princes* in 1573 in which he contended that in civil matters a prince's will must be restrained by law, that both prince and priest drew their authority from consent, and that both were made 'for the people's cause'.[16] Such talk was not new but it could now be heard from those inside the regime, rather than simply from those, like the Genevan or Louvain exiles, who stood beyond or against it.

Such ideas came together in their most compelling, if not necessarily most accessible, form in Richard Hooker's *Laws of Ecclesiastical Polity*.[17] Hooker was a priest and a logician who spent the last ten years of his short life writing what has been called 'the chief English prose work of the sixteenth century'.[18] The *Laws* is a more reasoned and generous publication than was usual for the time, with Hooker, although firmly anchored in the Protestant tradition, prepared to grant the millennium or so of Christian thought and tradition that predated the Reformation more weight than was common among Protestants.

His governing idea was law. All life – divine, angelic,

natural, supernatural, human, national, international, religious and secular – was related in one vast, ordered, reasonable system of law.[19] Law lay behind the harmony and reasonableness of creation. It stood in contrast to the whimsical or capricious rule of the individual. God's own nature, Hooker argued, was rooted in law rather than simply his unaccountable and incomprehensible will. God was not arbitrary in his intentions for, and dealings with, the world. This did not mean that his nature was accessible to the human mind. It was not. What it did mean was that his Word and his works were lawful, reasonable and would conform to those purposes that were evident to the human mind.

It was on this understanding of law that Hooker based his intervention in the vexed issue of who should interpret scripture. He had a particular animus against those Puritans who claimed to need no authority beyond that of their own conscience to interpret the Bible. This idea 'being once inserted into the minds of the vulgar sort, what it may grow unto God knows', he worried, prophetically. Elevating the personal opinion of the uneducated individual over the wisdom and learning of the ordained majority was a disgrace that beckoned religious and political chaos. Such 'insolency must be repressed,' he insisted, 'or it will be the very bane of Christian religion.'[20] The Bible, Hooker argued, could only be understood through the prism of reason and law, and standing within the stream of ecclesiastical tradition. It was the corporate judgement of Church over time rather than the individual's opinion that was the rightful arbiter of scripture.

It was also this understanding of law that enabled him to engage profitably in the broader issues of Church and civil government. Hooker rejected the view of some Calvinists that God reveals his law only through scripture. He also rejected the view that only that which could be located in scripture could serve as a valid basis for human law. Such views justified the Puritan argument that certain practices of the Church of England were unacceptable because they were not found in scripture, an argument he ridiculed.

Hooker had no quibble with the idea that scripture was complete and sufficient with regard to salvation. But there was a great deal else about which it was not entirely clear, matters that were 'indifferent' to salvation. This had implications for the way in which the godly monarch should rule. Just as those who thought that they could find in the Bible an answer to every conceivable religious question were demeaning God's true purposes, so those who searched for answers to every social and political question and then expected the monarch to force them into legislation did the same. It was simply not the business of the monarch, even the godly monarch.

Hooker's understanding of law did not, therefore, lead him to the rigid political hierarchy of the homily on obedience but to a subtler articulation of royal power. He devoted book eight of the *Laws* to a defence of royal supremacy of the Anglican Church, as part of which he outlined the limitations on royal power.[21] First, as no contemporary would have denied, there was the supremacy of Christ, the King of Kings. No king could act above or outside that. Second, again uncontroversially, there was law. Everything and everyone, including the monarch, was under the rule of law.[22] Finally, more significantly, there was the understanding that the monarch was supreme over any particular member of the body politic but not over the body politic itself. The monarch, in other words, was only truly sovereign when acting with rather than without, or, worse, against parliament. The ruler may be superior to the individuals over whom she ruled but the commonwealth as a whole was superior to the ruler. Hooker was concerned primarily with the governance of the Church, but as he saw the Church and the commonwealth occupying the same space, the broader political implications of his *Laws* were clear. Although he carefully distanced himself from contemporary ideas of elective monarchy and never imagined that parliament should serve an executive rather than merely representative function in the body politic, he was still advocating limitations on the monarchy from within the Protestant tradition and, significantly, within the political mainstream.

Although one of the first people to give 'Anglicanism' serious intellectual weight, Hooker had little impact in his time. It was not until after his death that he gained respect, finding a particular admirer in the philosopher John Locke.[23] In the meantime, his reasoned defence of law and the Elizabethan settlement would be drowned out by the very voices he most feared.

5

'A people set at liberty':
Divine right and democracy

'The King becomes a natural Father to all': divine right

James I considered himself to be a theologian. Following the murder of his father and the imprisonment of his mother, he was educated by George Buchanan, a highly respected humanist, poet, scholar and Calvinist, who instilled in him a love of learning and a distrust of Puritans. Calvinist doctrine had penetrated further and more thoroughly in Scotland than it had south of the border but had shaken off none of the factious air it had acquired mid-century. Scotland may have experienced a Reformation as widespread and thorough as any in Europe, but the threat of Protestant rebellion had not disappeared. Just beneath the surface of the Reformers' repeated affirmations of loyalty to the godly prince, there lay a stubborn insistence on the individual's conscience before God. No temporal authority could rest easy.

This lurking political defiance was compounded by France's changing religious landscape and the further impetus it gave to resistance theory. The Huguenots, or French Protestants, had long lived a precarious existence in France, recognised and protected by senior French figures with little love of the Huguenots themselves but less to gain from their persecution. Open conflict erupted in the 1560s, culminating in what came to be known as the St Bartholomew's Day Massacre when, in 1572, over 50,000 Protestants were killed in cities across the country. French Protestants had long been aware of arguments justifying resistance to the governing authorities. Now they needed them.

In appropriating such arguments for themselves, Huguenots wanted to avoid articulating what could have been seen and dismissed as narrow and sectarian, or socially anarchic, reasoning.

As a consequence, they deliberately drew on scholastic, legal and constitutional ideas, and in particular those relating to natural law, the moral structure of creation that was supposedly inscribed on every human heart and discernible through the judicious, guided use of reason.

Rejecting Lutheran ideas that tyrannous rulers were sent to punish the people's sins or that the punishment of tyranny should be left to providence, the Huguenots argued that the original state of humanity was one of fundamental liberty rather than political servitude. In the words of one tract: '[We are all] free by nature, born to hate servitude, and desirous of commanding rather than yielding obedience.' Peoples exist prior to their rulers. 'Even today,' it claimed, 'it is possible to find a people without a magistrate but never a magistrate without a people.'[1] This made the people morally, as well as chronologically prior to their leaders. Kings needed to remember that 'it is due to the people, and for the sakes of the people's welfare, that they exercise their power.' This was a long way from democracy. Good government demanded order and order was impossible if everyone decided the course of events. Nevertheless, even if it were mediated through governors, the point remained that the people had a *right* to resist tyranny by force.

Although based primarily on legal and scholastic sources, Huguenot thinking still drew explicitly on the Bible, for instance using the example of Saul's election as King of Israel to argue how a king demanded not only God's selection but also the formal acclamation and support of his people. That recognised, it is notable that 'the main foundations of the Calvinist theory of revolution were in fact constituted by their Catholic adversaries.'[2]

These ideas of political resistance were to prove influential, not only in France and the Netherlands, which was shortly to face similar problems, but also in Scotland. Scotland was Calvinist in a way that Huguenots could only dream of but it was led, for much of the 1560s, by a Catholic monarch, James I's mother, Mary. Her presence catalysed the debate about whether a people could legitimately remove a lawful monarch. One of the powerful voices to answer in the affirmative was James's tutor, George Buchanan, whose *The Right of the Kingdom in Scotland* was started in 1567 and published twelve years later.

Buchanan drew on a number of continental ideas, arguing that the original state of humanity was not only pre-political but pre-social, and that the commonwealth arose directly out of people's decisions. Politics was, in effect, created by a contract. Buchanan even talked about the 'whole body of people' coming together to elect someone to deal with the affairs of the community. Crucially, the people did not alienate their sovereignty in this transfer of authority. The implication of Buchanan's argument was that if the people had come together to 'elect' a ruler, they could also come together to depose him. Thus the king was less like a king and more 'like a guardian of the public accounts'.[3] When Buchanan's interlocutor in *The Right of the Kingdom in Scotland* asked him about Paul's injunction to obey rulers in Romans 13, Buchanan brushed the criticism aside, saying that one cannot allow a single verse of scripture to outweigh all evidence of law and philosophy and, in any case, Paul was not enunciating any universal maxim but rather only speaking of his own time and place. The contrast with Luther and Tyndale could not be stronger.

Critics thought that arguments such as these tended inevitably towards anarchy. James was among them and his high view of royal authority was, in measure, a reaction against these political ideas that put people before monarch. James was convinced that a monarch's rule did not depend on the transfer of sovereignty from people or even, as more moderate Elizabethan apologists had it, on the consent of parliament. As far as he was concerned, the king was answerable to God alone.

Although the divine right of kings is, to the modern mind, a quintessentially medieval idea, its English zenith came in the first half of the seventeenth century, when both James I and his son, Charles, held the view passionately and used it to justify their controversial policies. In a way that paradoxically aped Huguenot theories of resistance, the idea of the divine right of kings rested not so much on the revealed will of God in scripture but on natural law. The traditional Protestant doctrine, that human reason was too fraught by sin reliably to detect natural law, fell away. Natural reason detected natural law which pointed to natural order.

'Order of superiority and subjection is the instinct of purest nature,' the Bishop of Rochester explained. Earth was marked by 'superiority and subjection not only between man and all other creatures, but between man and woman', just as heaven was marked by 'order among blessed Angels'. Even in the 'innocence' of Eden 'there was a subordination of one to another, though without pain as now it is.'[4] According to this view, the earliest societies had been patriarchies. Adam's authority had been not just fatherly but kingly. The original state of man was patriarchal-political, not of voluntary association between free individuals who transferred their sovereignty to a nominated ruler.

In this sense, the divine right of kings was simply part of the natural social framework. In marriage, a husband's authority was not transferred to him by his wife. In a family, parents' authority did not derive from their children's consent. In a household, masters did not owe their status to any contract with their servants. Power, authority and status resided with God alone who, in his wisdom, gave them to those whom he chose. This was simply the natural law of creation.

This logic was frequently equated with the Ten Commandments whose simple moral clarity was read as an articulation of natural law. There were problems with this equation. Everyone held that the principle of self-defence was a fundamental element of natural law but it was a principle absent from the Decalogue. Such problems notwithstanding, the Ten Commandments were commonly drawn upon to defend the divine right of kings, on the understanding that each command had implications beyond its immediate sense. Thus, the fifth commandment, 'Honour thy father and thy mother', was taken to refer to all forms of civil obligation, including obedience to the king.[5] The king was, after all, the father of the nation.

Further biblical justifications were hard to come by. Apologists quoted Proverbs 8:15, 'By me kings reign, and princes decree justice', and Psalms 82:6, 'I have said, "Ye are gods; and all of you are children of the most High".' Recognising that latter quote meant the king's *authority* was divine, not the king himself. And, of course, there were the mandatory references to Romans 13:1. But beyond this, the Bible was not greatly used. Indeed, as Johann Sommerville has observed, 'absolutists believed that their theory could be expressed in – and proved by – purely rational arguments.' Pagans, who had never had any contact with the revealed will of God, were not exempt from and indeed often instinctively obeyed the natural laws of social and political obedience. 'The obligation to obey kings – and other superiors such as fathers – could not have arisen through Scripture alone. The Bible confirmed but did not create duties.'[6]

Such absolutist views were common among clergy in the seventeenth century, and formed the basis of King James's mental world. They did not mean that the king was wholly unaccountable, a law unto himself, or that he could legitimately practise arbitrary government. Rather, they meant, in the words of one contemporary, that 'God had trusted the King with the government of his kingdom . . . [and that] he is answerable for it . . . But not to his subjects.'[7]

James himself articulated the doctrine with admirable clarity in a number of books and speeches. God 'made you a little God to sit on his Throne, and rule over other men', he told his son in a book of advice entitled *Basilikon Doron*, meaning 'Royal Gift', published in 1599.[8] 'By the Law of Nature the King becomes a natural Father to all his Lieges at his Coronation,' James explained to his readers in *The True Law of Free Monarchies*.[9] Like any good father, that meant the king was 'bound to care for the nourishing, education, and virtuous government of his children', to take 'all the toil and pain that the father can', and 'to foresee all inconveniencies and dangers that may arise towards his children'. 'As the Father's chief joy ought to be in procuring his children's welfare', so the king's joy was to serve the good of his people. Yet, what the people's good consisted of, how it was to be achieved and who should hold the king to account over it were none of the people's business. 'Although I have said, a good king will frame all his actions to be according to the Law; yet is he not bound thereto but of his good will,' James explained.

Like any good divine right theorist, James justified himself primarily through appeals to natural law and reason. He did, however, back up his opinions with scripture, including an odd reading of Israel's own call for a king. This, it will be remembered, was in the teeth of opposition, not only of God, who interpreted it as a rejection (1 Sam. 10:19), but also of the prophet Samuel, who warned the people at length about how a monarch would exploit them: 'He will take your sons, and appoint them for himself, for his chariots, and to be his horsemen . . . he will take your daughters to be confectionaries, and to be cooks, and to be bakers . . . he will take your fields, and your vineyards, and your oliveyards, even the best of them, and give them to his servants . . .'

Historically this passage had been explained by royalist apologists as outlining what would happen if the people chose the wrong king. James, however, did not so much apologise for the passage as quote it, in *The True Law*, in full and approvingly, seemingly deaf to its tone of warning. The king, in his view, was called to serve the good of his people but was under no obligation to listen to them. His subjects were called to obedience, with prayers and tears their only weapons of resistance. The English found themselves under a doctrine of political obedience with which Luther or Tyndale would have been comfortable, except for its largely unbiblical justifications. Much that had gone before, from the exhortations of the Marian exiles to the ruminations of Elizabethan theologians, faded from memory.

'Touch not mine anointed': the King James translation

The critical exception was the Geneva Bible. Although Elizabeth's bishops had tried to replace it with their own official Bishops' Bible, their attempt had failed. The Bishops' Bible went through fourteen editions before Archbishop Parker's death in 1575. His successor at Canterbury, Edmund Grindal, was better disposed towards the Geneva version and enabled its first English printing in 1576. Thereafter, it went through numerous new editions and became the dominant translation for the next half-century, not only shaping this most significant era of English literature, but also informing political thought up to and during the English Civil War. And it was this that led to the Hampton Court conference of 1604 and the programme to publish a new, altogether safer version.

The origins of the Hampton Court conference lay in the Millenary Petition, so called because it was allegedly signed by 1,000 Puritan clergymen, which was presented to the new king on his way to London in 1603. The petition set out demands for a more fully reformed Church, focusing on the 'burden' of 'human rites and ceremonies', such as the signing of the cross in baptism and the use of a ring in marriage, which were deemed unbiblical. As a means of addressing their demands, and hopefully healing the Protestant divisions that had never been far from the surface of the Elizabethan Church, James called and presided over a conference at Hampton Court in January 1604.

Puritan hopes were high when the conference met on Saturday 14 January but, by the time it was drawing to a close on Monday evening, the small Puritan party was disaffected, each of its requests having been diplomatically refused by the king and not so diplomatically refused by the Puritan-loathing Bishop Bancroft. Towards the end of the afternoon, the Puritan leader, John Reynolds, suggested – it is not clear why – that a new translation be authorised. Bancroft at first snubbed the idea but James was more positive, seeing in it a way of placating the Puritans, driving out the Geneva version and dealing with the threat of the Catholic Douai-Rheims translation. A new official version would allow the authorities to regain control of this most important text, in much the same way as Henry VIII and Thomas Cromwell had tried to in the 1530s. In particular, it would allow for the removal of marginalia, many of which James considered to be 'very partial, untrue, seditious and savouring too much of dangerous and traitorous conceits'.[10]

Bancroft was given control over the process, selecting translators, setting their terms and reviewing the final text. He also set out the rules for translation, specifying that the only permissible marginal notes were those needed to explain difficult Greek or Hebrew words; insisting that traditional ecclesiastical words like 'Church' were to be preferred over more contentious, modern ones like 'congregation'; and stating that the translators were to follow the Bishops' Bible as their rule of thumb (itself a re-working of the 1540 Great Bible), although permitting them to draw on earlier versions when 'they agree better with the Text'.[11]

Over the next seven years, the forty-seven translators, working in six companies based in London, Oxford and Cambridge, translated and edited the full text, and appended a lengthy note 'to the reader' justifying the need for, and nature of, the new translation.[12] The result was a more respectable translation, free of seditious notes, of any mention of

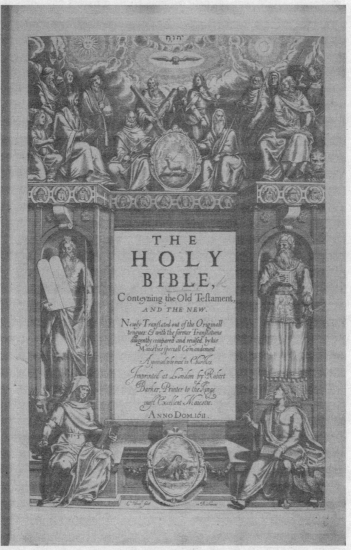

Fig. 6: Title page of King James Bible (1611)

the word 'tyrant' (a favourite of the Geneva exiles) and graced, on its frontispiece, by 'a sense of ordered massivity', the front page illustration being dominated by an impenetrable carved stone wall (Fig. 6).[13]

At first, the reception of King James's version was muted. The Geneva translation continued to sell well. However, official weight was behind the new translation and, under pressure, domestic printing of the Geneva version ceased in 1616. Printing continued in the Netherlands, whence copies were imported, but both Charles I and his archbishop from 1633, William Laud, disliked the Geneva version intensely, and for patriotic and economic reasons (they argued that the cheap, good-quality Geneva imports were putting English printers out of business) the Geneva version was banned. The last edition was printed in 1644.

Although the 1640s witnessed the publication of a Soldier's Pocket Bible, which comprised extracts from the Geneva version, there was no turning away from the official edition during the Interregnum. The King James Version was here to stay, its success finally secured with the Restoration of the monarchy and the Church of England in 1660. The battle for the English Bible, which had so influenced and been influenced by political life since the 1520s, was settled in favour of a large, heavy, official, 'authorised' version. In the *textual* tussle between freedom and order, order had won.

'A run-of-the-mill provincial backwater': Jerusalem in Dorset

For all the supposed Puritan sedition in the early years of the seventeenth century, it should be remembered that virtually no Puritan actively sought the overthrow of the monarchy or the political order. Puritans were as sure of the authority of the husband over his wife, the father over his family, the master over his servants and the king over his subjects as were royalists. They shared the widespread fear of democracy and denounced Anabaptism as much as any Anglican divine. Few were republicans. If we seek a simple conflict between authoritarian royalists and freedom-loving Puritans in the early seventeenth century we will be disappointed.

The point of contention was not so much the fact, or even nature of, royal authority as its religious responsibilities. The Elizabethan settlement had given the monarch considerable authority over the Church, which was not being deployed to complete the Reformation in the way most Puritans wanted. Worse still, it was now being used to elevate clerics, most notably Archbishop William Laud, whose theology and attitude to liturgy and ceremony was in direct tension with the Puritan vision.

This was a particularly acute problem in Scotland where the Presbyterians insisted on greater ecclesiastical autonomy than did the English. As far as many Scots were concerned, the Church was a self-governing institution, independent of the civil magistrate in spiritual matters, and ruled not by bishops (whom the king appointed) but by a hierarchy of assemblies, with elected pastors and lay elders at every level, whose job was to teach doctrine and impose discipline. It was this understanding of the Church, as an autonomous body within society largely free of temporal interference – paradoxically close to the vision that inspired Pope Gregory VII in the eleventh century – that formed the basis of the National Covenant of 1638, which was drawn up and signed in the wake of Charles I's attempt to impose the English Prayer Book on the Scottish Kirk. And it was this understanding that provided the spark that set the country aflame with civil war.

When the country stumbled into civil war, Scotland in 1639, and England in 1642, few imagined that ten years would see the king on the executioner's block. Many people, the godly among them, objected to Charles's high-handedness, his Catholic queen and (as they saw it) crypto-papist court, his support for Laud and other anti-Calvinist ecclesiastics, and his willingness to ride roughshod over the fundamental liberties of his subjects because of his conviction of his divine right. But it was not having a king per se that was the problem. For Puritans at least the problem was the way in which the king's actions thwarted their attempts to create a reformed, godly society.

The very idea of a reformed, godly society terrifies us today, epitomising every reason why religion and politics should not mix. However, those rare instances in which Puritans did gain the reins of power in England and work towards their vision of a New Jerusalem are revealing, and expose a less abhorrent and more familiar society than the caricatures prepare us for. One such instance was Dorchester, a regional market town of around 2,000 people in Dorset.

Dorchester, like most other places, suffered from periodic fires that destroyed many homes, shops and inns. One of these, on 6 August 1613, was particularly severe, razing 170 houses, around half the town. Eight years earlier one of the town's three parishes had received a new rector, John White, a passionate Puritan, who was typical of those Anglicans who were determined to reform the Church of England from within. When the town burned down in 1613, White and his allies deemed it a judgement from God and took the opportunity to work towards a godly Reformation.[14]

Before the fire Dorchester suffered from the standard social problems of the time. There were those that the godly were famed for objecting to: fiddling, dancing, may-poling, bear- and bull-baiting, swearing, Sabbath-breaking, playing sports, general lewdness, absence from church and trouble during services. Beyond, there was a range of sins and evils that Dorchester's new governors took no less seriously: poverty, drunkenness, antisocial behaviour, assault, theft, vagrancy, domestic violence, pre-marital sex, illegitimacy, desertion, incest, rape and infanticide. In an age in which private behaviour was thought to affect to the functioning of a community, Dorchester's Puritans fretted about these social problems and set about addressing them all.

Historically, such problems had been dealt with in traditional ways, through a combination of poor laws, private charity and general indifference. White and the Puritan hierarchy could not be indifferent to such sins, however, as every one was a stain on a would-be godly people. They embarked upon a broad social reform which lasted for much of the next forty years. Good social order was enforced. Idleness, immorality, vagrancy and promiscuity were punished. There was a sharp decline in illegitimacy. Churches were enlarged. Drunkenness was tackled, although the campaign against excessive drinking and unlicensed ale houses was one of the town's most conspicuous failures. The regular study of scripture was enjoined, church attendance enforced and travelling theatrical companies banned. There were also numerous attempts to enforce household discipline and parental authority, initially through mediation and then, if that failed, through the courts.

Beyond the attempts to reform personal morality, which they recognised as the bedrock of any stable society, the Dorchester

Reformers set up a new 'hospital' in which up to fifty children were fed, clothed, educated and taught a trade, for which they were paid a weekly wage. The scheme was not unique to Dorchester but it was conspicuously successful there and even, on occasion, stretched to include adults, such as the weaver Nicholas Cox who was sent to the hospital because he neglected his wife and children, and whose earnings were paid directly to his wife so he could not drink them away. The town set up several schools, almshouses for the elderly and sick, and a Fuel House to provide fuel for the indigent. It gave money and food directly to the elderly, infirm and deserving poor, paid for paupers' funerals and apprenticed orphans. The town hierarchy also engaged in market-fixing during bad harvests, restraining food prices and distributing emergency stocks of grain when deemed necessary.

All this cost a great deal of money, which was raised in two ways. The first was a massive outpouring of private charity. White and his fellow Puritan pastors coaxed from their parishioners a level of giving that was unmatched in England, including disproportionately large donations for victims of plague and fire elsewhere. The second means of raising and managing funds was more ingenious. The town hierarchy built a municipal brewery in which surplus funds were invested and which, coincidentally, helped to control the town's drink trade. 'The Brewhouse', as it came to be known, became the biggest industrial operation in town and was even used by some as a bank. Its profits were considerable and distributed every year to the poor at Christmas.

All in all, seventeenth-century Dorchester turned into a cross between the Society for the Reformation of Manners and the modern welfare state. Its enterprises, both personal and communal, were generally successful, although there was resistance from various quarters throughout. This was not simply on account of the intrusion into people's lives. In an age when illegitimacy, drunkenness or desertion burdened everyone in the community there was no wholly private sphere. Rather the 'vision of the reformed new Jerusalem required the imposition of policies of economic and cultural coercion that were deeply threatening' to some in Dorchester, in particular the poorest and the richest.[15] The Reformers created an ordered society but at the cost of freedom.

The Civil Wars disrupted Dorchester's civic reform, as did the death of John White in 1648, but the post-war period saw further attacks on poverty and ignorance, including the rebuilding and repair of the Brewhouse, the Fuel House, the hospital and the town's school buildings. It also saw the development of new schemes including a project for the education of poor children and a remarkable health-care programme in which the town defrayed medical costs, covered the bills of various doctors and apothecaries, and even paid the physician, Dr Losse, a stipend of £8 a year for treating poor patients. As David Underdown, whose historical research put Puritan Dorchester on the map, has remarked, 'For a brief moment in history Dorchester had something very like a municipal health service.'[16]

Dorchester's governors never regarded their Reformation as being incompatible with monarchy and, indeed, they appear to have been unhappy with Charles's execution and the ensuing religious and political chaos. However, after the Restoration, life was more difficult for those who espoused the theological convictions that had driven Dorchester's reforms and these, accordingly, died slowly throughout the 1660s and 1670s, along with the Puritans who had inspired them.

'That man of blood': killing the king

Dorchester proved easier to govern than the country. When the godly gained national power in the later 1640s they attempted to reform the country in a similar way by means of parliamentary Acts for which they have become infamous. The Adultery Act of 1650 imposed the death penalty for adultery and three months' imprisonment for fornication. In the same year, the Blasphemy Act pronounced on Sabbath-breaking, drunkenness, swearing and blasphemy, threatening to imprison those who professed that such things 'are not things in themselves shameful, wicked, sinful, impious, abominable and detestable'. For the most part, however, the godly Reformation that Dorchester experienced made little headway in England.

The reasons were only in part due to the sheer scale and unmanageability of a nation as opposed to a town. They were also, significantly, due to the fact that the godly could not agree on what a fully reformed, biblical society should look like. Legislation against murder, adultery or Sabbath-breaking was reasonably straightfor-ward. Such practices were prohibited in scripture and unacceptable among any Christian people. Outlawing them was uncontroversial, although quite how draconian the punishments should be, and how successful a law against fornication could ever be, was more contentious.

Beyond such issues of personal morality, however, it was hard to agree precisely what a godly society entailed. The radical religious groups that mushroomed in the late 1640s and 1650s may have been numerically tiny but were of far greater significance than their numbers alone indicate. Many were deemed thoroughly disreputable (and not just by conventional Anglicans) but they were indicative of an important, wider phenomenon: differences of opinion that could not simply be dismissed as heretical: legitimate heterodoxy. In time, awareness of a variety of acceptable opinions among the godly would mark a turning point for the role of the Bible in English politics and, indeed, a turning point for English politics as a whole. For the first time, the call for tolerance, or at least liberty of conscience, albeit a limited call, would be heard not from the political periphery but from its centre.

Initially, none of this was expected. Charles I had been so success-ful in unifying the opposition to him that their differences of opinion seemed largely irrelevant. The Bible's message against marrying alien queens, especially if they were of the wrong faith, could not have been clearer. Yet, shortly after coming to the throne, Charles married Henrietta Maria, daughter of Henry IV of France and, as it tran-spired, a public proselytiser in a way that James I's converted Catholic queen, Anne of Denmark, had not been. The Bible's message against idolatry was, if anything, clearer. Yet Charles favoured and elevated Archbishop William Laud and his fellow bishops, whose attitude to ceremony, public prayer, the altar, vestments and the sacrament was judged by many Puritans to be little better than idolatry. The Bible's message against tyranny had been repeatedly highlighted in the now suppressed Geneva translation. Yet Charles's conviction of his divine right enabled him to ignore his subjects' property rights and even personal liberty as he attempted to raise money without the aid of parliament. When the Church of England, meeting in Convocation in 1640, passed new canons, including an affirmation of the divine right of kings and of the doctrine of non-resistance, concerns multiplied and opposition, particularly in Scotland, further solidified.

Many of these concerns were voiced in the Fast Sermons, which marked national days of fasting and repentance, and had become a regular feature of parliament by the end of James I's reign. The majority of these, or at least the majority that found their way into print, drew on the Old rather than New Testament, and did so in such a way as to allow speakers to make unambiguous political points under the cover of biblical exegesis. In such sermons, Egypt stood for any land in which the tyrannous oppressed the godly and from which the godly had escaped, while always being tempted back towards it. Babylon stood as a place of idolatry, oppression and corruption into which the sin of the godly had led them. The Antichrist was the Pope. Pharoah was a typical ruler deaf to God's message; Nebuchadnezzar and Belshazzar rulers whose pride and arrogance were justly punished by God. Korah, Dathan and Abiram were rebels against a worthy leader who had received God's word. Jeroboam, Omri, Ahab and Manasseh were kings who had done evil in God's sight. Herod was their New Testament counterpart. The Pharisees were Church of England prelates.[17]

It would be a misreading of the Puritan mind, ascribing to it an unmerited cynicism, to assume that Fast Day preachers, or indeed any other sympathetic parliamentarians, used the Bible simply as a vehicle for their political programme. The Bible was far too important, too foundational, too dangerous to be exploited in this way. Rather, those who saw Charles I as Pharaoh or Belshazzar, or the nation as stumbling back into Egypt read scripture as a living text whose stories, places, characters and metaphors offered a map to navigate contemporary events.

Nowhere was this more important than in the execution of Charles himself. In the wake of the First Civil War, Charles I came to be labelled a 'man of blood'. This was more than just an insult or a vague accusation that he had brought violence to the land. The idea that shedding human blood was a profound act of injustice was deeply rooted in the Bible, and linked to the idea that humans were made in God's image. In the words of Genesis 9:6: 'Whoso sheddeth man's blood, by man shall his blood be shed: for in the image of God made he man.' Killing had consequences and the fact that the king had dragged the country into a murderous civil war, in which tens of thousands died, had momentous consequences. These were spelt out in Numbers 35:33, which read: 'So ye shall not pollute the land wherein ye are: for blood it defileth the land: and the land cannot be cleansed of the blood that is shed therein, but by the blood of him that shed it.' If England were to be a godly nation, it could not remain defiled by blood.

The General Assembly of the Kirk of Scotland had publicly warned Charles in 1645 that he must repent of his blood-guiltness 'which cleaveth fast to your throne'.[18] When the Second Civil War broke out in 1648, caused largely by the king's intransigence and his secret negotiations with the Scots against the English, the conclusion seemed inevitable. Pamphlets were printed recalling that God condemned Saul and Ahab to death for disobeying his orders to kill wicked kings, and claiming that God would deal similarly with those who, knowing the king's blood-guilt, still wished to sign a treaty with him. The regicides felt able to reject traditional formal legal procedure in the name of the higher justice they were pursuing. Numbers 35:33 was cited by the prosecutor at the king's trial. Only the king's death could purify the land. It seems unlikely that the Bible was 'primarily responsible' for the execution of Charles I, as historian Christopher Hill once claimed.[19] However, it is beyond doubt that it did provide a coherent and credible series of ideas that made the regicide not only possible but justifiable and, according to its own 'higher' standards, lawful.

All in all, a remarkably detailed and comprehensive biblical code language and logic was deployed in the 1640s. It was used by all sides but proved particularly important for those who felt unable to criticise monarch and crown directly. The language helped keep opposition to Charles anchored within a particular conceptual framework, related to the struggles of the godly against idolatry, corruption and tyranny. Crucially, however, it was a language of opposition, able to bind together the disparate forces allied to parliament against an arbitrary and arrogant monarch. It was not, however, able to provide that opposition with a programme for reform when those powers were curtailed and eventually removed. 'The ambiguities of the words

Antichrist, Babylon and Egypt helped to preserve unity among supporters of Parliament in the early days of the Civil War. But when it came to post-war settlement, the vulgar intruded with their own political and social ideas.'[20]

'Every sect saith, Oh! Give me liberty': the joy of sects

Sects – a misleading term wrongly suggesting complete detachment from the mainstream Church – had been a feature of English Protestantism from the 1540s, but it was only with the breakdown of censorship and the system of Church courts a century later that they emerged into the light.[21] Church attendance could no longer easily be enforced, nor assemblies to hear radical preachers punished. For the first time in English history, anyone who wanted to get into print – and could persuade a printer that there was money in his publication – could. The social and political ramifications were immense. As Bishop Hall told the House of Lords in December 1641, London and its suburbs hosted 'no fewer than four-score congregations of several sectaries, instructed by guides fit for them, cobblers, tailors, felt-makers, and such like trash'.[22]

The chaos of the First Civil War helped to multiply groups, tracts and radical ideas in a way that shocked the godly, whether they were Parliamentarian or royalist. In 1643 the Westminster Assembly of Divines was charged with reforming the national Church and bringing some order to the anarchic religious landscape. However, it faced a great deal of dissension over the issue of Church government, with 'Independents' unwilling to accept a Presbyterian system and instead placing a non-negotiable emphasis on the independence of each congregation. Although the assembly finally offered parliament a plan for a Presbyterian national Church in 1645, Independents in parliament and the New Model Army determined that the religious freedom of sects should not be curtailed and the plan came to little.

In reality, the number of sectaries is unlikely to have been above 2 per cent of the population, but it was a noisy and disturbing 2 per cent, which helped change the nation's religious and, indirectly, its political landscape for good. In a sermon published in 1640 entitled *The Sufficiency of the Spirits Teaching without Humane-Learning,* the cobbler Samuel How argued that although learning was useful to scholars, lawyers and gentlemen, the pulpit was better suited to uneducated persons as they were more open to the Spirit's teaching, which was what really mattered for understanding the mind of God. It is not clear how much rhetoric there was in this. Leading radicals were often educated and literate, and their reputation as unlettered and therefore unsullied by sophistry may owe something to self-presentation, as well, of course, to the criticism of the 'truly' learned.[23] Either way, however, How's point had appeal. People – *all* people – should read the Bible and decide *for themselves* what it meant, rather than be spoon-fed by the learned.

It was a sentiment readily supported by scripture, as sectaries knew. Galatians 1:12 saw St Paul emphasising the fact that his revelation had been personal rather than through any human system: 'For I neither received it of man, neither was I taught it, but by the revelation of Jesus Christ.' A proof text for the freedom for which radicals fought was provided in 1 Peter 2:9, although more obviously in the Geneva translation than the King James one. Whereas the King James read, 'But ye are a chosen generation, a royal priesthood, an holy nation, a peculiar people,' itself implying a degree of emancipation, the Geneva translation declared, 'But yee are a chosen generation, a royall Priesthoode, an holy nation, a people set at libertie.' Galatians 3:28 was treated as a fundamental statement not only of Christian freedom but also of equality: 'There is neither Jew nor Greek, there is neither bond nor free, there is neither male nor female: for ye are all one in Christ Jesus.' James 5:1 was a favourite verse for those intent on 'levelling' society: 'Go to now, ye rich men, weep and howl for your miseries that shall come upon you.' Altogether the New Testament, if read under the light of the individual conscience rather than the constricting tutelage of spiritual or temporal authorities, offered vast resources – if no coherent programme – for a politically and socially subversive movement.

And there were plenty such movements, most known to us through the abusive terms with which they were labelled at the time. The most notorious were the Ranters, who believed – or were believed to believe – that they were free from all legal and moral constraints. In what may have been a deliberate reaction against the Calvinist emphasis on human depravity, they contended that they had been liberated from sin and the constraints of flesh and morality by the Spirit. To the pure in spirit, like themselves, all things were pure. There was no moral law. They believed that matter was eternal, God was 'reason', scripture full of contradictions and that the biblical Christ unimportant. Only the spiritual Christ, who lived in believers, mattered. Not surprisingly they scandalised respectable opinion, which circulated with lurid descriptions of their sexual misconduct. Persecuted, the movement died out in only a few years.

More successful, though hardly more respectable at the time, were the Quakers, so named (again abusively) because, after the fashion of Isaiah 66:2, they were said to quake at the word of God. Initially not the pacifist organisation they were to become (founder George Fox once advised Cromwell to sack Rome), they also claimed to be led by an inner spiritual light, rather than by clergy or Bible. This encouraged them to flout conventional customs, although in a way wholly different to the Ranters. Quakers refused to doff their caps to social 'superiors' and addressed them with the familiar 'thou' rather than the respectful 'you'. They interrupted church services and challenged clergy to debate. Informal, spirit-led worship meant that anyone, including women, could speak. Although they too suffered persecution, they survived the Interregnum and Restoration in their tens of thousands.

Many such 'sects' promoted political ideas that were too novel or eccentric to gain any popular purchase. Two groups, however, the Levellers and the Diggers (or 'True Levellers') were different. The Diggers were inspired by pamphleteer Gerrard Winstanley. He believed, like John Ball before him, that 'not one word was spoken at the beginning that one branch of mankind should rule over another, but selfish imaginations did set up one man to teach and rule over another.'[24] His and the Diggers' critique of inequality was focused on land tenure, in particular private land-ownership. In the beginning, Winstanley wrote, 'the whole earth was common to all without exception.'[25] The subsequent division of land, as the strong took what had once been 'a common treasury' was not, according to Winstanley's unorthodox view, a result of the Fall so much as actually part of the Fall itself, a tragedy and crime that was still being enacted.

The coming of Christ, which, like many, Winstanley expected imminently, would herald an earthly reign in which 'none shall lay claim to any creature and say, "This is mine, and that is yours, This is my work, that is yours"; but every one shall put their hands to till the earth, and bring up cattle, and the blessing of the earth shall be common to all.'[26] Winstanley consequently advocated a form of Christian communism, based on the promised reversal of the Fall and the practice of the early Church as described in Acts 4:32–7. Unusually, Winstanley and the Diggers put their ideas into practice, founding and living in a commune in St George's Hill in Surrey, until the frightened local landlords destroyed it.

The Levellers were not a religious 'sect' in the same way as the Diggers. Unlike other sects, their objectives, in as far as they had easily definable objectives,[27] were not based solely on a biblical vision for society. They deployed arguments from natural law and reason at least as often as they did from scripture. Nevertheless, the Bible remained close to the heart of their ambitions. A large but disparate group, many belonging to the New Model Army, the Levellers formed around several leading radicals, in particular Richard Overton, William Walwyn and John Lilburne. Overton was a General Baptist, at least for a period, although one with views that were at the time considered somewhat unorthodox. Walwyn avoided denominational labels and was renowned as a clever and sophisticated writer, a reputation that earned him frequent accusations of atheism, a charge he denied. Lilburne was more obviously religious in his convictions, an orthodox Calvinist until converting to Quakerism in later life, peppering his writing with biblical references and allusions.

With such leaders, it is hardly surprising that the biblical vision underpinned much Leveller thought and activity. Lilburne spoke of God engraving the golden rule of Matthew 7:12 upon his heart. Overton declared, 'I was not born for myself alone but for my neighbour as well, and I am resolved to discharge the trust which God hath reposed in me for the good of others.'[28] Walwyn wrote of how the essence of Christianity lay in 'universal love to all mankind without respect of persons, opinions, societies . . . churches or forms of worship'.[29] Between them they were convinced that all people were created equal and that none had the right to rule over others without those others' assent. Both convictions were firmly anchored in fundamental biblical principles.

The Levellers' political agenda included religious toleration, extended suffrage, a reformed legal system and the abolition of the House of Lords. 'All power is originally and essentially in the whole body of the people of this nation,' declared the tract *The Case of the Army Truly Stated*. 'Their free choice or consent by their representers is the only original or foundation of all just government.' The document *Agreement of the People* worked through the implications of this, advocating a redrawing of constituencies to suit the population better, bi-annual elections, a ban on conscription and universal obedience to the law.[30] These ideas were subsequently debated at Putney church in October and November 1647, in which Colonel Thomas Rainsborough famously said that 'the poorest he that is in England hath a life to live, as the greatest he . . . [and] every man that is to live under a government ought first by his own consent to put himself under that government.'[31] Such sentiments, which drew on similar debates about Church government – did authority reside with ministers and elders only, or in the entire congregation? – were no less shocking in the tumultuous mid-century atmosphere than they had been earlier in the century, however. Other, more influential, participants argued forcefully that the economically dependent could and should have no stake in the nation's governance.

In addition to a reformed parliament, the Levellers also argued for (a measure of) religious toleration. 'Liberty of conscience [should be allowed] for every man . . . to worship God in that way, and perform Christ's ordinances in that manner as shall appear to them most agreeable to God's word,' Walwyn insisted.[32] This was also the position of the individual who came to dominate the political landscape during the Interregnum. For a man whose every thought was saturated with scripture, Oliver Cromwell's own religious beliefs are notoriously hard to pin down. Unlike many of his Puritan contemporaries, he did not keep a spiritual diary or journal. He wrote no story of personal conversion, despite probably having had one in his thirties. He issued no personal credo, never discussed any of the thousands of sermons he heard and never commented on any books, other than Walter Raleigh's *History of the World*, which he recommended to his son. His beliefs can only be constructed through his public pronouncements.

More significantly, Cromwell cannot be associated with any of the factions or sects that flourished at the time. He showed a sincere aversion to sectarianism, which he thought was not only socially and politically dangerous but – far more importantly – in express defiance of God's plans. Instead, he declared himself to be largely indifferent to the form in which godliness came. What was important was the godliness itself. 'Whosoever hath this faith, let his form be what it will.'[33]

This is key to understanding Cromwell's advocacy of a liberty of conscience during the 1640s and 1650s. If the godly were 'men that believe the remission of sins through the blood of Christ', rather than men who were Presbyterian or Independent, the compass of toleration should extend across factions – although not that far across.[34] Liberty of conscience could be justified for Presbyterians, Independents and Baptists, possibly for Anglicans, but only questionably to Quakers, and certainly not to Roman Catholics or Socinians.[35] In the words of one commentator, Cromwell was 'not so much a promoter or defender of the sects, as a man enamoured of godliness but indifferent to its forms, provided they fell within the limits of mainstream, evangelical, Trinitarian Protestantism'.[36]

Those limits are, to us, absurdly tight, making the liberty of conscience that was being advocated hardly worth having. This was tolerance for people like me. Unlike John Locke who, as we shall see in the next chapter, understood tolerance as a good in itself, Cromwell promoted liberty of conscience as a necessary evil, a means of securing the unity of the godly. He was continually frustrated and disappointed when the sects failed to respond accordingly. 'Every sect saith, Oh! Give me liberty. But give him it, and to his power he will not yield it to anybody else.'[37] Cromwell persevered, however, attempting to keep the peace between different godly groups. Crucially, the idea of tolerance, limited as it was, was being voiced not from the political periphery but from its centre. Cromwell's vision of the liberty of conscience may have been pragmatic rather than ideological but it was nonetheless 'paving the way for the religious plurality of the modern state'.[38]

'Learn obedience to reason': Milton and Hobbes

The radical movement of the 1640s and 1650s had a broad anti-intellectual streak to it. That did not mean that it was an anti-intellectual movement or that it failed to attract any educated opinion, however. John Milton was among the most erudite and cultured men of his time and became one of the most eloquent defenders of political radicalism. He also provided one of the most forceful arguments for biblically rooted political freedom in English history.

The son of a Catholic convert, Milton was educated at St Paul's School and at Christ's College, Cambridge, where he was deeply unhappy. A fifteen-month tour of France and Italy in 1638–39 confirmed in his mind his future as a man of letters but was interrupted, at least on Milton's own somewhat dubious account, by the growing political tensions at home. He entered the fray with five pamphlets written in 1641 and 1642 that attacked the Church's episcopal government. He followed these with four more that advocated divorce and that were apparently motivated by his own recent, impetuous and initially disastrous marriage to a girl half his age. He subsequently wrote a number of tracts attacking censorship, and defending the regicide and the new political order, some of them while in the employment of the new Commonwealth.

Milton was intensely biblical. His prose, like his better known verse, was saturated with scriptural quotations and reasoning. An early tract against 'Prelatical Episcopacy' argued that we must make 'the Gospel our rule, and Oracle', treating it as the authority against which all other authors, such as the Church fathers who advocated episcopacy, should be judged.[39] His tracts on divorce were often little more than exercises in biblical exegesis, as he attempted to reconcile apparently contradictory positions on the subject. His 1649 work *The Tenure of Kings and Magistrates* drew on Protestant theories of popular sovereignty and resistance, and then supported them with pages of biblical examples. The tract outlines the dangers of, and necessary limitations upon, kingship, from which Milton concluded that 'a republican form of government . . . [is] better adapted to our human circumstances than monarchy.'[40] In one of his last publications, *The Readie and Easie Way to Establish a Free Commonwealth*, published as his republican dreams were dying around him, he insisted that 'the whole Protestant church allows no supreme judge to rule in matters of religion, but the Scriptures; and these [are] to be interpreted by the Scriptures themselves, which necessarily infers liberty of conscience.'[41] Not only is Milton the most biblical of England's major poets, but he is also one of its most biblical political thinkers.

That political thought, and the biblical and theological reflection that formed it, had as its lodestar the idea of liberty. The gospel is 'God's proclamation of our freedom', not simply 'inward freedom' but also 'political freedom'.[42] Drawing on numerous biblical texts, in particular Matthew 20:25–6,[43] Milton argued that Protestant Christianity meant – or should have meant – freedom from religious and political authority, and even from certain social conventions.

Milton adopted a rule of biblical interpretation that was based on two principles: 'nature' and 'charity'. This was most obvious in his divorce tracts. Milton faced a complex problem in these. How do you reconcile biblical texts that tell you that 'it is not good that the man should be alone' (Gen. 2:18); that 'it is good for a man not to touch a woman' (1 Cor. 7:1); that a man may 'write [his wife] a bill of divorcement . . . [if] he hath found some uncleanness in her' (Deut. 24:1); and that 'whosoever shall put away his wife, except it be for fornication . . . committeth adultery' (Matt. 19:9)? Which texts take priority over which and how do you judge? The Church's answer had usually been clear: Christ's commands take precedence over all others. But that put Milton, advocating divorce, in a difficult position. In consequence, he argued that theologians had interpreted the words of Christ erroneously, partly because they ignored that fact that Christ himself said he had come not to abrogate the law of Moses (Matt. 5:17–19) and partly because Christ's words should be interpreted according to the principles that he himself embraced, meaning the principle of love or 'charity'. Thus, reading scripture should involve 'consulting with charity, the interpreter and guide of our faith'.[44] 'We cannot safely assent to any precept written in the Bible, but as charity commends it to us,' he wrote in *The Doctrine and Discipline of Divorce*.[45]

'Nature' was almost an adjunct to this principle of charity. The 'two prime statutes' of nature are 'to join it self to that which is good and acceptable and friendly; and to turn aside and depart from what is disagreeable, displeasing and unlike'.[46] The principle of charity that must guide our reading of the Bible directs us to an ethic in which embracing the good and avoiding the 'displeasing' serves as the guiding principle. Thus, although St Paul says some demanding things about sex and marriage in 1 Corinthians 7, he also makes some allowances for 'the present distress', allowing Milton to remark 'the Apostle adds a limitation . . . which he gives us doubtless as a pattern how to reconcile other places by the general rule of charity.'[47] As with divorce, so with wider political considerations: 'if charity be . . . excluded . . . how yee will defend the untainted honour of your own actions and proceedings?' Milton wrote to parliament in 1643.[48] If a command seemed harsh or insensitive, it should be read through and reconciled according to the principles of charity and nature.

Milton thus drew a radical political, ecclesiastical and social agenda from scripture, in much the same way as less reputable sectaries did, but with a good deal more sophistication. The idea behind both agendas was the same: God gave his salvation to individuals, and it was up to those individuals to work out their salvation for themselves. Milton appeared unconcerned about the anarchic potential of all this, expecting a degree of noise and turmoil. Sects and schisms 'are but the throws and pangs that go before the birth of reformation'.[49] Indeed, they were reminiscent of early Christianity itself. 'The Primitive Christians in their times were accounted such as are now call'd Familists and Adamites, or worse.'[50]

In defending such factionalism, Milton was also practising a form of self-defence. He had been working for many years on a *magnum opus* entitled *De Doctrina Christiana* (Of Christian Doctrine), which was written in Latin and remained unpublished until found in the Old State Paper Office in Whitehall in 1823. This was Milton's proudest achievement, drawing on around 8,000 biblical texts and comprising his *Summa Theologica*. It shared the basic premises of Protestantism, such as the divine inspiration of the Bible, its sufficiency as an arbiter of faith and its clarity, even to the unlearned, in matters pertaining to salvation. Despite this, it was a profoundly – unpublishably – unorthodox book, in which Milton spoke out not only against tithes and episcopacy, but also against the sacraments, infant baptism, the immortality of the soul and, most dangerously, the Trinity, which he called 'a bizarre and senseless idea'.[51] Milton clearly knew that unfettered biblical and political freedom led to some dangerous places.

By way of rebalancing the scales, Milton placed clear emphasis on the importance of sincere personal piety and discipline. 'The liberation of all human life from slavery [is possible] provided that the discipline arising from religion should overflow into the morals and institutions of the state,' he argued.[52] 'If you think slavery an intolerable evil, learn obedience to reason and the government of yourselves.'[53] As things turned out, he was to be bitterly disappointed. The English people were more traumatised than liberated by the events of the 1650s and appeared not to value political or religious freedom as much as he did. Republicanism collapsed in 1659 and 1660, but Milton held on tenaciously and bravely to his beliefs. As the situation became more desperate, so did he. In *The Present Means, and Brief Delineation of a Free Commonwealth*, written in early 1660, he intimated to George Monck, the leader of the army in Scotland who had emerged as the most powerful man in the country, that he should be prepared to maintain political liberty *against* public opinion, by force if necessary.[54] In his second edition of *The Readie and Easie Way to Establish a Free Commonwealth*, printed when the game was all but up, he returned to this problem of a people that did not want the political liberty he sought for them, and he arrived at a similar conclusion. Ultimately, Milton's hopes – that the political liberty he derived from the Bible would prove sufficiently desirable so as to be self-sustaining – proved ill-founded. As a last resort, he was prepared to countenance the use of force to impose freedom on an unwilling population.

There is an interesting comparison to be made between Milton and his contemporary Thomas Hobbes. Both were accomplished classicists, both loathed their time at university, both travelled around and were influenced by those whom they met on the Continent, both were irreconcilably hostile to Catholicism, both embraced a form of mortalism, the idea that the soul dies (and is resurrected) with the body, and both recognised that Christianity offered a powerful source of personal and political freedom. Where they differed was on the desirability of that freedom. Both wrote political treatises that were saturated with biblical texts – *Leviathan* cited over 650 – but to very different ends.

Hobbes was born in 1588, the son of a clergyman who left his parish and home after assaulting a parishioner. He was educated in Malmesbury and at Magdalen Hall in Oxford, where he was immersed in arid Aristotelian logic-chopping for which, along with universities in general, he acquired a lifelong loathing. He then entered the service of William Cavendish, soon to be Duke of Devonshire, with whose family he remained connected for seventy years (he died aged ninety-one). As tutor to Cavendish's son, Hobbes had access to several great libraries, met a number of leading European thinkers, encountered and admired Euclid's geometry, and absorbed a new scientific intellectual climate. This proved crucial to his later political philosophy, which sought to work out the nature and extent of sovereignty from first principles. As he wrote in his introduction to *Leviathan*, his long and controversial *magnum opus*, 'seeing life is but a motion of Limbs . . . why may we not say, that all Automata . . . have an artificial life? [Thus] that great Leviathan called a Commonwealth, or State . . . is but an Artificial Man . . . in which, the Sovereignty is an Artificial Soul, as giving life and motion to the whole body.'[55]

Hobbes reasoned in *Leviathan* that 'nature hath made men . . . equal, in the faculties of body, and mind' but that 'from this equality of ability, ariseth equality of hope in the attaining of our Ends' which led inevitably to conflict.[56] 'In such condition,' he reasoned, 'there is no place for Industry; because the fruit thereof is uncertain . . . no Culture of the Earth; no Navigation . . . no commodious Building; . . . no Knowledge of the face of the Earth; no account of Time; no Arts; no Letters; no Society; and which is worst of all, continuall feare, and danger of violent death.' This life was, famously, 'solitary, poore, nasty, brutish, and short'.[57] Writing as he was in the late 1640s, he had good reason for such a bleak view.

The only solution to this dilemma was for people to surrender their natural right to defend themselves to a sovereign power who would guarantee public order. Unlike earlier Protestant theories of government in which sovereignty ultimately remained with the people, Hobbes's system dictated that once the people had made their covenant with a ruler, the ruler held authority. This was a permanent endowment, not a lease of sovereignty. Moreover, Hobbes's sovereign had no obligations to his people, who could not hold him to account for anything he might do.

This did not mean the sovereign did not have duties. He did, 'namely the procuration of the safety of the people'.[58] This meant that the sovereign was 'obliged [to fulfil those duties] by the Law of Nature, and to render an account thereof to God, the Author of that Law, and to none but him'.[59] In this way Hobbes developed a theory of political authority that combined elements of, but managed to alienate advocates of, both divine right and contractarian schools of political thought. The ruler was accountable to God alone, not his people. But he was ruler not by divine right but by political contract. And he need not even be a king: 'The office of the Soveraign, (be it a Monarch, or an Assembly,) . . .'.[60]

There was a problem, however, and it had to do with religion. Hobbes recognised, as he could hardly fail to have done, that religious beliefs bred such powerful convictions, not least relating to personal freedom, that they threatened to tear the state apart. Writing in *Leviathan* about 'those things that weaken, or tend to the dissolution of a Commonwealth', Hobbes remarked that 'as [t]here have been Doctors, that hold there be three Souls in a man; so there be also that think there may be more Souls, (that is, more Sovereigns,) than one, in a Commonwealth.'[61] The consequence of this was disastrous for any attempt to erect a supreme sovereign authority or Leviathan.[62]

> Where one is Soveraign, [and] another Supreme; where one can make Lawes, and another make Canons; there must needs be two Commonwealths, of one & the same Subjects; which is a Kingdome divided in it selfe, and cannot stand. For notwithstanding the insignificant distinction of Temporall, and Ghostly, they are still two Kingdomes, and every Subject is subject to two Masters.[63]

Hobbes's solution was a form of Erastianism, the doctrine whereby the Church is subservient to the state, which had been influential in the English Reformation. Hobbes's Erastianism, however, was extreme and unusual in so far as it was driven by political rather than theological considerations. It was also fortified by the way in which Hobbes re-read Christian doctrine in such a way as to strip it of all that might enable it to challenge the state. It was this re-reading that was to earn him the label 'atheist', which he was unable to shake off despite many protestations to the contrary.

Hobbes dedicated considerable space in *Leviathan* to debunking or redefining a wide range of orthodox and more folkish Christian beliefs. Miracles should be understood not as divine interruptions of natural laws but as 'strange' events which may – or may not – indicate the hand of God. 'The same thing, may be a Miracle to one, and not to another.'[64] Religious dreams were similarly discredited. 'To say [God] hath spoken to [a man] in a Dream, is no more than to say he dreamed that God spake to him.'[65] The kingdom of God was redefined as an earthly phenomenon, 'properly [God's] civil sovereignty over a peculiar people by pact'.[66] Angels, ghosts, demons and invisible spirits were demystified. Most importantly, the ideas of divine judgement, eternal life and damnation were renegotiated, as they, more than anything else, threatened the authority of Leviathan. 'It is impossible a Commonwealth should stand, where any other than the Sovereign, hath a power of giving greater rewards than Life; and of inflicting greater punishments than Death.'[67]

It is in this spirit that Hobbes dealt with the Bible. He was careful not to overstep the mark, commenting at one point that 'I see not therefore any reason to doubt, but that the Old, and New Testament, as we have them now, are the true Registers of those things, which were done and said by the Prophets, and Apostles.'[68] Having acknowledged that – how sincerely is debatable – his method throughout *Leviathan* was to measure the Bible rather than using the Bible to measure the world, as his contemporaries were wont to do.

Part three of *Leviathan* begins, after a short chapter on the principles of Christian politics, with a much longer examination of the 'number, antiquity, scope, authority, and interpreters of the books of Holy Scriptures'. Starting with the Old Testament canon Hobbes admits, 'I can acknowledge no other Books of the Old Testament, to be Holy Scripture, but those which have been commanded to be acknowledged for such, by the Authority of the Church of England,' before immediately going on to discuss how St Jerome and Josephus did in fact recognise rather different canons.[69] Analysing Old Testament authorship, he wrote that 'the five Books of Moses were written after his time,' basing his conclusion on the fact that 'we read in the last Chapter of Deuteronomy . . . concerning the sepulchre of Moses, "that no man knoweth of his sepulchre to this day,"' which rather suggested 'that those words were written after his interment'.[70]

The idea that there was post-Mosaic material in the so-called books of Moses was not new in seventeenth-century Europe, but Hobbes went further to apply the same analysis to the books of Joshua, Judges, Ruth, Samuel and Kings, using the same logic throughout. In the book of Numbers, he observed, 'the Writer' (i.e. not necessarily Moses) 'citeth another more ancient Book, Entitled, The Book of the Warres of the Lord', a fact that implies that earlier, perhaps more reliable texts lie behind the extant ones. Hobbes's observations are so obvious as to be unremarkable to us today but they were deeply disquieting to his contemporaries who were simply not used to the Bible being scrutinised in this way.

Hobbes was less sceptical about the New Testament, acknowledging the documents were written by authors who had known (and written only shortly after) Christ himself. However, he was more circumspect about the formation of the New Testament canon, remarking that 'the Council of Laodicea is the first we know, that recommended the Bible to the then Christian Churches . . . and this Council was held in the 364th year after Christ.'[71] The real issue for him, however, was not when the canon was formed but who authorised it. 'It is a question much disputed between the diverse sects of Christian religion, from whence the scriptures derive their authority . . . [whereas] the question truly stated is, by what authority they are made law.'[72] His answer was predictable: 'that of the Commonwealth, residing in the Sovereign, who only has the Legislative power.'[73]

Overall, Hobbes's reassessment of scripture subtly undermined its unity, cohesion and authority, 'transform[ing it] into a complex artefact containing elements of different, kinds and different derivations'.[74] This has encouraged much speculation about Hobbes's own beliefs, with different critics seeing him as an orthodox Protestant, a proto-deist or even a crypto-atheist. It is certainly hard to ascribe to him anything other than heterodox Christian beliefs. However, his own opinions are largely irrelevant. The important point for him was that religion was valuable not for its truth but for its utility to the Commonwealth. The freedom inherent in Protestant Christianity made it dangerous rather than valuable.

'I do not expect to be taught by bibles': the end of an age

Both Milton and Hobbes, in their own very different ways, contributed to the transformation of the role of the Bible in English politics that occurred around 1660. Milton's impact was accidental. A passionately biblical thinker, he was part of a movement that elevated the individual conscience or the personal experience of Holy Spirit above the Bible itself. The intellectual fervour of the time saw numerous commoners do this. 'I do not expect to be taught by bibles or books, but by God,' said Jacob Bauthumley, a New Model Army soldier and lay preacher.[75] Six soldiers went as far as publicly to burn the Bible at Walton-on-Thames in 1649, claiming 'the Bible containeth beggarly rudiments, milk for babes' but now 'Christ . . . imparts a fuller measure of his spirit to his saints than this [the Bible] can afford.'[76]

By insisting that the Bible should be interpreted according to the guide of 'charitie' and nature, Milton opened the way for not only the individual's conscience to be the final arbiter of what the Bible meant but for what the individual deemed to be charitable or natural to be the judge. Personal taste became the final court of appeal. If a text appeared too difficult or unappealing or challenging, it could be simply judged uncharitable or unnatural and ignored. This was not necessarily Milton's intention, but the fact that Milton's aim of writing a defence of Protestant orthodoxy resulted in an unpublishably heterodox book gives a good example of how good intentions did not guarantee desired results.

Hobbes's impact was more deliberate. Whether Hobbes really did want to discredit the Bible or whether he simply wanted to disarm it so as to fit into his political scheme is uncertain. Either way, his treatment of the text helped to undermine its authority. In the intellectual commotion of the time, others did something similar, asking whether the Fall of man, Virgin Birth, resurrection, ascension and Second Coming should be read allegorically. These two trends – the elevation of personal conscience over the biblical text, and scepticism towards that text – helped to change the role of the Bible in post-Restoration politics. Three others contributed.

The first was that the political Bible had become tarnished by its association with radical politics. Although by no means all radical politics was driven or guided by a biblical agenda, much was. The men who had dragged the nation into civil war, at least as the Restoration saw it, were driven by their biblically inspired fanaticism. Those who had killed the king had justified their actions, in part, with biblical texts. It would be a long time before the Bible, or rather those who appealed to it as self-evidently authoritative, would throw off the guilt of association.

The second was the failure of millenarian politics.[77] Apocalyptic beliefs had a long and often bloody history and reached a climax with execution of King Charles in 1649, the logic of which was as millenarian as it was generally biblical. Not only would the nation be cleansed if the 'man of blood' were executed but the godly might at last begin their rule. The final chapters of Revelation had spoken of the destruction of idolatrous kings which would herald the reign of the saints.[78] In the words of Christopher Hill, not only can we see January 1649 as the 'high point of radical millenarianism' but also 'the high point of Biblical influence on English politics'.[79] The millennium did not arrive and the subsequent decade can be measured by its continued postponement. The Rump Parliament that followed Charles's death was charged with the task of promoting the millennial rule of Christ. When it failed to deliver, the Barebones Parliament that followed it was confronted with a similar mission. Cromwell, who had opened the Barebones with a powerful millenarian address, faced the same expectations and when his pragmatism disappointed, he was identified by some with one of the horns of the beast of Revelation.[80] His death and the political confusion of 1659–60 gave a last spur to millenarian hopes but these were devastated by the peaceful and popular Restoration of the monarchy. Millenarian hopes did not die. Indeed they seem to be indestructible, if subsequent history is to be believed. But they were thoroughly discredited, and with them the biblical literalism and fervour on which they fed.

The final blow to biblical politics came with a decline of Providentialism, the belief that events are controlled and predestined by God. This wasn't – or wasn't just – superstition. It had biblical warrant. The godly, Cromwell among them, liked to quote Matthew 10:28–9,[81] to show how God governed 'every particular passage' of our lives.[82] Biblical or not, it was beset with problems. Events could be very difficult to read. Was defeat an indication that your cause was wrong? Could it not be an exhortation to perseverance? Such difficulties were compounded by more general problems, for example the way natural events had a frustrating habit of affecting the godly and the wicked indiscriminately.

Such difficulties notwithstanding, Providential thinking ran deep in the Parliamentary camp, so that when the cause died with the Restoration, all could see that either God favoured the monarchy or that Providential thinking was deeply flawed. Providentialism had an easy way out of this problem, and indeed many Puritans interpreted the events of 1660 as a punishment for their sins. But the total failure of their cause made even this excuse inadequate. Providentialist thought remained alive among those who found themselves in power after the Restoration and who were able to argue that God had indeed been in charge. But it lost much of the intensity it had exhibited during the Interregnum. The apparent refutation of Providentialism, at least among the most militantly biblical political camp, helped further erode the biblical foundations on which it rested.

Between them these five factors – the elevation of conscience, the emergence of biblical scepticism, the association of the Bible with radical politics, the failure of millenarianism and the apparent refutation of Providentialism – conspired to weaken the hold of biblical thinking on national politics after the Restoration. The (albeit implicit) expectations that had been born with William Tyndale and the early English Reformers, that the vernacular Bible would bring a compelling clarity to domestic politics, proved false. Ironically, however, the plurality of religious opinions that it did bring proved in the long run to be more profitable. After 1660, the influence of the Bible would remain profound and pervasive but it would also be subtler, less prominent and, increasingly, have to work alongside other intellectual frameworks.

6

'Under our vines we'll sit and sing':
Restoration and reason

Radical politics did not die with the Restoration and the revolutionary Bible was not silent after 1660. Some sectaries still compared
Charles II to Nebu and Ahab.[1] Others, like the Fifth Monarchist
Thomas Venner, continued to issue radical manifestos. As late as
1694 there was, according to the diarist John Evelyn, 'a great rising
of people in Buckinghamshire, upon the declaration of a famous
preacher . . . that our Lord Christ appeared to him . . . told him he
was now come down, & would appear publicly at Pentecost.'[2] These,
however, were diary-worthy exceptions. The overwhelming desire
was for a return to political stability. Religious enthusiasm was
denounced. Antichrist became a vulgar word; fanatic a term of abuse.

The Bible remained central to national politics but it was no longer
exclusively or unquestionably authoritative. Recent history had
shown that its teaching needed to be mediated by the respectable and
reasonable. Attempts to build a heavenly city on English earth were
abandoned. The English, latterly the British, remained a chosen
people, as the events of the next half-century would confirm, but it
was a rather different kind of divine election than that which had
shaped post-Reformation politics.

'Delivering this kingdom from popery and
arbitrary power': a biblical identity

The initial response to the events of the previous two decades was
moderate. Only a handful of sectaries were executed. Charles II
seemed conscious of, and determined to avoid, the mistakes of his
father. Such moderation was not to last. The 1662 Act of Uniformity
required Church ministers to be ordained by a bishop, subscribe to

the 39 articles, give their full assent to the revised Prayer Book and to repudiate the Solemn League and Covenant, the document drawn up during the First Civil War which sought, among other things, to further the Reformation. It also mandated the payment of tithes and the solemnisation of baptism, marriage and funerals at the parish church, making attendance there compulsory.

The Act of Uniformity was one of a series of discriminatory laws that came to be known as the Clarendon Code. A year earlier the Corporation Act had compelled all municipal officials to reject the Solemn League and Covenant, to receive communion according to the rites of the Church of England, and to take the Oaths of Allegiance and Supremacy and of non-resistance. The Quaker Act of 1661 made it illegal to refuse to swear oaths as required by law. The Conventicle Act of 1664 forbade unauthorised religious meetings of more than five people who were not members of same household.[3] The Five Mile Act of 1665 prohibited those 'nonconformist' clergy from preaching, teaching or coming within five miles of a city, incorporated town or parish in which they had served, unless they took an oath of non-resistance.

Between them these Acts comprised a determined effort to turn England back to its pre-Civil War days by imposing severe civil disabilities on all who would not conform to the doctrines and articles of the Church of England. The terms were unacceptable to many and nearly 1,500 ministers left their posts in the 1660s. The exodus had little effect. The following decade saw the passing of two Test Acts, animated by growing fears of Roman Catholicism, which required all holders of civil or military office to take the Oaths of Allegiance and Supremacy, to receive Anglican Communion and to repudiate the doctrine of transubstantiation. Despite the fact that the nonconformist community comprised no more than 10 per cent of the population, and the Catholic one little more than 1 per cent, the Restoration authorities were determined to impose religious and civil order on the nation.

This process was aided by the revision and establishment of the Book of Common Prayer and by the now unquestioned dominance of the King James Bible. In the half-century following the Restoration, 237 editions of the King James Version were printed, and no new translations attempted.[4] The powerful association of Church and monarchy, and both with political order, was further reinforced by the developing cult of King Charles the Martyr. The day of his execution, 30 January, became one of national humiliation and entered the Anglican liturgy alongside the anniversaries of the Gunpowder Plot (5 November) and the Restoration of Charles II (29 May). Each provided an occasion for innumerable sermons to expound on the link between God, king, Church, order and harmony, and to explain how the Almighty sometimes punished the wicked by letting them get their own anarchic way, but how he ultimately remained sovereign, punishing those who dared to touch his anointed, in his own good time.

Charles II had a high opinion of his office and of himself but was not personally responsible for the persecution of Nonconformists. He believed religion to be a fundamentally private affair and presided over a notoriously dissolute court. Moreover, his brother James's Roman Catholicism and his own inclination to Rome disposed him towards a degree of toleration.

James's Catholicism, exposed by the Test Act, began to worry public opinion in the 1670s, when it looked likely that he would succeed to the throne. The situation divided the political class into two parties, a 'Tory' one that formed around the court and established Church and favoured James to succeed Charles, and a 'Whig' one, led by the Earl of Shaftesbury, which gathered around a broader Protestant identity and was determined to exclude him. Charles repeatedly dissolved parliament to prevent it passing an Exclusion Bill and explained his actions in a declaration that was read from every pulpit in country.

James eventually succeeded Charles in 1685, peacefully and with minimal protest. Fears of Catholic power remained high, however, and were redoubled when, in October that year, Louis XIV revoked the Edict of Nantes, forcing France's vulnerable Protestants to choose between conversion, persecution and exile. Many chose exile and fled to England where they settled as living examples of the arbitrary and autocratic government that the freedom-loving Protestant English associated with Roman Catholicism.

For his part, James worked towards religious toleration for

Nonconformists as well as Catholics, for which he received noncon-formist thanks and a measure of loyalty. In April 1687 he issued his own Declaration of Indulgence, removing all civil disabilities for non-Anglicans and allowing freedom of worship in what was the most far-reaching attempt at religious toleration the century had seen. Such toleration alarmed the established Church, which saw in it an attempt to circumvent its authority. When James ordered the declaration to be read from every Anglican pulpit the following year, the Church protested and seven bishops, including Archbishop William Sancroft, submitted a petition to the king explaining the clergy's act of disobedience and asking him to reconsider his religious policies. The bishops were arrested and tried for seditious libel, but their cause was a popular one, and their stance and eventual acquittal helped to foment opposition to the king. When the queen gave birth to a son, James Francis Edward Stuart and the Catholic succession became secure, the opposition moved.

A number of senior statesmen approached William of Orange, a Dutch Calvinist who was recognised as the leading opponent to Europe's most powerful Catholic monarch, Louis XIV, and assured him of English support should he attempt to take the crown. William was married to Mary, James's daughter and heir, who had been brought up a Protestant and had been first in line to the throne before James's son was born. William saw himself and was seen by others as a champion of law, liberty and Protestantism. He made it clear that he supported liberty of conscience, even for Roman Catholics, and freedom to worship for Nonconformists, although not the repeal of the Test and Corporation Acts.

William raised a force, landed in Torbay on the symbolically powerful date of 5 November and advanced quickly to London. James's meagre support rapidly disappeared and he escaped to France where he was welcomed by Louis. The Commons voted that James had abdicated and that the throne was vacant, although not everyone was happy with this legal fiction. A few months later parliament issued a Declaration of Rights which spelled out James's misdeeds, happily associating the king's tyranny with his Catholicism and his subjects' much abused liberty with their Protestantism.

The Declaration of Rights formed the basis of the Bill of Rights which did two things that were to shape the English theo-political landscape for the next century and a half. The first was to effect a rapprochement between Anglicans and Nonconformists. In spite of the many tensions between these Churches, the prospect of Catholic succession brought them together. Dissenting ministers and moderate Anglicans made common cause, which was made real in the Toleration Act of 1689. This held nothing for non-Protestants, let alone non-Christians, but it did exempt from punishment those Nonconformists who were prepared to take the Oath of Allegiance, and allowed dissenting clergy to practise their ministry if they signed up to thirty-six of the Thirty-Nine Articles and registered their meeting places with authorities. Given that William himself was not an Anglican, some degree of toleration was inevitable. The manner in which it occurred, however, helped baptise English Protestantism as chosen specially by God.

'It hath pleased Almighty God to make [William] the glorious instrument of delivering this kingdom from popery and arbitrary power,' declared the Bill of Rights. English monarchs since Henry VIII had been lauded as David, Solomon, Joshua, Hezekiah or Deborah at their accession. William and Mary were duly accorded the same honour, God having quite obviously raised up a new Moses to deliver his people from their Popish captivity. Given the events of the 1680s this comparison seemed more than routine flattery. The English had long claimed the mantle of a chosen people. The events of 1689 appeared to justify their claims.

The second impact of the Bill of Rights and the events it crowned was to cement in the English mind a firm anti-Catholicism. Catholicism, long identified with arbitrary and cruel government, was now treated as almost incompatible with being English. Hence, the Bill of Rights insisted that 'it is inconsistent with the safety and welfare of this Protestant kingdom to be governed by a popish prince,' and demanded that people swore an oath against the 'damnable doctrine' that princes excommunicated by the Pope 'may be deposed . . . by their subjects'. To be reliably English was to reject the authority of the Bishop of Rome.

The link between these two factors – Protestant unity and Catholic opposition – was the Bible, the nation's founding political icon. The freedom of a (theoretically) unmediated relationship with God through his Word, which was the foundation stone of Protestantism, served as the basis for the political freedoms that the nation celebrated. This was well drawn in William and Mary's coronation, the service of which was remodelled to highlight the importance of their faith. For the first time, a copy of the Bible was carried in procession to Westminster Abbey. The king and queen had to swear, as none of their predecessors had, to rule according to the 'true profession of the gospel, and the Protestant reformed religion by law'. Once crowned, Bibles were handed to each 'to put you in mind of this rule and that you may follow it'. The new king's personal faith was, in reality, somewhat tepid but his public image was one of Protestant piety. Unlike his worldly predecessors he would not permit infidelity or anti-religious ridicule at court. He ordered national fasts, issued proclamations for the suppression of vice and witnessed the passing of the Blasphemy Act in 1698. The first English missionary societies, the Society for the Propagation of the Gospel in Foreign Parts (SPG) and the Society for Promoting Christian Knowledge (SPCK), were both founded during his reign.

His successor, Queen Anne, was more sincere, having been raised as a strict Anglican and her reign saw the last attempt to impose religious unity on the nation, such as closing the loophole of 'occasional conformity' by means of which dissenters circumvented the Toleration Act.[5] It was a short-lived and unsuccessful campaign, unpopular with many people and abandoned when the throne had passed to George, the Lutheran Elector of Hanover, in 1714. Most people viewed the blind eye that had been turned to the practice of occasional conformity as simply a way of unifying a Protestant people, something that became more important with the Act of Union joining the kingdoms of England and Scotland in 1707. The new nation needed a collective identity to be something more than a political aspiration and that identity was located in Protestant Christianity. In the words of the historian Linda Colley, 'Protestantism was the foundation that made the invention of Great Britain possible.'[6]

Inevitably this identity borrowed heavily from the Bible. The Jacobites and the French were regularly identified as Assyrians, and

Britain with Jerusalem. Isaac Watts published a translation of Psalms in 1719 in which he rendered Israel as 'Great Britain'. When, in 1745, Charles Stewart and Scottish Highlanders were on the march in the last Jacobite rebellion of the century, Presbyterian ministers in the Lowlands rallied the faithful by quoting Ezekiel 38:15–16: 'thou shalt come from thy place out of the north parts, thou, and many people with thee, all of them riding upon horses, a great company, and a mighty army:/ And thou shalt come up against my people of Israel . . .' One, reasonably typical, victory sermon marking the Peace of Paris and end of the Seven Years War in 1763 was entitled 'The triumph of Israelites over Moabites, or Protestants over Papists'. George Handel proved the master of this milieu, regularly inserting comparisons between his patrons and the heroes of the Old Testament.[7] His oratorios were all based on the delivery of God's people from tyrants. 'Zadok the Priest', the anthem he composed for George II's coronation in 1727, has been sung at every subsequent coronation.

A state poem, published in 1716, effortlessly elided two of the most salvific prophecies of the Old Testament, Micah 4:4 and Isaiah 9:6, with praise of the nation's new, safely Protestant, king.

> Under our vines we'll sit and sing,
> May God be praised, bless George our King;
> Being happy made in every thing
> Both religious and civil:
> Our fatal discords soon shall cease,
> Composed by George, our prince of peace;
> We shall in plenty live at ease,
> In spite of popish envy.[8]

The fact that King George could be readily identified with Christ without alarm shows the way in which British identity was forged through Protestant Christianity. It shows also that the rhetoric that identified the nation with God's chosen people, which had been so popular with radical Puritans in the seventeenth century, did not disappear in the 1660s. Rather it endured and became hugely popular over the following century. It endured, however, in a significantly modified way. While the mid-century Puritans had used the biblical idea and rhetoric of election to cajole, bully and force the nation into godliness, the English and then British of the late seventeenth and early eighteenth centuries used the same idea to sanction the status quo. The events of the eighty or so years following 1688 saw awkward successions negotiated, reformed religion preserved, political freedoms secured, plots discovered, invasions avoided, rebellions defeated, wars won, profits generated, and scientific and intellectual progress made – all events quite clearly evidence of divine favour. The British were self-evidently chosen by God, and so it was only natural for them to appropriate characters and images from Old Testament Israel to articulate and justify that sense of election. The Bible explained the nation's success and justified the way things were.

'The care of souls cannot belong to the civil magistrate': the quest for toleration

The toleration established at the Glorious Revolution was expedient, but it was not only expedient. The year 1689 also witnessed the publication of a work 'concerning toleration' and its roots in biblical Christianity, which was to become the most enduring statement on the subject in English political history.

John Locke studied at Christ Church, Oxford, where he pursued medicine and came under the influence of John Wilkins, the first secretary of the Royal Society. Having grown up during the Civil War and Interregnum, Locke was, like most of his contemporaries, acutely aware of the perils of religious freedom and social disorder, and was initially disposed towards authoritarian government. 'Grant the people once free and unlimited in the exercise of their religion and where will they stop?' he asked rhetorically. [9] His so-called first tract on government, written in late 1660, argued that the civil magistrate could lawfully determine the nature of things indifferent to religious worship and that he could impose his decision on religious communities. 'All things [should] be done decently and in order,' he argued, quoting St Paul, as God had left it 'to the discretion of those who are entrusted with the care of the society to determine what shall be order and decency'.

At the same time as he advocated the godly magistrate, however, Locke also observed that 'scripture speaks very little of politics anywhere . . . and God doth nowhere by distinct and particular prescriptions set down rules of governments and bounds to the magistrate's authority.'[10] This was the theological seed from which the doctrine of toleration grew, as Locke explored in a briefer, Latin tract on government written shortly after and defending the first. 'Christ himself, often lighting on occasions of discussing this matter [of governmental and civil power], seems to refuse deliberately to involve himself in civil affairs and, not owning any kingdom but the divine spiritual one as his own, he let the civil government of the commonwealth go by unchanged.'[11] This other-worldly nature of the Christian religion, as Locke saw it, opened up real possibilities for political toleration.

In 1665 Locke went to the lower Rhineland on government business. To his surprise, the Catholics and Catholic priests he met were not the political monsters of the English imagination. He even remarked to a friend, 'I have not met with any so good-natured people or so civil, as the Catholic priests.'[12] Just as important, he saw how people of different creeds could live peacefully together. 'They quietly permit one another to choose their way to heaven,' he wrote to his friend, Robert Boyle.[13]

Shortly after returning to England, Locke entered the employment of Anthony Ashley Cooper, later to become the first Earl of Shaftesbury. Cooper was one of the country's leading statesmen, an adviser to Charles II and then his leading opponent. It was in Shaftesbury's employ, in 1667, that Locke wrote an *Essay Concerning Toleration*. This understood human nature in somewhat less bleak terms than his earlier tracts on government. In contrast with those, the essay argued that the magistrate did not have the right to command matters of worship as they had 'no more certain or more infallible knowledge of the way to attain [heaven] than I myself'.[14] It placed a greater stress on the limits of government and advocated tolerance of those purely speculative opinions that did not threaten to disturb the peace of the state.

The problem was that then, as now, the line between purely speculative opinions and those that did threaten the peace of the state was far from obvious. To the late seventeenth-century mind it was abundantly clear that neither atheism nor Roman Catholicism were purely speculative opinions. Both threatened the political and social order, although for different reasons. Indeed, it was dubious whether even differences of opinion between Protestant Churches, such as the status of the Thirty-Nine Articles or the position of the communion table, were purely speculative. The hope for toleration, for discerning a genuine line between speculative and threatening opinions, lay in the fact, which Locke had pointed out in his first tract on government, that there is no political template in the New Testament.

Locke was forced into exile when, in 1675, there appeared *A Letter from a Person of Quality, to his friend in the Country*, which criticised Charles II for being increasingly absolutist and arbitrary. Condemned and burned by the Lords, the publication was attributed to Locke, although he probably only had a part in writing it. While abroad, Locke met a number of biblical scholars and encountered some early works of biblical historical scholarship. It was there that he also wrote his influential *Letter Concerning Toleration*, which developed his earlier thoughts on the subject but was to remain unpublished until 1689.

Locke was by no means the first to make a principled case for toleration in seventeenth-century England. Before 1640 a small number of radical Puritans had argued that religious toleration should be extended to all who did not endanger the civil peace or safety of the commonwealth. Thomas Helwys wrote in 1612 that the king's power 'extends to all the goods and bodies of his servants', but not to their spirits. This meant that toleration should be granted to all peaceable religions: 'Let them be heretics, Turks, Jews, or whatsoever it appertains not to the earthly power to punish them in the least measure.'[15] Leonard Busher made a similar argument two years later: 'the king and parliament may please to permit all sorts of Christians; yea, Jews, Turks, and pagans, so long as they are peaceable, and no malefactors.'[16]

These could be dismissed as pure self-interest, coming as they did from those on the religious margins of society. However, the creeds for which some advocated toleration suggests there was something more involved. When William Walwyn called for the toleration of 'all professions whatsoever' in 1641, he included Socinians and papists.

He later suggested that even those 'so far misinformed as to deny a Deity, or the Scriptures' should be tolerated.[17] This was clearly not self-interest.

The fact that such arguments for toleration made frequent appeals to biblical history and ideas also suggests that this was a matter of principle rather than pragmatism. Central to the argument was the nature of the early Church. In the apostles' days, the Baptist Richard Laurence pointed out, Christians had dwelt among 'Heathens and Pagans, Turkes and Jews' without persecuting or prosecuting them for their error. Why should contemporary Christians not do the same?[18] Those Puritans who advocated toleration insisted that such an attitude was intrinsic to Christianity, rather than merely an accident of its origins. Contemporary Christians should practise a similar humility, meekness and charitable toleration as their primitive ancestors. In doing so, they would merely be imitating their Lord, who had instructed his followers to turn the other cheek and return love for violence. They liked to cite the example of Luke 9, when Jesus rebuked those disciples who had wanted to call down fire on a Samaritan village, in order to show how Christ had commended love even for those of a different creed. They cited the parable of the wheat and the tares in Matthew 13, in which Christ explained how the godly and ungodly were to be allowed to grow peacefully alongside one another in the world until God separated them and judged them. They cited St Paul's teaching that the Christian's weapons were spiritual rather than worldly (2 Cor. 10, Eph. 6), that charity suffered long and was kind (1 Cor. 13), and that the 'servant of the Lord must not strive, but be gentle unto all men . . . in meekness instructing those that oppose' (2 Tim. 2:24–5).

Behind this emphasis on peace, humility and the New Testament Church, there lay a more profound theological shift. Whereas the fundamental Reformation position on the role of the magistrate rested on the analogy between Old Testament Israel and modern Christian nations, certain Puritan groups recognised *themselves*, and not the people among whom they dwelt, as latter-day Israelites. Only a small number of Christians were truly the people of God. The rest were unredeemed, in spite of appearances. 'The National Church of the Jews cannot be a pattern for us now,' insisted Henry Robinson.[19]

A truly Christian nation was, thus, a contradiction in terms. 'Where hath the God of heaven, in the gospel, separated whole nations or kingdoms, English, Scotch, Irish, French, Dutch, &c, as a peculiar people and antitype of the people of Israel?' asked Roger Williams.[20] Such thinking freed the magistrate from his responsibility for religion, and allowed him to concentrate on matters more suited to his function, such as 'the defence of persons, estates, families, [and] liberties of a city or civil state'.

In spite of his Puritan background, there is no evidence that Locke was influenced directly by any of these Baptist thinkers. What he advocated, however, echoed many of their arguments, in particular the shift in emphasis from the Old Testament model to the New. The key difference between them was circumstantial, but no less important for being so. Locke, though critical enough of monarchy to have been in effective exile for a decade, was a respectable, intellectual Anglican, untainted by the disreputable enthusiasm of the Puritans. He advocated tolerance from a position of political, intellectual and theological centrality, which could not be easily dismissed as extremist or self-serving.

Locke deployed pragmatic arguments in the *Letter*, arguing that persecution did not work and that magistrates were not capable of judging rightly in such cases. However, he subsequently acknowledged that these arguments were vulnerable. The *Letter*, although published anonymously, attracted much attention, especially from the Anglican clergyman Jonas Proast, to whom Locke subsequently spent much time responding. Proast argued that the idea that force does not work was demonstrably false. If not to make minds up then force could at least be deployed to make them more receptive to the truth. Locke conceded this but did not shift his overall position, except to make it rest more fully on principled, theological arguments.

These theological arguments were established in the original *Letter* (his replies to Proast meant that there were eventually four), and frequently echoed the concerns of the radical tolerationists earlier in the century. Salvation was personal, not a matter for political authorities. 'No man can so far abandon the care of his own salvation as blindly to leave to the choice of any other.'[21] Governing authorities are ignorant of the truth, ignorant of the state of men's souls and have only the bluntest and least appropriate instruments to hand. 'The care of souls cannot belong to the civil magistrate, because his power consists only in outward force.'[22]

The Old Testament was not an example to follow because the British were not *the* chosen people. God was 'in a peculiar manner the King of the Jews'.[23] That was why 'he could not suffer the adoration of any other deity,' as such adoration 'was properly an act of high treason against Himself'.[24] And even within Israel allowances were made. 'David and Solomon subdued many countries . . . [yet] amongst so many captives taken . . . we find not one man forced into the Jewish religion and the worship of the true God and punished for idolatry.'[25] The example of those conquered foreigners who chose to become part of Israel was particularly instructive. 'If any one . . . becoming a proselyte, desired to be made a denizen of their commonwealth,' Locke observed, 'he was obliged to submit to their laws; that is, to embrace their religion.' The important point was that 'this he did willingly, on his own accord, not by constraint.'[26]

If there was this leeway within Old Testament Israel, it was clear that in the age of Christ, in which the Church inherited the mantle of God's people and there were no such things as Christian commonwealths, a Christian magistrate had no duty imposing his religion on his subjects. Rather, it is 'above all things necessary to distinguish exactly the business of civil government from that of religion and to settle the just bounds that lie between the one and the other'.[27] Locke briefly examined what the business of civil government was, explaining that it was 'by the impartial execution of equal laws, to secure unto all the people in general and to every one of his subjects in particular the just possession of these things belonging to this life.'[28] The focus of the essay was not the function of government, however, but its limitations: 'It neither can nor ought in any manner to be extended to the salvation of souls.'[29]

This went a long way towards justifying toleration but it still left unanswered a critical objection on which tolerationism had long foundered. 'The public good' may well be 'the rule and measure of all law-making', as Locke insisted, but everyone alive at the time thought that religion directly affected the public good.[30] It was no good arguing that the magistrate did not have a right to interfere with purely religious matters, if there were no such thing as purely religious matters. If religion was a worldly matter, it couldn't be so readily tolerated.

Locke responded to this by defining carefully what religion comprised. 'A church . . . I take to be a voluntary society of men, joining themselves together of their own accord in order to the public worshipping of God in such manner as they judge acceptable to Him, and effectual to the salvation of their souls.'[31] Such a definition allowed him to prise religion sufficiently far from politics for it to become safe and for toleration to become workable. 'The Church itself is a thing absolutely separate and distinct from the commonwealth . . . He jumbles heaven and earth together, the things most remote and opposite, who mixes these two societies, which are in their original, end, business, and in everything perfectly distinct and infinitely different from each other.'[32]

This allowed Locke to draw a crucial distinction between sins and crimes, religious transgressions and political ones. Some religious opinions were merely opinions and not threats to political order and could therefore be tolerated, whether held by a Roman Catholic, Jew or even a 'heathen'. 'If a Roman Catholic believe that to be really the body of Christ which another man calls bread, he does no injury thereby to his neighbour. If a Jew do not believe the New Testament to be the Word of God, he does not thereby alter anything in men's civil rights. If a heathen doubt of both Testaments, he is not therefore to be punished as a pernicious citizen.'[33]

This was not to say that *all* religious opinions were mere opinions. The Roman Catholic belief in transubstantiation might have been harmless enough but its belief in papal authority was not. 'That Church can have no right to be tolerated by the magistrate which is constituted upon such a bottom that all those who enter into it do thereby ipso facto deliver themselves up to the protection and service of another prince.'[34] A similar point could be made of Islam which, Locke believed, knew no distinction between religious and political opinions. 'It is ridiculous for any one to profess himself to be a Mahometan only in his religion, but in everything else a faithful subject to a Christian magistrate, whilst at the same time he acknowledges himself bound to yield blind obedience to the Mufti of

Constantinople.'[35] And just as the Roman Catholic or Muslim creed fatally weakened a subject's loyalty to his prince, so did an atheist's, whose word simply could not be trusted. 'Those are not at all to be tolerated who deny the being of a God. Promises, covenants, and oaths, which are the bonds of human society, can have no hold upon an atheist. The taking away of God, though but even in thought, dissolves all.'[36]

This formula managed to clear away a stubborn objection to toleration – that the magistrate had a duty to regulate anything that interfered with the public good, which included religion – but it came at a heavy price. 'The only business of the Church,' Locke declared at one point, 'is the salvation of souls, and it no way concerns the commonwealth, or any member of it, that this or the other ceremony be there made use of.'[37] Christianity, properly understood, was a matter of personal moral conduct and worship that affected, and was of concern to, no one beyond the individual believer and his God. If that template was adhered to, all would be well. 'If each of them would contain itself within its own bounds – the one attending to the worldly welfare of the commonwealth, the other to the salvation of souls – it is impossible that any discord should ever have happened between them.'[38]

Locke acknowledged that all may not be well and that it was possible, if unlikely, that 'the magistrate should enjoin anything by his authority that appears unlawful to the conscience of a private person.'[39] In those circumstances and those alone, political resistance was permitted. In the meantime, benign magistrate and politically enervated Church could rub along happily together.

Locke shared many arguments, texts and examples with radical tolerationists earlier in the century. Both were biblically rooted and derived the weight of their arguments from the New rather than Old Testament.[40] On occasion it is difficult to discern who exactly is talking. But there was one crucial difference. Writing from the social and theological margins, the radical tolerationists were under no illusion about the potential, indeed the likelihood, of tension between Church, as properly understood, and the magistrate. Their toleration recognised how antagonistic Christ's message and his followers could be to people among whom they sojourned. Locke's Christianity was no less sincere but it was far safer: established, private and, above all, reasonable. His arguments for toleration were to prove more successful than those of the sectaries that preceded him, but so was his vision of the Church as a dependable prop for the existing political order.

'To understand political power . . . we must consider what state all men are naturally in': justifying equality

Locke's *Letter Concerning Toleration* was published in the same year as his *Two Treatises of Government*, which were no less biblical or influential. Like the *Letter*, the *Treatise* had also been written several years earlier, having been occasioned by the publication of a tract by Sir Robert Filmer on the divine right of kings.

Filmer was a minor country gentleman who had died in 1653. A lifelong royalist, he had written several essays defending a high view of kingship but had remained obscure until Locke responded to him posthumously. *Patriarcha, or the Natural Power of Kings* had been written around 1640 but was only published in 1680, to coincide with the Exclusion Crisis. It offered a lengthy argument against the idea that 'mankind is naturally endowed and born with freedom from all subjection, and at liberty to choose what form of government it please.'[41]

Filmer drew on, and argued with, familiar thinkers and texts, including Aristotle, Ballarmine, Bodin, Suarez and 'and all those who place supreme power in the whole people', but he based much of his argument on biblical ideas.[42] The king's authority derived ultimately, he argued, from Adam who commanded 'lordship . . . over the whole world', and the patriarchs whose paternal authority was also political, their 'acts of judging in capital crimes, of making war, and concluding peace, [being] the chiefest marks of "sovereignty" that are found in any monarch'.[43]

This paternal-political power was confirmed by the Decalogue, in particular the reading of the fifth commandment so favoured by divine right theorists: 'We find in the decalogue that the law which enjoins obedience to kings is delivered in the terms of "Honour thy father."'[44] It was confirmed by examples from Israel's history, in particular the dubious reading of 1 Samuel 8 favoured by James I, and by examples from the gospels, in particular Christ's injunction to render to Caesar what was Caesar's.[45] And it was confirmed by the teaching of the Epistles, in particular what Paul and Peter had to say about political obedience. Although Filmer did not hang his case on biblical arguments alone, the impression *Patriarcha* gave was that the Bible insisted upon the divine right of kings and that those who thought otherwise, especially those who might go as far as to attempt to exclude a monarch from power, were unbiblical and unchristian.

Locke was a minor player in the Exclusion Crisis, a sincere Christian and a keen biblical scholar, all of which animated him against Filmer, and provoked him into writing his *First Treatise of Government*. This comprised a detailed rebuttal of Filmer's arguments, taking on his 'scripture-proofs', in particular those relating to the arguments from Genesis, to which Locke devoted rather more space than Filmer. Locke's tone was consistently sarcastic and he frequently complained about Filmer's sloppy use of scripture, his lack of secure biblical foundations and his theological non-sequiturs. Much of this was simply the conventional rhetoric of political polemic but it was also indicative of his frustration with Filmer's arguments. Locke objected not simply to the divine right of kings but to its supposed biblical justification, and in his sustained demolition of Filmer's arguments he was 'trying to give the world a lesson in the difference between *arguing* from scriptural revelation and simply assembling various verses and catch-phrases in an opportunistic political tract'.[46]

In successive chapters he attacked Filmer's contention that political authority derived from the nature of creation, from God's donation of that creation to Adam, from Adam's supposed dominion over Eve, and from the dominion he had as father over his children. Thus, of the idea that Adam's creation by God gave him political authority, Locke remarked Adam 'could not, *de facto*, be by providence constituted the governor of the world, at a time when there was actually no government, [and] no subjects to be governed'.[47] Of the idea that God's gift of 'dominion ... over every living thing that moveth upon the earth' justified political power, Locke observed first that this gift did not include dominion over other humans and second, and crucially, that 'God, in this donation, gave the world to mankind in common, and not to *Adam* in particular.'[48] And of the idea that Adam's political sovereignty derived from Eve's subjection he pointed out that this was in fact 'a punishment laid upon Eve', rather than the intended state of affairs.[49]

Locke tackled Filmer's use of the fifth commandment with gusto, pointing out that he liked to quote 'honour thy father' without ever adding the following two words 'and mother'.[50] The omission was important and not unique, as Locke also pointed out that the donation of Genesis 1:28 was not to 'him', as Filmer implied, but to 'them', meaning Adam and Eve and, by implication, humanity. This was perhaps Locke's single most important and constructive scriptural argument. Further, he pointed out that the donation of Genesis 1:28 was linked inextricably with the creation of humanity, two verses earlier, in God's image. Locke pointed out that just as God gave dominion to 'them' rather than 'him', he made 'them' rather than 'him' in his own image.[51] His conclusion was profound. 'Whatever God gave by the words of this grant, it was not to Adam in particular, exclusive of all other men: whatever dominion he had thereby, it was not a private dominion, but a dominion in common with the rest of mankind.'[52]

Quite how radical this was is best seen not in Locke's arguments against the divine right but his arguments for sexual equality. This argument was based on the plural reading of Genesis 1:26–8 ('them' rather than 'him') but supported by a battery of other biblical texts and ideas, beginning with the Decalogue's honouring of father 'and mother' and continuing through the law, prophets and New Testament.[53] He ridiculed the idea the man was supreme over woman because he was created first, pointing out that this argument would 'make the lion have as good a title to [dominion]' as man.[54] And he demolished the idea that male supremacy was justified because God made woman out of man by showing how this argument would in fact legitimise joint authority, as 'no body can deny but that the woman hath an equal share, if not the greater, as nourishing the child a long time in her own body out of her own substance.'[55] If Filmer tried to give the impression that the Bible overwhelmingly supported the divine right of kings, Locke tried to do the same not simply for political equality but for sexual equality.

Locke did not go all the way towards equality between the sexes. He acknowledged male supremacy on account of Eve's role in the Fall and God's consequent proclamation in Genesis 3:16.[56] But even here he ameliorated the curse, pointing out that 'there is here no more law to oblige a woman to such a subjection, if the circumstances either of her condition, or contract with her husband, should exempt her from it, than there is, that she should bring forth her children in sorrow and pain, if there could be found a remedy for it.'[57] In a similar vein, in his *Second Treatise of Government*, which was published with the *First*, Locke wrote that husbands and wives, 'will unavoidably sometimes have different wills', and where conflict occurs 'the last determination . . . naturally falls to the man's share, as the abler and the stronger.'[58] However, he immediately proceeded to attenuate the impact of this by arguing that it applies only to 'the things of their common interest and property', thereby 'leav[ing] the wife in the full and free possession of what by contract is her peculiar right, and giv[ing] the husband no more power over her life than she has over his'.

Locke's *Second Treatise*, unlike his *First*, demonstrates little interest in theological debate, preferring instead to work through the implications of his biblical arguments in questions of property, political society and the legislative power of the commonwealth. It is for this, alongside his *Letter Concerning Toleration* and his *Essay Concerning Human Understanding*, which was also published in 1689, that Locke is most fêted. However, there could be no *Second Treatise* without the foundations of the *First*. As Locke himself observed in the latter book, 'to understand political power right, and derive it from its original, we must consider, what state all men are naturally in'.[59] This original state was neither an accident nor self-evident. Rather it was the basis – indeed, the only reliable basis – for Christian ideas of freedom, worth and equality.

> Men being all the workmanship of one omnipotent, and infinitely wise maker; all the servants of one sovereign master, sent into the world by his order, and about his business; they are his property, whose workmanship they are, made to last during his, not one another's pleasure: and being furnished with like faculties, sharing all in one community of nature, there cannot be supposed any such

subordination among us, that may authorize us to destroy one another, as if we were made for one another's uses, as the inferior ranks of creatures are for our's.[60]

Locke justified this view not only by the creation stories of Genesis 1–3 but also by the gospel itself. Salvation, he insisted, was accessible to all, no matter how poor, vulgar or ill-educated. Christianity, he remarked in *The Reasonableness of Christianity*, 'is a religion suited to vulgar capacities'. Indeed, Jesus and St Paul even suggested that the philosophically sophisticated were 'shut out from the simplicity of the gospel; to make way for those poor, ignorant, illiterate, who heard and believed promises of a Deliverer'.[61] Thus human equality was based not only on fundamental foundations of how we are created but also on the no less fundamental foundations of how we are redeemed.[62]

'Reason is the only foundation of all certitude': reason and revelation

Although Locke was to prove immensely popular and influential in the decades after his *annus mirabilis*, one should not read back into the early eighteenth century today's unanimous admiration for him. Nor should one imagine that his arguments settled the debate over the obedience due to political authority. Even after James II had fled the country and William and Mary assumed the throne, there remained serious differences of opinion, the perpetuated, if modified, divisions that marked the Exclusion Crisis a decade earlier. Whigs contended that James had broken his contract with the people, the contract that was enshrined in the coronation oath, and that it had therefore been lawful to depose him. Tories, by contrast, were ambiguous about the Revolution and chose instead to understand James's desertion as an abdication of the throne.

For some even this formulation of events was not enough. About 400 Anglican ministers, including Archbishop Sancroft, rebelled against the Revolution and refused to swear allegiance to the new monarchs. These Nonjurors, as they were called, disliked James as much as anyone else but had sworn allegiance to him and were adamant that to do the same for William and Mary would be to swear a false oath and commit perjury. The Nonjurors left the Church and rapidly became a political irrelevance but their perceived quandary persisted. If government had divine origin, as the New Testament and, in particular, Romans 13 seemed to suggest, no matter how warranted or providential the Glorious Revolution may have been, it was still illegitimate. The alternative, which some Whigs recommended, that government was lawful on account of its existence or its alleged contract with the people alone, was not only too threatening for most people but seemingly unbiblical. The principle of consent was not enough as it all too easily undermined authority and lent itself to destabilisation. Mere power was not the same thing as genuine authority.

The tension was resolved, at least in part, by a careful reading of the two classic New Testament texts on government, Romans 13 and 1 Peter 2:13–18. Romans 13:1 read: 'For there is no power but *of God*: the powers that be are ordained of God.' The meaning was clear: government was divine. However, 1 Peter 2:13 read: 'Submit yourselves to every ordinance *of man* for the Lord's sake.' The difference was instructive and allowed people to draw a distinction between the divine obligation to submit to government per se and the right, indeed the divinely sanctioned right, to determine what *form* that government should take. In the words of Robert Lowth, Bishop of Oxford: 'Government in general is the ordinance of God: [but] the particular Form of government is the ordinance of man.'[63] This proved to be a satisfactory agreement, not least as it legitimised the settlement of 1689 which virtually all agreed was providential. The Bible, correctly mined and interpreted, provided the authority to justify the status quo. Everything depended on the interpretation being reasonable.

The fundamental problem that had underlain so much of the factional politics of the seventeenth century – who should interpret the Bible and how – was settled, seemingly satisfactorily, by the end of the century. On the one hand, it was self-evidently true (now) that the average person could not be trusted to adjudicate on its meaning. That way lay anarchy. The Bible could not be removed from popular hands – to do so would have been to strike at the heart of what it meant to be British – but those popular hands could be prevented from wielding any power. Religion that refused to conform to the established order could be restricted to the private realm. On the other hand, the idea that the monarch should be the judge of biblical meaning, although less politically worrying, had its own problems. As the series of crises that marked James II's accession and reign indicated, not even a king could be trusted to read scripture in the right way.

Instead, taking a cue from broader intellectual trends, 'reason' became established as the only acceptable arbiter of biblical truth. Once again Locke led the way. In Chapter 19 of his *Essay Concerning Human Understanding* he wrote that 'reason is natural revelation, whereby the eternal Father of light and fountain of all knowledge, communicates to mankind that portion of truth which he has laid within the reach of their natural faculties.'[64] Revelation, Locke insisted, was genuine and necessary but, in reality, little more than 'natural reason enlarged by a new set of discoveries communicated by God'. Moreover, and crucially, the authenticity of revelation was to be judged by reason. 'Reason vouches the truth of [revelation], by the testimony and proofs it gives that they come from God.'

Locke explored these ideas in greater detail in *The Reasonableness of Christianity* which he published anonymously in 1695. This saw him picking his way between 'two extremes'.[65] One held that 'all Adam's posterity [was] doomed to eternal, infinite punishment, for the transgression of Adam, whom millions had never heard of', a position so incompatible with 'justice or goodness of the great and infinite God' that it 'shook the foundations of all religion'. The other, inflamed by revulsion at such divine callousness, insisted that 'there was no redemption necessary', thereby making 'Jesus Christ nothing but the restorer and preacher of pure natural religion . . . [and] doing violence to the whole tenor of the New Testament'.

Locke tried to navigate between enthusiastic and Socinian extremes by undermining both. The Bible, he argued, was 'a collection of writings, designed by God, for the instruction of the illiterate bulk of mankind'. It was 'to be understood in the plain, direct meaning of the words and phrases' rather than in the 'learned, artificial, and forced senses . . . put upon them, in most of the systems of divinity'. The 'great proposition' of apostolic Christianity – Locke largely limited himself to the gospels and Acts of the Apostles – was about 'whether [Jesus of Nazareth] was the Messiah or no?' It was 'assent to that . . . which distinguished believers from unbelievers' in the earliest Church, and it was in this article of faith that the essence of Christianity lay.[66] Salvation was necessary, *pace* the Socinians, but, *pace* the enthusiasts, it was not a complex matter for endless, angry wrangling.

In spite of acknowledging that 'human reason unassisted failed men in its great and proper business of morality,' *The Reasonableness of Christianity* was accused of advocating the very thing he was trying to undermine. [67] The book was reported by the Grand Jury of Middlesex for denying the Trinity, and encouraging Socinianism and atheism. Locke's own reasonableness was not enough for some of his more fiercely orthodox critics, many of whom could find heterodoxy under every stone. The 1690s were alive with such fears. In 1696 John Toland had published his influential *Christianity not Mysterious*. 'Reason is the only foundation of all certitude,' Toland asserted.[68] 'All the doctrines and precepts of the New Testament (if it be indeed Divine) must consequently agree with Natural Reason, and our own ordinary Ideas.'[69] To think otherwise was little more than 'a blameable Credulity'.[70]

It was attitudes like these that gave rise to the 1698 Blasphemy Law, which was specifically directed against those who denied the divinity of the Bible. It appeared to have only a limited effect. Anthony Collins, an admirer of Locke, published a *Discourse of the Grounds and Reasons of the Christian Religion* in 1724, which advocated freedom of enquiry and religious toleration on the grounds that it was possible to interpret the Bible in a vast range of incompatible ways. Thomas Woolston's *Discourses on the Miracles of our Saviour* (1729) argued that the New Testament miracles were self-evidently too fantastic to be understood literally, containing instead a spiritual truth, such as the mystical union between Christ and the believer. Mathew Tindal's *Christianity as Old as Creation* (1730) argued that 'the Religion of Nature is an absolutely perfect Religion; and that external Revelation can neither add to nor take from its Perfection,' and that 'they, who, to magnify Revelation, weaken the Force of the Religion of Reason and Nature, strike at all Religion.'[71] When revelation and reason stood in opposition to one another, it was clear which must give. 'Tho[ugh] the literal sense of the Scripture be ever so plain, yet it must not stand in Competition with what our Reason tells us of the Nature and Perfections of God.'[72]

For a while deism – the belief in a God who set creation in motion but was otherwise shorn of all his distinctively Christian characteristics – seemed liked a genuine menace. Deistic tracts were often very popular: Woolston's *Discourses* sold 30,000 copies. Most, however, were instantly and forcefully answered by the erudite and orthodox, and as a result their clever but rather bloodless arguments failed to make an impression beyond educated circles. The immediate threat seemed to fade in the 1730s.

In a subtler way, however, their arguments were effective. Biblical criticism of the type found in Collins's or Woolston's tracts was not entirely new. Hobbes had been gesturing in their direction eighty years earlier. The deists helped draw the issue out from the shadows. Their publications drove attention to the Bible, putting various texts under the spotlight of public scepticism and casting doubt over their reliability. Holy scripture was made a topic for pamphleteering, manhandling the sacrosanct and leaving it less impressive in the process. Defenders of orthodoxy had to rely on the idea of figurative language a little too often for comfort.

Deists and Churchmen agreed on the fundamental point that reason was the basic criterion for judging scripture. No less a figure than Archbishop Tillotson was quoted on the front page of the 1702 edition of *Christianity not Mysterious* saying, 'We need not desire a better Evidence that any man is in the wrong, than to hear him declare against Reason.' The dispute between deist and orthodox was about the extent to which revelation was reasonable. The fact that revelation was to be judged by reason was not in dispute.

The effect of this was to enervate still further the influence of the Bible on political thought. It was just a short step from elevating 'reason' to the position of arbiter over revelation, to treating the Bible as a source of texts and ideas that legitimised that which was apparently self-evidently true. The state poet could call George 'our Prince of Peace' because the events of 1688 and 1714 were clearly providential, ordered by God. Britain could be described as a land where people sat and sang under their vines because it was enjoying a peace and prosperity that could only come from God. Preachers could use Romans 13 and 1 Peter 2 to distinguish between the fact of government and the form of government because that was what the Glorious Revolution required of them. And even Locke, sincere and industrious in his biblical studies, could argue for toleration because he reasoned that a properly spiritual Church would never have cause to challenge a properly constituted political authority.

The Bible was not politically toothless in this period. Locke's doctrines of toleration, of human equality and of sexual equality were all firmly rooted in biblical thought and all angrily refuted by various contemporaries. The Bible could still challenge the status quo. But in the century after the Restoration and, in particular, after the Glorious Revolution, the fundamental political function of the Bible was to show how right everything was.

PART 3

Relocating the Kingdom of God

7

'The inestimable price of Christ's blood':
Evangelicals, abolitionists, revolutionaries, economists

*'Politics are Satan's most tempting and alluring baits': Apolitical
animals*

> Long my imprisoned spirit lay,
> Fast bound in sin and nature's night;
> Thine eye diffused a quickening ray
> I woke, the dungeon flamed with light;
> My chains fell off, my heart was free,
> I rose, went forth, and followed Thee.

Evangelicals appreciated freedom. Charles Wesley's famous hymn celebrated the intense sense of deliverance that many evangelicals claimed to have experienced and that became a cornerstone of evangelical identity and theology. To be an evangelical was to know the grace of God, utterly unmerited, freely given, eternally liberating.

And yet many evangelicals were also known as 'Methodists', a term coined to ridicule the way in which they followed a systematic 'method' in their pursuit of holiness. The limitless freedom of the gospel demanded a disciplined response of prayer, fasting, fellowship and charity. Liberty necessitated honesty, integrity and industry. It was a paradox that would affect the shape of evangelical politics.

Evangelicalism was (and is) a complex phenomenon, defying easy definition. In many ways, its distinctiveness lay less in its content than its emphases. According to its leading historian, David Bebbington, it had four.[1] First, evangelicalism emphasised the need for conversion, a resolute turning away from sin and towards God, which ideally could be pinpointed to a specific moment. Second, there was a crucicentrism, a focus on Christ's sacrifice on the cross, the atonement by means of which sin was forgiven, new life offered and the individual put right with God. Third, there was activism. Evangelical Christianity demanded an assiduous personal response. Thomas Chalmers, the leader of the Free Church in Scotland who proved immensely influential in the early nineteenth century, remarked of the early days of his ministry, 'a minister may enjoy five days of uninterrupted leisure', but was reputed, after his evangelical conversion, to have visited 11,000 homes in his parish in a single year.[2]

Finally, there was the evangelicals' biblicism. In contrast to those quasi-deists who elevated reason over revelation, and those High Church Anglicans who emphasised the institution of the Church, albeit a Church called to the service of the state, evangelicals placed their trust in the Bible. This trust did not at first necessitate a belief in biblical inerrancy or the conviction that scripture must be interpreted literally. Charles Simeon, the influential evangelical vicar of Holy Trinity, Cambridge, had as high a view of scripture as anyone in the early nineteenth century but could still admit that it contained 'inexactness in reference to philosophical and scientific matters'.[3] The hardening of the evangelical attitude to the Bible came much later, largely in response to the 'higher criticism' that questioned its historicity and reliability. For its first century or so, evangelicalism merely served to reinstate the emphasis on the Bible that had distinguished many of the seventeenth-century sectaries, with whom they were often compared.

As that comparison implied, there was some concern that evangelicalism was politically dangerous. It certainly had the potential to be so. Not only was there its unfashionable emphasis on the Bible, the source of so much political instability in the previous century, but there was the fact that, at least at first, evangelicalism was a theologically, ecclesiastically and socially marginal movement.

Theologically, eighteenth-century evangelicals stood outside the mainstream. They were not anti-rational, as such. John Wesley once remarked that 'it is a fundamental principle with us that to renounce reason is to renounce religion.'[4] Rather they insisted that human reason was inadequate. Salvation lay in the gospel alone. If this was some way from the Puritan theology of the previous century, it was further still from the unchallenging rational theology of the age.

Ecclesiastically, evangelicals, although many were Anglicans, commonly criticised the established Church not so much for the *fact* of establishment as for its effect on clergy. Respectability and comfort drained them of evangelistic and pastoral energy. The trappings of state recognition – tithes, sinecures, pluralism, lay patronage – were not exactly wrong in themselves. Rather, they were symbolic of an ecclesiastical body that had lost sight of Bible, cross and salvation.

This, in turn, helped marginalise evangelicalism's social presence. As the Church of England was less dominant in urban areas, where social deference was also weaker, evangelicalism became a disproportionately urban, middle and lower class artisan movement, appealing to those people over whom the Anglican Church had a weaker hold. Accordingly, the authorities often saw it as a potential social threat and sometimes refused to ordain young men with evangelical credentials.

If early English evangelicalism did pose a (latent) social threat, it offered no political one. This was not so much because it placed an unusually high premium on biblical commands to obey the authorities, as because politics was deemed incapable of addressing humanity's biggest dilemma. Human sin rather than human suffering was the problem; Christ's cross rather than political endeavour the solution. What was needed, first and foremost, was personal repentance; what was anticipated was eternal joy rather than earthly justice.

If this appeared to close the door on political engagement, it also left open a gap that, in time, would open wide enough to accommodate political action on a massive scale. In so far as social deprivation could be identified with sin or political injustice became a bar to the gospel remedy, both became targets for evangelical action. Politics could not save souls, but it could damn them. Evangelicals determined that it would not.

For the first half-century or so, then, English evangelicalism was apolitical on principle, a principle that informed and was informed by how the Bible was read.[5] Did Jesus not decline to judge between two warring brothers in Luke 12?[6] Had he not abjured politics when tested on the Temple Mount in Matthew 22?[7] Did not Paul tell Timothy in his second letter to him, 'No man that warreth entangleth himself with the affairs of this life'?[8] Moreover, 'if Christians were quiet when under the government of Nero and Caligula and when persecuted and hunted like wild beasts,' observed John Newton, former slave trader and now rector of St Mary Woolnoth in London, 'they ought to be not only quiet but very thankful now.'[9]

The Christian calling was to proclaim Christ, not to reform the political world. 'The Lord has not called me to set nations to right but to preach the Gospel, to proclaim the Glory of his Name, and to endeavour to win souls,' said John Newton in 1793.[10] Or, in the more visceral words of the Revd Thomas Jones, 'Politics are Satan's most tempting and alluring baits.'[11]

'You were not chosen by the freeholders to preach the Gospel': the emergence of political evangelicalism

This began to change in the 1770s, when nearly ninety years of British military success, overseas expansion and economic growth came to a humiliating end with the loss of its American colonies. The same decade witnessed the passing of the first Catholic Relief Act, by means of which Roman Catholics were permitted to purchase land legally and their priests freed from the threat of arrest and imprisonment, in return for taking an oath of allegiance designed to be acceptable to them. It was not a huge measure but it was enough to resurrect Protestant fears and provoke a reaction, culminating in the Gordon Riots of June 1780 when 60,000 Londoners marched on parliament, attacked foreign embassies, burned Catholic chapels and killed over 200 people. The riots set the tone for a decade in which the nation found itself facing imperial problems in India and Ireland, war with France, Spain and Holland, and a vastly increased national debt, which necessitated higher and deeply unpopular levels of taxation. In a relatively short space of time the seemingly divinely ordained sense of political order, military success and national self-assurance was undermined. People became sceptical about providence or, at least, unsure whether providence was always beneficent. Perhaps God was chastening his people as he had Israel?

Neither such crises nor their theological interpretations necessitated a *political* response. Indeed, many Christians read the signs of the times as a warning against the nation's infidelity and radicalism and advocated prayer, fasting and piety as the only appropriate action. Others, however, believed that national repentance demanded a political element. Sir Richard Hill, the country's first evangelical MP, took his seat in parliament in 1780 and was publicly committed to furthering the cause of Christianity in national life. His speeches quoted from the Bible at length, eagerly sought biblical parallels for contemporary events and were judged by many to sound more like sermons than parliamentary addresses. It was a mark of how politics had changed since the seventeenth century that Hill was widely criticised for his parliamentary sermonising. 'You were not chosen by the freeholders to preach the Gospel, but to attend to their interest,' a constituent once wrote to remind him. '[Please] drop the language of the tabernacle, and assume that of a Senator and a Gentleman.'[12]

The Bible remained a major feature on the nation's political landscape but its role was now markedly different. No longer was it treated as a self-evidently authoritative and relevant text, whose presence in public debate was sufficient, necessary or even welcome. To a growing number of political radicals it represented the intolerable complacency of the English *ancien régime* against which they fought. To everyone else it still defined and validated the nation's social and political order. But that did not mean it belonged in parliamentary debate. Its function now was more to inspire and inform those political figures and movements who deemed it authoritative and pertinent. Henceforth biblical politics was a subtler, more reasoned affair, blending scriptural arguments with those from economic theory, political strategy and national self-interest.

This is not to claim that the political Bible was no longer deployed in an abrasive or unadorned way. It certainly was, such as when evangelicals set about generating moral indignation about the slave trade or, as we shall see in Chapter 9, when Christian radicals did the same thing about the Poor Laws. In those instances, biblical arguments about human equality or the evil of poverty were treated as incontestable, and biblical rhetoric was deployed to inspire commitment and action. But these were particular circumstances, in which some Christians were attempting to generate moral indignation and political action among others. In broader, more representative public forums, such as the House of Commons, the language and logic of 'the tabernacle' were marginalised in favour of more publicly accept-able arguments. Few doubted what moved and guided political figures like William Wilberforce or Henry Thornton but, at the same time, few wanted to be reminded what that was every time they rose to their feet.

'God hath made of one blood all nations of men': the abolition of the slave trade

In the half-century after Hill took up his seat, at least 120 evangeli-cal MPs entered the House of Commons. Sizeable as this was, it was the thirty or so known, without overwhelming affection, as the 'Saints' who had the greatest impact on national life. Most were members of, or close to, the so-called Clapham Sect, a loose group of evangelicals that extended beyond parliament to include clergy-men, colonial governors, bankers, philanthropists and authors, which was centred on Clapham, then a village three miles south-west of London. William Wilberforce, the sect's unofficial leader, had led a mildly dissolute life until his conversion in 1785–86. Deterred from relinquishing public life by his close friend the Prime Minister William Pitt, Wilberforce dedicated himself to politics, famously writing in his journal in 1787: 'God Almighty has set before me two great objects, the suppression of the Slave Trade and the Reformation of Manners.'[13] It was the first of these that was to prove evangelical-ism's political mettle.

The transatlantic slave trade had been conducted in a piecemeal way since the mid-sixteenth century but had grown from an ad hoc, essentially piratical venture to a vast, lucrative, officially sanctioned industry by the mid-eighteenth. The precise figures are disputable but it is estimated that by the turn of the nineteenth century British slave ships had transported over 3 million slaves to the Americas, about half a million of whom died in transit. The trade was condoned by almost everyone. Slavery was clearly practised in the Old Testament and clearly permitted in the New. It was sanctioned, even promoted, by the British state. It was extremely profitable. Few people beyond those who ran the ships actually knew what was involved. Sincere Christians involved in the trade could salve their conscience by treating slaves a little better than was the norm. And nearly everyone enjoyed the cheap sugar. Slavery was simply the way of the world.

A few individuals objected to the cruelty practised by slave and plantation owners. George Whitefield warned the more brutal slave owners in the American South with the words of James 5:1: 'Go to now, ye rich men, weep and howl for your miseries that shall come upon you.'[14] He was, however, more circumspect about the slave trade[15] and he was positively affirmative about slavery itself, his reasoning being thoroughly biblical: 'As for the lawfulness of keeping Slaves I have no doubt, since I hear of some that were bought with Abraham's money & some that were born in his house, and I cannot help thinking that some of those servants mentioned by the Apostles in their Epistles, were or had been slaves.'[16]

There were a few voices crying in the wilderness, most of them Quaker. The minutes of the Quakers' London Yearly Meeting of 1727 record an early – perhaps the earliest – corporate condemnation of the trade with a range of objections that became frequent from the mid-century onwards.[17] 'The Slave-trade [is] destructive to the natural Rights of Mankind; who are all ransomed by one Saviour, and visited by one divine Light, in order to Salvation: A Traffick calculated to enrich and aggrandize some, upon the Misery of others; in its Nature abhorrent to every just and tender Sentiment, and contrary to the whole Tenor of the Gospel.'[18] The Quakers were not entirely alone. The seventeenth-century Puritan Richard Baxter had declared that slave traders were 'fitter to be called devils than Christians', and from the mid-1760s the Anglican evangelical Granville Sharp began to write and campaign vigorously for slaves and against the trade. However, until the late 1780s the typical attitude was that of John Newton who was converted while captaining a slave ship in the 1750s, but sought to work through his new-found evangelicalism by treating his cargo humanely, rather than by changing professions, still less laws.[19]

A combination of factors conspired to change this state of affairs, not least a growing awareness of what the trade involved, and in May 1787, twelve men, including Sharp, a young Thomas Clarkson and a number of long-standing Quaker campaigners, met in London, formed the Committee for the Abolition of the Slave Trade and recruited Wilberforce to lead the parliamentary campaign. The campaign was supported by a range of extra-parliamentary activities, including a vigorous pamphlet war, a boycott of rum and sugar, and hundreds of petitions with millions of signatories. It was a vast and unprecedented movement, which made the argument for abolition on a number of fronts.

One of these was the humanitarian. The abolitionists gathered reams of evidence, often at great cost, detailing the unimaginable cruelty of the trade. Tales of legalised abduction, incarceration, rape, torture and murder transcended every ideological divide. The campaign was not conducted only on a humanitarian level, however. Wilberforce's 1807 *Letter on the Slave Trade* was entirely typical in the way it deployed economic and political arguments alongside humanitarian ones. Because the issue touched on questions of human dignity, equality, rights and duties, however, economic and political arguments often pointed beyond themselves to fundamental ethical, and therefore theological, commitments. Indeed, what was striking about abolitionism was quite how theological the campaign was and how many biblical arguments it employed.

Of central importance was the idea of human unity and brotherhood. 'Oh fool! See the 17th chapter of the Acts, verse 26: "God hath made of one blood all nations of men, for to dwell on all the face of the earth",' exclaimed the freed slave and abolitionist, Olaudah Equiano.[20] Just as Locke had argued for human equality by means of universal accessibility of the gospel, so did the abolitionists. Granville Sharp wrote how 'a Negro, as well as any other man, is capable of becoming "an adopted son of God"; and "heir of God through Christ"; a "temple of the Holy Ghost"; [and] "an heir of Salvation".'[21]

Then there was the idea of liberty. The Exodus revealed God's aversion to systems of oppression and bondage. The limited 'spiritual' liberation that some Christians had offered to slaves was quite inadequate, as the escape from Egypt demonstrated. Freedom was a gift of the creator, won at enormous cost by his Son. To deprive anyone of it by force was to deny God himself.

There was the example of Christ himself. Abolitionists frequently quoted Jesus' own mission statement from Luke 4, itself a quote from the prophet Isaiah: 'The Spirit of the Lord is upon me, because he hath anointed me . . . to preach deliverance to the captives . . . to set at liberty them that are bruised.' Christ's oft-quoted 'Golden Rule', of Matthew 7, was also widely used, instructing Christians to view the world from the other side of the trade. Thus, Abraham Booth visualised himself, his family and thousands of his fellow countrymen 'kidnapped, bought, and sold into a state of cruel slavery'.[22]

And, of course, there was the belief in divine judgement. The idea that God would punish individual sinners was obvious. The ex-slave and abolitionist Ottabah Cugoano warned slave masters that if they did not repent they would 'meet with the full stroke of the long suspended vengeance of heaven'.[23] Equiano reminded the author of a pro-slavery pamphlet: 'Remember the God who has said, "Vengeance is mine, and I will repay" (not only the oppressor, but also the justifier of the oppressor).'[24]

The abolitionists did not have it all their own way. Indeed, one of the reasons why biblical arguments played such a significant part in the campaign was that there were other Christians who argued that the Bible sanctioned the trade. These tended to dwell heavily on the Old Testament. Genesis 9 told the story of Ham, Noah's son and the father of Canaan, who 'saw the nakedness of his father' and was cursed for his sin. 'Cursed be Canaan; a servant of servants shall he be unto his brethren.' Africa, it was believed, was peopled by Ham's descendants. Negroes were therefore naturally slaves.

As if this were not enough, the story of Israel itself contained plenty of examples of 'the Licitness of the Slave-Trade' as the Revd Raymund Harris's popular pamphlet of the same name pointed out.[25] Detailed analyses of Abraham, the Mosaic law and the tale of Joshua showed how 'the Slave-Trade has the indisputable sanction of Divine Authority.'[26] Harris also spent time, albeit somewhat less, proving the licitness of the trade from New Testaments texts, although his tone and arguments in doing so were conspicuously weaker. Thus he cited silence as evidence in his favour. 'If the Writings of the New Testament mention nothing . . . in vindication of the Slave-trade, neither do they in reality and truth mention any thing in condemnation of it.'[27] In as far as he cited positive justifications for the trade in 1Timothy 6:1[28] and Philemon 10–11,[29] he deliberately elided the 'servanthood' of the King James translation with the contemporary phenomenon of slavery, and then blurred this with the slave *trade*.[30]

It was not a persuasive argument but such shards of New Testament evidence, combined with the rather more robust examples from the Old, meant the abolitionists had serious biblical battles to fight. Arguments from silence could be easily dismissed. Neither 'the sanguinary despotism of Nero' nor 'the sports of gladiators' was condemned by the apostles but no one doubted their opposition to them.[31] Single texts apparently justifying slavery could be traded. Slavers might search the Mosaic law for texts to legitimise their trade, Cugoana pointed out, but in doing so they deliberately ignored those that made it a capital crime.[32] As for the references to Paul, it was all very well to point to his implicit acceptance of slavery in 1 Timothy 6 but slavers rarely mentioned his condemnation of 'menstealers' alongside murderers, whoremongers, liars and perjurers in the same letter.[33]

Specific pro-slavery arguments were answered in a subtle and often forensic way, abolitionists teasing out the details of the texts to undermine their opponents. The Old Testament clearly did allow the buying and selling of slaves, Thomas Gisborne conceded, but it did so within very narrow constraints, such as for the just punishment of a crime, for a specific period of time, without the enslavement of dependants, and only under humane conditions. The modern slave trade had totally failed to respect these conditions, therefore necessitating its own abolition.[34] 'The Servitude which the Jews, by the Mosaic Law, were permitted to exact of their Brethren . . . was very much limited,' Sharp noted. 'They were not to be treated as Bond Servants but as Hired Servants . . . the Servitude could not lawfully be extended beyond Seven Years . . . and . . . in every other case, it was absolutely unlawful to hold a Brother Hebrew in Slavery.'[35] Similarly Paul 'did not entreat Philemon to take back his servant Onesimus "in his former capacity" . . . in order to render bondage "consistent with the principles of revealed religion"'. Rather, he expressly asked that Onesimus be received 'not now as a servant, but above a servant, a brother beloved . . . both in the flesh, and in the Lord'[36]

One of the more important manoeuvres necessitated by this theological hand-to-hand combat was the further divorce of the New

Testament from the Old as a basis for political thought. Abolitionists had no choice but to admit that the Mosaic law did sanction slavery, and although they countered this by qualifying the form and terms of the legalised slavery, they also insisted that the New Testament fundamentally altered the validity and weight Christians could attach to the Old Testament as a model for contemporary political life. This was not in itself a remarkable move, but it sat ill at ease alongside the popular idea of Britain as a chosen nation that lived under God's judgement. In effect it marked a further shift away from the political thought of the post-Reformation period, in which the life and law of Old Testament Israel was the centre of gravity, towards a political theology that came to dominate the later nineteenth and twentieth centuries, in which the spirit of Christianity and mission of the Church were the leading motifs.

The abolitionists' driving motivations were obvious to everyone. They deployed explicitly scriptural arguments, albeit elucidated with theological reasoning, with the passion of the Hebrew prophets. However, incontestable and inspiring as this was to anyone who had experienced the liberation of the gospel, it is noticeable that its deployment in public debate was somewhat circumscribed. The language and logic of the pulpit rallied troops but it did not necessarily win political battles.

In as far as pro-slavers drew on Christian arguments – which some did, even in parliament – abolitionists countered them, publicly and with force.[37] But otherwise these most biblically literate of politicians tended to avoid biblical language in public debate. Wilberforce expressed his desire to avoid the Bible in parliament although he was in no doubt that the weight of the biblical arguments was on his side.[38] When the final, victorious bill was first brought before parliament in 1806 it was sponsored not by abolitionists but by the government. Wilberforce kept a deliberately low profile, advising the Prime Minister to argue on the basis of national interest alone and to avoid the 'mistaken idea that it rests on general Abolition principles or is grounded on justice and inhumanity'.[39] In order that they might achieve their political objectives, these Christian politicians needed, if not quite to hide, then at least to translate and play down their Christian justifications. It was a sign of the times.

'The greatest Good arises from the greatest Order':
the French Revolution and Napoleonic Wars

If the 1780s had worried evangelicals into political action, the 1790s traumatised them. A month or so after King Louis XVI assembled the Estates General in May 1789, the commoners' estate seceded and declared itself the National Assembly. Within weeks public order had broken down, with mobs looting Paris and capturing the almost empty but iconic Bastille fortress. The National Assembly published its Declaration of the Rights of Man and of the Citizen in August. The nation crept towards chaos and irreligion.

The English reaction to these events was initially muted, even favourable. Many applauded it as evidence that the French were finally throwing off their burdensome (Catholic) political yoke and taking upon themselves the rather easier British (Protestant) model. Charles Fox declared the fall of the Bastille the greatest and best event in the history of the world and, in July 1789, the Commons proposed a day of thanksgiving to celebrate the revolution. Opinions soon changed. The constitutional monarchy fell and a politically febrile situation gave way to the September Massacres. Formerly excusable anti-clerical measures, such as the dissolution of religious orders and the compulsory oath of loyalty to the civil constitution, gave way to all-out hostility. The Church's right to impose the tithe was abolished, its property sold off. Revolutionaries razed churches, killed priests and attempted full-scale de-Christianisation through their imposition of the cult of Reason. Louis's execution, the Reign of Terror and the outbreak of war with Britain further entrenched the British Christian reaction. Already animated by Thomas Paine's *The Rights of Man*, Christian public opinion was further inflamed by the reports of French clerical refugees. Works like Augustin Barruel's *Memoirs Illustrating the History of Jacobinism*, published in London in 1797, popularised the idea that there was a widespread conspiracy to overthrow Christianity and the established order. Satires depicted French rebels crushing the Bible underfoot. 'Crush the wretch! Crush Christ, crush the religion of Christ, crush every religion that adores Christ,' cried Barruel's infidels.[40] So sensitive was public opinion that Wilberforce's yearly attempts to outlaw the slave trade were criticised as little more than English Jacobinism. Radicalism, insurrection and atheism became intimately linked in a way that was to shape English Christian politics for a generation.

The once-frequent references to the events of 1688–89 disappeared from Anglican sermons. In their stead appeared Christ the patriot, standing defiantly against the bloody atheism of the revolutionaries. Arguments from Romans 13 or Filmer's *Patriarcha* proliferated. Louis's execution placed a further premium on political order, provoking innumerable sermons on the subject. 'The greatest Good arises from the greatest Order, the greatest Order arises from the greatest proper Subordination,' observed one preacher after the king's 'murder'.[41] War with France cemented the union of religious duty and political loyalty. 'He that fights against his King, fights against God himself,' preached Thomas Biddulph in a sermon entitled, 'Seasonable Hints to the Poor, on the Duties of Frugality, Piety, and Loyalty'.[42]

The fact that national political life in all its forms was born, nourished and sustained by Christianity was repeatedly emphasised. 'All the great doctrines of our constitution are parts of our religion [just as] our laws are cradled in Christianity,' wrote the Norfolk cleric George Bruges.[43] Conversely, 'whatever strikes at the very root of Christianity tends manifestly to a dissolution of the civil government,' observed Chief Justice Raymond.[44] The pressure to conform to the doctrine of public order was particularly intense on those evangelicals who lay on the fringe of the established Church. Many were only too willing to respond. Wesley was clear that government was a trust 'not from the people but from God', and that in England it was delegated to the king as 'the fountain of all power'.[45] Wesleyan ministers, gathered at the Methodist Conference of 1792, agreed that 'none of us shall . . . speak light or irreverently of the Government under which he lives.'[46]

For those who lay beyond the fringe, the pressure was greater still. Given that many dissenters had backed the American colonists in the 1770s and that they dominated the anti-war movement of the 1790s, those evangelicals who sat in nonconformist churches felt a particular need to demonstrate their political obedience. The Baptist missionary William Carey, having held republican views as he sailed to India in 1793, repented of them four years later, writing that 'the Bible teaches me to act as a peaceful subject under the government which is established.'[47] Andrew Fuller, minister of the Kettering Particular Baptist Church, wrote in a pamphlet called *The Backslider* that 'there is scarcely any thing in all the New Testament inculcated with more solemnity than that Christians should be obedient, peaceable and loyal subjects.'[48]

It was in this spirit that evangelical MPs offered almost unqualified support for the various pieces of legislation that were intended to maintain public order. Wilberforce was particularly engaged in this area, speaking in favour of every single repressive statute proposed by the government between 1795 and 1819. He energetically supported the Treasonable Practices Act and the Seditious Meetings Acts of 1795, the Preservation of the Public Peace Bill of 1812, and the Seditious Meetings Bill and the Habeas Corpus Suspension Act of 1817. More striking still, he defended the Peterloo Massacre of 1819 in which the cavalry charged a crowd demanding parliamentary reform in Manchester, killing around a dozen people and injuring hundreds. To top it all, he then spoke against a proposal for an enquiry into the massacre on the grounds that any such enquiry 'would be called on to investigate the conduct of magistrates in their official capacity and that in so doing they would be obliged to examine men . . . who professed the new system of morality, who defied the laws of God and man'.[49] Such views earned him widespread criticism, not only from obvious adversaries like the radical paper *Black Dwarf* but also from other prominent and respectable Christians. Bishop Henry Bathurst of Norwich publicly accused him of being too fond of Romans 13, 'the support of which you seem to think of paramount importance to all the other Christian precepts of Christianity'.[50]

The weight that Wilberforce attached to strict political obedience, imposed by force if necessary, was extreme. None of the other Saints spoke anything like as frequently or as passionately in favour of the government's repressive acts. However, the fact that only one ever voted against them suggests that Wilberforce was closer to the evangelical norm than not. Political order was part of the divine order. It was sanctioned by scripture and made particularly necessary by the radical politics of the day. It was too important to risk.[51]

This politically repressive attitude was not limited to the years of revolution and war. Resistance to political change lasted long after the end of the Napoleonic Wars, powering the Christian opposition to electoral reform. The bishops were at the forefront of the anti-reform movement. Although they only rarely *spoke* against the Great Reform Act of 1832, in which the pattern of parliamentary seats was revised and the franchise (slightly) extended, twenty-one bishops voted against the bill and only two supported it.[52] Crowds were furious, demanding disestablishment and attacking bishops' palaces. At the second reading the following year, the bishops were more vocal and also more divided, twelve voting for the bill and fifteen against it. Even after the foreign threat had died away, the association of political obedience and Christianity forged in the fires of revolution, and justified by classic biblical texts of obedience, was strong, shaping the established Christian engagement with domestic political unrest.

Such arguments for *political* obedience were matched by ones for preserving the *social* order. These, of course, had never been far from the surface of Christian politics and had gained in importance since the 1780s. The social dislocation inherent in urbanisation and changed employment patterns; the growth of the press and of public associations as sources of information beyond the pulpit; the fear of the luxury, licentiousness and bad manners that came with a culture based on trade and industry rather than land and agriculture – all these had conspired to focus clerical attention on the need for social order. The events of the 1790s served to underline how corrupt and dangerous the times were and how very important it was to impose social order on the masses. Christianity, naturally, had the central role in this because, as one preacher observed, to rely on secular philosophy to restrain the passions was like binding a tiger on a thread.[53]

Countless publications, like Benjamin Rhodes's 1796 work *Discourse on Civil Government*, carefully described, in the words of its subtitle, 'the Duty of Subjects to their Sovereign, laid down, and enforced by the Scriptures, and the example of Primitive Christians'.[54] Just as Christianity authorised political order, so, in the words of Henry Best, a fellow of Magdalen College, Oxford, 'a sincere conviction of the truth of the Christian religion will be the firm support of social order.'[55] A hierarchical and unequal social order was inevitable and it was in everyone's interests that it was made to work well, rich and poor serving each other's good, rather than fighting one another.

The Bible offered plenty of examples of this divinely sanctioned order. 'The good Christian and the good citizen are but two parts of that undivided character pointed out by the Apostle in his "perfect man of God, thoroughly furnished unto all good works",' preached Charles Daubeny, referring to 2 Timothy 3:17.[56] Other clerics quoted Romans 14:7 ('For none of us liveth to himself') or more profitably 1 Corinthians 12. Paul wrote in his letter to the Corinthian church that 'God [hath] set the members every one of them in the body, as it hath pleased him' and 'those members of the body, which seem to be more feeble, are necessary.' It was a clear and incontestable example of how a Christian society was an organic whole, the health of which depended on every class discharging its duties conscientiously.

The French Revolution and Napoleonic Wars served to expose and amplify the Christian emphasis on political order in all but the most radical Christian quarters. Evangelicals, in particular Anglican evangelicals, were anything but immune. The fundamental equality of all, the founding motif of liberation from oppression, the oft-repeated Golden Rule, Christ's personal mission statement – each of these had as much potential to reshape domestic politics as it had the slave trade. Not entirely without reason had Wilberforce's critics accused him of Jacobinism for his unyielding insistence on liberty, equality and fraternity of African slaves. Yet, the events in France were to mute this line of thought and help steer Christian politics away from domestic reform and towards a stress on public order, imposed by force if necessary.

'He that will not work, neither shall he eat': political economy

A second, less dramatic but equally powerful influence on the form that Christian politics would take in the nineteenth century came in the science of political economy. This proposed theories of production, distribution and market exchange that explained the seeming inevitability of poverty, inequality and competition, as well as the existence of private property and wage labour. Although not a new discipline, it received a significant boost through the work of the clergyman Thomas Malthus, whose 1798 essay, *The Principle of Population*, showed that population growth 'is indefinitely greater than the power in the earth to produce subsistence'.[57] The result was that population was forcibly kept down, by 'severe labour and exposure to the seasons, extreme poverty, bad nursing of children, great towns, excesses of all kinds, the whole train of common diseases and epidemics, wars, plague, and famine'.[58] From this basis Malthus and others demonstrated how poverty, except for a minority, was inevitable and redistribution pointless. 'No possible contributions or sacrifices of the rich . . . could for any time prevent the recurrence of distress among the lower members of society,' Malthus reasoned.[59] Inequality was a fact of life. 'It is the nature of property not only to be irregularly distributed, but to run into large masses,' observed influential theologian William Paley.[60] Competition was part of the natural order and self-interest was the only feasible guiding light. 'The greatest economic good is rendered to the community by each man being left to consult and labour for his own particular good,' commented Thomas Chalmers.[61]

On the surface this understanding of life, in which misery, poverty, inequality, competition and self-interest were an acceptable part of the natural order, was somewhat difficult to reconcile with Christianity. Yet, in the early years of the nineteenth century a number of influential Christian thinkers, including Malthus, Paley, Thomas Chalmers, Richard Whately, latterly Archbishop of Dublin, and John Bird Sumner, latterly Archbishop of Canterbury, did just that. The fundamental idea behind their baptism of political economy was that the discipline revealed God's laws for human society in the same way that Newton had revealed his laws for nature. The moral world was as ordered, consistent and harmonious as the physical one. Commerce, government and true religion were parts of one grand master plan. The union of the Christian idea of providence, the Newtonian idea of divine order and the Enlightenment ideas of progress showed how that plan was God's way of ruling – and improving – the world. For those who had eyes to see, the poverty, inequality, competition and self-interest that political economy revealed to be facts of life were, in fact, evidence of God's goodness and wisdom. To interfere with them was to deny him.

Thus it could be proven that poverty, inequality and self-interest were actually necessary social goods. Man, as Malthus described him in his *Essay*, was naturally 'inert, sluggish, and averse from labour unless compelled by necessity'.[62] He needed, in Sumner's words, 'a still more powerful desire', such as poverty or hunger, to help him overcome his 'inherent principle of indolence'.[63] If poverty was the stick, the carrot was inequality. 'It is not . . . by what the Lord Mayor feels in his coach, but by what the apprentice feels who gazes at him, that the public is served,' wrote William Paley.[64] Private property enabled the whole system to work and was thus sacrosanct. 'It is to the established administration of property, and to the apparently narrow principle of self-love, that we are indebted for all the noblest exertions of human genius, all the finer and more delicate emotions of the soul, for everything, indeed, that distinguishes the civilised, from the savage state,' effused Malthus.[65]

It was self-interest that made communal life possible. 'The problem of supplying with daily provisions of all kinds such a city as our metropolis,' explained Richard Whately, '[is] accomplished far better than it could be by any effort of human wisdom, through the agency of men, who think each of nothing beyond his own immediate interest.'[66] It was much more efficient than any deliberately co-operative or co-ordinated effort. The free market had a hidden hand and it was God's. 'To buy in the cheapest and sell in the dearest market, the supposed concentration of economical selfishness, is simply to fulfil the command of the Creator.'[67]

This logic had an obvious appeal to rational theologians of the eighteenth century who preferred reason to revelation, and nature to scripture, and who worked hard to understand the laws by means of which God governed the world. But it also had an allure for evangelicals, whose theological premises were rather different. As the historian Boyd Hilton has written, 'the centrepiece [of evangelicalism] was an "economy of redemption" in which souls were bought in the cheapest market and sold in the dearest.'[68] The evangelical cross was a place of exchange, where the wretched sinner traded his 'filthy rags' for Christ's riches. Crucially, though, that divine economy could only work if left to operate freely, unfettered by human action that might distort the exchange. God allowed the world to run on laissez-faire lines, so that people could freely choose the salvation made available to them.

Reconciling political economy with evangelical theology was, therefore, reasonably straightforward. Reconciling it with biblical teaching was harder, and the Bible is notable for its silence or at least its muted presence in many of the Christian defences of political economy. Scripture could be mined for occasional supporting verses, such as the curse of Genesis 3:19, 'in the sweat of thy face shalt thou eat bread', or Paul's injunction to the Thessalonians, 'He that will not work, neither shall he eat.' Christ's 'Blessed are the poor' argument could be twisted to good effect, as Adam Smith did when he argued that 'in what constitutes the real happiness of human life [the poor] are in no respect inferior to those who would seem so much above them.'[69]

For the most part, however, the absence of biblical texts endorsing the poverty, inequality, competition and self-interest that political economy had revealed as part of God's supposedly intended order, led the Christian political economists to draw on texts exhorting personal responsibility, of which there were rather more. The Bible, Thomas Chalmers pointed out, contains 'many pointed admonitions, that each should provide for himself, and for his own household'.[70] There was Paul's advice in 1 Timothy 5, indicating that charity was the preserve of families: 'if any provide not for his own, and specially for those of his own house, he hath denied the faith, and is worse than an infidel.' Then there was the example of the five foolish virgins in Matthew 25 who 'went forth to meet the bridegroom . . . [but] took no oil with them', and who ended up being rejected by the bridegroom. Thomas Spencer remarked of them that 'if when their lamps were gone out, the foolish virgins could have claimed a right to a share in the oil which the wise had provided, then would others have been led by their example, to be equally careless and improvident.'[71]

Such texts certainly helped baptise the ideas of political economy, but there was still the rather awkward figure of Christ himself. Here Christian defenders of political economy sometimes found themselves wriggling. Christ, they pointed out, might have cured people of disease on many occasions, but he only actually relieved hunger twice. Indeed, he refused to perform the miracle of the loaves and fishes a third time. Christ freely instructed and healed but 'we read of no extraordinary, or gratuitous, supply of food; except in the wilderness, where there were no ordinary means of human industry,' reasoned Thomas Bernard, one of the founders of the Society for Bettering the Condition of the Poor.[72] In any case, had not Christ said, 'ye have the poor with you always'? Had not the apostles refrained from dispensing charity on the grounds that 'it is not reason that we should leave the word of God, and serve tables'?[73] Chalmers even used Christ's words in John 6:27 – 'Labour not for the meat which perisheth, but for that meat which endureth unto everlasting life' – as an argument against charity.

The difficulty that preachers and theologians had in legitimising political economy with much more than a limited number of biblical texts did not stop the system from becoming received Christian wisdom in the early nineteenth century. In so doing, it set two key parameters that would help shape Christian and, in particular, evangelical politics for decades. First, it insisted that there was little point in *legislating* against poverty. Not only was it logically impossible to make charity compulsory, for 'an action to be virtuous must be voluntary', but it insisted that to do so was incompatible 'with the nature of man, and with the state of discipline and trial which his present existence is clearly designed to be'.[74] Malthus' *Essay* had demonstrated 'that all endeavours to embody benevolence into law, and thus impiously as it were to effect by human laws what the Author of the system of nature has not effected by his laws must be abortive'.[75] Such an 'ignorant struggle against evil really enlarges instead of contracting the kingdom of evil'.[76] It was this thinking that informed the infamous and widely hated New Poor Law of 1834, which sought to abolish *ad hoc*, outdoor poverty relief and replace it with workhouses that were so grim that they would serve as a deterrent to idleness just as much as a relief of destitution. More generally, such thinking set the tone for social thinking about poverty for over half a century.

Second, it insisted on the critical importance of moral restraint among the masses. Malthus had emphasised that moral restraint was the main 'preventative check' against misery for the many. Prudence, responsibility, sobriety, frugality, industry, diligence, fidelity and chastity were all practical as well as spiritual imperatives. There was, according to Chalmers, an 'inseparable connection between the moral worth and economic comfort of a people'.[77] It was vitally important for everyone, not least the poor themselves, that they should behave. Failure to live responsibly brought misery on all. Malthus advised:

> If any man chose to marry, without a prospect of being able to support a family, he should have the most perfect liberty so to do . . . [but] he should be taught to know, that the laws of nature, which are the laws of God, had doomed him and his family to suffer for disobeying their repeated admonitions; [and] that he had no claim of right on society for the smallest portion of food, beyond that which his labour would fairly purchase.[78]

'What shall we abolish next?': morality and integrity

The irrefutable logic of political economy lent particular emphasis to evangelical conviction that personal reformation was the only serious solution to social problems. Evangelicals were not entirely against using legislation to address such problems, however. In the celebrations following the passing of the Abolition Bill in 1807, Wilberforce had 'playfully' asked Henry Thornton, 'Well, Henry, what shall we abolish next?' 'The lottery, I think,' Thornton replied solemnly.[79] Nearly twenty years later, he was proved right when the 170-year-old state lottery was closed down. Evangelicals played a part in this, although they did not have as significant a role as later Victorian chroniclers believed.[80] For over fifty years economists had warned that gambling diverted the resources and attentions of the poor away from their necessary labours. Some evangelicals, like Thomas Buxton, were adamant in their opposition, but the majority were lukewarm and the parliamentary campaign against it was led predominantly by non-evangelicals. Ultimately, economic and political concerns, along with old-fashioned paternalism, were as much behind the lottery's demise as evangelical moralising.

It was a similar story regarding blasphemy and obscenity. The Blasphemous and Seditious Libel Act of 1819 allowed magistrates to seize unsavoury publications and provided for more punitive measures against their authors but, eagerly supported by many evangelicals as this was, it was simply part of the so-called Six Acts that were introduced by the Home Secretary Lord Sidmouth in the wake of the Peterloo Massacre. There was, of course, no doubting the evangelical disapproval of sexual immorality but, in as far as this had a legislative impact, it was delayed and somewhat unexpected. Their preoccupation with sexual propriety, for example, would lead evangelicals later in the century to campaign for mining legislation (as miners of both sexes worked scandalously stripped to the waist), against overcrowding (as overcrowding led to incest) and for an end to the health inspection of prostitutes (on the grounds that the Act appeared to sanction sexual immorality). Given how very seriously evangelicals judged sexual misconduct this was meagre fare.

It was the same story even with regard to Sabbath observance. The Old Testament was clear that God punished his people for flouting the Sabbath and no contemporary nation could claim the mantle of godliness if it ignored the Sabbath. The French had been notoriously lax when it came to observing the holy day and look what had happened to them. Even here, however, legislative efforts were muted. Wilberforce drew up a bill in 1792 to obstruct Sunday travel but he knew that it would never pass the Commons, and only went through with it 'since perhaps it might be right though nothing further were to follow from it to bear a public testimony to the cause of God'.[81] Other attempts were piecemeal, such as shaming the country's first evangelical Prime Minister, Spencer Perceval, into giving up the practice of summoning parliament on a Monday, so as to avoid the need to travel on a Sunday. Not a single measure to secure stricter observance of the Sabbath was passed between 1799 and 1833.

Political economy proved that there was no point in trying to legislate against poverty or inequality. Christian theology showed that only conversion could change hearts, lives and communities. And practical wisdom suggested that there was little chance of evangelical morality being imposed by law in any case. As Henry Thornton noted in his diary: 'it seems a difficult question to say how far we who know ourselves to be a minority and differ as such could press our own system on the legislature.'[82] Legislation was largely redundant as a means of tackling social problems. In its stead, evangelicals' preferred method for reforming public manners and securing social order was the 'society'. Although societies could be dated back to the deist scare of the 1690s, they took off with real force in the final years of the eighteenth century. Such societies campaigned against everything from bull- and bear-baiting, public houses and gambling, through sports clubs, horseracing, theatre and novels, to more or less anything that violated the Sabbath. It was evangelical societies rather than evangelical laws that created Victorian culture.[83]

This passion for reforming manners earned evangelicals criticism, ridicule and the reputation for being against everything and for nothing. Whereas the Chartists campaigned for an extended franchise and annual parliaments, evangelicals, it was argued, had no coherent positive social agenda, preferring instead to worry themselves into a frenzy over modern novels or Sunday sports. It also earned them the reputation for energetically persecuting the poor person's pleasures while turning a blind eye to those of the rich. The journalist William Cobbett, implacable in his criticism of Wilberforce, exclaimed, 'I feel for the careworn, the ragged, the hard-pinched, the ill-treated, and beaten and trampled upon labouring classes . . . to whom . . . you do all the mischief that it is in your power to do.'[84] The essayist Sydney Smith did the same when he renamed the Society for the Suppression of Vice, altering it to the Society for Suppressing Vices of Persons whose Income does not exceed £500 per annum.

There was much to justify this criticism, but also much to undermine it. Evangelicals regularly attacked the sins of the rich with as much force as those of the poor. Richard Hill talked about 'tax[ing] the vices, follies and luxuries of mankind to the utmost; but spar[ing] trade and commerce . . . industry, and as much as possible . . . the poor', a maxim that led him to advocate taxes on card games, hair powder, wine and other upper-class frivolities.[85] Other evangelicals attacked the practice of duelling, as upper-class an offence as any. Under the conviction that private immorality incapacitated a man for public office whatever his background, the Saints effectively forced George III's second son, the Duke of York and Commander-in-Chief of the army, to resign his post for having a sordid affair that involved his mistress selling army commissions. Whether dealing with the vices of the poor or the sins of the rich, the evangelical criteria of honesty and integrity remained firm.

It was this concern with honesty and integrity that led many evangelicals to work for one particular type of reform. The issue on which Wilberforce and his evangelical colleagues most often came out against the government was, surprisingly, economic reform. The Saints consistently supported measures aimed at tackling abuses in the administration and reducing public expenditure.[86] Sir Charles Middleton remodelled the entire civil administration of the navy when he was comptroller. James Stephen steered through reform of Chancery law. Henry Thornton produced an important treatise on currency reform and was an active member of the 1807 committee to examine ways of controlling public expenditure. Charles Grant initiated significant economic reform in the East India Company and commissioned an enquiry into bribery. Henry Bankes persistently criticised government waste and extravagance. Wilberforce himself drew up a list of public matters he wished to see rectified, which included the buying of army commissions, corruption in the judicial system, the failure to punish abuses and misconduct in executive servants, and the appointment to senior office of self-evidently inept people simply on account of their family connections.[87] He helped secure the impeachment of Viscount Melville, First Lord of the Admiralty, in 1805 for the misappropriation of public money, an impeachment that undermined Pitt's government and some thought contributed to the Prime Minister's early death the following year. He even worked to enforce a measure of economy on the royal family, especially on its more profligate members, opposing the government proposal in 1795 to raise the Prince of Wales's income by £25,000 in order to pay off his debts.

It was in this spirit that evangelicals engaged in the question of electoral reform. Changing the system of representation was not an obvious moral issue in the same way as the slave trade or parliamentary corruption. Evangelical MPs were thus often lukewarm about parliamentary reform, at least in the early days. Many, however, came round to support it. In House of Commons divisions on the issue from 1820 onwards all but five of the Saints voted consistently in favour of reform, sometimes, provocatively, on explicitly biblical grounds. Thomas Macaulay quoted from scripture in the House of Commons in October 1831 to justify reform, in response to which one Colonel Sibthorp immediately stood to correct him on the grounds that 'the tenor of the observations which he made was in direct contradiction to the precept which the Scriptures inculcated – namely, obedience to superiors, and a proper respect for all orders of society.'[88]

In spite of such jousting in the chamber, political reform of this kind was never an evangelical crusade. Electoral corruption was another matter. 'Too often [election] is a mere contest of the purse, and all the money is spent on the promotion of all sorts of individual wickedness, domestic misery and political mischief ... [where] drunkenness and bribery gain the day,' complained Wilberforce.[89] When Spencer Perceval sought to water down the 1809 Anti-Bribery Bill, which made it an offence to sell or offer to sell any seat in the Commons or to give or accept a bribe in return for a vote, the Saints fought for it to be retained in its full form. Wilberforce, Thomas Babington and Henry Thornton were among the tiny minority of MPs who supported the far-reaching Election Bribery Bill of 1811. Not surprisingly, the primary appeal of the Reform Bill to those Saints who did choose to support it was less the extension of the franchise and more because it swept away the 'rotten boroughs' that typified the parliamentary corruption they loathed. The fact that these causes were usually solitary ones, pursued by individuals with particular interests rather than by political evangelicals en masse, testifies that neither financial probity, nor parliamentary integrity, and still less parliamentary reform, had the appeal of abolition. Nevertheless, the fact they were pursued is an important corrective to the picture of political evangelicals determined to squeeze the vice, and the fun, from the lives of the poor.

By the start of Victoria's reign evangelicals had lost the political reticence that had once characterised the movement and were engaged in a bewilderingly wide range of campaigns. In as far as there was any unifying theme to their activity, it was that political endeavour, like everything else, had to be seen from the perspective of God's eternal kingdom. Everything that humans did was to be viewed in the light of the salvation that had been won at inestimable cost and was now freely offered by the Son of God. Accordingly, anything that obscured or obstructed that salvation needed to be removed. Hence, personal sins and the slave trade, despite being so very different, could fall into the same category as objects that cut the individual soul off from Christ. If something could be identified as a sin that jeopardised the individual's soul, it was to be an object of political endeavour.

This was to remain the key in which evangelical politics was played out in the nineteenth century. As that century proceeded, however, there was to emerge a greater emphasis on the corporate, ultimately parliamentary, responsibility for removing those sinful obstacles, as well as an increasingly alarming scrutiny of the very document that underpinned evangelicalism in the first place.

8

'Everything for time, and nothing for eternity': Education, empire and eclipse

'I seldom read except in my Bible and ledger': charity and education

Political economy insisted that institutionalised charity was against God and nature. Many Christians concurred. But *Christian* political economy insisted that personal charity was an imperative. Attempting to legislate suffering out of existence was a waste of time, but attempting to alleviate it through personal generosity was a non-negotiable Christian duty.

This was not hair-splitting. Personal charity could discriminate between the deserving and the undeserving poor, rescuing some from their misfortune without rewarding others for their indolence. Moreover, personal charity, if conducted in the right spirit, could minister to the rich as well as the poor. That spirit was willing and committed rather than forced or arbitrary. 'Our object is not to anni-hilate charity,' remarked Sumner, 'but to render it profitable both to the giver and receiver.'[1] 'God wants not money alone,' observed Edward Irving. 'The silver and gold are [already] His . . . He wants your heart.'[2]

Thus it was that Wesley urged Christians, once they had provided for necessities, to give away everything else for fear that they would otherwise be robbing God and the poor, making themselves 'account-able for all the want, affliction, and distress which they may, but do not remove'.[3] Wilberforce usually gave away over a quarter of his income, anonymously if possible, and Henry Thornton up to 85 per cent of his. Babington ran a soup kitchen every winter for the poor of Leicestershire. Thomas Buxton set up a shop in Spitalfields to sell cheap food. Charles Barclay established savings banks for the poor in Southwark.

Charity did not simply mean individual charity. The growth of evangelical philanthropic organisations made the Victorian age what it was. It has been estimated that three-quarters of all charitable organisations set up in the nineteenth century were evangelical in character.[4] There were charity schools, ragged schools, Sunday schools, mothers' meetings, soup kitchens, maternity charities, crèches, blanket clubs, coal clubs, clothing clubs, boot clubs, provident clubs, goose clubs, slate clubs, medical clubs, lending libraries, holiday funds, penny banks, saving banks, visiting societies, temperance societies and pension societies. Some grew to be national institutions, such as Dr Barnardo's Homes, the Mothers' Union, the Shaftesbury Society, the YMCA and the Probation Service.[5] Not without reason did the 1895 Charities Commission report remark that 'the latter half of the 19th century will stand second in respect of the greatness and variety of Charities created within its duration, to no other half-century since the Reformation.'[6]

Charity included education. Hannah More spent the 1790s founding schools in the Mendip Hills in which the children of farmers and labourers were taught to read. The objective was to open the Bible to illiterate locals and, in the process, to underline their obligation to social superiors. Sunday schools expanded rapidly from the 1780s for similar reasons. More was not alone in her objectives. Bishop Pretyman-Tomline remarked in 1794 that education was 'the most effectual means of preventing turbulence and discontent, and of securing a due obedience to the civil magistrate'.[7] Not everyone agreed. Many were convinced that education made French-style revolutionary sentiments or, at least, general uppishness more rather than less likely. That was certainly the view of many of the farmers whose charges More educated, who often believed that learning would make children lazy or demand more than their station in life. Education, even when deployed for the sake of social order, was a risky and potentially liberating enterprise.

That risk was diminished, slightly, when the poor were taught to read the right material. In the first instance this meant the Bible, but the Bible was a notoriously difficult and dangerous book, as apt to advocate freedom as it was respect for authority. While she was setting up her schools, More wrote a series of so-called Cheap Repository

Tracts. Originating in an attempt to rebut Paine's *Rights of Man*, these short booklets, issued at a rate of three a month between 1795 and 1798, offered cheap, accessible and compelling stories that inculcated deference, obedience, solidarity, restraint and hope – of the right kind – among the lower orders. The tracts were enormously popular – over a million were sold – and they spawned many others that continued the task, shepherding readers away from the political temptations that stalked the land, such as the memorably named Paineite speaker Mr Judas Mac'Serpent from one story, and into safer textual pastures. 'I seldom read,' one fictional master-manufacturer told an employee who wished to miss work so he could attend a radical meeting and discuss rights of man, 'except in my Bible and ledger.'[8]

The examples of charity work and education illustrate well how evangelical energies were channelled and concentrated in the public realm. It was because political hierarchies and political economy reflected the divine order, and therefore could and should not be remodelled, that evangelicals tended to eschew direct political means of addressing social problems such as poverty. Instead, and within these accepted parameters, evangelicals expended huge energies in feeding, clothing, housing and teaching the poor. Poverty, inequality, destitution and ignorance could not be eradicated. They were part of God's good order, and it would be a sin to try. But they could and must be ameliorated, as much for the sake of the individual who dispensed charity as the one who received it.

'I have a great mind to found a policy upon the Bible': Sadler and Shaftesbury

Charity, education and personal reformation remained the fundamental evangelical tools for addressing social issues until the 1830s, when a legislative response to poverty and need first began to mark evangelical politics. Two parliamentarians in particular were identified with the change.

Michael Sadler was a Tory MP who had been brought up in the Yorkshire coalfields and experienced directly the brutality of mining and mine owners. He had little time for the confidence of political economy or its theological apologists, remarking in 1829, 'it is not to

God, but to man that [suffering and distress] are attributable.'⁹ He attacked laissez-faire thinking and called for politicians to interfere with the free operation of industry and commerce in order to help the helpless. He argued that the legislature should 'exhibit itself in the attitude of a kind parent, who, while exulting in the strength and vigour of his elder born, still extends his fostering care to the young and helpless branches of his family'.¹⁰ It was this spirit of Christian paternalism that led Sadler to campaign for child workers, limiting their working day to ten hours, and banning work for children under nine.

It was a similar brand of Christian paternalism that inspired Anthony Ashley Cooper, latterly the seventh Earl of Shaftesbury, to follow Sadler's lead and pursue factory reform and many other causes through parliament. Born in April 1801 and therefore firmly in the second generation of evangelical parliamentarians, with no memories of the French Revolution and wars to scare him into political repression, Shaftesbury was motivated by two key factors. The first was his paternalism. According to Shaftesbury, everyone in society, not least the rich, had a role and a responsibility to discharge. 'Property and station had their duties as well as their rights,' he told the House of Commons in 1843.¹¹

The second inspiration was his evangelicalism. From a mildly religious background, he experienced an evangelical conversion in 1826.¹² His was an intensely biblical evangelicalism. He wrote in his diary around the time of his conversion: 'I have a great mind to found a policy upon the Bible,' and in the evangelical *Record* a decade later: 'Let us then, as Protestants, stand by that which alone was the pillar and ground for truth – the Bible, the whole Bible and nothing but the Bible.'¹³

Shaftesbury's evangelicalism was shaped by an intense premillennialism, which he adopted in the 1830s. Millenarian beliefs, as noted earlier, had lost their political teeth in the later seventeenth century but retained a power over the popular imagination that was intensified by the evangelical revival. Such beliefs drew their power and shape from Revelation 20, in which St John describes seeing 'an angel come down from heaven' and 'la[y] hold on the dragon . . . which is the Devil . . . and bound him a thousand years.' During this millennium, those 'that were beheaded for the witness of Jesus . . . and which had not worshipped the beast ... lived and reigned with Christ', after which time Satan was unbound and went 'out to deceive the nations . . . .[and] gather them together to battle'.

John's lurid vision had inspired political movements for centuries.[14] Eighteenth-century evangelicals, influenced by the rationalism and optimism of the time, believed that the millennium of saintly rule would be arrived at slowly through conversion and social progress, after which Jesus would return, bringing with him the resurrection of the dead and the Last Judgement. This quiet and confident postmillennialism, so-called because Jesus was expected after the millennium rule of the saints, was shaken by a number of factors at the turn of the nineteenth century – the French Revolution and Wars, domestic political and social unrest, the relative failure of missionary work (at least by the standards of initial expectations), the influence of Romantic thought and a growing awareness that industrial progress came at a human cost. Such factors bred a different view of the millennium, in which Jesus was expected before the reign of the saints, his coming being preceded not by steady improvement but by social deterioration, and being marked by a cataclysmic upheaval. Many of the premillennialists who held this view lost themselves in endless speculation about when Jesus was due and what signs would indicate his arrival. Shaftesbury avoided the worst excesses of such speculation and took instead from these beliefs the conviction that when Christ returned he should not be found idle. 'The time is short . . . the period of the great conflict for all nations is coming on,' he noted in 1857. 'That nation and Church alone will stand upright which are found engaged in the service of their Master.'[15]

These two factors – paternalism and premillennial Protestantism – inspired and informed Shaftesbury's political action, but they were joined by a humanitarianism that had hitherto played a less powerful role in evangelical politics. Time and again Shaftesbury's diaries record his concern for basic human happiness. 'By God's blessing, my first effort has been for the advancement of human happiness,' he noted in 1828.[16] 'Every sign prevented, and every pang subdued, is a song of harmony to the heart,' he remarked of his work for the Lunatic Commission.[17]

These various motivations shaped his political engagement in important ways. Some of these he shared with the earlier generation of evangelical politicians. His Protestantism oriented him against the repeal of the Test and Corporation Acts in 1828, against Catholic emancipation the following year, against the emerging Oxford Movement,[18] against the grant to the Catholic seminary at Maynooth in 1845[19] and against the 'Papal aggression' of the early 1850s.[20] It oriented him towards long-standing evangelical concerns such as observance of the Sabbath, with Shaftesbury managing to stop the Sunday post, albeit briefly. And it placed upon his heart a strong sense of a Christian nation that would be accountable to God for its sins. Thus, he considered the fire that destroyed the Palace of Westminster in 1834 a moral judgement on the nation and deemed the appalling conditions in the nation's mills and mines, 'perfectly intolerable [for a country] that professes to call itself Christian'.[21] Like his political evangelical forebears, Shaftesbury stressed the responsibility of the rich to the poor and saw in reform movements like Chartism a threat to the divinely ordained social order. 'If those who have the power will be as ready to abate oppression as those who have suffered will be to forgive the sense of it,' he told the House of Commons, following a report on the atrocious conditions of mines, 'we may hope to see the revival of such a good understanding between master and man, between wealth and poverty, between ruler and ruled.'[22]

What marked Shaftesbury as different from earlier generations of political evangelicals was his willingness to put moral energy into a legislative format. His premillennialism marked a turn away from the eminently reasonable and predictable God of the eighteenth-century, postmillennial mind. God was now one who interfered with his creation, rather than simply allowing it to run on immutable, rational lines. Personal sin and moral failure lurked behind poverty and deprivation just as much for Shaftesbury as for earlier evangelicals, but he was less impressed with the excuses of political economy and therefore more willing to interfere with the laws that trapped people in their deprivation. This was most clearly evident in his determination to protect chimney sweeps[23] and to limit the working day in factories and mines, but it could also be seen in less obvious areas, such as in his opposition to vivisection. 'On what authority of Scripture, or any other form of

Revelation . . . did they rest their right to subject God's creatures to such unspeakable sufferings?' he asked the House of Commons during a debate on the Cruelty to Animals Bill in 1879. 'The animals were His creatures as much as we were His creatures; and "His tender mercies", so the Bible told us, "were over all His works".'[24]

Shaftesbury did not abandon charitable activity for parliamentary work. He was involved in a huge range of philanthropic concerns from the Ragged Schools Society to the Shoeblacks Brigade. The representatives of some 200 voluntary societies attended his funeral in Westminster Abbey in 1885. Rather, his paternalism and premillennial evangelicalism enabled him to overlook the laws of political economy and embrace legislation as a way of implementing his Christian concerns.

'Open a path for commerce and Christianity': mission and empire

Shaftesbury, like the Saints before him, was passionately committed to Christian mission and it was here that evangelicals showed the greatest commitment to, and consistency about, the role of legislation. Laws could not change hearts, still less bring the penitent sinner to conversion, but they could clear the obstacles that stood in the way of conversion. It was an attitude that would transform the English understanding and government of their growing empire.

Despite originating, in historian Niall Ferguson's memorable phrase, 'in a maelstrom of seaborne violence and theft', the British Empire had always been tinged, however faintly, with moral purpose.[25] No matter how criminal or corrupt its enterprises, they were Protestant enterprises and growing up, as the empire did, in the shadow of the vastly bigger and more powerful Catholic empires of Spain and Portugal, this was important. The sixteenth-century scholar Richard Hakluyt described being shown a map and a Bible by his cousin, who then directed him to Psalm 107:23–4, which told how 'they that go down to the sea in ships, and occupy [do business] by the great waters, They see the works of the Lord, and his wonders in the deep.'[26] God was to be found over the face of the waters.

Such Protestant inspiration remained firmly in the background however, as economics and politics dictated strategy and determined a laissez-faire attitude to the cultures among which the British traded and over which they slowly, almost accidentally, began to govern. Warren Hastings, to take one well-known example, was appointed by the East India Company as the first Governor-General of India, in which capacity he founded a *madrasa*, sponsored the translation of several Islamic texts, studied Persian and Hindi, wrote a preface to a translation of the *Bhagavad Gita* (which he commissioned) and was then impeached (although finally acquitted) on grounds of corruption. It was a combination of sympathies, interests and conduct that would have been unthinkable a century later.

Hastings's impeachment was part of a transition in which the extensive and oft-threatened presence of the East India Company in south Asia was increasingly underwritten by a British military presence, thereby putting the company under ever greater political scrutiny. Governors-General would henceforth be appointed by the crown and the culture of the company changed from one of perquisites and oriental corruption to one of salaries and British virtue. Economic expediency, in which local cultures were respected, tolerated or exploited according to circumstance, gave way to imperial principle, which sought to civilise, redeem and open up territories for missionaries.

The turn of the nineteenth century witnessed a furious growth of overseas missionary societies. Although some, like the Society for the Propagation of the Gospel in Foreign Parts, had been in existence for decades, missionary activity had been sporadic in the eighteenth century. This changed in the 1790s, with the formation of the Baptist Missionary Society in 1792, the (latterly London) Missionary Society in 1795 and the Society for Missions in Africa and the East, latterly the Church Mission Society, in 1799. These early years of overseas missionary activity were marked by enormous enthusiasm and confidence, which was tied up with the turn from rational to evangelical theology. As one London Missionary Society sermon of 1819 confidently put it:

> If then you would arrest the savage in the desert; if you would detain him from the chase; if you would rivet him to the spot, and hold him in the power of a spell that is altogether new to him, do

not begin with cold abstraction of moral duties, or theological truths, but tell him of Christ crucified, and you shall see his once vacant countenance enlivened by the feelings of a new and deep interest.[27]

Mission and empire thus became natural partners. Did not God say, 'Ask of me, and I shall give thee the heathen for thine inheritance, and the uttermost parts of the earth for thy possession'?[28] Did not Revelation prophesy how 'the kingdoms of this world are become the kingdoms of our Lord, and of his Christ; and he shall reign for ever and ever'?[29] The expansion of the British Empire was clearly no accident. There was 'a high trust to be turned to God's glory', a moral and spiritual responsibility, only the discharging of which would guarantee the continued success of the empire.[30]

This was not to say they were easy partners. The weighty moral responsibility that evangelicals placed upon the expanding empire exasperated many, burdening commercial operations and straining local relations beyond toleration. This was most obviously the case for slavery. Slavery continued to make good business sense, even after the trade had been abolished. It remained, however, an evangelical *bête noire*. Societies warned their missionaries to heed Paul's teaching on political obedience and on the slave's duty to his master. They were not to entangle themselves in political affairs, to speak out against colonial authorities, to challenge slave owners or to foment rebellion. Most obeyed, at least initially, but contact with slavery often bred revulsion for the institution, which, on a purely practical level, was found to be all but incompatible with evangelism. Missionaries regularly fell out with slave owners who suspected them of inciting insurrection, and frequently placed restrictions on their activities.

The Congregational missionary John Smith argued with plantation owners about the physical maltreatment of slaves and the fact that they were compelled to work on a Sunday. In this atmosphere, even teaching slaves to read, let alone preaching a gospel of liberation, was regarded as subversive.[31] Smith was not a revolutionary but his interference in Demeraran colonial affairs, which soon deteriorated into open rebellion, led to him being court-martialled in 1823 for conspiracy to rebellion, after which he was sentenced to death.

Although George IV commuted his sentence, he died in jail, provoking uproar in England. Missionaries may have been officially apolitical, but their activity could not but have serious political implications. It was in this confrontational atmosphere that their presence provoked John Dyer, secretary of the Baptist Missionary Society, to declare in 1831 that 'Either Christianity or slavery must fall.'[32] Within a few years he was proved right.

It was a similar story elsewhere. Missionaries took up the cause of Canadian Indians who had been promised land by the British government, in return for help fighting Americans, but had later been cheated. They condemned the opium trade in China, which they saw as a crime against God and felt as a severe impediment to mission. They fought for the interests of natives in Australia, New Zealand and the South Pacific, who were regularly exploited by Western settlers. A young Charles Darwin sailing through the area on the *Beagle* in 1834 wrote his first published article defending missionaries, and commented in his *Voyage of the Beagle* that 'the march of improvement, consequent on the introduction of Christianity through the South Sea, probably stands by itself on the records of the world.'[33]

Darwin also remarked that 'human sacrifices . . . the power of an idolatrous priesthood . . . infanticide . . . [and] bloody wars, where the conquerors spared neither women nor children . . . had [all] been abolished' by missionary activity, an observation that pointed towards the flip side of the newly moralised, imperial coin.[34] The same biblical inspiration that freighted imperial aspirations with the duty to free slaves and defend the weak from political and economic exploitation also produced an attitude to indigenous cultures, in particular indigenous religious cultures, that was as implacable as it was contemptuous. Thus, Wesleyan missionary William Shaw would explain the behaviour of the Xhosa people of southern Africa during the Sixth Frontier War of 1834-35 by means of Paul's description of utter ungodliness in Romans 3:10-18. Only millennia of heathenism, during which time 'the light of traditional knowledge concerning God and moral subjects has been growing more and more dim,' could account for their 'state of almost total darkness'.[35]

It was idolatry that particularly exercised missionaries. The Bible was visceral and uncompromising in its attitude to idol worshippers,

Paul placing idolaters in grim company.[36] Such an understanding was to shape imperial policy profoundly, if intermittently, throughout the nineteenth century, most visibly and calamitously in India. During the eighteenth century, missionaries had required a special licence from the East India Company to operate in south Asia. The company was often reluctant to give it to men who they thought would destabilise the cultures in which they worked. At the time of the company's charter renewal in 1793, Wilberforce had tried to insert a clause requiring it to maintain 'a sufficient number of school masters and missionaries in their territories'.[37] The attempt was a failure but when the charter came up for renewal twenty years later the Clapham Sect threw its weight behind the campaign, collecting nearly half a million signatures in favour of introducing Christianity to India. The campaign was largely successful, although the requirement for missionary licences remained. When this was abolished in 1833 the subcontinent was fully open to missionaries.

One of the 1813 petitions explained how those peoples that were 'in the most deplorable state of moral darkness, and under the influence of the most abominable and degrading superstitions', had a 'pre-eminent claim on the most compassionate feelings and benevolent services of British Christians'.[38] In India that 'most deplorable state of moral darkness' took three particular forms: female infanticide; thagi, the cult of assassin priests, who were supposed to strangle innocent, unwary travellers; and, supremely, sati, the act of (supposedly voluntary) self-immolation of Hindu widows on their husbands' funeral pyres. Each of these was described in vivid detail as typifying the 'abominable' idolatry that oppressed the people, and were deployed as incontestable arguments for the civilisation, which often meant Christianisation, of the land. God had placed an onerous responsibility on British shoulders, which often meant British soldiers, to ensure that darkness was banished from the land. Commerce, Christianity and civilisation went together, refashioning the British attitude to their empire in their wake.

The Indian Mutiny of 1857–58 changed this, but only slightly. Despite being caused in large measure by the high-handed attitude to local religious cultures, it provoked a storm of anti-Indian feeling in Britain, particularly among evangelicals who were convinced that the problem had been too little Christianisation of the subcontinent rather than too much. Imperial power thought otherwise, however. The governorship of India was transferred to the crown, which had no intention of permitting the same level of evangelistic activity as the East India Company had been compelled to accept.

The focus merely shifted, however. Within months of the Mutiny, David Livingstone was telling Cambridge students how he was returning to Africa 'to try to open a path for commerce and Christianity', imploring them to 'carry out the work which I have begun'.[39] The white man's burden had not been alleviated by the changed circumstances within the empire's greatest province. It remained more or less the same, only now dragging him south rather than east. As the historian of missionary activity Brian Stanley has observed, 'as more and more of those who ruled and administered the empire came to accept that imperial rule could be justified only in terms of its contribution to social reform, educational progress and the advance of Christianity, the diffusion of Christian, liberal and democratic values became an increasingly prominent goal.'[40] It was in this way that the Bible made its most significant political impact in the nineteenth century, not at home but overseas.

'Making numerous and ardent politicians': the nonconformist conscience

The nineteenth century closed with a burst of concentrated Christian political activity such as had not been seen for a century. Commonly associated with the 'nonconformist conscience', it was, in effect, the last great flowering of political evangelicalism, and it was inspired and shaped by a Prime Minister who was an Anglo-Catholic (rather than a Nonconformist), a staunch defender of the established Church (rather than a disestablishmentarian) and by the turn of the century dead.

William Gladstone was raised an evangelical. He drifted from his youthful faith as he set out on a political career that was to last sixty-three years, but that career was nonetheless marked by characteristically evangelical concerns: severe spiritual discipline, a preoccupation with sin, intense self-examination, unyielding demand for personal integrity and efficiency, and an on-going interest in theological debate that marked him as one of the most self-consciously Christian Prime Ministers of the century. No longer an evangelical, his Christianity was as biblical as that of any lifelong evangelical. A collection of his articles, *The Impregnable Rock of Holy Scripture*, was published in 1890, when he was aged eighty-one and shortly to assume his fourth premiership.

His passage from evangelicalism towards High Church Christianity, with its greater emphasis on sacraments, apostolical authority and the community of Christ, was part of a wider journey of opinion in the general direction of freedom. Having entered parliament in 1832 as a High Tory, vehemently opposed to the Reform Bill, he came slowly to accept the need for, and then actively pursue, the extension of the franchise. Impressed by the patience and self-control of manufacturing labourers laid off due to the economic slack caused by the American Civil War in the 1860s, he became convinced that the people were morally worthy of political freedom.

Under the influence of Robert Peel, he came to promote free trade and to campaign for an end to the Corn Laws, which prohibited the import of foreign wheat until the price of the home-grown equivalent reached an appropriately high level. In this he was a fellow traveller with many Nonconformists, who committed themselves to the campaign for cheap corn with an enthusiasm second only to their devotion to the abolition of slavery.[41] The Anti-Corn Law League had been founded in 1838 and was supported, inspired and led by a number of dissenting, although not necessarily evangelical, ministers. It was known for its Christian rhetoric. Envelopes were decorated with biblical texts.[42] Supporters regularly cited Proverbs 11:26: 'He that withholdeth corn, the people shall curse him.' When free-trade agitator John Buckmaster began his campaign to convert the agricultural labourers and rural artisans to the cause of free trade, he focused on 'the anti-Scriptural character of the Corn Laws', arguing that 'if the Corn-Laws had been in existence when Jesus Christ was on earth He would have preached against them.' The argument resonated with his audience. 'They talked familiarly about Jesus Christ,' he observed, 'as if he were a farm labourer keeping a family on nine shillings a week.'[43] Repeal of the laws was close to the nonconformist heart and Gladstone's conversion to the cause in the 1840s earned him a place there too.

His commitment to freedom outlived the repeal of the Corn Laws in 1846. His first and most famous budget of 1853 massively reduced the level and complexity of trade tariffs, thereby diminishing the state's interference in trade. He sought unsuccessfully to abolish income tax, and placed considerable emphasis on the need to retrench government expenditure and to maintain the highest level of financial rectitude and efficiency. He disliked and avoided the bellicosity that marked Benjamin Disraeli's international politics, much preferring to apply his free trade principles to international politics. Removing regulation helped colonial trade and alleviated Britain from the responsibilities of running its dominions, he argued. The bonds of empire should be bonds of affection rather than legislation or military intervention.

Economic freedom was matched by a concern for religious liberty. Gladstone moved from arguing that the role of the state was to defend the established Church to advocating religious emancipation, whether that was through abolishing compulsory Church rates in 1868, disestablishing the Church of Ireland the following year or arguing for the admission of the atheist Charles Bradlaugh into the House of Commons in the 1880s.[44]

This combination of political emancipation, free trade, economic probity, international peace and religious freedom was to prove immensely appealing to the nation's Nonconformists. Having finally shrugged off the suspicions that had dogged them for two centuries they became, in the later Victorian period, more 'powerful a force in the nation [than at any time] since the days of the Long Parliament'.[45] That force was marked by 'a fascination amounting to fetishism' for William Gladstone and his Liberal Party.[46] Like the Saints of a century earlier, late Victorian nonconformist evangelicals sought to move political mountains. Unlike them, they sought to do so through a particular political party.

The other difference between late nineteenth-century political Nonconformists and early nineteenth-century Saints was that the former were convinced that the state could, and should, promote the moral welfare of its citizens. The conviction was a new one, not least for Nonconformists who not only shared evangelical reservations about the efficacy and morality of politics, but who also remained culturally rather marginal in the early Victorian period, and therefore ill-positioned to steer legislation through parliament. By the 1860s, their social respectability gave them the security to campaign politically, and the Contagious Diseases Acts gave them the cause to do so. Designed to prevent the spread of venereal disease in the armed forces by providing for compulsory three-monthly examinations of prostitutes within a fifteen-mile radius of towns in which the army or navy was stationed, the legislation scandalised the nonconformist conscience. Not only was it deeply hypocritical, all but criminalising women while ignoring male sin, but, worse, it effectively gave state sanction to sexual immorality. Debates about whether or not it was effective were irrelevant. The question was 'whether expediency or right is to govern a Christian people.'[47] Such was the force of the collective indignation that the Acts were rapidly suspended and then abolished, leaving Nonconformists with a sense that the law was in itself a moral force and, moreover, one that was amenable to suasion.

Thereafter outrage at the scandal of juvenile prostitution helped raise the age of consent from thirteen to sixteen. Shock at the effects of alcohol helped transform the temperance movement from a personal moral crusade into one that made repeated, although unsuccessful, calls for regulation. Apprehension at the ruinous consequences of gambling, then turning from a leisure pursuit of the moneyed into a mass industry, led to pressure to prevent publication of betting odds in newspapers. When Andrew Mearns, secretary of the London Congregational Union, published *The Bitter Cry of Outcast London* in 1883 he drew nonconformist attention to the grim reality of poverty, the degrading housing conditions and, crucially, the seeming omnipresence of brothels in the capital.[48] His revelations energised another moral outcry, leading to a Royal Commission on Housing of Working Classes and a new chapter in housing policy.

As these examples suggest, nonconformist politics was primarily the politics of outrage and protest. Although it sympathised with the broader Gladstonian agenda, holding financial rectitude, free trade and personal integrity in high esteem, political energies were roused against sin and a rather narrow understanding of sin, at that.

The exception was education, which saw the climax of nonconformist political activity in the early years of the twentieth century. This has been a long-standing point of tension between Anglicans and Nonconformists, who disagreed over the extent to which any publicly funded school system should favour the established Church. The issue became so iconic, and so neuralgic, that many Nonconformists campaigned for wholly secular schooling rather than risk any denominational bias, thereby presenting the spectacle of some intensely biblical individuals fighting for the Bible to be kept out of schools.

The issue had been rumbling along for decades but emerged with particular force in the 1890s. An Act passed by the Conservative government in 1902 tried to rationalise the situation but made it worse, at least as far as the Nonconformists were concerned, by requiring them to pay for denominational school teaching they didn't agree with *and* send their children to those schools. The Nonconformists headed for the barricades. The issue became a political crusade to match that against the Contagious Diseases Acts. Many refused to pay the rates and some were sent to jail for nonpayment, thereby earning their cause publicity and sympathy. The Liberal opposition promised to repeal the Conservative legislation, further cementing the already massive nonconformist support base, and helping to bring the Conservative government to a crashing defeat in 1906. Nonconformist elation soon turned to frustration and disenchantment, however, as the new Liberal government proved unwilling or incapable of resolving the issue, which wasn't fully settled until the Butler Education Act of 1944.

The nonconformist battle over education was, in their mind, a fight for freedom, the lodestar for dissenting politics since the seventeenth century. It was marked by precisely the same tone of uncompromising moral outrage that had inspired their campaigns against drink, gambling and sexual licence. It was also marked by a loyal commitment to the Liberal Party that was to prove costly. The experience with education had showed that the Liberal Party could disappoint. No matter how much moral energy and political weight Nonconformists had thrown behind the cause, the party they had chosen to back had not been able, or willing, to deliver.

More worrying was the fact that directing so much energy through narrow political channels was proving to be short-sighted. Heavy investment in political crusading could, it seemed, come at the expense of evangelism. Late Victorian Christians worried incessantly about the health and future of English Christianity but it was only in the Edwardian age that there emerged firm evidence that numbers were, in some denominations, declining. There was much soul-searching and a widespread sense that Nonconformity had become too political. Having spent too much time 'making numerous and ardent politicians, it has made scare any saints'.[49] It was all very well celebrating the fact that there were 181 nonconformist MPs sitting in the 1906 parliament, up from 53 in 1868, but if that rise had come at the expense of emptying pews, the future looked bleak.

'The godless, non-Bible system is at hand': the waning of evangelical politics

The fight over the Contagious Diseases Acts and state education showed how evangelicalism remained a political force to be reckoned with in the late nineteenth and early twentieth centuries. However, as the Victorian age progressed, it began to face problems that would come to weaken its political impact. The problems were many and varied, but clustered around a single issue: how to respond to change.

All political movements, no matter how apparently homogeneous, have fault lines and for political evangelicalism, unified by its fidelity to and reliance on scripture, the fault line was biblical, specifically how it should respond to those political, social and intellectual changes that had biblical implications. The earliest of these related to Catholic emancipation. The debates about this were as much about expediency and pragmatism as about theological principle, and when they were about theological principle the argument could cut both ways. The fundamental question was whether Catholics could be trusted to be good citizens. Although the Catholic teaching on papal supremacy suggested they could not, George Canning spoke for many in 1825 when he said, 'for a good subject of the state, whose safety I am to provide for, I . . . would unquestionably prefer the man who insists on the necessity of good works as part of his religious creed, to him who considers himself controlled in all his actions by a preordained and inexorable necessity.'[50] It was an argument that ingeniously used the weight of Protestant theology against itself: works rather than faith made a man trustworthy. Whether they agreed with Canning's logic or not, many people were persuaded of the need for Catholic emancipation. Of the twenty-six Saints who took part in parliamentary divisions on the subject between the first attempt to pass legislation in 1812 and the final passage of Roman Catholic Relief Bill in 1829, eighteen voted consistently for emancipation, four consistently against and four changed sides.

The Saints, however, were not necessarily typical of evangelical opinion. Spencer Perceval had warned in 1805 that 'if, in my conscience, I believe [Roman Catholics] to be superstitious, idolatrous . . . and an abomination before God, surely my conscience will not acquit me, if I do anything myself, or compel others by my vote to do anything, for the very object and purpose of preaching, propagating or perpetuating such opinions.'[51] Although clearly not the Clapham view, it was nonetheless one that many evangelicals held through the emancipation battles, which were to prove enormously divisive.

While Wilberforce remained in parliament there was a semblance of evangelical political unity, but once he had left divisions became more obvious. A more conservative evangelical group emerged around a new journal, the *Record*. These so-called Recordites were determined to defend and preserve the explicitly biblical, Protestant foundations of parliament and country, fighting Catholic emancipation and any other measure that might dilute or corrupt the nation's Protestantism.

When one such Recordite was shouted down in parliament in 1824 as he petitioned for stricter observance of the Sabbath, the *Christian Observer* lamented how 'no man can stand up in a professedly Christian Assembly . . . and advocate any point involving the highest interests of the community, upon the broad principles of the Bible, without exposing himself to the risk of contempt or ridicule.'[52] This was not strictly true. Six years later Robert Grant introduced a bill to repeal all civil disabilities against Jews, thereby allowing them to sit in parliament, by arguing, on broad biblical principles, that 'it was the duty of the House in reference to this question, to do justice and love mercy.'[53] Emancipation of the Jews was not, however, what the *Christian Observer* had in mind when it complained about the biblical silence within Westminster.

The Recordites, fearing no ridicule and motivated by a burning conviction that the nation needed urgently to repent, fought their cause with uncompromising and explicit biblical logic and rhetoric. Seeing the cholera outbreak of 1831–32 as divine punishment for the national apostasy implicit in Catholic emancipation, one Recordite MP succeeded in having a clause inserted in the preamble of a precautionary measure against cholera that read: 'in order to mark and acknowledge the visitations and power of Divine Providence'.[54] Another, Spencer Perceval Junior, moved for a day of national prayer and fasting on several occasions, declaring that 'he would force the House of Commons to declare whether they would bow their knee to God.'[55] Such antics reached a memorable climax when, on 20 March 1832, as the Commons was engaged in the third reading of the Reform Bill, Perceval entered the chamber 'looking like he had just escaped from Bedlam'. 'In whose name do you sit here?' he demanded of the MPs. The Leader of the House tried to move an adjournment but Perceval was not to be distracted from his purpose 'to warn you of the righteous judgment of God which is coming on you, and which is now near at hand'. He harangued the frustrated and embarrassed MPs for forty minutes.[56]

The Recordites were never a large block in parliament, achieving eleven members in total. They were fixated on a narrow set of issues relating to the defence of the Protestant establishment and motivated by an apocalyptic vision of divine wrath, and this helped alienate them from many fellow evangelicals, not to mention other Christians. But the manner in which they reacted against what they saw as the compromises and concessions that parliamentary evangelicals were now willing to make, prefigured the wider challenge that political evangelicalism would face in the nineteenth century.

As the century progressed, Victorian England changed the way it engaged with the Bible. Theologically there was a shift away from what Boyd Hilton has called the 'Age of Atonement' to an 'Age of Incarnation', which we shall explore in greater detail in the following chapters. The world turned away from hell, at least in the brutally physical and eternal format envisaged by many evangelicals. It turned away from the idea of substitutionary atonement in which God punished Christ instead of wicked sinners. And it turned away from a God of judgement to a God of sympathy. Theologians reinterpreted parables. The parable of the talents, according to A.B. Bruce, Professor of Apologetics at the Free Church College in Glasgow, was not a warning about wickedness and disobedience but rather a tale about being timid, over-cautious and unwilling to discharge responsibilities.[57] Others shifted their centre of parable gravity, away from those of the talents or the unjust steward, to the tale of the prodigal son or the Good Samaritan. These, they argued, were the best means of understanding God. When the Revised Version of the Bible was published in 1881, it rendered Romans 5:11 – 'we also joy in God through our Lord Jesus Christ, *by whom we have now received the atonement*' in the King James – as 'through whom we have now received reconciliation'. Charles Gore, an influential scholar and bishop, spoke for many when he wrote many years later of 'a very widespread rebellion of conscience against everything in the current religious tradition which described the action of God as tyrannical, arbitrary and cruel'.[58]

Such changes, although sometimes promoted by evangelicals, did much to undermine the foundations of the evangelical mind and, by association, evangelical politics. But there was more and worse. The gradual acceptance of Higher Criticism, which subjected the Bible to intense and often revisionist scrutiny, scandalised many evangelicals. The most notorious of Higher Criticism's publications, the 1860 volume, *Essays and Reviews*, provoked a controversy far greater than that over Darwin's *Origin of Species* which was published a few months earlier. Such Higher Criticism undermined one of the fundamental tenets of the Reformation, that the scriptures were as open to the unlearned as they were to their educated brethren. Worse, it undermined the basic reliability of the Bible itself. Accordingly, it bred serious tension between those evangelicals who were prepared to accommodate the new criticism and those who were not and who, in turn, placed ever greater emphasis on the Bible's inspiration, inerrancy and sufficiency. The whole process led to a kind of siege mentality, a turning inward, away from the world that came to be seen as threatening.

Such a mentality was accompanied by the further decline of post-millennialism, particularly among Anglican evangelicals, in favour of a far more pessimistic premillennial thought. The emergence of socialism and secularism confirmed that the world was set on a downward course, and the only faithful response was to stay and keep watch until Jesus chose to return. Many evangelicals turned away from the world, favouring a 'holiness movement' which claimed that the faithful could enjoy complete victory over sin, through a life of purity, piety, absolute submission to God and detachment from a corrupt and damned world. The job of evangelicals was to preach the gospel, not heal the world. God 'tells us plainly, not that the development of the Kingdom will bring the King, but that the King himself must come to establish the Kingdom', remarked G.E. Morgan in 1919, highlighting the most important fault line in contemporary political Christianity.[59]

Above and beyond such theological trends, there was the (not unconnected) shift away from voluntary and moral solutions to social problems. Just as the world turned away from hell, it also turned away from the idea that personal sin was the source of social problems. Environment and circumstances were just as culpable. Evils could be systemic as well as individual, thereby opening up the possibility that human endeavour might eliminate such problems rather than simply alleviate or endure them. The idea that society could be transformed for good grew in popularity at the expense of the earlier, inflexible scheme of sin, trial, endurance and judgement. What the world needed was not eternal salvation so much as temporal improvement. Thus, of the iconic Education Act of 1870, which made education between the ages of five and twelve compulsory (from 1876) and funded by rates, Shaftesbury remarked apocalyptically:

> The godless, non-Bible system is at hand; and the Ragged Schools, with all their divine polity, with all their burning and fruitful love for the poor, with all their prayers and harvests for the temporal and eternal welfare of forsaken, heathenish, destitute, sorrowful, and yet innocent children, must perish under this all-conquering

march of intellectual power. Our nature is nothing, the heart is nothing, in the estimation of these zealots of secular knowledge. Everything for the flesh, and nothing for the soul; everything for time, and nothing for eternity.[60]

As the state took over more social responsibilities, replacing voluntary, religious activity with statutory, secular obligations, there was less room for the Church in which to operate. As Gladstone had observed as early as 1856, 'the day you sanction compulsory rating for the purpose of education you sign the death warrant of voluntary exertions.'[61] This was a slow process. It was by no means opposed by all Christians. Indeed much of it was grounded in and justified by Christian theology, as we shall note in the following two chapters. But that theology sat uncomfortably with many evangelicals, with the result that many abandoned politics altogether in the twentieth century.

Overall, the evangelical Christian impact on nineteenth-century political and social thought was immense and immensely more complex than is sometimes assumed. As with every other manifestation of English (and British) Christianity through the ages, it was informed by the contours of its time, moulded by ideas and events that amplified or moderated its innate characteristics. Although clearly driven by the same theological considerations that had characterised the eighteenth-century revival – sin, cross, salvation, response – it was also shaped profoundly by contemporary conditions, whether political, economic or intellectual. Political evangelicalism took the form it did at least as much because of the French Revolution, the theories of Malthus or the seemingly providential spread of the British Empire, as because of its focus on the Bible or the cross.

Like previous incarnations of political Christianity it drew on the Bible for its inspiration and energy. Unlike the incarnations of the sixteenth and seventeenth centuries, however, it did so more hesitantly and less explicitly. Scripture worked under the surface of arguments, informing their logic and providing their rhetorical power rather than comprising the arguments themselves. It inspired and guided individual endeavours rather than commanding universal agreement and deference. Evangelicals recognised this. They knew that the Bible was no longer the self-evidently authoritative document that they or their Protestant forebears thought. And they also recognised that the level of biblical knowledge among their peers, particularly in parliament, could not now be assumed. When the Quaker MP John Bright spoke in favour of Gladstone's Reform Bill in 1866, accusing an opponent of retiring 'into what may be called his political cave of Adullam', many members of the House did not know where or what the cave of Adullam was.[62] That would not have happened in Cromwell's time.

9

'Jesus Christ was the first Chartist':
Christian radicalism

'Our resistance is glorious': early radicalism

Their position outside the Anglican mainstream meant that the dissenting Churches always had the potential for political radicalism. Politically excluded, religiously restricted[1] and sometimes the object of mob violence, Nonconformists had some reason to be antagonistic. Such factors, combined with an emphasis on the Bible rather than on traditions that tamed it, a theology that majored on the religious liberty due to each individual conscience and a preference for congregational structures that undermined hierarchy and were in their own way democratic, made dissenters the eighteenth century's natural radicals.

In reality, dissent was politically quiescent at least for the first sixty years of the century. Once the High Church/Tory spasm in the reign of Queen Anne had passed, the security of Nonconformists was largely assured. Whig administrations passed measures that attenuated the legal impositions placed on dissenters.[2] More importantly, the practice of occasional conformity was winked at and dissenters regularly found themselves in public office. The perception of inequality and exclusion was greater than the reality. Dissenters had limited cause for radicalism.

This began to change in 1760s. The new king, George III, was more positive towards the Tories, who disliked Nonconformists, than his predecessors had been. Dissenters themselves, having enjoyed public office for decades and, in their own minds, proved themselves trustworthy, made attempts to dismantle the Test and Corporation Acts and relieve dissenting clergy from the need to subscribe to the Thirty-Nine Articles.[3] They failed and that failure, accompanied by other factors, in particular the American War of Independence, nudged them towards radicalism.

Given the religious ties between British Nonconformists and many American settlers, it was only natural that the former should adopt the latter's cause when conflict arose. Not all dissenters were pro-American, nor all Anglicans against the cause of independence, but the majority of dissenting MPs took the side of the colonists. As far as they were concerned, taxation without representation equated to slavery and the cause of their brethren in America – English dissenters consciously identified themselves with the colonists – was therefore a godly one, on a par with the religious liberties dissenters themselves had long pursued.

The Bible was one source among many for nonconformist radicalism, taking its place alongside natural law and appeals to English history. When it was deployed it was done in a way that would have been familiar to Protestants of the mid-seventeenth century. Thus, in 1778, James Murray, a popular Calvinist Presbyterian minister in Newcastle, preaching on the story of Eglon, King of Moab who occupied Israel for eighteen years, commented:

> This is as much as can be said for any unjust taxations; they are no more than political robberies, committed by persons in power upon those who have not might to oppose them. Very likely the king and people of Moab might pretend that they had taken Israel under their protection, and were not obliged to protect them for nothing; they therefore might pretend that they had a right to impose taxes upon them.[4]

The parallel would have been obvious to all listeners. Others wrestled with Romans 13 or 1 Peter 2, in the fashion of the Marian exiles 200 years earlier, concluding 'the only question on the subject of resistance is, whether we resist a lawful or an unlawful authority . . . if it be an unlawful authority we resist, our resistance is glorious.'[5] Or, in Murray's pithier, poetic words, 'When fools wear crowns, and tyrants' sceptres sway,/Then subjects sin not though they disobey.'[6]

Such pro-American sentiments could, on occasion, shade over into outright political radicalism. Dissenters were usually eager to voice their loyalty to the crown, unwilling to undo nearly a century of political progress. But that loyalty was sometimes visibly circumscribed. 'Kings are no gods of my adoration,' George Walker, a Nottingham-based Presbyterian, preached. 'They weigh not a feather in my scale against the public good . . . if [they] or whatever exalted individuals, will not enter . . . into this benevolent view, they ought to be considered and treated as mere expedients of public good, and be made subservient thereto.'[7] Such sentiments had been acceptable since the time of Locke, of course, but when put in incendiary terms by dissenting ministers just as the nation was losing its American colonies they sounded far more dangerous – although not as dangerous as they were soon to become.

As noted in Chapter 7, many clergymen, dissenting and established, initially welcomed news of the French Revolution. Enthusiasm quickly faded, however, and in the ensuing atmosphere of near hysterical fear and aggressive patriotism, it was a brave, almost suicidal and invariably heterodox Christian soul who publicly defended the cause of revolution and equality. Samuel Taylor Coleridge was one such soul. In 1795 he delivered a series of lectures in Bristol on 'Revealed Religion: Its Corruptions and Political Views'. These followed on from three earlier 'moral and political' lectures, for which he had been accused of Jacobinism and had received death threats. They were hardly less contentious.[8] Coleridge stressed the revolutionary nature of Christ's message for the poor and oppressed, and the need for equality, suggesting that true followers were forbidden all property and could not even enter commerce. This was provocative stuff, not least in the commercial capital of the West Country. Coleridge was better at pointing out the faults and failures in other systems than he was at building up his own. His later *Statesman's Manual*, despite being subtitled *The Bible the Best Guide to Political Skill and Foresight*, was not especially constructive, being described by his biographer Richard Holmes as 'the most obscure and disorganised short work that [he] ever published'.[9] Coleridge was to exert a considerable influence on nineteenth-century Christian political thought, but it was an older, more conservative and more philosophical Coleridge rather than the provocative dreamer of the 1790s.

Coleridge was not entirely alone in drawing on scripture to defend revolutionary sentiments around the turn of the century. Dissenting ministers, especially Unitarians, published sermons and pamphlets (often anonymously) arguing that Christianity demanded the kind of equality that the, admittedly misguided, revolutionaries in France were pursuing. James Pilkington, a Unitarian minister from Derby, published a pamphlet in 1795 entitled *The Doctrine of Equality of Rank and Condition examined and supported on the Authority of the New Testament, and on the Principles of Reason and Benevolence.* This argued that 'Jesus' preaching was to bring mankind as nearly as possible to an equality of rank or condition,' and that his action was to show how 'marks of distinction' were 'inconsistent with that equality, which belonged to them as brethren, and as the children of that great common parent, who is no respecter of persons'.[10] Pilkington was prepared to concede that there were 'several discourses' in the New Testament that showed that Christ wished the 'worldly circumstances of mankind' to be 'nearly, if not entirely equal.' But if near-equality was not quite a good as actual equality, it was certainly much better than the state of extreme inequality that most clergy currently admitted.

Those inclined to follow where Coleridge and Pilkington led were confronted by the need to answer the familiar biblical texts, which supposedly commanded political quiescence or obedience. The former charge was easy to deal with. Robert Hall mocked the idea that Jesus' refusal to take on the role of civil magistrate demanded Christian renunciation of politics. 'On this ground the profession of a physic is unlawful for a Christian,' he observed, 'because our Lord never set up a dispensary.'[11]

When it came to the charge of obedience, preachers and pamphleteers responded by re-reading and contextualising passages to show that neither Paul nor Peter actually demanded passive obedience. One anonymous dissenter argued of Romans 13 that respect for magistrates and obedience to local laws were precepts 'more suitably addressed to Jewish converts, who, from the prejudices of their early habits, must be particularly averse to the political interference of a heathen magistrate'.[12] Another, Noah Hill, contended that there was no way Nero or Caligula or even some more modern princes could be considered 'God's ordinance, as David was'. Rebellion, it appears, was not as serious an offence as had been imagined.[13]

For the most part, however, such dissenting voices were isolated in a political wilderness. The threat lined up against Britain and, if the reports of Catholic exiles were to be believed, Christianity was too great. The fact that Thomas Paine, one of the greatest of these threats, bolstered his largely secular arguments for the rights of man with religious references, made the Christian radical case more rather than less problematic. Paine claimed that the origin of the rights of man dated from the creation of Adam and that although God had given man equal rights, clerics had subverted them.

Paine made good use of the Genesis creation story in a way similar to Locke's treatment of it a century earlier.

> The Mosaic account of the creation, whether taken as divine authority or merely historical, is full to this point, the unity or equality of man. The expression admits of no controversy. 'And God said, Let us make man in our own image. In the image of God created he him; male and female created he them.' The distinction of sexes is pointed out, but no other distinction is even implied. If this be not divine authority, it is at least historical authority, and shows that the equality of man, so far from being a modern doctrine, is the oldest upon record.[14]

Such biblical arguments were not liable to persuade critics and the fact that Paine openly acknowledged that Jesus the man preached excellent morality and the equality of mankind did not improve matters. The most popular and infamous English infidel of the age could not be right. No matter how Lockean his analysis of the creation story and, no matter how much he professed to admire Christ's teaching, if Paine saw in scripture a doctrine of equality that legitimised events on the Continent, then he, and with him that interpretation of scripture, was almost certainly wrong.

'Jesus Christ the Only Radical Reformer': arguments for political reform

Moral panic did not end with the defeat of Napoleon, and the decades after 1815 were as difficult for Christian radicals as those before. The association of blasphemy, atheism and sedition was firm in the British mind. Radicalism was simply unchristian. For the radicals' part, when prominent evangelicals like Wilberforce eagerly supported repressive government legislation, and less prominent clerics like the Revd William Hay read the Riot Act at Peterloo, the association of Christianity with civil tyranny was secured. Christian radicals were left with an awkward middle ground to occupy. They did this, however, with considerable skill and, in the same way as George Canning had used Protestant theology to challenge Protestant political assumptions, radicals used scripture and in particular the New Testament to undermine the official Christian insistence on passive obedience to the magistrate.

Numerous radicals used Jesus Christ against those who were supposed to represent him. The radical paper the *Gorgon* insisted that Christ taught peace but 'his followers, from Wilberforce to Canning, are passionately fond of war.' Christ exemplified poverty and humility but 'his followers are generally distinguished by their pride, ostentation, and avarice.' Christ tolerated the mistakes of others whereas 'the persecuting spirit of his followers is generally and in proportion to their zeal.'[15] The anonymous author of *A Sermon for the Conversion of the Bishops to Christianity* described himself as a 'true and sincere Christian, as understood by the Gospels', and asked pointedly:

> Would any apostle recognise a brother in the Bench of Bishops with the precepts of the Gospels? Which of you in his high estates, seeks to give meat to the hungry and drink to the thirsty – to clothe the naked – to visit the sick – and to come to those in prison? How many of you are to be found waiting on your unfortunate brethren in the hospitals, prisons, and houses of correction, and ministering unto them?[16]

The association of the bishops with the Pharisees was not uncommon. 'In their phylacteries in the House of Lords, [the Bishops] pass laws to consign the poor and helpless to ignorance and captivity,' the author remarked. One wit published an advertisement offering a £500 reward to anyone who could produce a religious leader who actually fitted the description offered by Paul in 1 Timothy 3.[17]

Some radicals used similar arguments to call for an extended franchise. John Wade's *Black Book* of 1820 described Christ as 'the great radical reformer of Israel'.[18] John Cartwright called Jesus 'the Great Reformer' and 'a Jewish Jacobin of old' and argued that, just as Jesus had laid the foundations for Christianity among the poor, so should parliamentary reform be extended to include such poor.[19] If, Cartwright argued, God considered even the humblest man competent to judge for himself the means of eternal salvation, and good laws were simply the means of temporal salvation, it followed that the English constitution should involve the people in legislation. Here was Tyndale's ambition for even the ploughboy to know scripture and salvation for himself coming home to roost.

Christian history was put to similar effect. In his 1820 publication *Why are we Poor?*, the pseudonymous Roger Radical argued that the labouring classes were like the 'primitive Christians . . . when all the potentates of the earth, all the rich, and the grandees were their enemies, and cruelly persecuted them to death'. These 'ragged radicals', however, had the last laugh, 'triumph[ing] . . . over their proud oppressors, and plant[ing] the triumphant banner of the cross on the site of the capitol of ancient Rome . . . Let the apostles of liberty preach up the CHRISTIANITY OF POLITICS,' he exhorted.[20]

Just as Christ and Christian history were used against the establishment, so were the Prayer Book and the Christian creeds. Various publications parodied catechisms, creeds and prayers as a way of invoking the notion of true biblical religion against that of the established Church. The most famous instance was that of William Hone whose work ended up marking a significant moment in the freedom of the press. Hone grew up in a traditional, Bible-dominated household in the 1780s. Inspired by events in France, he turned his back on orthodoxy and the Bible, which he came to view as a source of moral wisdom rather than divine revelation. He worked as a bookseller, publisher, satirist and investigative journalist, although his business ventures were rarely successful. In 1817 his short-lived journal the *Reformists' Register* attacked establishment hypocrisies and ridiculed leading public figures by means of parodying the liturgy and the Athanasian Creed, in the form of the Sinecurist's Creed. He was tried for his efforts, on the grounds that bringing the Prayer Book and

Christianity into contempt harmed public morals. However, he defended himself pugnaciously at his trial, adopting a deliberately Christian stance, repeatedly referring to Christ as 'Our Saviour' and accusing his persecutors of neglecting the true precepts of Christianity. Despite standing before hostile judges he was acquitted.[21]

As the example of Hone suggests, it was not simply Protestant dissenters who used scripture against the established order that it apparently legitimised. Richard Carlile was one of the most notorious of early nineteenth-century infidel radicals, frequently prosecuted for blasphemous publications and parodies. He openly called himself an atheist and denounced Christianity, rather than simply the Church, calling it 'a human institution generated in fraud and fable'. His followers were of the same opinion yet that did not stop one from published a pamphlet in 1838 called *Jesus Christ the Only Radical Reformer*. This contained a catechism of reform that began:

> What is Radical Reform? A change in human nature from all its evil passions and errors
>
>> How is this to be accomplished? By Jesus Christ
>>
>> What is Jesus Christ? The Spirit of God, as reason or the intellectual principle incarnate and working in man[22]

This was hardly orthodox theology but is notable for the way in which Christ, however interpreted, could be a resource of even infidel radicalism.

At the other end of the theological spectrum, there were safer and more establishment figures who used the Bible against the repressive political Christianity that was shaping the post-Napoleonic period. Henry Bathurst, Archdeacon of Norwich, wrote to Wilberforce in 1818 complaining about post-war politics and Wilberforce's support of them. In doing so, he made the thoroughly radical case that 'the world was made, and Government, like the world, for all equally to enjoy its blessing. The Almighty cannot sanction a monopoly of enjoyment to a few.' He went on to make the same argument as John Cartwright had done. 'Christianity,' he admitted, 'does not meddle much with the interior arrangement of human government; but its analogies at least ought to be observed. Salvation is offered to all. All souls are equally dear in the sight of God . . . Should not the justice and equity of human government correspond?'[23] Although private, the argument informed Bathurst's public life. Not surprisingly, he failed to follow his father on to the bishops' bench.

Bathurst was not the only establishment figure to deploy such arguments. Thomas Gisborne, Prebendary of Durham, defended the Reform Bill on the grounds that 'every man is bound to do to every other man as he would wish the other to do to him.'[24] Vicesimus Knox, a headmaster of Tonbridge School, argued that those Church leaders who set their faces against reform would, had they lived at the time of Christ, 'have joined with the high priests and rulers to crucify [him] . . . prosecut[ing] and persecut[ing] him for sedition and high treason'.[25]

Such establishment Christian radicalism was, however, rare. Knox, Gisborne and Bathurst were engaged in no less dangerous a game than Wade, Hone or any of the other Christian radicals who felt compelled to publish their work anonymously. Although none risked being burned alive, the situation was reminiscent of the years between Wyclif and Tyndale in which the Bible was both the foundation for, and greatest challenge to, the existing political order.

'Did Christ come to teach the doctrines of Malthus?': attacking political economy

Radicals made extensive use of the Bible in their campaigns for factory reform or against the New Poor Law. Factory reform was, as noted in Chapter 8, a particular concern of Christian Tories like Richard Oastler and the Earl of Shaftesbury. But it was also, naturally, a cause among Christian radicals, the difference being that radicals tended to emphasise the rights of the poor whereas the Christian paternalists focused on the obligations of the rich.

As with the cause of political reform, Christ was widely cited. His stories, in particular the parable of the Good Samaritan and the parable of Lazarus and the rich man; his teaching, in particular the Beatitudes and the words in Matthew 25 ('I was an hungred, and ye gave me meat'); and, supremely, his example were all used to show up the callous, merciless, fundamentally unChrist-like nature of the

New Poor Laws.[26] 'Art thou a Christian?' asked one agitator rhetorically. 'Then look into the law of Christ: read through his words – imbibe his spirit, for thou knowest "he loved" children, and "suffered them to come unto him, that he might bless them".'[27]

There was a similar message in the 1832 play *A Vision of the Trial of Mr Factory Longhours* by Cavie Richardson, in which one of the witnesses was called to the stand to discuss the gospels.

> Judge: Well, Mr Lovechild. As you are to be sworn upon the Gospels, as to the truth of your evidence, pray what do the Gospels contain?
>
> Mr Lovechild: The words and deeds of our Lord and Saviour Jesus Christ.
>
> Judge: Repeat me, will you, some of the words of Jesus Christ, and such as bear upon the subject before the court.
>
> Mr Lovechild: 'Whatsoever ye would that men should do unto you, do ye even so unto them.' – 'Be ye merciful as your father who is in heaven is merciful.'
>
> Judge: What do you consider in the acts of Jesus Christ to justify you in giving evidence against the Prisoner?
>
> Mr Lovechild: Jesus Christ went about doing good; his life was a continued series of acts of benevolence, justice, and goodness; but this man so far from imitating the example of Jesus Christ has acted with the cruelty of the Devil.[28]

If factory reform provided one target for Christian radicalism, so did the New Poor Law. Here the range of victims extended from children to entire families. The range of villains extended from Mr Factory Longhours to the assortment of workhouse owners, politicians, utilitarians and Christian political economists who ran and justified the system. And the range of sins extended from overwork to poverty, hunger, family break-up and public humiliation. The Poor Law 'is Mammon's Law!' exclaimed Samuel Roberts, a manufacturer in Sheffield who campaigned energetically for the protection of chimney boys, the abolition of capital punishment and the abolition of slavery. It is 'the Law of him, who displaying to his weak and wicked victims, the riches of this world exclaims, "All these will I give thee if thou wilt oppress thy poor neighbour whom God has commanded thee to cherish; and in spite of Him, fall down, worship, and obey ME!'"[29]

Arguments did not rest on the New Testament alone. The Old Testament, radicals insisted, spoke about creation being for the good of all. After the flood, God 'spread Nature's carpet beneath their feet', and proclaimed 'all is yours, it is mine in chief, but yours in trust . . . if you are the children of Adam, children of God, then every inch of this earth – every blade of grass – every ear of corn which swells the harvest with golden growing ripens, is YOURS.'[30] Such arguments were used to inform a labour-value form of theology, in which God's creation was abundant but only made valuable by labour, which turned its potential into fruitfulness. As Abraham Hanson put it: 'their labour was the source of all property – they performed that labour by the physical power of their bodies, they derived that power from none but God.' Therefore, and naturally, it was those who put in labour who should have the first claim to the fruits of creation.[31] Workers had a right to far more than they actually received.

These arguments were bolstered by examples from the corporate life of Israel. In 1838 a translation of the pre-eminent medieval rabbi Moses Maimonides' book *The Laws of the Hebrews, relating to the Poor and the Stranger* was published. It argued that the obligation to feed the poor that was to be found throughout the Torah amounted to their *right* to be fed.[32] The book precipitated other, similar essays, which drew on Maimonides' arguments, such as *The Judaic-law: as opposed to English military-law, gaol-for-debt-law, the pauper-law, and factory-slave-law*. Preachers quoted Old Testament verses to show 'the greatest crime on earth is unjustly keeping back from another that which they have a right to have at your hands.'[33] Working men carried banners proclaiming Psalm 37:3: 'dwell in the land, and verily thou shalt be fed.'

Particular play was made of the role of the family in the Old Testament. Political economy, based on Malthus's demography, made fecundity a curse and the New Poor Law, based on political economy, ruthlessly separated those couples and families it consigned to the workhouse. Yet in the Old Testament, radicals pointed out, large families were seen as a blessing. God's command in Genesis had been 'be ye fruitful and multiply'. 'Has that law [to be fruitful] ever been repealed?' asked one preacher rhetorically. 'Did Christ come to teach the doctrines of Malthus?'[34] A piece in the *West-Riding Herald* suggested that perhaps the marriage ceremony should be changed to read 'until death or the Poor Law Commissioners do us part'.[35]

For all the Old Testament's power, however, it was the New Testament that provided the strongest, most authoritative and most uncompromising message. And it was from the New Testament that there emerged an idea of supreme importance that would transform the Christian political landscape in the nineteenth century. 'Among the Poor the Saviour was born, with the Poor he died,' said Samuel Roberts in 1839. 'To the poor he preached, by the Poor were his doctrines embraced and propagated, the Poor he fed, even by miracles, for the Poor he wept, and in the cause if the poor he constantly laboured.'[36] God had come in person on earth, dwelling among the lowest of the low. Human life, even that of the most despised, was dignified, even sanctified, by the incarnation.

'A political Saviour and a political martyr': Joseph Rayner Stephens

Radicals insisted that Christ was a political figure and the Bible a political book. The leading advocate of this message and, indeed, the most prominent Christian radical of the time was Joseph Rayner Stephens.

Stephens was born in 1805, the son of an impeccably orthodox Wesleyan minister. Having held clerical posts in Stockholm, Cheltenham and Newcastle-under-Lyme, he moved, in 1832, to Ashton-under-Lyme, an area dominated by cotton mills. He rapidly came into conflict with the Wesleyan authorities over his passionate disestablishmentarianism and he resigned from the Wesleyan ministry in 1834, thereafter leading a largely working-class group of supporters that became known as Stephensites.

Stephens openly lamented the lack of prophets in his own day, quoting Ezekiel 22:29–30 approvingly[37] and consciously adopted the manner and message of an Old Testament prophet in response. 'If Jeroboam deserved to be destroyed by the sword,' he preached in

February 1839, 'the high places and principalities and powers of England deserve a thousand times heavier blow.'[38] He was not afraid of naming sinners and was blunt in the extreme in his treatment of them. Having become involved in the Ten Hours movement in 1836, which sought to limit the factory working day to ten hours, his condemnation of factory exploitation led him into open war with the mill owners in his congregation. When they nailed a placard to his Stalybridge Chapel, which read 'Stephens's evangelical cotton manufactory and lunatic asylum for turned-off parsons', he responded by preaching a sermon in which he called mill owners murderers and swindlers and denounced the existing factory system as contrary to the Word of God.

He turned a similar fury on religious leaders, insisting that ministers were not only shirking their prophetic duty but shutting out the poor by humiliating, class-ridden seating arrangements, endless collections, incomprehensible sermons and by refusing to challenge their wealthy oppressors who sat comfortably in their pews. When over 100 workers were sacked from local factories for supporting him in 1838, he shared his stipend with them. He refused to become sole trustee of those chapels that had been financed from working-class pennies, insisting that the subscribers should have the control.

Stephens was not such a firebrand that he could not, on occasion, sound like a Tory paternalist. He railed against 'the spread of infidelity' and 'the practical atheism of the age', and against political economy, which substituted material considerations for spiritual, and placed individual interests over unity and community.[39] The 1834 Poor Law was wicked not simply because it treated poverty like crime and burdened millions with misery, but also because it effectively destroyed the principles of reciprocal obligation and harmony that should characterise Christian charity. He deemed politics of only limited use. 'Acts of Parliament or recorded laws . . . can do nothing to renovate, reform, or improve a nation,' he wrote in 1840. The locus of real change lay within the individual. 'It is the direct and immediate influence of individual character upon those, with whom we have . . . to deal in our own respective . . . relations in life, that is to effect the practical good we profess to seek.'[40] And he had as powerful a sense of imminent divine judgement as any Recordite premillennialist.

We are now arrived at the period when God is saying to us for the last time, 'How often – how often would I have gathered you as a nation, taken you under my especial protection, as a hen gathers her brood under her wings, but ye would not!' God, in my judgment, is now giving England her last opportunity; we are now at the eleventh hour of the day of our salvation.[41]

Yet, for all such similarities there was an aggressive, even violent, radicalism to his message that located him firmly beyond the Tory paternalist and mainstream evangelical camps. Stephens was clear that when the stamp of God's authority was obviously absent in a law, such as the New Poor Law, resistance was wholly legitimate. He openly used Old Testament examples to justify active resistance to the governing authorities, in a way that would have been familiar to the Protestant exiles of the mid-sixteenth century. Of Shiprah, Puah and the other Israelite midwives who disobeyed Pharaoh in Exodus 1, he said, 'would that every mother in England were a rebel like the mother of Moses, and refuse to acknowledge the laws of Commissioners and Guardians.'[42]

His rhetoric could be as provocative as any infidel street revolutionary. 'If the rights of the poor were trampled underfoot,' he once declared, 'then down with the throne, down with the aristocracy, down with the bishops, down with the clergy, burn the church, down with all rank, all title, and all dignity.'[43] In the most notorious case of such preaching, he said, 'Newcastle ought to be and would be one blaze of fire, with only one way to put it out, and that with the blood of all who supported this abominable measure [i.e. the New Poor Law].' He justified such belligerence by reference to Genesis 9:6, arguing 'if [the Poor Law commissioners] by law . . . should shed the blood of the poor, by the law of God their blood is to be shed in return,' but this did little to defuse the ensuing scandal.[44] It is not surprising that G.J. Holyoake, the most militant secularist of the time, wrote an admiring life of Stephens, entitled *'Preacher and Political Orator.'*

Such admiration notwithstanding, Stephens was clear that his radicalism was thoroughly biblical. 'It has been my practice,' he wrote in the *Champion*, 'to apply the rules of God's commandments to various institutions of our modern social system.'[45] The Bible was a fundamentally political document. 'You have nothing in the Word of God exclusively religious,' he declared. 'Religion and politics in the Word of God are always united. Social, political, and divine wrath are always connected in the Word of God.'[46] The Exodus was, he insisted, 'a political deliverance, a social emancipation'.[47] The Old Testament prophets were political radicals. Jesus Christ was the supreme reformer. 'The Jesus of the Bible I look upon as the great social reformer, and the regenerator of the human race . . . He was . . . a political Saviour, and therefore a political martyr.'[48]

Stephens was not an original thinker and his treatment of Bible, prophets and Christ was of a piece with earlier Christian radicals, albeit spoken with particular rhetorical force. His significance lies partly in his prominence as a Christian radical. No preacher fought more loudly or aggressively for the rights of the poor. But it also lies partly in his insistence that the kingdom of God was here and now. Evangelical as his roots were, Stephens firmly rejected any idea that Jesus had come to deliver immortality rather than life. 'How can we judge the blessings of eternal life unless we have an earnest, a foretaste of those blessings in our mouth, in our belly, on our back, over our heads, in our arms, and dancing around our knees here upon earth?' he asked. The incarnation was about the here and now, not the somewhere else. 'What is it all about if the coming of Christ have nothing to do with this world, but with the other?' Christ came to establish, 'not the kingdom hereafter but the kingdom from heaven here on earth'.[49]

This recognition pointed to a fundamental difference between Christian radicalism and the political evangelicalism alongside which it flourished. Political evangelicalism was a large and varied phenomenon, and any generalisations about it are liable to be partial and inadequate. There were many evangelicals, particularly among the labouring classes and within denominations like the Primitive Methodists, who would have agreed with much of what Stephens preached. Many *were* Christian radicals. And yet, the public face of political evangelicalism was more readily associated with the likes of Wilberforce and Shaftesbury. It was more Anglican, more secure, more authoritarian.

As the example of Stephens shows, there could be numerous points of similarity between Christian radicalism and this kind of Anglican political evangelicalism, such as a shared horror of infidelity or the conviction that the Church belonged at the centre of national life. Yet, there were also significant differences. It was not simply that political evangelicalism was socially well established, whereas Christian radicalism was socially marginal, indeed disreputable. Nor was it that political evangelicalism was given to preserving political and social order, whereas Christian radicalism was prepared to challenge it, or that evangelicalism emphasised the responsibilities of the rich, while Christian radicalism stressed the rights of the poor.

Instead, the fundamental difference related to the understanding of the kingdom of God. For most evangelicals the kingdom was located *post mortem*. Life on earth was a trial, albeit an incomparably important one, for that final destiny. Politics played a part in that trial and at times the part it played – if filtered through the premillennialist, Protestant paternalism of someone like Shaftesbury – could sound uncannily similar to Christian radicalism. But the point of reference remained the individual preparing himself for divine judgement and its consequences.

Much Christian radicalism was an inchoate reaction against cruelties, often justified by biblical references, witnessed daily. It was an instinctive rather than intellectual approach. Moreover, it would be wrong to imagine that Christian radicals were necessarily less concerned with salvation, judgement and heaven than evangelicals, among whose number many would count themselves. However, in as far as there was a unifying theme in their thought, one that distinguishes them from mainstream political evangelicalism, it was that the kingdom of God was not simply limited to life *after* death. Taking their cue primarily from the life and teaching of Christ himself, Christian radicals located the kingdom firmly on this side of death or, more accurately, on both sides of the divide. The kingdom of God was among us or, rather, it should have been among us. Stephens's importance was that, although undoubtedly a visceral and impulsive preacher, his rabble-rousing was founded on the idea that the kingdom of God was located on earth not in heaven. It was an idea that was to become central to British Christian politics once it had been articulated more subtly and by more reputable thinkers.

'The Bible is especially "The People's Charter"': Chartism

Stephens played an important early role in the movement that was to see the climax of early nineteenth-century Christian radicalism. Chartism took its name from the People's Charter of 1838, which called for universal male suffrage, secret ballots, equal constituencies, annual parliaments, salaried MPs and no property qualification for parliament. As a mass, predominantly working-class movement it was seen as a serious threat by governing authorities and established Church alike, of which it was particularly critical. Stephens spoke at a number of early Chartist meetings, was arrested in 1839 and, despite denying that he was a Chartist, was sentenced to prison for eighteen months.

Chartism had a broad streak of anti-clericalism running through it. Chartists often drew a parallel between the corrupt Jewish priests of the New Testament and contemporary clerics who 'rob God and the poor, and say "wherein have we robbed thee?"'.[50] These are 'the disciples of Him,' one Chartist draper contemptuously remarked of well-heeled Anglican bishops, 'who hath not where to lay his head'.[51] It was not, however, an anti-Christian movement. Rather, its frequent complaint was that Church and nation were not Christian enough. 'We are not converted to Christianity yet,' stated Henry Solly bluntly in his pamphlet *What Christianity Says to the Present Distress*.[52] Our task is 'to deliver the religion of Jesus Christ from the disgrace brought upon it'.[53] The nation needed revival and Chartism was to be its source. 'Politics led religion astray and politics must bring her back again. By the Charter alone can the deformed be transformed.' Such was the symbiotic relationship between Christianity and Chartism that some could remark that 'no man can be a Christian unless he be a Chartist and vice versa . . . in working out our political redemption, we are actually at the same time working out our spiritual salvation.'[54]

In this context the Bible was not simply a political book, but a proto-Chartist document. 'What is [the Sermon on the Mount] but a manual of Chartism – a manual for Chartists?' asked the *Northern Star*. 'The Bible is especially, "The People's Charter", drawn up by the King of Kings, and sealed with the blood of his only Son,' declared

Benjamin Parsons.[55] As with earlier radical movements, Christ himself was the central focus. Just as the Bible was an early Charter, so Christ was the first Chartist. The *Northern Liberator* recorded how, in September 1839, a group of Chartist prisoners were assembled in the prison chapel for a service. After the officiating clergyman had given a short sermon 'on the virtues and excellence of Jesus Christ', one of the prisoners known as Radical Jack 'stood up and with a loud voice exclaimed: "Sir, Jesus Christ was the first Chartist. He was the best man that ever came into the world. He taught the doctrines of humility and equality, and even instructed men to sell their garments and buy a sword."'[56] He was awarded three days' solitary confinement for his outburst.

The sword reference was carefully chosen. The Chartist proclamation of Christ was sometimes prepared to ascribe to him violent inclinations, justifying their claim through his words in Luke 22:36: 'he that hath no sword, let him sell his garment and buy one.'[57] Thus one Mr North told a Chartist meeting in Bradford, 'Christ tried moral force, and when he found that failed, what did he say? Why he said, "if t'hesn't gotten a sword, go an sell the' co[a]t and b[u]y one": an I'll give ye t'same advice.' He immediately addressed the obvious theological criticism. 'Some said this meant the sword of the spirit, but it was a sword that cut a man's ear off.' His conclusion, which referred to the practice of separating families in the workhouse, was as provocative as Stephens's apocalyptic warning to Newcastle. 'They were told to increase and multiply, and Christ said that no man was to part man and wife; but our laws say that they are to be parted. If he died fighting in their cause he should die fighting for the laws of God and Christ.'[58]

This reformist critique of Christianity led Chartists to adopt and adapt Christian language, logic and liturgy for their own ends. They commonly spoke about the 'factory child' or the 'Union pauper', fusing biblical and contemporary categories. They published innumerable articles with titles like 'Defence of Freedom as a Religious Duty', 'On the Christianity of Chartism', and 'Religious Politics'. They held open-air camp meetings that were closely modelled on

Methodism, incorporating hymn-singing, prayers, biblical exhortations and sermons. At least three specifically Chartist hymn books were published, with hymns like the one sung at the Peep Green demonstration in 1839:

> God is our Guide! From field, from wave
> From plough, from anvil and from loom
> We come, our country's rights to save.
> And speak a tyrant faction's doom!
> And hark! We raise from sea to sea
> The sacred watchword, Liberty!
> We will, we will, we will be free.[59]

The Chartist relationship with existing Churches was a complex one. The 1839 Peep Green demonstration concluded with the resolution 'not to attend any place of worship where the administration of the services are inimical to civil liberty'. This led to a degree of ecclesiastical separatism, campaigners founding a number of Chartist churches and Chartist Sunday schools, in which prayers adapted from the Book of Common Prayer were used and where revolutionary and apocalyptic sermons were preached.

The Chartists did not simply disengage from mainstream Churches, however. They also chose to challenge them by using biblical precepts against them. When the House of Commons rejected a petition in support of the Charter with over 120,000 signatures in July 1839, the Chartist mood darkened and energies turned towards public action. Much of this was centred on churches. Chartist leaders would inform local clergy in advance that they and their followers would attend the service on Sunday. Hundreds, sometimes thousands arrived early and filled the pews, including those that were rented out to the wealthy and respectable. The protesters would carry banners bearing scriptural messages, such as 'He that oppresseth the poor reproacheth his Maker: but he that honoureth him hath mercy on the poor,'[60] or 'What mean ye that ye beat my people to pieces, and grind the faces of the poor? saith the Lord God of Hosts.'[61] Alternatively, banners would proclaim messages like 'The voice of the people is the voice of God' or answer scriptural questions like 'Who devour

widows' houses and make long prayers?' with a simple portrait of a
bishop and the words 'wolves in sheep's clothing'.[62]

In announcing their intention to mob the church, Chartist leaders
would often ask the minister to preach on a specific text with radical
implications, such as Nehemiah 5:3,[63] Exodus 20:9,[64] Isaiah 3:14–
15,[65] Amos 8:4–8,[66] Matthew 19:21,[67] or, most popularly, James
5:1–6.[68] Occasionally such challenges were accepted, such as when
the vicar of St James' Bradford preached on Proverbs 22:2 ('The rich
and poor meet together: the Lord is the maker of them all'). Other
vicars preached on the recommended texts but flatly refused to admit
that they had any connection with the contemporary situation. One
Dr Whittaker accepted the challenge to preach on James 5 but insisted
that while the Roman rich might have been culpable, to castigate the
contemporary wealthy would be 'the grossest injustice'.[69]

Most preachers simply ignored the requests and spoke on what
they had intended. Some not only ignored the invitation but chose
deliberately antagonistic verses and preached deliberately provocative sermons. Edward Goodwin of Sheffield spoke on Proverbs 24:21
('My son, fear thou the Lord and the king: and meddle not with them
that are given to change') and advised the Chartists to 'return to a
sound mind, to loyal, peaceable, and industrious habits, and to a serious and diligent pursuit of those "better things which the gospel of
Christ held out to them."'[70] Some were blunter still. The junior curate
of Ashton rejected suggestions for his sermon and announced as his
text, 'my house is a house of prayer but ye have made it a den of
thieves.'[71]

Even when thus provoked, the Chartists conducted themselves
with dignity and propriety. Violence was very rare and limited usually
to fights between indignant churchgoers who found their rented pew
occupied by Chartist protesters. When preachers deliberately ignored
or berated their newly enlarged and political congregations, the
worst their audience did was heckle or stand up and leave en masse.
More usually, they would wait and listen patiently and leave peacefully at the end. Their actions demonstrated not only their own moral
authority but also their contempt for churchmen who cared little for
their plight.

In time, the ecclesiastical authorities formed resistance to these mass visitations and even, in some instances, stationed guards at church doors, a measure that provoked extreme indignation among the protesters.

> 'To the poor the Gospel is preached'. 'Whatsoever ye do unto one of the least of these, my brethren, ye do it unto me', said the holy Jesus during his sojourn upon earth, and the Church professes to follow his maxims up by dubbing itself the 'Poor Man's Church'. Yet no 'straight gate or narrow way', but a band of armed policemen, and a host of special constables, backed by a troop of dragoons, in readiness if wanted, shut up the entrance to the Church, and the garb of poverty was a sufficient reason for exclusion.[72]

The measure proved successful, however, and the church demonstrations ground to a halt. The Chartist movement presented parliament with another petition, this time of over 3 million signatories, in 1842, and a third, with around 2 million, in 1848. Both were rejected and the movement died with a whimper after a widely anticipated and feared mass rally on Kennington Common in April 1848. Chartist Christianity died a similar death, the Chartist Church losing the edge of its anti-institutional criticism by becoming somewhat institutionalised itself, and the whole movement losing its Christian rhetoric in favour of a more narrowly political tone in the 1840s.

Nevertheless, it stood as the climax to a tradition of Christian radicalism that emerged in the difficult years around the turn of the nineteenth century and struggled through decades of political oppression, economic hardship and ecclesiastical disapproval to bequeath to later decades an important legacy to Christian politics. That legacy was as profound as it was untidy. It insisted that the Bible was a political text, 'the best political book in the world' according to Samuel Cook. It contended that pastors should be political animals.[73] 'Unless a priest of the living God be a politician in the pulpit,' declared Joseph Rayner Stephen, 'he has no business there at all.'[74] It was thoroughly biblical in a way that would, eventually, help legitimise reformist politics in the public mind and rescue it from the charge of godlessness. It was willing to use Christian arguments against the Church in such a way as would, again in time, help provoke an ecclesiastical re-evaluation of political engagement. It helped shift the locus of sin away from purely individual weakness or wickedness and towards the social conditions that shaped, and destroyed, so many lives.

Crucially, it brought Christ himself centre stage, orienting Christian political thought not around the idea of a godly nation, nor around the famous texts of political obedience, nor around a vacuous doctrine of economic providence hastily baptised by Christian economists, but around the Son of God and his life on earth. Christian radicals trod a treacherous path, assailed on one side by clerics who told them they were ignoring or abusing their spiritual duties, and on the other by more secularised radicals who thought their talk of moral reformation and of God's judgement simply blunted the case for practical reform. It was perhaps because of this precariousness that Christian radicalism never achieved any unity of thought and had nothing of the coherence of more conservative Christian arguments. Yet, that did not prevent it from serving as a key source for later Christian political thought.

10

'He meant us to do secular work in His name': Church and kingdom

'We were all members one of another': Tractarianism

The repeal of the Test and Corporation Acts in 1828 and Catholic emancipation the following year cast shadows over the Church-State relations that had apparently been settled over a century earlier. Henceforth many who had no attachment to, and little affection for, the established Church would be in a position to legislate for its government. Parliamentary supremacy over ecclesiastical matters was unproblematic (for established clerics at least) when that parliament was merely the temporal side of one national coin, stamped with more or less the same mark as the Church's spiritual side. When, however, that temporal side began to look somewhat different, difficulties arose.

The changed circumstances led more ecclesiastics to emphasise the Church's independence from the state, insisting that its authority derived not from its political establishment but from its apostolic succession, and denying the right of anyone not committed to the Church to interfere in its internal affairs. Sentiments like these helped create the opinion among later historians that Tractarianism, or the Oxford Movement, which sought to reinvigorate the Church in light of these changes, was an apolitical movement, driven by men whose motivations were located beyond the temporal and whose interests were ecclesiastical rather than political.[1] This was not so. The very assertion of the Church's independence from the state was a political act with significant implications for the ordering of society. 'Strictly speaking, the Christian Church, as being a visible society, is necessarily a political power or party,' observed John Henry Newman in a book on early Church history. 'In truth, the Church was framed for the express purpose of interfering, or, (as irreligious men will say,) meddling with the world.'[2] The Tractarians, through their journalism, sermons and didactic novels, were eminently political, although in their own terms.

The Tractarian understanding of the Church had implications for Church-State relations. The Church was the independent, authoritative, visible body of Christ on earth. It antedated the state, was founded by a higher authority, and was commissioned for a higher purpose. Popular views, which saw it as the nation's conscience or a department of state with responsibility for guarding the nation's moral health and thereby its political security, were indefensible. 'As if the purpose of our Lord's coming were merely to instruct men in this or that duty, or to make them respectable members of society,' wrote the clergyman and latterly convert to Roman Catholicism Frederick Oakeley contemptuously.[3] The job of the Church was not 'to make men good members of society, honest, upright, industrious and well-conducted'. It was to make them 'Saints'.[4]

This did not preclude establishment but nor did it necessitate it. 'The parting of the State from the Church is no light matter,' reasoned Edward Pusey, a leading early Tractarian. '[But] to the state it is suicide.'[5] Establishment was acceptable if it meant the state was 'incorporated' (a favourite word) into the Church, rather than partnering with it, still less controlling it. As Thomas Mozley, writing in *British Critic*, from 1837 an organ of Tractarian thought, said, 'the State is a member, or an organ, or a child, of the Church,' sanctified by doing what Christ's body dictates it should.[6] This view was justified by scripture, although usually in a somewhat crude, proof-texting way and, more importantly, through the Tractarian reading of Church history.[7]

If this sounded medieval in its ambitions, it was. Tractarian claims could, at times, sound rather like those of Gregory VII. 'The destiny of the Christian faith is nothing short of universal dominion,' claimed Henry Wilberforce, youngest son of the abolitionist, in his 1838 book, *The Parochial System*. Its task was 'to regulate the fate of churches and nations'.[8] English queens, just like holy Roman emperors, stood under divine judgement. 'One there is, Who is higher than all the kings of the earth ... from Whom all rulers, whether in Church or State, derive their authority.'[9]

All Christian thinkers would have agreed with this, at least in theory. The crucial difference was that with their high view of the Church, the Tractarians used this logic to pass judgement, explicitly, severely and frequently on what they understood to be the misdemeanours of the state. A world away from the Christian radicals and Chartists, both theologically and socially, they assumed a similar prophetic mantle. In the words of the historian who has done most to recover the political thought of the Tractarians, 'Pusey's anxiety over the condition of England informed sermons which read like despatches from an anti-capitalist jihad.'[10]

Given their theological foundations, it is not surprising that the most significant criticism levelled at the state was ecclesiastical. A series of events in the mid-nineteenth century – the saga of the Jerusalem bishopric of 1841,[11] the Gorham judgement of 1850,[12] the Matrimonial Causes Act of 1857,[13] the Irish Church Disestablishment Act of 1869[14] and the admission of the openly atheist Charles Bradlaugh to parliament in 1886[15] – all strained the Tractarian relationship with the state, compelling some to leave the established Church altogether. However, their criticism was as much social and political as it was ecclesiastical.

They were scathing about political economy, which Samuel Bosanquet called 'the philosophy of Antichrist'. Political economy was grotesquely selective in its reading of the Bible, they complained. It heard the first part of Deuteronomy 15:11, for example – 'For the poor shall never cease out of the land' – but completely ignored that longer, latter part: 'therefore I command thee, saying, Thou shalt open thine hand wide unto thy brother, to thy poor, and to thy needy, in thy land.' Pusey used Jesus' moving words in Matthew 25 to savage every aspect of its teaching.

> I did not take in little children in Thy name, but they were provided for; they were sent, severed indeed from father or mother to the poorhouse, to be taught or not about Thee, as might be; I did not feed Thee when hungry, political economy forbade it, but I increased the labour market with the manufacture of luxuries; I did not visit Thee when sick, but the parish doctor looked in on his ill-paid rounds; I did not clothe thee when naked, I could not afford

it, the rates were so high, but there was a workhouse for Thee to go to; I did not take Thee in as a stranger, but it was provided that Thou mightest go to the casual ward.[16]

Sound and socially respectable High Church characters from didactic Tractarian novels sounded like apocalyptic radicals. 'There is more misery than ever among the poor,' remarked the central character in *The Warden of Berkingholt* by Francis Paget. 'Their patience is exemplary: but a time must come, when, if things go on as they do at present, their patience will be exhausted; they will have borne, still they can bear no longer.'[17]

The landscape and culture created by political economy were a disgrace. Manufacturing towns were visions of hell where chimneys symbolically replaced spires. London was condemned for 'its frightful contrasts of extreme luxury and extreme misery'.[18] Legitimate trade had become a form of idolatry, the worship of Mammon. How could men speculate on markets when God was promising a '"hundredfold" return on earth, with eternal life into the bargain?' asked Henry Wilberforce rhetorically.[19]

Worse still was the treatment of the poor. Tractarian sermons and novels constantly beatified the poor, praising them for their forbearance and calling them the treasure of Christ's Church. They utterly rejected the idea that poverty implied moral failing, preferring instead to identify the poor with Christ himself in a way that would have been familiar to contemporary Christian radicals. 'White sepulchres are the streets of our cities,' Pusey denounced. 'They are beautiful outwardly, but within, but a few yards from all that pomp, luxury, and self-indulgence . . . Christ, as He Himself says, lies, an hungered, athirst, naked, sick, unvisited.'[20]

Not surprisingly, the workhouse was a particular target, partly for its discomforts and partly for its indiscriminate use. Inequality was similarly denounced, again partly for its dehumanising effects on the poor and partly because it exemplified class alienation. The state of the poor 'is the greatest disgrace to humanity – let alone the name of Christian which we profess – that ever has existed since the world began', said Bosanquet with a little exaggeration. 'The separation and estrangement of the richer orders from the poorer, is indescribably greater in this country, which professes the religion which makes all men brethren, than it ever was in any country professedly or practically heathen.'[21]

The Tractarian critique was not born of theory or ignorance – a great many Tractarians drew on their parochial experience to write authoritatively about poverty – and did not (always) remain at the level of generality and caricature. Pusey, for example, in a commentary on the Minor Prophets of the Old Testament, used his entry on Hosea 12:7 – 'He is a merchant, the balances of deceit are in his hand: he loveth to oppress' – to attack the 'truck system' in which labourers were obliged, on pain of dismissal, to buy their goods from particular shops at inflated prices. 'When . . . wages are paid in necessaries priced exorbitantly, or when artisans are required to buy at a loss at their masters' shops, what is it but the union of deceit and oppression?'[22]

Such experience and specificity notwithstanding, Tractarian solutions were rarely detailed or practical, at least in the political sense. This too was on account of the theological foundations from which they were working. In the fashion of most Christian politics of the time, not least the evangelicals whose early influence on some Tractarians was significant, Tractarianism did not understand social problems as being amenable to legislative remedies. Rather the problem was primarily spiritual and moral, in which regard the Tractarian solution shared something with evangelicalism, whose insistence on generosity and self-denial was much admired.

It was, however, different in one important, long-lasting and fundamentally theological respect. The Tractarian understanding of the Church placed much weight on incarnation and fellowship. Christ had dwelt among us, thereby sanctifying life. Tractarians talked enthusiastically about 'the marvellous fact of His Incarnation, that crowning mystery, whereby GOD-HEAD and Manhood, whereby matter and spirit are indissolubly combined'.[23] His presence on earth was more tangible than Protestant theology had allowed and was communicated to the believer through the administration of the sacraments, rather than scripture alone.

Moreover, God's presence in the Church itself made the body of Christian believers a true communion, in which 'all members of Christ are made members of one another ... members of the Christian family.'[24] Thus when Newman insisted that silk-weavers of Spitalfields 'deserved to be helped because they were baptised', he was making an inclusive rather than an exclusive point.[25] Simply being a member of the Christian family was enough to justify practical help.

The location for this communion, and therefore for the charity it demanded, was the local parish. Tractarians raged against the New Poor Law and, to a lesser extent, evangelical societies for the relief of poverty, because they removed from the local parish tasks that were properly the Church's. The Tractarian solution to the 'Condition of England' demanded not only attentiveness to the Church's teaching but a relocation of charity from a national to a parochial basis. The local parish was of supreme interest to the Tractarians, who saw in it the harmonious homogeneity they supposed had characterised pre-Reformation England. They took their pastoral responsibilities very seriously and innovated influentially, commonly introducing a daily service, simple preaching, auricular confession and an offertory wherever they ministered. The fact that this entailed them adopting an aggressively inhospitable attitude to Nonconformists in their parish, whom they viewed as little better than heretics, did not strike them as in any way undermining their rhetoric of inclusion.

Crucially, they modelled the kind of society they wished to see at large. This meant a number of things, foremost among them the removal of box pews and the campaign against pew rents, 'the rotten boroughs of our churches' in the words of Thomas Mozley.[26] The church was a place of true spiritual equality; it could not be one of material distinction. Tractarian novels tell of pews ripped out to the indignation of spiritual villains. In one, Francis Paget's *Milford Malvoisin*, the Tractarian vicar Mr Till is confronted by the pompous Mrs Tuff who tells him, 'if I can't sit in a pew, I shan't come to church.' Mr Till responds with a lecture on how pews are an offence to God and Church, how 'we were all members one of another . . . high and low, rich and poor,' and how there won't be pews in heaven. Mrs Tuff is horrified. 'You would not have one Heaven for the Rich and another for the Poor? Well, really, I never heard anything so shocking! ... You a clergyman, Sir! and preaching such levelling, jacobinical, democratic, radical doctrines.'[27]

The levelling didn't end with pews. *Milford Malvoisin* closes with Mr Till preaching on a favourite Chartist text, James 2:2–6, and warning his congregation 'if they wish to save themselves and their neighbours from the fate of those who despise "Christ's little ones" they will read with awe, the Apostolic warning, and act upon it promptly and decidedly.' The five uncompromising verses are then printed in full and in capitals by way of the novel's conclusion.[28]

Radicalism and rhetoric of this kind were not limited to Tractarian novels. The *British Critic* printed articles in which contributors talked about 'the right of the Christian poor . . . to a sufficient and dignified maintenance, without disgrace or confinement . . . [a right that] we hold to be at least as good and demonstrable as that by which our Sovereign wears her crown, or any land-owner received the rent of his land, or the parson his tithe.'[29] When Lord John Russell as Home Secretary approved arming of private citizens in the face of Chartist agitation, the *Critic* seethed, remarking that if 'blood [were to be] shed in our streets . . . shocking though it may be, we really think it would be better for the peace of the country that it should be the blood of those who were the first openly to arm and drill, viz. the "Armed Associations."'[30] John Rayner Stephens could not have come up with something more incendiary.

One can take the parallel too far. Tractarians may have publicly exonerated rank-and-file Chartist protests but their objectives were fundamentally different. They sought to establish God's order on earth, primarily through the parochial unit as seen through medieval-tinted spectacles. The job of the Church was to deal with the causes of sin rather than the symptoms, which helps to explain why most of their practical solutions, such as a renaissance of the squirearchy, Sabbath recreation, national 'holydays', village fairs and the generally amiable culture of the mythical Middle Ages were not remotely practical.

The Tractarians, at least in their more radical moments, recognised that the poor had a just claim to be fed, clothed and cared for, but understood this as the responsibility that Christian men and women had to one another simply by dint of being members of God's Catholic Church. They also believed that the poor should be resigned to inequality. Heaven was their true and final compensation. In Frederick Oakeley's words:

It may be said that the Gospel is the enemy of riches (which, in a certain sense, is true) and represents all men as free and equal, (which is also true), and therefore that the worldly distinctions which we see around us are irreligious . . . But this were to mistake altogether the nature of Christian equality, and to measure it by a mere worldly rule.[31]

Spiritual equality undermined material inequality rather than insisted on material equality.

Such important qualifications aside, Tractarian rhetoric could be as fierce and radical as anything preached at a Chartist sermon. As Frederick Oakeley said in 1840, the rich 'roll at their ease in splendid carriages along streets of palaces . . . [while] there are poor around them to whom their crumbs were a feast . . . No wonder if to such, the Bible is a distasteful Book . . . I do not scruple to say . . . it is also a levelling Book.'[32]

'The Kingdom of Heaven is the great practical existing reality': Conservative Christian Socialism

Two days after the anticlimactic Chartist rally on Kennington Common in April 1848 copies of a poster began to appear in London, headed 'Workmen of England!'. It spoke of the miserable conditions under which the working classes laboured but implored the Chartists to 'turn back from the precipice of riot'.[33] France had recently experienced another, albeit far less traumatic, revolution and the English authorities, which included the majority of the Anglican clergy, were worried that England was heading in the same direction.

The poster was an attempt to defuse the situation. It was the work of a barrister and two Church of England clergymen. The youngest was John Malcolm Ludlow. Born in India in 1811 and brought up by a radical widow in France, he had moved to England in 1838 and experienced an evangelical-style conversion the following year. Never an evangelical proper, he was nonetheless as biblical in his thinking as he was French. At the age of twenty he wrote in French a book that explained how Christianity was the fulfilment of whatever was good in socialism, and he subsequently introduced to his colleagues the principles and methods of the co-operative groups he had encountered in France.

The second was Charles Kingsley, the twenty-eight-year-old vicar of Eversley in Hampshire. Impulsive, passionate, provocative, Kingsley was a Romantic and a visionary. He was later to write to Charles Darwin on the publication of *The Origin of Species* a letter gushing with such theological praise that Darwin quoted it in subsequent editions of the book. A powerful preacher and a novelist of some repute, his mind was theologically threadbare, 'innocent of great intellectual insight' according to Edward Norman.[34] Although schooled for a kind of Tory paternalism, he had a great deal of sympathy for the plight of working men, remarking autobiographically at the end of his novel *Alton Locke*, published in 1850, 'if to be a Chartist is to love my brothers with every faculty of my soul – to wish to live and die struggling for their rights, endeavouring to make them, not electors merely, but fit to be electors, senators, kings and priests to God and His Christ . . . then I am a seven-fold Chartist.'[35]

The third was John Frederick Denison Maurice, born in 1805, the son of a Unitarian clergyman. His family life was marked by religious division, his mother and sisters becoming Calvinist evangelicals, and this helped engender in Maurice a lifelong fear and loathing of Christian disunity. He himself converted to Anglicanism in 1831 and was ordained three years later, before serving as a chaplain at Guy's Hospital, where he was immersed in the suffering of the English working class, and then as chaplain at Lincoln's Inn, where he met Ludlow. Although praising and drawing on both evangelical and Tractarian traditions, he criticised both for sectarian tendencies and did his best to avoid 'joining a party in the church'.[36] Maurice was made a Professor of English Literature and History at the newly established King's College, London, in 1840, and then Professor of Theology there in 1846, roles that he combined with pastoral duties and from which he would be forced to resign over his controversial views on eternal life.

Ludlow, Kingsley and Maurice formed the kernel of the Christian Socialist movement, which flourished, in its first incarnation, between 1848 and 1854. Alarmed by but also sympathetic towards

Chartism, the Christian Socialists set about, through their short-lived journals, *Politics for the People* and the *Christian Socialist*, and a series of *Tracts on Christian Socialism*, articulating what they understood to be the proper Christian response to the social unrest that was plaguing England. This could, at the time, sound like Christian radicalism of the purest kind. 'Instead of being a book to keep the poor in order, [the Bible] is a book, from beginning to end, written to keep the rich in order,' opined Kingsley under the pseudonym Parson Lot, going on to quote the biblical admonitions so favoured by the Chartists. 'It is our fault,' he continued, that 'We have used the Bible as if it was a mere special constable's handbook – an opium dose for keeping beasts of burden patient while they were being over-loaded.'[37] Such sentiments were as much Kingsley – impassioned, idealistic, incendiary – as they were Christian Socialism which, under the theological tutelage of Maurice, was more measured and nuanced. What the early Christian Socialists lost in radicalism, though, they made up in a theological sophistication that was to prove their legacy.

Maurice's background gave him an ability to navigate and draw on different theological traditions. While positive about evangelicalism he felt it had made a fundamental error by making 'the sinful man and not the God of all grace the foundation of Christian Theology'. This emphasis bred a kind of individualism, in which personal salvation trumped all other concerns, thereby making people insensitive to the needs and desires of others, an insensitivity that was ultimately responsible for anti-Christian movements.

> Men feel that they are not merely lost creatures; they look up to heaven above them, and ask whether it can be true that [their sinfulness] is the whole account of their condition; that their sense of right and wrong, their cravings for fellowship, their consciousness of being creatures having powers which no other creatures possess, are all nothing. If religion, they say, will give us no explanation of these feelings, if it can only tell us about a fall for the whole race, and an escape for a few individuals of it, then our wants must be satisfied without religion. Then begin Chartism and Socialism, and whatever schemes make rich men tremble.[38]

Such individualism also helped foster the doctrine of competition that dominated economic thought. Although he claimed that 'we are not setting at naught the principles of political economy but are vindicating them from a mean and dishonourable perversion of them,' Maurice was clear that 'the present system of trade' was premised on a competitive individualism that eroded the Christian bonds that tied society together.[39] It was difficult to see how political economy could be reconciled with this vision of Christian society.

Maurice was to adopt a fundamentally different approach to biblical politics, made up of several strands. The first was to take the infinite goodness of Christ rather than corrupting sin of Adam as the foundation for human nature. Evangelicals, he wrote, 'make sin the ground of all theology, whereas it seems to me that the living and holy God is the ground of it'.[40] The ineradicable human tendency towards moral failure remained strong, but it was no longer primary.

Second, and closely related, was an emphasis on Christ's incarnation as a counterbalance to the evangelical focus on his atonement. The incarnation was the centrepiece of history, in which God dwelt among and shared the sufferings of his creation, thereby sanctifying it and granting it a spiritual significance that a concentration on atonement, judgement and other-worldly salvation lost. Christ's sacrifice remained crucial, but Maurice saw it not as the delivery of individual souls from damnation but as a way of revealing and securing the basic order of creation. In the great annual act of atonement in the Old Testament, he wrote, 'the whole people were taught that God, who had accepted them as a holy people to Himself, purified them, as a body, of that which had set them at war with Him. The individual Israelite could not be satisfied with his own sin-offering or peace-offering, unless he was thus assured that he belonged to a redeemed and purified society.' The New Testament atonement told the same story, only writ on a cosmic scale. This revelation of an underlying communion, within the Godhead and between God and his creation, was 'the revelation of an order which sustains all the intercourse and society of men'.[41]

Third, and again linked, there was a focus on the kingdom of God. Maurice straddled the gap that had threatened to swallow so many Christian radicals in the early nineteenth century, on the one side of which was the kingdom of God as entirely other, restricted to the hereafter, to be anticipated with patience and perseverance, and on the other side of which was the secular radical cry that this was mere humbug, a distraction from the proper human task of building heaven on earth, here and now.[42] For Maurice, Christ had inaugurated his kingdom – 'The Kingdom of Heaven is to me the great practical existing reality which is to renew the earth' – and the job of Christians was to recognise this and participate in it.[43]

The unifying path that ran through these various theological fields was that of fellowship. Humans had a divinely implanted desire for communion with one another just as they did with God. The incarnation had established a community, a 'brotherhood' of humankind that was both 'divine and human'. It was a 'permanent communion which was not created by human hands, and cannot be destroyed by them'.[44] This relativised all other social, political, even ecclesiastical identities and commitments, creating an 'influence strong enough to overpower the tendencies to rivalry and division which exist among [men]'.[45] As Maurice wrote in the first edition of *Politics for the People*, published less than a month after the Kennington Common rally: 'an Everlasting Father has revealed Himself to men in an elder Brother, one with him and with us, who died for all . . . therefore we can feel to each other as brothers; we can look upon all you whom we address in this paper, nobles, shopkeepers, labourers, mechanics, beggars, aristocrats, democrats, people of every class and party, as brothers.'[46]

The Christian Socialists were as good as their word on this. Ludlow persuaded the antichristian Chartist leader, Walter Cooper, to hear Maurice preach at Lincoln's Inn, and Cooper was sufficiently moved to suggest Maurice meet some of the men who had been on Kennington Common. When they did, the Chartists were impressed. Working men like them had rarely engaged with an Anglican clergyman on this level – they met in a coffee house – and still less one who took the time to listen to them and acknowledge their complaints, let alone one who told them he thought the primitive Church in Jerusalem had been communistic, and that although the state could not be such, the Church should be 'in principle'.

For all this apparent social equality and theologically grounded radicalism, however, neither Maurice nor the other early Christians Socialists were radicals or even, for that matter, socialists. Maurice himself had self-confessed 'anti-democratical heresies' and was determined, as were his peers, to defend both monarchy and aristocracy. More seriously and certainly more directly connected to his theological arguments, Maurice exhibited what Ludlow called an extreme 'system-phobia'.[47] Not only had he no interest in large-scale government intervention in industry, or in the redistribution of wealth, or in the extension of the franchise, or in trades unions, but he had a prevailing antipathy towards anything that sought to restructure society. The epithet 'socialist' was a deliberate provocation rather than a sustained political programme.

As far as Maurice was concerned, such ambitions were wholly inappropriate for an ordained minister to propound. They were liable to lead to precisely the kind of division he feared. They were likely to be ineffectual. Worst of all, they were contrary to the organic order of God's creation. If the kingdom of God was already in existence on earth, planning fundamental changes to institutions that were part of the kingdom was to betray God's own plans. In this regard Maurice shared the evangelical conviction that personal moral reform was more appropriate, more effective and more Christian than those 'certain scientific arrangements' that would supposedly remedy social ills.[48] Maurice, like his fellow Christian Socialists, was fundamentally conservative in his attitude.

What Maurice did do was try to effect a change of attitude. He once said of himself in a letter to Ludlow, 'my business, because I am a theologian, and have no vocation except for theology, is not to build but to dig, to show that economy and politics . . . must have ground beneath themselves . . . society is not to be made anew by arrangements of ours, but is to be regenerated by finding the law and ground of its order and harmony, the only secret of its existence, in God.'[49] Regeneration could only be achieved by recognising the communion that was the basis of divine and human life in its current form, rather than as it would some day be.

That meant inculcating among the rich 'a greater recognition of poor men as men, and not merely as poor'.[50] It also meant listening to what God was saying through the working classes rather than condemning their activity out of hand. 'God seems to me to speak to us in the present time through the feelings which have been excited . . . in the minds of the working-men,' Maurice wrote. 'Their impulse to co-operation, their plans for effecting it, if we take them aright, may be the means He designs for reviving the true feeling of Christian fellowship and brotherhood which has departed from us.'[51]

Christian Socialism also meant recognising that the whole nation was in this together. 'The whole country must look for its blessings through the elevation of its Working Class . . . we must all sink if that is not raised.'[52] If this sounded like the Christian nationalism of a Tory paternalist like Shaftesbury,[53] it serves to remind us Christian conservatism informed Maurice, just as evangelicalism and Tractarianism had done. His genius was as much in synthesis as originality. Maurice's Christian Socialism meant advocating a society marked by co-opera-tion rather than competition, collective endeavour rather than solitary industry, public good rather than private profit, fellowship rather than individualism. It was a moral and educative 'socialism' rather than economic or political.

On paper the first Christian Socialists achieved precious little. *Politics for the People* ran for seventeen issues in the summer of 1848. Although some articles tackled overly political subjects like the exten-sion of the franchise, the need for improved sanitation, the pertinence of political legislation and events in post-revolutionary France, the overall tone was apolitical in the sense that Maurice preferred. The journal contested the idea that an extended franchise would solve anything. It criticised Chartist tactics, like the Kennington Common meeting, for being illegal and politically immature. It pointedly rejected both 'legislation' and 'socialism' as anything other than superficial and inadequate answers to England's real problems.

In as far as *Politics for the People* advocated any 'solutions' they were at best hopeful and at worse naïve or, on occasion, ridiculous. The authors commonly recommended honest and open dialogue between clergy and different classes as the only way to foster and develop the common Christian fellowship that the nation needed. Only through regular, sincere, face-to-face meetings would antago-nism between classes be resolved. Less helpfully, they counselled moral regeneration as a way of alleviating social problems. Kingsley suggested, for example, in two articles on the National Gallery, that workmen ought to acquire an interest in the visual arts as a way of gaining respite from 'the ugly colourless things which fill the workshop and the factory'.[54] It was a suggestion on a par with some of the Tractarians' more medieval ideas.

The *Christian Socialist*, which appeared in only eight issues between 1850 and 1851, was more focused than its predecessor, founded, edited and largely written as it was by the more practically minded Ludlow. It offered a more coherent and pragmatic Christian vision of socialism, without losing the fundamentally moral approach to politics. It attacked political economy and argued that Christianity was incompatible with a system of trade and industry based wholly on the profit motive. It also stressed that socialism had to rest on Christian moral grounds of righteousness, sacrifice and fellowship, and that godless socialism was thus inherently unstable.

The one practical solution that the Christian Socialists did favour was the co-operative society, in which workers owned and profited from their work. The Rochdale Society of Equitable Pioneers had recently been founded, and the Christian Socialists helped establish some dozen workers' associations around London that were reasonably successful for a brief period. Ludlow energetically pursued the idea in the *Christian Socialist* but he also wanted the state to interfere directly in economic matters, and it was his frustration with Maurice's total unwillingness to commit himself to any concrete political action or recommendations that helped fracture the group after only six years. Ludlow wanted to implement a socialist agenda, politically if possible, whereas Maurice really wanted to Christianise socialism and socialise Christianity. The ultimate difference was over the nature of the kingdom of God. Maurice saw it as existing and merely awaiting recognition and participation, whereas Ludlow understood it as a goal to be achieved, by political means as well as personal. Eventually, assailed by criticism from without (he was dismissed from his chair at King's in 1853 for unorthodox views on hell) and division from within, Maurice stood away from the Christian Socialists to concentrate on education for working men, and the movement died in his wake.

In the immediate term, Maurice, Ludlow, Kingsley and their circle were largely ineffective. Given that, with the partial exception of

Ludlow, they had no programme to implement, however, this is not the criticism it might be. Their real success was partly in announcing to the Church and world that (established) Christianity could engage positively with socialist thought and working-class men, and partly in locating a theological framework that could serve to give justification and coherence to what had hitherto been a rather disorderly body of Christian radical thought.

'He meant us to do secular work in His name': the spread of socialist ideas

England saw no organized Christian Socialist group for nearly a quarter of a century after 1854. Maurice turned his attention from co-operatives to working men's education and Kingsley all but renounced his former socialist concerns. Only Ludlow remained active, supporting unions and taking part in the foundation of the Christian Social Union of 1889. More important than the individuals, however, were their ideas, which inspired and guided a number of late Victorian Christian 'socialists'. Three merit particular mention.

Hugh Price Hughes was the founder and editor of the *Methodist Times*, a celebrated preacher and one of the most influential Nonconformists of the late nineteenth century. Once described as 'a Day of Judgement in breeches', he wrote in his book *Ethical Christianity*: 'we have deadened our consciences and paralysed our energies by explaining away passages that refer to this present life.'[55] As far as he was concerned, Christ was one of 'the greatest revolutionists the world has ever seen',[56] and had come 'to reconstruct human society'.[57] Although not directly influenced by Maurice, he recognised that 'it will be impossible for us to evangelize the starving poor so long as they continue in a starving condition.'[58] He was thus concerned to promote social reform, listing in 1889 nine social evils 'against which we must wage ceaseless war', a list that prefigured Beveridge's five giants: pauperism, ignorance, drunkenness, lust, gambling, slavery, Mammonism, war and disease.[59] Rather than simply address this problem through personal and voluntary measures,[60] however, he recognised the need for a political response. 'A profound instinct has taught the masses of the people that if

Christianity is not applicable to politics, Christianity is an antiquated delusion,' he wrote in *Ethical Christianity*.[61]

Hughes's Christ, like Maurice's, was a safe radical, 'essentially a man of the people – a working man', who 'came to save the Nation as well as the Individual'.[62] His Christianity was personal *and* social. Only regenerate men could make 'Christian laws and Christian policies and Christian institutions', Hughes wrote in *Philanthropy of God*.[63] Yet the nation could not expect to see regenerate men emerge from unregenerate circumstances. Thus slum clearance was necessary, 'a part of true religion'. And if slum clearance was necessary, so was 'securing laws which will absolutely prohibit such buildings'. He urged London County Council to build houses and public baths for the poor and to break monopolies in the food trade that kept them impoverished and hungry. He drew the line, however, at 'warm clothes, [for which] the poor must help themselves'.[64]

Hughes was not shy of using legislation to reform the conditions in which people lived, reasoning that just as the Mosaic law had moralised the people of God, so could contemporary law work likewise. 'The statute-book is the national conscience,' he remarked in *Social Christianity*.[65] On occasion, he even hinted at the possibility of wealth redistribution. 'I am in favour of all legislative and social changes by which the fruits of human industry may be more widely distributed among the industrious.'[66] Hughes did, however, have serious doubts about the competence of the state and the materialist bent of much socialist thought, and was clear that his ultimate object lay way beyond the competence of politicians and legislators. 'Both the Bible and History teach me that the human race is not going to be evangelised either by Politicians or by Schoolmasters,' he wrote in *Philanthropy of God*.[67]

Hughes is the most prominent example of nonconformist Christian Socialism in the later nineteenth century. A fellow traveller, yet significantly different in many other ways, was Brooke Foss Westcott, a conservative biblical scholar who, from 1870, held the Chair of Divinity at Cambridge University. Chaplain to the queen from 1875 and a canon at Westminster Cathedral after 1883, Westcott was a thoroughly Anglican, thoroughly establishment figure and, as such, did more than almost anyone else to give Christian Socialist ideas public respectability. Westcott had limited knowledge of working-class conditions. He kept his distance from the reality of politics, had little interest in its details, and believed that legislation should be 'the last and not the first thing in social reform'.[68] Although he did not get on well with Maurice when they were both professors in the 1870s, his teaching – that the incarnation consecrated the material world, that all men were brothers, that endeavours in this world had lasting significance, that the kingdom of God was 'not simply the deliverance of individual souls [but] the establishment of a Divine Society' – had a distinctly Mauricean ring to it.[69]

Westcott was the first president of the Christian Social Union, an Anglican organisation, set up by himself, Charles Gore and Henry Scott Holland in 1889. The CSU avoided party politics and political commitments, preferring instead to analyse social problems and suggest broad principles in response. Accordingly, its direct political impact was minimal. However, its success and Westcott's importance lay in the way it spread and legitimised Christian Social thought through the established Church around the turn of the century. Despite being largely apolitical himself, Westcott, along with Gore and Scott Holland, was as responsible as anyone else for the dominant tone of Christian politics in much of the twentieth century.

A third figure, as different from Hughes and Westcott as they were from each other, was Stewart Duckworth Headlam. Born in 1847, he was educated at Eton and Cambridge where he attended lectures by Maurice. 'Long before the Fabian Society was founded I learnt the principles and was familiar with the title of "Christian Socialism" from Maurice and Kingsley,' he wrote later in his Fabian tract on Christian Socialism.[70] Headlam was ordained curate of St John's in Drury Lane in 1872 where he championed the cause of disreputable theatricals in a way that scandalised opinion and angered his bishop. The following year he moved to Bethnal Green where he immersed himself in the poverty of the East End, conditions in which many Anglo-Catholic priests of the time chose to live. Headlam was himself deeply influenced by Anglo-Catholicism and his social thought was shaped by its concerns, in particular the incarnation and the vision of the Church as an autonomous, spiritual society that embodied and enacted the life and work of Christ.

He had a talent for provocation. Quite apart from the disreputable thespian company he kept (including Oscar Wilde at time of his trial) he embraced Fabianism, was friendly with the atheist MP, Charles Bradlaugh, and publicly accepted the critical modernist approach to the Bible, not as scandalous a position as it had been two decades before but still controversial. He was prohibited from preaching in 1878, following a lecture defending theatrical art, and then had his licence removed altogether when he appeared on the same platform with the Irish republican Michael Davitt. This was a considerable blow given Headlam's Anglo-Catholicism but it did not significantly alter the course of his work. In 1877 he founded and became warden of the Guild of St Matthew, the first corporate Christian Socialist presence in England since 1854 and organised it into a national body with nearly 400 members by the early 1890s.

Headlam's writing and addresses for the guild were as Christ-focused as those of any nineteenth-century radical. Jesus was 'the social and political emancipator, the greatest of all secular workers, the founder of the great Socialistic society for the promotion of right-eousness, the preacher of a Revolution', he wrote in *The Sure Foundation*.[71] His teaching exhibited 'solidarity, brotherhood, co-operation, socialism'.[72] His miracles were fundamentally actions of social welfare, 'distinctly secular, socialistic works . . . for health against disease, [for] restoring beauty and harmony and pleasure where there had been ugliness and discord and misery'.[73]

Headlam tirelessly emphasised that Christ had had little to say about the afterlife, certainly in comparison with what he had to say about the present one. Christ's kingdom was undoubtedly an earthly rather than a purely spiritual one. His words 'tell of a Kingdom of Heaven to be set up upon earth, of a righteous Communistic Society'.[74] Those who deemed to call themselves Christians were called to go and do likewise. 'Christ meant us to be an organised society, to work for the physical as well as the moral and spiritual well-being of the Humanity He lived and died to save . . . He meant us to do secular work in His name,' Headlam wrote.[75] The Church existed 'for doing on a large scale throughout the world those secular, socialistic works for which Christ did on a small scale in Palestine'.[76] The Mass was a 'Feast of National Emancipation', baptism 'the great sacrament of equality'.[77]

Headlam thus combined three of the key streams of nineteenth-century Christian political thought: Jesus as radical, the earthly kingdom of God and the role of the Church. He was, however, rather more specific in his recommendations than most of his Christian Socialist peers. Unencumbered with institutional ties after being dismissed from his curacy, Headlam felt free to advocate specific, political ideas. He was vocal in his support of Henry George's 'Single Tax' scheme whereby the taxation of land would increase to the point at which the state was receiving the full value of an economic rent, which Headlam justified by reference to egalitarian land laws of early Israel. He joined the Land Reform Union because, as he liked to explain, 'the earth is the Lord's ... [and] therefore not the landlord's.'[78] He campaigned for an extended franchise, the repeal of blasphemy laws, disestablishment, universal secular education, collective bargaining and trades union rights, a minimum wage and a maximum working day, state redistribution of wealth and, latterly, better housing. Not without reason does the historian Edward Norman call Headlam, 'the first really serious Socialist, in the modern sense, in the Church' and his Guild of St Matthew, 'the first Christian body in England to achieve some real insight into the dynamics of Socialism'.[79]

Overall, Hughes, Westcott and Headlam give some indication of the gradual spread of Christian social thought in England around the turn of the nineteenth century. In many ways, this was no more unified or united than the Christian radicalism earlier in the century had been. But it was more widespread and more acceptable, if not yet quite respectable.

'Christianity and Socialism are almost interchangeable terms': Labour and the Labour Church

By the late 1890s most denominations had a socialist society and the nation had its first Christian Socialist MP. Keir Hardie was cut from very different cloth than Headlam or Hughes, let alone Westcott or Maurice, his poverty-stricken upbringing informing his Christianity rather than any formal theological education.[80] 'The more a man knows about theology, the less he is likely to know about Christianity,' he once commented.[81]

Brought up by atheist parents, Hardie converted in 1878. His Christianity, like his socialism, was formed by his brutal childhood, and accordingly was expressed in the tone of earlier Christian radicals. It was motivated by the vision of human equality, as articulated in Genesis. 'You are God's children,' he told a group of miners in 1885. 'Your work is mining but the blackest work to which a man may put his hand can never disguise or blot out the image of him in whose likeness he was made.'[82] This was thoroughly Lockean, not that Hardie would have known or cared. Moreover, just as Locke's reading of Genesis was filtered through the gospels, so was Hardie's. Towards the end of his life, in a talk delivered to strikers and their families entitled 'What Think ye of Christ?', he exhorted them, 'Oh, men and women, in the name of the God whom ye profess to believe in, in the name of Jesus of Nazareth who died to save your souls, how long do you intend to submit to a system which is defacing God's image upon you?'[83] Human equality was based on the redemption of God the Son as much as it was the creation of God the Father.

Although he spurned theological niceties, Hardie's socialist Christianity was explicitly biblical. His book *From Serfdom to Socialism* spoke admiringly about the Mosaic land laws, the ban on usury and Israel's treatment of debtors, remarking that although these 'cannot perhaps be described as socialistic in the modern sense of the word . . . they were quite as drastic in their way as are many of the socialistic proposals of our own day'.[84] He cited the prophets as beholding the tears of the oppressed and fighting fearlessly for their cause, arguing that 'clearly the modern system of wealth accumulation, which is rooted and grounded in land monopoly, usury, and the fleecing of the poor, finds no support in the Old Testament scriptures.'[85] Above all, like the Christian radicals before him, he placed enormous emphasis on Christ himself, *From Serfdom to Socialism* beginning with a discussion on the Sermon on the Mount. 'Christ recognised clearly that the possession of private property came between man and his welfare both for time and eternity,' Hardie warned.[86]

Hardie used such arguments to condemn the Church of his time, as radicals had done before him. Addressing the Congregational Union of England and Wales in 1893 he claimed that 'Christianity today lay buried, bound up in the cerements of a dead and lifeless theology. It awaited decent burial, and they in the Labour movement had come to resuscitate the Christianity of Christ, to go back to the time when the poor should have the gospel preached to them, and the gospel should be good news of joy and happiness in life.'[87] His address caused uproar but did nothing to weaken Hardie's hold on the parliamentary seat for West Ham that he had won the previous year.

Thus it was that, at the turn of the twentieth century, Christian radical ideas, filtered through the theology of the early Christian Socialists, and popularised by a range of Christian thinkers who otherwise would have agreed on little, were coming of age. 'I claim for Socialism that it is the embodiment of Christianity in our industrial system,' Hardie claimed, and although only few would have agreed with such a stark analysis the idea that the nation's industrial system badly needed to reflect better its Christianity was gaining ground.

It was, however, in precisely this triumph that there lay dangers for Christian politics. For provocateurs like Headlam, secularism, socialism and sacramental Christianity elided into one. 'In our view Christianity and Socialism are almost interchangeable terms,' opined the *Christian Socialist Journal*, which Headlam established, in 1883. Headlam and Hardie may have been unusually blunt in their association of Christianity with socialism, but the logic on which they drew was increasingly widely held. The kingdom of God slid, at least rhetorically, from being something that straddled life and afterlife to something that could, and should, be realised on earth as it is in heaven. Hell and heaven became descriptions of earthly rather than eternal states. The task of Christians moved from worship towards welfare.

Many radically minded Christians thought God was choosing to work through the secularists and socialists as a way of bringing about his kingdom because the Church itself had so abjectly failed in its task. One preacher carefully interpreted the parable of the vineyard in Matthew 20:1–14 in precisely this way. 'At the eleventh hour the Lord ... goes again to the market-place ... amongst the dregs of society, amongst those whom we call the enemies of society, that He may fetch forth real saviours and cultivators of society' – the dregs and enemies being the 'revolutionists', radicals, socialists and agitators, by whom 'society has been saved and quickened with new and fuller life.'[88]

All of which begged the question, what was the point of Christianity? If heaven and hell were simply earthly states; if Jesus' kingdom was entirely of this world; if God was working to establish his kingdom by the labour movement, or secularists, or any means other than his Church, why attend church? This problem was most clearly visible in the short-lived Labour Church, founded in 1891 by John Taylor, a Unitarian minister who had resigned to set up the movement on account of the failure of other Churches to support the Labour movement. The Labour Church was 'the Labour Movement in its religious aspect' and began with high hopes, a service of over 5,000 people accompanying the foundation of the Independent Labour Party in Bradford in 1893.[89]

Labour Church theology comprised the staple fare of Christian radicals and socialists: a focus on Jesus the radical, on human brotherhood, on the earthly reality of the kingdom of God and on the sense that God was immanent in the whole world. Like Hardie, it was deliberately anti-theological, seeing in theology the attempt to tame Christianity's radicalism and suppress its revolutionary potential. Christ, according to Sam Hobson's 1893 booklet, *Possibilities of the Labour Church*, 'was essentially a practical teacher' who made clear his 'detestation of mere theology'.[90]

The movement was also antipathetic to doctrine, the third of its five principles stating that 'the Religion of the Labour Movement is not Sectarian or Dogmatic, but Free Religion, leaving each man free to develop his own relations with the Power that brought him into being.'[91] Even this was too demanding for some members. 'Neither religious faith nor want of religious faith should debar any man from joining our ranks,' argued Fred Brocklehurst in the *Labour Prophet*.[92] When the Labour Church debated whether to retain reference to God in public pronouncements it chose to retain it, by eleven votes to nine.

In the fashion of the Chartist churches of fifty years earlier, the Labour Church designed and conducted its own services and published its own hymn books. Those books, although popular, contained few traditional hymns and rather more socialist songs and romantic poems, many of which were thoroughly pantheistic in tone. Its prayers and benedictions were short and vague. The churches rarely bothered with Christian rites of passage and when they did they were adapted to the particular concerns of the Labour movement. They eschewed priest, pulpit and ritual and sometimes Bible, prayers and sung worship too. Central organisation was kept to a minimum for fear of crushing free spirit. The motto of the *Labour Prophet*, the Church's journal, having originally been 'God is our King', was replaced, after four issues, with 'Let Labour be the basis of civil society'.

At its peak in 1893 the movement boasted about 100 Labour churches. By 1902 there were only twenty. This rapid de-Christianisation and decline was doubtless due to the fact that many members were Christians who had staggered through some form of Victorian crisis of faith, and reached for ethical socialism or the undemanding theology of the Labour Church movement as a way of keeping hold of their Christianity. But it was also due to the movement's ideological proximity to the Labour movement. The Labour Church drew its strength from the Independent Labour Party, which in 1894 recommended that all its branches should form Labour churches. Indeed, some Labour churches were established simply to get round the law forbidding political meetings on Sundays. As there was usually precious little to distinguish between the Labour Church and the Labour movement, there soon seemed little point in attending a Labour church.

The Labour Church was an extreme example of the perils that awaited (some) Christian politics in the twentieth century. Identify the kingdom of God too closely with worldly politics, and you would risk losing it altogether. Equate it with the coming socialist order, and you might end up being doubly disappointed. There were warning voices. The chairman of the Congregational Union delivered a warning address in 1894 entitled 'The Secularisation of the Pulpit'. Nevertheless, there was little doubt in which direction the wind was blowing. When Archbishop Frederick Temple addressed a deputation of trades' societies in 1900 he affirmed a scheme proposed by Charles Booth that the state should pay a pension of 5 shillings a week to everyone over the age of sixty-five.[93] He had reservations but they did little to mask the unprecedented sight of an Anglican archbishop arguing for state support for the elderly on theological grounds. The religious and political worlds were changing.

11

'The role of the State in Christian Society is to encourage virtue, not to usurp it': Negotiating a new landscape

The disintegration of the Labour Church movement sounded a warning to Christian Socialism in the 1890s, and the experience of Liberal politics chastened Nonconformity a decade later. But it was the experience of the First World War that was really to shock the nation's Christianity.

The Church, in particular the established Church, emerged from the conflict with a reputation for bellicose nationalism that was to scar it for decades. In some instances it was well earned. Arthur Winnington-Ingram, Bishop of London, regularly called the conflict a 'Holy War', to fight in which was an honour. Such war-mongering was not limited to the bishops. William Robertson Nicoll, editor of *British Weekly*, probably the most powerful voice in evangelical Nonconformity at the time, was equally bellicose, greeting the armistice with the headline, 'Beholding the fallen Satan'.[1] Christians across the denominations were caught up in and celebrated the militaristic nationalism of the hour.

Theirs were not the only voices, however. Bishop Edward Talbot of Winchester punctured the jingoistic mood by asking, 'Have we no sin with us, of materialism, of boastful confidence in force and wealth of unchristian dislike or contempt for other peoples?'[2] Charles Gore, by then Bishop of Oxford and something of an Anglican elder statesman, warned in a sermon preached a matter of weeks into the war, that although 'the Bible is full of patriotic emotion, [it is] even more conspicuous the Bible is full of a great warning against the sufficiency of patriotism.'[3] Most prominently, Randall Davidson, the Archbishop of Canterbury, studiously avoided sabre-rattling. Privately, he wrote to, and met with, Prime Minister Herbert Asquith to protest about bombing reprisals against civilians and the use of poison gas by

British forces. Publicly, he insisted that 'there does exist what our opponents deny, a higher law than the law of any state, a deeper allegiance that can be claimed by any earthly Sovereign.'[4] And yet, for all that Talbot, Gore and Davidson said, it was Winnington-Ingram who was remembered.

It was a similar story at the coal face. Hundreds of chaplains served alongside the men in the trenches. Many were highly esteemed and some became cult figures, most notably Geoffrey Studdert Kennedy, popularly known as Woodbine Willie for his endless supply of cigarettes. Yet by the 1920s Kennedy either was or was believed to be something of an exception. The popular post-war image of the chaplain was of someone who, at best, was part of the system that had resulted in slaughter or, at worst, had actively justified and encouraged it. The Church was seen as an instrument of the state, the rector as a recruiting sergeant. The conjunction of the Bible, Communion Table and Union Jack in almost every church in the country was deeply symbolic.

For the Church's part, the experience of war further eroded the belief in providence, as the seemingly inexorable military and economic success that had marked previous decades came to a grim halt. Just as alarming was the discovery that the nation's Christianity might be even more superficial than was feared. A report on the religion of trench soldiers, published in 1919, concluded that many felt that 'there is little or no life in the Church at all, that it is an antiquated and decaying institution, standing by dogmas expressed in archaic language, and utterly out of touch with modern thought and living experience.' The Churches, they believed, 'are more and more governed by the middle-aged and the elderly . . . [their] ministry professionalised and out of touch with the life of men, deferring unduly to wealth'. Most tellingly, they did 'not see any real differences in the strength and purity of life between the people who go to church and the people who do not'.[5] The problem facing the free Churches – too many Liberal politicians, too few nonconformist saints – was deeper and wider than the free Churches alone.

'In order to believe in human equality it is necessary to believe in God': between the wars

Recognising this motivated the established Church, not only to re-energise its evangelistic endeavours but also to engage in a form of politics that took greater account of the lives and needs of the working classes. During the war the Church commissioned a series of reports as part of a National Mission of Repentance and Hope, the last of which was entitled *Christianity and Industrial Problems* but widely known simply as 'the Fifth Report'.[6] It put forward five principal ideas: that Christian ethics were binding on social relations and not just on individuals; that true wealth lay not in material goods but in the quality of person; that personality is sacred; that service was a Christian duty; and that the Church should act corporately.

Although there was little that was radically new in these ideas, the report applied them in such a way that made it the clearest expression of its quasi-socialist approach to the nation's problems to date. Discussing unemployment, industry, education and labour, it advocated an economic system based on co-operation for public service rather than competition for private gain and argued that industry should make paying a living wage and providing for adequate leisure time its top priorities. 'An examination of the facts compels the conclusion that the existing industrial systems makes it exceedingly difficult to carry out the principles of Christianity,' remarked Archbishop Davidson in his preface.[7] The Fifth Report was a long way from the concrete proposals demanded by many, not least the record fifty-nine Labour MPs elected in 1918, but this was intentional. The Russian Revolution, the founding of the British Communist Party in 1920, the strengthening trades unions and the rise of Labour militancy terrified many Christians, helping to drive an already apolitical and intellectually weakened evangelicalism further from public life. In such circumstances what was remarkable about the Fifth Report and the tradition of Christian social thinking to which it gave the archiepiscopal imprimatur was not the benevolent vagueness for which it was criticised, but the fact that it was as socialist in tone as it was.

Precisely how socialist Christian social thinking should be or, more accurately, how that thinking should manifest itself, was to dog

Christian political thought throughout the inter-war period. On one side were those who saw co-operation as best implemented through small-scale, localised and voluntary activities. This thinking was led by the so-called 'Christendom movement', which saw in the thought and corporate life of the Middle Ages a model for the modern, industrialised world. Although not as naïve as the neo-medievalism favoured by some Tractarians, it fed on the same disenchantment with modernity, emotionally and aesthetically antipathetic to urbanisation, industry and commerce.

Christendom ideas spread across denominations but were particularly prevalent at the Catholic and Anglo-Catholic end, finding their ablest expositors in Hilaire Belloc and G.K. Chesterton. Belloc's influential pre-war book, *The Servile State*, argued that European civilisation had progressed from a pagan civilisation that had been based on two classes of people – property-owning free citizens and dispossessed slaves – through a period, roughly equated with the Middle Ages, in which slaves were transformed into serfs and serfs into small-holding peasants.[8] Subsequently, however, it had slid back into unfreedom as the Reformation and Industrial Revolution had deprived commoners of the property that ensured liberty and had pressed them into capitalist captivity.

Not surprisingly, Belloc did not see collectivism as a solution to this problem, its ambitions to centralise and control exacerbating the 'servility' imposed on people by capitalism. Only a decentralised system in which property and the means of production were widely dispersed among the mass of citizens would secure economic and political freedom. Christendom thinkers recognised, as did all major Christian social thinkers at the time, that co-operation rather than competition was what society needed. However, that co-operation needed to be small-scale and voluntary, modelled on the guild culture of the Middle Ages. The solution of centrally co-ordinated co-operative endeavours threatened to be worse than the problem, undermining the ability of individuals and groups to work meaningfully together in solving the problems they faced.

On the other side of the debate were those who favoured state intervention as a means of ensuring national co-operation. At the radical end were those clerics like Conrad Noel, vicar of Thaxted in

Essex, who spoke of 'Christ the communist', and Hewlett Johnson, the so-called 'Red Dean' of Canterbury, who was uncritical in his adulation of the Soviet Union, despite having been to Moscow twice.[9] These were extreme cases, however, whose extremism did not help the cause of Christian Socialism.

Far more influential were two men who arrived as schoolboys at Rugby on the same day, went up to Balliol College, Oxford, in the same year and remained friends for life, R.H. Tawney and William Temple. Tawney was the most politically influential lay Christian of the early twentieth century. Primarily an economic historian, he worked as a lecturer at the London School of Economics between 1917 and 1931, during which time he drafted the Church of England's Fifth Report, contributed to several Labour manifestos and wrote three immensely important books, *The Acquisitive Society* (1921), *Religion and Rise of Capitalism* (1926) and *Equality* (1931).[10]

Although he joined the Fabian Society in 1906 and the Independent Labour Party in 1909, Tawney did not share many socialist assumptions. In particular, he was convinced that the social and political problems that the nation faced were fundamentally moral and spiritual. Capitalism was wrong not because it was inefficient but because it was morally unacceptable, treating people as means (to profit) rather than as ends in themselves. The 'Commonplace Book' he kept before the First World War makes clear the Christian foundations of his socialism. 'The essence of all morality is this,' Tawney wrote in 1913, 'to believe that every human being is of infinite importance, and therefore that no consideration of expediency can justify the oppression of one by another.' This was not a self-evident truth. 'It is only when we realise that each individual soul is related to a power above other men, that we are able to regard each as an end in itself,' he insisted, concluding, 'in order to believe in human equality it is necessary to believe in God.'[11] This was the basis for Tawney's socialism, creating the conditions for 'the social order [to be] judged and condemned by a power transcending it', but it was also the basis for his socialist reservations. If the problem was spiritual at heart, political and economic reform could only ever be palliative. Failing to recognise that could lead to the cure being worse than the ailment.

To this extent, he was a fellow traveller with many Christendom

thinkers. However, he parted company from them in several important ways. His understanding of economic history prevented him
from embracing the sometimes rather naïve medievalism of
Christendom thinkers. He did not share their intense aesthetic
distaste for the trappings of the modern, industrialised world. Most
significantly, his experience of the First World War alerted him to the
possibility, indeed the necessity, for large-scale, co-ordinated social
action to deliver the kind of change that many of those who had
fought wanted.

Tawney believed that the contemporary 'acquisitive society' made
'the individual the centre of his own universe and dissolves moral
principles into a choice of expediencies'.[12] This was unacceptable
according to his Christian vision of objective human equality and
divine moral judgement. Instead, he understood property rights as
limited and contingent upon the discharge of public obligations. Just
as political power had been made accountable to the community, so
should economic power, wealth without function being transferred
'to bodies representing those who performed constructive work'.[13]
He sought, along with others within the Christian social tradition, to
provide the conditions by means of which all might have the opportunity to flourish morally and spiritually. Unlike most who had gone
before him, however, he believed it was necessary to use state intervention to create those conditions.

Tawney gave Christian Socialism the academic credentials that his
friend William Temple was willing to draw on. Born in 1881, the son
of Archbishop Frederick Temple and therefore the only man to
succeed his father in that role, Temple junior had a lifelong interest in
social Christianity. President of the Workers' Educational Association
from 1908, secretary to the National Mission of Repentance and
Hope in 1916, and subsequently Bishop of Manchester and
Archbishop of York, he gave Christian Socialism the ecclesiastical
credentials to match Tawney's intellectual testimonial.

He had to work hard. His leftish enthusiasms worried many in the
establishment, not least Churchill who chose him for Canterbury in
1942 not because he liked him or his politics (he didn't) but 'because
he was the only half-crown article in a sixpenny-halfpenny bazaar'.[14]
Temple was convinced that the kingdom of God was an earthly

phenomenon that demanded political action, as well as a spiritual reality that transcended earthly affairs. His early book, *The Kingdom of God*, published in 1914 when he was still headmaster of Repton, argued that the level of inequality in Britain was unacceptable. Although not concerned with outlining a political programme, there was little doubt where his theology led him. The Christian state ought to be 'socialistic'. 'Whether it will take the form of direct ownership, or of state control of privately owned capital' was, he claimed, 'irrelevant'.[15] The point was that the competition that underpinned the whole system was little more than 'organised self-ishness'.[16] Christian politics demanded that co-operation replace competition as the prime virtue, and there was no doubt which party did this.

Temple joined the Labour Party in 1918 but resigned on assuming the see of Manchester three years later. He lost none of his political vigour, however, and was the motivating power behind the Conference on Christian Politics, Economics and Citizenship (COPEC) in Birmingham in April 1924. This involved twelve commissions, each drafting a preparatory volume, which were then presented to, and discussed by, a total of 1,400 delegates from across the denomina-tions. The assembly, chaired by Temple, heard messages of encouragement from Ramsay MacDonald, Stanley Baldwin, Herbert Asquith and the king, together with a rather lukewarm one from Archbishop Davidson who was unimpressed with Temple's mission-ary zeal.

'We bear on our hearts the burden of unemployment, and in our consciences the challenge which tells us that where such things happen God's Kingdom is not yet come on earth as it is in heaven,' Temple proclaimed in his opening address.[17] The conference called 'on all Christian people to do all in their power to find and apply the remedy for recurrent unemployment', 'to press vigorously for . . . effi-cient housing schemes, whether centrally or locally', and 'to seek an immediate extension of education facilities' by increasing the school leaving age and reducing class sizes.[18] In this regard, it was clearly cut from the same cloth as the Church of England's Fifth Report or Temple's own lectures on the kingdom of God. Its significance was as a powerful symbolic demonstration that the Churches, while not exactly advocating a socialist agenda, were willing to support significant social reform.

Much of Temple's energy over the following years was devoted to ecumenism but he remained politically engaged. He organised a conference on Church, community and state at Oxford in 1937 and another at Malvern in January 1941, in which 200–300 Anglican clergy and laity discussed 'how Christian thought could be shaped to play a leading part in the reconstruction after the war is over'. Malvern made genuinely socialist noises. It passed proposals for the state provision of decent housing, family allowances, increased wages, milk and one meal a day at school, education to the age of eighteen, unemployment provision, representation for workers on the directorates through the unions and two days of rest per week. The ideas informed Temple's most significant publication, *Christianity and Social Order*, which sold 140,000 copies when published as a Penguin Special in 1942. In under 100 pages this set out primary and second principles for Christian politics. The former comprised the basic Christian story of God's purposes and humanity's 'dignity, tragedy and destiny', while the latter encompassed the ideas of freedom, social fellowship and service. The final chapter of the book laid out 'the principles by which the Christian tradition would lead us to direct human life', concluding with six 'objectives' that Christians were 'to call upon the Government to set before itself'.[19] The book's appendix then offered suggestions to achieve what Temple was careful to call '*a* Christian social programme'. Small wonder that Temple and his book were seen as major influences on William Beveridge's report on state welfare provision then being prepared. Temple was Beveridge's 'warm-up man', in the words of the (critical) historian Corelli Barnett.[20]

Eminent as they were, Temple and Tawney did not speak for all the Church of England, let alone all the churches of England. Members of the Christendom group, although playing an active part in COPEC and Malvern, were unhappy with, and often abstained from votes on, its resolutions. Some prominent Christian figures were more antagonistic still. Herbert Hensley Henson, the Bishop of Durham, denounced COPEC and insisted that the world could be redeemed only through the redemption of individuals. Lord Hugh

Cecil, an influential Anglican layman and Conservative politician, argued that Christ was not a social reformer and that 'there is immense difficulty in applying the teaching of revealed religion directly to the problems of social and political organisation.'[21] Such criticisms notwithstanding, there was no doubt that the social Christianity of Tawney and Temple was now the dominant feature on the Christian political landscape.

'I would always stress the spiritual rather than the political foundations of democracy': defending Christian civilisation

Today is Trinity Sunday. Centuries ago words were written to be a call and a spur to the faithful servants of Truth and Justice: 'Arm yourselves, and be ye men of valour, and be in readiness for the conflict; for it is better for us to perish in battle than to look upon the outrage of our nation and our altar. As the Will of God is in Heaven, even so let it be.'[22]

So ended Winston Churchill's first broadcast to the nation as Prime Minister, on 19 May 1940. The text he quoted to rouse his people was from 1 Maccabees 3:58–60, a book confined to the English Apocrypha since the Reformation. It was not his only biblical excursion. In an address to the nation two months later he intoned how 'bearing ourselves humbly before God, but conscious that we serve an unfolding purpose, we are ready to defend our native land . . . Here in this strong City of Refuge which enshrines the title-deeds of human progress and is of deep consequence to Christian civilisation; here . . . we await undismayed the impending assault.'[23] Visiting Coventry after the city was annihilated in November 1940 he quoted Hosea 8:7: 'They have sown the wind, they shall reap the whirlwind.' To the Commons the following January he spoke about 'the whole English-speaking world are passing through a dark and deadly valley', recalling Psalm 23.[24] Churchill knew his Bible.

That Bible, however, was a mine of rhetorical rather than religious inspiration. Churchill lost his cradle Christianity early on and passed through 'a violent and aggressive anti-religious phase', which, he said, 'had it lasted, might have made me a nuisance'.[25] The fact that it did not last he put down to his 'frequent contact with danger', in which, 'whatever I might think and argue, I did not hesitate to ask for special protection.' Those experiences did not lead him back to Christianity. His wartime secretary, John Colville, noted that a Westminster Abbey sermon of September 1940, at which Churchill was present, 'contain[ed] much alliteration, many fiery denunciations, a good deal of politics and no Christianity – which was what Winston had come to hear.'[26] Instead, Churchill's regained faith was in a providential God with a general interest in England and a particular interest in Winston Churchill. When staying with Herbert Asquith in October 1911 he was invited to become First Lord of the Admiralty. Churchill described how, later that evening, he turned to a Bible that happened to be on the table in his room and opened it at random only to discover a passage from Deuteronomy 9 in which God assures the Israelites of victory. 'It seemed,' he wrote, 'a message full of reassurance.'[27] Destiny, history, civilisation and providence merged and found their climax in a story in which Churchill was the lead player.

Christianity played a key part in that story. 'What General Weygand called the Battle of France is over. I expect that the Battle of Britain is about to begin. Upon this battle depends the survival of Christian civilisation,' Churchill told the House of Commons in his 'Finest Hour' speech on 18 June 1940.[28] He was not alone in this talk of Christian civilisation. Indeed, such rhetoric had played an increasingly important role as the 1930s had proceeded. Stanley Baldwin, three times Prime Minister in the inter-war years, said in 1934 that 'if freedom has to be abolished and room has to be made for the slave state, Christianity must go because slavery and Christianity cannot live together.'[29] This was not simply political opportunism. 'I would always stress the spiritual rather than the political foundations of democracy,' Baldwin told a Congress on Education for Democracy in New York in August 1939, having left power. 'It is a recognition of the dignity of man and of his individuality, and that dignity and individuality are his as a child of God.'[30]

Lord Halifax, a prominent Anglo-Catholic Conservative who was close to Baldwin, published a selection of his speeches and broadcasts in August 1940, which sounded a similar note. Arnold Toynbee lectured in the Sheldonian Theatre at Oxford on 'Christianity and Civilisation' in May 1940. *The Times* visited the subject in several editorials during the year. The Ministry of Information told its Religious Division to impart 'a real conviction of the Christian contribution to our civilisation and of the essential anti-Christian character of Nazism'.[31] The 'crusade' in defence of Christian civilisation was central to the story that the British told themselves about the war.

Perhaps ironically, the Churches were among the quieter voices in this chorus. The country observed several Days of National Prayer and Thanksgiving to mark the various crises and supposed deliverances in the run up to, and early years of, the war. But, as a rule, the Churches were notable for their reluctance to bang the military drum. Haunted by memories of the First World War and stung by the criticism of their conduct in that conflict, churchmen sought to avoid war at almost any cost.

Moreover, the way in which European fascists played the anti-'Godless Communist' card made the more conservative churchmen particularly reluctant to condemn them. Few clerics actively supported Hitler but equally few stood out resolutely against him. Only those who were really well informed about the state of Germany, like Arthur Jones, Dean of Chichester, took a firm stance against the regime. Jones sent telegrams to the archbishops of Canterbury and York following Munich asking them 'to voice the conscience of England in protest against the most shameful betrayal in English history'.[32]

Chichester was also to provide the most antagonistic ecclesiastical stance during the war. Its bishop, George Bell, had been Randall Davidson's chaplain during the Great War and was influenced by the archbishop's conduct. Bell was convinced that the Church was not the state's 'spiritual auxiliary', as he put it in a 1939 article on 'The Function of the Church in Wartime', going on to say that it 'must not hesitate, if occasion arises, to condemn the infliction of reprisals, or the bombing of civilian populations, by the military forces of its own nation'.[33] This is precisely what Bell did, making a principled and unpopular stand against the British obliteration bombing campaign. Few bishops actually approved of the campaign – Bishop Mervyn

Haigh of Coventry was the exception and many thought he was unduly influenced by what had happened to his own city – but few actively opposed it. Archbishop Lang denounced the deliberate targeting of civilians in 1941 when it was a largely theoretical issue and Temple took a similar view, although he was prepared to accept the official line that this was not government policy. Bell, by contrast, was vehement and uncompromising in his opposition, writing in *The Times* in April 1941 that it was 'barbarous to make unarmed women and children the deliberate object of attack'. He made the same point, more forcefully still, in the House of Lords on 4 February 1944, in a speech that was to become his legacy.[34] 'George,' Bell's friend Lord Woolton told him beforehand, 'there isn't a soul in this House who doesn't wish you wouldn't make the speech you are going to make . . . But I also want to tell you that there isn't a soul who doesn't know that the only reason that you make it, is because you believe it is your duty to make it as a Christian priest.'[35]

Expediency, Bell argued, was simply not the issue. Even if obliteration bombing were to shorten the war or break German morale (Bell did not think it would) 'to justify methods inhumane in themselves by arguments of expediency smacks of the Nazi philosophy that Might is Right.' The war was a war of ideologies not of people and must therefore be won ethically as well as militarily. The Allies stood for something greater than power. 'The chief name inscribed on our banner is "Law".' Only by using power that 'is always under the control of law' could the Allies hope to win. 'Why is there this blindness to the psychological side?' he concluded aggressively. 'Why is there this inability to reckon with the moral and spiritual facts? Why is there this forgetfulness of the ideals by which our cause is inspired?'[36]

Bell was hardly typical of the bishops. Indeed, he made his speech partly because Temple did not. Churchill detested him and denied him Canterbury when Temple died. But he is nevertheless symbolic of the more qualified stance that the Churches took in relation to the Second World War, just as the equally atypical Arthur Winnington-Ingram of London was symbolic of the ecclesiastical attitude to the earlier conflict. The Churches were as determined as Churchill, Baldwin or Halifax to see the nation's Christian civilisation defended.

But although they were in little doubt as to the justness of the cause, they did not wave the flag with quite the same instinctive vigour as they had a generation earlier.

'The Church's function is best exercised not by passing judgements': another reformation of manners

Much of the wartime discussion of Christian civilisation focused on the need to protect it from internal threats as well as external. In its leader of 17 February 1940 *The Times* declared it would be of little use to fight 'as we are fighting today . . . at immense cost to safeguard religion against attack from without if we allow it to be starved and neglected from within'.[37] Toynbee, lecturing in Oxford, spoke of how the nation had been living on reserves of spiritual capital for a number of generations, clinging to Christian practice without possessing Christian belief, and that the next generation was beginning to discover the cost of this 'wasting asset'. George Orwell was more succinct. 'We have got to be children of God,' he wrote in *Time and Tide* in April 1940, 'even though the God of the Prayer Book no longer exists.'[38]

In the initial post-war period such concerns seemed exaggerated. The 1950s witnessed something of a Christian renaissance, with C.S. Lewis, T.S. Eliot, W.H. Auden, Graham Greene and Dorothy Sayers pre-eminent in literature, Maurice Powicke, E.F. Jacob, May McKisack, Richard Southern and Lewis Namier in (especially medieval) history, and Donald MacKinnon, Elizabeth Anscombe, Peter Geach and Michael Dummett in philosophy. The Church presided over the coronation in 1953, as it had every coronation for over 1,000 years, reasserting its position at the heart of national life, newly affirmed and bound together by an ancient Christian ceremony. The immediate post-war Labour government established a 'welfare state', whose ambitions appeared to be the fulfilment of Christian social thought and whose very name was first coined by William Temple.[39] The succeeding Conservative government was largely supportive and although without obvious debt to Christian social thought, was thoroughly Anglican in composition, including Harold Macmillan, Rab Butler, Viscount Hailsham, Alexander

Douglas-Home, Edward Heath, Walter Monckton and Enoch Powell. Such factors, combined with the enormous publicity and apparent success of the Billy Graham mission in 1954, seemed to indicate that the nation's Christianity, and political Christianity within it, was secure and earlier fears about wasting spiritual capital ill-founded.

It was not so. Beneath the apparently tranquil surface of a gentle Christian renaissance, British religion was far more fragile than was assumed. Congregation sizes, having slipped in most nonconformist denominations for a generation, began to fall precipitously across the board, only the Catholic Church resisting the trend and even then only for a generation. The cultural Christianity about which clergy had fretted for generations had a precarious hold on the people. The passing of the 'pagan' German threat took with it the rhetoric of needing to protect and preserve Christian civilisation. The emergence of a welfare state effectively disinherited the Churches of their historical role in welfare provision, leaving Christianity a religion whose social functions now clustered round a limited number of personal rites of passage. Perhaps most importantly, an unprecedented and rapid rise in affluence further eroded its apparent relevance just as it loosened the social bonds that had kept the nation together.

A new generation of political leaders emerged, whose formation and worldview owed little to Christianity except in so far as they saw in it, and in establishment Christianity in particular, a force of reaction against which they fought. This was most obviously so in the Labour government of the 1960s, which was not only profoundly different from its Conservative predecessor but also from Attlee's government of the 1940s. Harold Wilson may have had slightly more religious feeling than Clement Attlee but those with whom he surrounded himself had rather less than Attlee's peers. Hugh Gaitskell, Aneurin Bevan, Anthony Crosland, Richard Crossman and Roy Jenkins replaced George Lansbury, Arthur Henderson, Stafford Cripps and James Chuter Ede.

It is not entirely clear how far it was this change in political personnel that was responsible for the epochal social legislation of the 1960s, or how far the legislation was simply catching up with a culture that had changed beyond recognition without anyone in the much-derided establishment actually noticing.[40] Either way, the significance of the decade is not debated. In an astonishingly short period of time, the more or less Christian legislative framework for personal behaviour that had shaped the nation's morals for decades, and in some cases centuries, was swept aside. Betting and Gaming Acts in 1960 and 1968 allowed off-course betting shops, bingo halls and commercial casinos to be set up, and led to a vast increase in gambling. The 1961 Suicide Act decriminalised the taking of one's own life. The 1965 Murder Act suspended the practice of capital punishment for murder for five years before it was finally abolished in 1969. The 1967 Sexual Offences Act decriminalised homosexual activity in private between consenting males aged over twenty-one. The 1967 Abortion Act legalised abortion up to twenty-eight weeks when it had been entirely illegal for a century and a half. The long-standing role of the Lord Chamberlain in censoring theatrical productions was abolished in 1968. The following year the Divorce Reform Act expanded the limited criteria under which divorce had been permitted, essentially adultery, desertion, cruelty and insanity, in the process intending 'to eliminate fault and guilt as the basis of divorce'.[41] Although the reforming zeal passed with the first Wilson government, the direction was set and led, in time, to further liberalisation of laws surrounding blasphemy, gambling, homosexual practice, credit and Sunday trading. In the words of Andrew Holden who charted the social legislation of post-war Britain in meticulous detail: 'in 1945 the criminal law largely reflected traditional Judeo-Christian morality in the context of the rapidly industrialising society of late Victorian Britain, when laws concerning abortion, marriage and divorce, the protection of children, homosexuality, alcohol and licensing were all stiffened by the rising affluence of religious, and particularly nonconformist, moral concern.'[42] A generation later it did not.

This unprecedented and unprecedentedly rapid reformation of manners was seen by many to tear up centuries of Christian legislation. Many Christians objected. Had not Christ said, 'whosoever shall put away his wife, except it be for fornication, and shall marry another, committeth adultery'?[43] Had not God commanded, 'Whoso sheddeth man's blood, by man shall his blood be shed'?[44] Such proof-texting was limited to the political periphery, however. Those who campaigned most vigorously against the reforms recognised that direct biblical appeals would have only the most limited appeal and preferred instead to talk about public decency, responsibility and morality. Foremost among them was Mary Whitehouse who came to prominence with her 'Clean up TV' campaign in 1963. Through a series of meetings, petitions, campaigns and private prosecutions, Whitehouse and her National Viewers' and Listeners' Association campaigned fiercely and in the face of much ridicule against public obscenity, bad language and pornography, becoming the public face of the Christian response to the 1960s social earthquake. Iconic as she may have been, Whitehouse's was not the only or even the typical Christian response to the legislative changes. In a sense, she was to the 1960s and 1970s what Arthur Winnington-Ingram was to the 1910s or George Bell to the 1940s. In actual fact, relations between her organisation and the mainstream Churches were usually tense and often acrimonious. The Churches were often appalled by the apocalyptic language and tone of moral superiority adopted by the NVLA, while it, in turn, was exasperated by the (usually Anglican) ecclesiastical unwillingness to adopt a hard line on such obviously clear-cut moral issues.[45] Thus, Michael Ramsey's secretary was horrified by and instantly declined the invitation for the archbishop to support the vividly named Campaign for National Disgust in 1971.

It was not that Ramsey or many other leading figures from the Anglican, Catholic or nonconformist Churches liked or supported the programmes or publications that so enraged the NVLA. Rather, they saw the issue differently in two key ways. The first was over the question of the appropriate *ecclesiastical* response to the social upheavals. In a statement made to the British Council of Churches in April 1971 Ramsey remarked: 'I believe that the Church's function is best exercised not by passing judgements on particular incidents. It is not for the Church to have an index of prohibited books or films. It is the Church's function to state the Christian moral principles which bear upon present problems and to expose the trends which make for evil.'[46] The Church, in particular the established Church, was not to function like a campaigning organisation but rather to draw attention to the moral conceptions and misconceptions that formed the culture in which obscene films and publications were created and consumed.

The second difference between Church and campaigners was that the former was more acutely aware of the plural nature of contemporary British society. Thus, just as the Churches had been a little reluctant to join the 'Christian civilisation' chorus of the 1940s, they were reluctant to join the 'Christian culture' chorus of the 1960s and 1970s. This was evident in their response to a number of the social reforms of the time. In some instances, such as the reformation of gambling laws or abortion, their response was both antagonistic and largely unified. In others, there was a studied balance that reflected the Churches' understanding of social change. Thus, although suicide had long been understood in Christian theology as an act of rebellion against God, wilfully destroying what he had graciously given, its decriminalisation was supported by churchmen. Both archbishops and the majority of Lords Spiritual spoke *for* the Sexual Offences Bill when it came before the Lords in 1965 and Michael Ramsey was even a vice-president of the Homosexual Law Reform Society. Giving evidence to a Joint Select Committee on the abolition of theatre censorship, the Church of England concluded that 'it would be morally healthy for the nation both if responsibility for maintaining standards were transferred to the theatrical profession itself and also if the adult population were faced with the choice of condemning by withholding patronage.'[47]

It was not that clerics had decided to throw in the moral towel and simply go with the flow or that they had renounced theology in favour of market mechanisms as the only legitimate means of ethical adjudication. Rather, established clergymen in particular recognised that it was no longer appropriate, if it ever had been, to enforce specifically Christian morality by law. Thus, the Wolfenden Committee, whose 1957 report so influenced the Sexual Offences Act, drew on the report of the Church of England Moral Welfare Council published in 1952 entitled *The Problem of Homosexuality*, which outlined the difference between sin and criminality.[48] Homosexual practice was an offence according to traditional Christian morality and should be treated as a sin, but that did not make it a crime even in a country so formed by that Christian moral vision. In a similar way, the report of Archbishop Ramsey's group on divorce law reform, *Putting Asunder*, recognised that 'in a modern plural society the concept of human law is very different from that which is obtained when the traditional theology of law was being formulated', and therefore recommended that 'breakdown of marriage' be substituted for 'matrimonial offence'.[49] In both instances, Church statements recognised that British society was not Christian, or at least not in the way that it had long been held to be.

The significance for Christian politics of the social and moral upheavals of the 1960s and beyond was not so much in the shift from a Christian to a utilitarian framework, from the idea that law should be rooted in a Christian concept of virtues to the idea that it should be rooted in the 'no harm' principle. Instead, it was in the implicit and sometimes explicit recognition that national and Christian ethics could no longer be seen as coterminous. The nation was morally plural now. The law needed to recognise this and get out of the business of making people good and into the business of permitting them to express themselves in whatever way they saw fit, providing it didn't 'harm' other people, whatever that meant. The enormity of that change for a nation that had been formed over the centuries on Christian principles seemed hard to overstate: hence the angry and horrified response from many Christians and social conservatives. In reality, it often *was* overstated. What was undone in the 1960s was not, in fact, Christian morality per se so much as a particular brand of high Victorian Christian morality. Nonetheless, the forced recognition of the newly pluralised moral landscape was traumatic for many, who viewed it as little short of calamitous.

'Something else had gone wrong spiritually': political reinvigoration

So it was that about three-quarters of the way through the twentieth century the influence of the Bible on national politics was in an unfamiliar place. Although clearly present, it was wholly submerged, guiding and informing certain political players rather than intruding into open debate. Such submersion was both necessary and appropriate, but it risked a form of cultural amnesia in which the fundamental principles on which political ethics rested were ignored and forgotten, before finally being dismissed as irrelevant.

The direction in which biblical reflection on social and political issues had guided many over the previous half-century and more was towards a welfare state. This was now firmly established and widely supported by Christian leaders. 'Christians should welcome [it as] the embodiment of the principle, "Bear ye one another's burdens and so fulfil the law of Christ",' wrote Cyril Garbett, Archbishop of York. There was, however, a concern that dogged this moment of triumph. The apparent success with which the welfare state fed the hungry, housed the homeless and healed the sick removed from the Church many of its historic responsibilities, in the process blunting its political edge, which had always been defended and justified by its immense social presence. Biblical reflection, particularly on themes of equality, dignity, co-operation and service, had drawn many towards the solution of a co-ordinated welfare settlement, but that settlement threatened to make redundant the Christian politics that had informed it.

If the precise function of Christian politics was thus under question, the Christian culture in which it was situated was seeping away. The reforms of the 1960s had dismantled legislation that confirmed, in its breach if not honour, that the nation was Christian. If Christian doctrine, as understood by most leading churchmen, was now embodied by the state's economic policies, it was now ignored in its personal, moral stance. Personal liberty replaced Christian morality as the lodestar. The result was that Christian politics often adopted a siege mentality, either content with or uninterested in welfare politics, and animated primarily by the social and moral reformation that was going on around it. The reputation that Christians were interested solely in questions of sex, Sabbath and censorship was formed.

Wider trends were more ominous still. Church attendance was now reporting year-on-year falls. Sociologists confidently predicted the imminent demise of religion worldwide. Evangelicalism remained intellectually defensive and politically cocooned. Theological liberalism grabbed headlines, proclaiming the need to update doctrine so that it remained relevant or announcing the death of God altogether, in so doing helping to enervate still further the Christian capacity for political critique. Only Roman Catholicism remained numerically steady and theologically invigorated, in the process generating a level of political engagement that had been largely absent for centuries. Beyond that, few in 1970 would have predicted a vibrant future for Christian politics.

And yet the fourth quarter of the twentieth century did not go quite the way that many living at the end of the third assumed it would. There was a slow but perceptible change in the theo-political climate that was part of a much broader set of trends, as religion emerged as a major political force globally, the post-war welfare consensus broke apart and the direction of British history shifted towards pluralism rather than secularism. Given the size and complexity of these trends, the slow reinvigoration of domestic Christian politics cannot be ascribed to any one single phenomenon or individual. Nor, however, can it be divorced from individuals, and especially not from Margaret Thatcher.

Thatcher was brought up in a devout, evangelical Methodist home. Her theological interests remained long into her premiership. Asked by the journalist Hugo Young in 1983 what she was reading, she replied, 'Right now I'm re-reading *The Ten Commandments*, by the Archbishop of York . . . I'm always trying to read a *fundamental* book . . . I read quite a lot of theological work.'[50] Five years later she resolved to read the Old Testament through, informing her staff of her progress and admitting that she had found it rather 'gory'.[51] Biographers have differed over how much Christianity influenced her politics. As far as she was concerned the answer was a great deal. 'I never thought that Christianity equipped me with a political philosophy,' she told an audience at St Lawrence Jewry in 1977, but 'it did equip me with standards to which political actions must, in the end, be referred.' Her 'whole political philosophy' was 'based' on 'what are often referred to as "Judaeo-Christian"' values.[52]

It was not so much Thatcher's theological interests or literacy that helped refashion the theo-political landscape, however, as her repeated insistence on exposing the moral foundations beneath politics, in the process questioning the form they had taken for a generation or more. In her first conference address as Conservative Party leader in 1975 she carefully placed the country's economic situation, 'serious as [it] is', in a wider, moral context. 'Economic problems never start with economics,' she said. 'They have much deeper roots in human nature.'[53] 'I was not going to make just an economic speech,' she later wrote. 'The economy had gone wrong because something else had gone wrong spiritually and philosophically.'[54]

That 'going wrong' was a drifting away from the virtues that, in her mind, were embedded in the Judaeo-Christian religion, specifically the nonconformist Christianity in which she had grown up. These were 'hard work, self-reliance, thrift, enterprise' and 'self-discipline, responsibility, pride in and obligation to one's community'.[55] Thatcher understood that such public virtues were not free-floating but rested on, and were shaped by, their spiritual foundations. 'Freedom will destroy itself if it is not exercised within some sort of moral framework, some body of shared beliefs, some spiritual heritage,' she told St Lawrence Jewry. For Britain that framework was Christianity. 'Christian religion . . . is a fundamental part of our national heritage . . . we are a nation whose ideals are founded on the Bible.'[56]

She was clear that those foundational biblical ideals were not monolithic but comprised a delicate balance. 'There are two very general and seemingly conflicting ideas about society which come down to us from the New Testament,' she observed. One was 'that great Christian doctrine that we are all members one of another expressed in the concept of the Church on earth as the Body of Christ, [from which] we learn our interdependence.' The other was that 'we are all responsible moral beings with a choice between good and evil, beings who are infinitely precious in the eyes of their Creator.'[57] It was from this delicate theological balance that Christian politics was formed. Acknowledge this as she did, and protest that she did not believe 'that Socialist theory and Socialist practice as we know them are contrary to the New Testament', it was clear that Thatcher saw the scales tilted very heavily in one direction. 'I wonder whether the State services would have done as much for the man who fell among thieves as the Good Samaritan did for him?' she asked pointedly.[58]

Thatcher's Christianity stood outside the long-dominant tradition of social Christianity. It took its cue from and resembled the political evangelicalism of the nineteenth century. Christianity taught her that 'what mattered fundamentally was Man's relationship to God, and in the last resort this depended on the response of the individual soul to God's Grace.'[59] 'The fundamental purpose on earth is to improve your own human nature and disposition,' she told the *Catholic*

Herald in 1978.[60] This was the theological foundation of her politics, much as it had been for the Saints and other political evangelicals. The individual stood before God responsible for the conduct of his or her own life. It was this that bred discipline, industry, pride and responsibility. In as far as the more corporate reading of Christianity as translated into socialist politics interfered with this, it not only wrecked the nation's economy but it morally infantilised its people and, presumably, endangered their spiritual health. 'The role of the State in Christian Society is to encourage virtue, not to usurp it.'[61]

Although chary of assuming the pulpit too often, not least after she had entered Downing Street, she never hid her Christian convictions and was willing on occasion to engage in what amounted to full-on biblical exposition. The most famous instance of this was her so-called 'Sermon on the Mound', a speech to the General Assembly of the Church of Scotland in May 1988 where she made an extraordinarily explicit *apologia* for her beliefs. 'Speaking personally as a Christian', she began by outlining three 'distinctive marks' of Christianity; three marks which, in good Christian fashion, were actually one.

> First . . . from the beginning man has been endowed by God with
> the fundamental right to choose between good and evil . . . second,
> that we were made in God's own image and, therefore, we are
> expected to use all our own power of thought and judgement in
> exercising that choice . . . and third, that Our Lord Jesus Christ,
> the Son of God, when faced with His terrible choice and lonely
> vigil chose to lay down His life that our sins may be forgiven.[62]

Christianity, as Thatcher told John Humphrys who had tried to catch her out in a pre-election radio interview the previous year, was fundamentally about choice.[63] The speech proceeded to explain that the Christian faith was founded on the acceptance of 'the sanctity of life, the responsibility that comes with freedom and the supreme sacrifice of Christ', and not 'because we want social reforms and benefits or a better standard of behaviour'. Quoting the gospels twice,[64] St Paul twice[65] (and alluding to him a third time),[66] the book of Leviticus once[67] and the Ten Commandments (twice),[68] referring to the Genesis creation narrative,[69] C.S. Lewis, an unnamed preacher and two hymns,[70] the address was remarkable, even by Margaret Thatcher's standards.

Thatcher herself was not solely responsible for the reinvigoration in Christian politics in the last years of the century, but the manner in which she repeatedly drew attention to the moral and spiritual foundations of politics did help catalyse the process. Perhaps ironically, this became most immediately obvious within Christian political thought itself or, more precisely, in the way in which the Churches, most famously the Church of England, offered a critical, theologically grounded response to Margaret Thatcher's own policies. Anglican bishops were not naturally hostile to the Thatcherite emphasis on personal responsibility and wealth creation, and Archbishop Robert Runcie was not an instinctively antagonistic or even an instinctively political figure. However, the established Church reacted against the theo-political imbalance it detected in Thatcherism and Runcie, who was inclined to find moral complexity in most issues, became an irritant to Thatcher's own moral clarity.

Tension between government and Church began early, and rapidly reached a low point when Runcie spoke about the grief of Argentinian as well as British mourners during the Falklands War thanksgiving service at St Paul's Cathedral in July 1982.[71] The Church subsequently challenged the government's refusal to apply economic sanctions against South Africa, spoke out in favour of the striking miners and played a key role in the coalition that defeated the 1986 Shops Bill which sought to deregulate Sunday trading (a bill that would have scandalized many nineteenth-century Nonconformists). It was, however, the Church's opposition to the government's economic policies that drew greatest attention. Interviewed in *The Times* in October 1984, Runcie offered measured support for policies of economic growth but insisted that 'if the human consequences of such aims mean unemployment on an unprecedented scale, poverty, bureaucracy, despair about the future of our communities, [and] inequitable sharing of the sacrifice called for, then the objectives must be called into question.'[72] Such opposition, magnified by the failure and disarray of the official opposition at the time, captured the front pages the following year with the publication of *Faith in the*

City, the report of the Archbishop's Commission on Urban Priority Areas set up in the wake of the 1981 Brixton riots.

The furious government response – Thatcher declared herself 'absolutely shocked' and one unnamed Cabinet minister described it as 'pure Marxist theology' – kept the report on the front pages for four days and helped it sell 83,000 copies.[73] In reality, although the report claimed that Marxist-flavoured liberation theology 'represents a challenge to us to look again at our own theological priorities', its theological analysis was limited, measured and almost timid, certainly in comparison with Thatcher's own.[74]

The report sought, in essence, to rebalance Thatcher's theological scales by emphasising the first of her 'general and seemingly conflicting ideas about society' derived from the New Testament, the one that had, they felt, been unduly ignored in government policies. It highlighted 'the concern for social justice and for the protection of the weak which pervades the Old Testament, and the repeated New Testament call to "share one another's burdens"'. This, it argued, 'authorize[d]' the Church 'to challenge the slogan of "efficiency"'. It compelled it to question 'the moral and spiritual effects of the modern consumer economy . . . [which came] perilously close actually to encouraging the sin of covetousness'.[75] In effect, the report argued, it was a narrow and harmful reading of the Bible that underpinned and justified, at least in Thatcher's mind, socially destructive economic policies.

The publication and popularity of *Faith in the City* did not mean that the Bible had surfaced from its long political submersion. The report was still empirical and technical in its focus – it would hardly have had the effect it did had it not been – and it was still couched largely in the language of 'public reasoning'. Its 'Theological Priorities' section came early on and was limited to twenty-two pages out of nearly 400. The biblical content of the report was deliberately flexible.[76] The theological tone was considerably less sermon-like than it was accused of being. In this regard it was entirely representative of the Church's wider political interventions in the 1980s. A study of the contributions made by bishops in the House of Lords during the Thatcher years found that 7 per cent of episcopal contributions in the House referred explicitly to biblical material and only

1 per cent did what the Sermon on the Mound had done, and engaged in a detailed examination of scripture.[77] Not even its critics – and there were many – could accuse the bishops of Bible-bashing.

The reinvigorated Christian politics of the 1980s was not, therefore, a return to early modern times in which the chamber resounded to the sound of Old Testament prophets. Nor, indeed, was it a sign that the nation was reversing the trends of the previous two decades and becoming more Christian. The 1980s saw pews emptying at a faster rate than even the 1960s and 1970s. Rather, *Faith in the City*, like many other Christian interventions in the decade, and like the dominant political figure of that decade herself, represented an ideological pluralising of society. By insisting that political and economic problems were at heart moral ones, and moral problems were at heart spiritual ones, Thatcher directed public attention to politics' hidden foundations. Perhaps ironically, given her own firm conviction that the nation was thoroughly Christian in its formation and ethos, that process inadvertently highlighted the fact that others, even Christian others, disagreed with her, either about the nation's Christian ethos or about what, if any, role it should play in contemporary politics.

The economic confrontation of the 1980s did what Church documents like *Putting Asunder* had done, albeit in a different context a decade earlier, and openly recognised that British and Christian morality were no longer one and the same. The political economic differences that ran through the nation were not now simply questions of which lever should be pulled in Whitehall to maintain the welfare state on its (divinely sanctioned) course, any more than the political moral ones were questions of what definition of adultery was sufficient to justify divorce. They were more profound, relating to fundamental questions of what is the state actually for, what role should competition and co-operation have in public life and, beneath them all, what is the objective of human life.

In the immediate term those differences of opinions would become less acute, at least in the economic realm, as the policies of John Major's administration elided into those of a New Labour one without obvious upheaval. But the intrusion of wider considerations – the fundamental moral challenges placed by medical and reproductive technological advances; by environmental degradation and the way we conceive humanity's role within creation; by terrorism and security threats and the temptation they offer to adopt an unduly authoritarian or military response; by devolution and unprecedentedly large-scale immigration and questions of national identity and social cohesion; by unprecedented levels of asylum applications and the question of our moral responsibility to vulnerable others; by previously uncommon religious practices and the question of quite how much religious freedom a liberal society can afford – would ensure that what the Canadian philosopher Charles Taylor has termed the 'deep diversity' of modern societies would remain a dominant feature on the landscape.

> *'The need to rule god-talk out was a symptom*
> *that it was coming back in': doing God*

It was a quirk of fate that one of the most publicly Christian Prime Ministers in British political history should be followed, within seven years, by another. Tony Blair's upbringing was a world away from Margaret Thatcher's. Christianity was largely absent from the childhood home. Blair's father was an atheist and he himself was brought up a Christian only in the most nominal way. When at Oxford, however, he met and was deeply impressed by Peter Thomson, an Australian Anglican priest. 'I had always believed in God,' Blair told the *Sunday Times* in July 1994, 'but I had become slightly detached from it. I couldn't make sense of it. Peter made it relevant, practical rather than theological. Religion became less of a personal relationship with God. I began to see it more in a social context.'[78]

Just as it is debatable what impact Thatcher's Christian faith had on her politics, so it is far from clear what Blair's had on his.[79] Blair himself claimed that 'the single most important thing [for me] . . . is the notion that people are members of the community, not simply individuals, isolated and alone. You are what you are in part because of others, and you cannot divorce the individual from the surrounding society.'[80] Such ideas were popular in the progressive circles in the late 1980s and early 1990s in which Blair moved, as a coterie of young Labour Turks sought to chart a course between old-style, statist socialism and individualistic

Thatcherism. But Blair's enchantment with so-called communitarian thought was also a legacy of John Macmurray, the Christian philosopher to whom Thomson introduced Blair at Oxford. As with Thatcher, the personal religious and public political happened to coincide, as Blair himself admitted.[81]

The real difference between Blair's religious convictions and Thatcher's lay not in the extent to which they influenced policy, but in the extent to which they could be wielded or even admitted in public. Blair's Christianity was genuine and deeply felt. Although never as bullish as Thatcher he never denied and, in the early days, was quite open about his faith and its social implications. 'Your religious beliefs aren't something that you shut away from the world but something that means you have to go out and act.'[82] This soon changed, however, as the diaries of his press secretary Alastair Campbell illustrate.[83] On Wednesday 20 March 1996, Blair agreed 'to do a piece on his religious beliefs for the Easter edition of the *Sunday Telegraph*.' Campbell was concerned. 'People knew he believed in God, if not perhaps how important it all was to him, but I could see nothing but trouble in talking about it.' He was proved right. The *Telegraph* 'splashed' the interview on the Saturday, prompting Campbell to sense a 'mini-disaster' with the media 'spin[ning] it as Blair allying Labour to God', which he was not doing. As predicted the story went 'pretty mega' and there were several bad editorials saying 'he was playing politics with God'. When Campbell eventually spoke to Blair, the future Prime Minister admitted he should never have done it and agreed not to do it again.

Blair was as good as his word, his undoubtedly serious and motivating Christian faith remaining the elephant in the Cabinet Room for the next decade. On occasions when he slipped – how deliberately? – his principled reticence was vindicated. When talking to Michael Parkinson in March 2006 about his decision to go to war in Iraq he said, 'In the end there is a judgement that, well, I think if you have faith about these things then you realise that judgement is made by other people, and also by—' He didn't get the chance to finish his sentence. Parkinson seized the scoop: 'What do you mean by that?' Blair's response was particularly faltering and did not major on the 'God' element:

I mean by other people, by, if you believe in God, it's made by God as well and that judgement in the end has to be, you know, you do your . . . When you're faced with a decision like that, and some of those decisions have been very, very difficult, as I say, most of all because you know there are people's lives, not just, this isn't a matter of a policy here or a thing there but their lives, and in some case, their death . . .[84]

The media response was as instant and unfavourable as it had been a decade earlier. Silence was clearly the only safe option.

Why the change? Why had Thatcher been able to be so very explicit about her Christianity when Blair's far more muted pronouncements were greeted with astonishment and hostility? The difference is not quite as significant as it may first appear. Thatcher's theo-political pronouncements were immensely controversial – she just didn't care – whereas Blair and Campbell were hypersensitive, especially in 1996, about media coverage of New Labour. That recognised, there was undoubtedly a change in political context from one Christian Prime Minister to the next.

That change had clearly much to do with the international scene, particularly the election of George W. Bush and the events of September 2001. The rise of religious rhetoric in US politics, meticulously charted by David Domke and Kevin Coe in their book *The God Strategy: How Religion Became a Political Weapon in America* and, in particular, its use by a Republican administration widely disliked by the British public helps to explain the increased British nervousness with God. When Donald Rumsfeld, the US defense secretary, and his team at the Pentagon apparently placed biblical quotations on the cover of their Iraq briefings to President Bush,[85] and Bush himself allegedly tried to sell the invasion to Jacques Chirac by using prophecies from Ezekiel concerning Gog and Magog, such nervousness turned to hysteria.[86] If this was what Christian politics was, we would rather not have it at all, thank you.

But the different reactions to Blair and Thatcher were also due to the recognition that Christian (indeed religious) politics was on the rise. Not only had it not failed to die the death predicted a generation earlier but it appeared to be more confident and more forthright than for many years. In the words of the philosopher Julian Baggini writing in *Public Policy Research*, 'when the UK Prime Minister's spokesperson [Alastair Campbell] remarked in 2003 that "We don't do God" what was striking was that until that point it went without saying that politicians don't overtly discuss religion [*sic*]. The need to rule god-talk out was a symptom that it was coming back in.'[87]

This was demonstrably so. Liberal theology, ascendant in the 1960s, was replaced by Radical Orthodoxy, a movement that stayed close to traditional Christian creeds and adopted a much more critical attitude to modernity.[88] Rather than go with the flow, theologians increasingly felt they had the right and resources to swim against it. After many years in the intellectual shadows, British evangelicalism began to regain its former vigour and, with it, a passion for political and social engagement. A growing number of evangelicals, once dispirited by the state of the world, angered by the compromise they saw in other Christians and convinced that the only appropriate response was one of personal repentance and conversion, now found their biblical fidelity directing them towards active public life.

Roman Catholicism, so long the denomination that dared only whisper its political name, was reinvigorated first by the Second Vatican Council in the 1960s and then by John Paul II, who dominated the world stage more than any other figure in the century's last two decades. His and the Church's role in the collapse of communism gave it particular political kudos. The publication of a number of influential social documents – from papal encyclicals like *Centesimus Annus* in 1991 to the 1996 report of the Catholic Bishops' Conference of England and Wales, *The Common Good and the Catholic Church's Social Teaching* – many of which were assembled into a *Compendium of Social Teaching of the Church* in 2005, gave the Church unparalleled weight and resources for its political engagement. And with Catholicism becoming the biggest denomination in the UK, congregations often being revivified by immigration, the Church spoke with a new confidence – a confidence that was, at the same time, badly dented by revelations of widespread child-sex abuse within the Church.

In the political arena, the Conservative Christian Fellowship was founded in 1990 and rapidly grew to a sizeable and influential body within the party. Its ambitions, according to its founder Tim Montgomerie, were to steer the party away from the 'narrowly economic' course it had adopted in the 1980s by adopting 'a moral case for conservatism' that 'could reignite the party's compassion'.[89] Although feared by some members of the party and all but exiled from power during Michael Howard's leadership, the CCF remained influential, not least through the non-religious think tank, the Centre for Social Justice, which several prominent Christians helped set up and which was headed by former Tory leader and Catholic Iain Duncan Smith.

On the other side of the House, the Christian Socialist Movement, re-founded in 1960, grew ever stronger, boasting among its members John Smith, Tony Blair and Gordon Brown. Although, like the CCF and the smaller Liberal Democrat Christian Fellowship, it too had critics within its party, the general disarray of Labour politics in the late 1980s, the prominence of many CSM members and the widely recognised historical influence of Christian Socialism on the Labour movement gave the CSM a secure seat round the party table.

An interesting measure of the fall and rise of Christian politics, or at least Christian Socialist politics, over the twentieth century can be seen in the preferred reading matter among Labour MPs. According to Mark Bevir, Labour MPs in 1906 claimed they had been most influenced by John Ruskin, the Bible, Charles Dickens, Henry George and Thomas Carlyle.[90] In 1962, when asked the same question, the influences were G.B. Shaw, H.G. Wells, G.D.H. Cole and Karl Marx. Thirteen years later Marx topped the list followed by R.H. Tawney, Shaw, Aneurin Bevan and H.G. Wells. In 1994, however, the list ran: Robert Tressell's *The Ragged Trousered Philanthropists*, R.H. Tawney, the Bible, Marx, John Steinbeck and George Orwell. After an absence of over half a century the Bible was back.

Given this resurgence it is not surprising that (some) secular-minded commentators and politicians were nervous about and tried to ward politicians off 'doing God'. It is far too early to know whether this uneasiness will harden into permanent antagonism, or whether, for example, the passing of the Bush administration or the actual conduct of political clerics and Christian politicians – engaging in reasoned, accessible and conciliatory debate rather than hacking and hurling biblical verses at opponents – will calm fears. The fact that Gordon Brown, Blair's chancellor and successor, was open about his Christian upbringing and 'moral compass', and willing to quote the Bible (albeit in a heavily rhetorical way) far more frequently than his predecessor, is certainly suggestive.[91] It implies, if no more than that, a willingness to attend to, and engage with, convictions that are drawn, even if at a distance, from a religious inspiration. Whether critics welcome and engage with such contributions or not, it appears that the age of Christian politics is far from over.

'We rejoice in the hopes of Jubilee': two celebrations

Tony Blair's premiership witnessed two very different jubilees. In June 2002 the nation and the Commonwealth celebrated fifty years of Queen Elizabeth II's reign. Over 12,000 people attended a Prom at Buckingham Palace (2 million applied for tickets) on 1 June and 12,000 more a pop concert there two days later. There were street parties held across the country and over 2,000 beacons lit worldwide. The royal family attended a private service at St George's Chapel and then, on 4 June, a National Service of Thanksgiving at St Paul's Cathedral, to which the queen rode in the Gold State Coach. The celebration weekend concluded with a royal address, a procession along the Mall and a flypast. The celebrations were judged a triumph.

This kind of jubilee has its own particular story. The biblical 'jubilee', as described in Leviticus 25, was a semi-centennial celebration in which debts were cancelled, families returned to their ancestral lands, the poor were redeemed by relatives and liberty was proclaimed across the land. Early on in Christian history the Hebrew word 'jobel', referring to the ram's horn that was blown to announce the 'jubilee', was confused with the Latin word 'jubilo' meaning 'I rejoice', thereby conflating the two subtly different concepts and obscuring the social and economic significance of the original, biblical jubilee.

Jubilee years were held in the Middle Ages, either on behalf of the papacy or of a particularly long-lived king, but they retained only a little of the original biblical meaning. On such occasions, papal indulgences were sold or debtors were released to mark the anniversary and to link society to the example of God's people. Such measures notwithstanding, however, the events were more celebration than liberation.

It was only in the nineteenth century that such public celebrations really took off, however, with the golden jubilee of George III in 1809. This witnessed an amnesty for those naval and military deserters who were now willing to rejoin their ship or regiment. Extra rations were issued to the forces. Prisoners of war were freed and returned home. Debtors were released from prison with public subscriptions paying their creditors. Public celebrations were held, such as the one in Brighton where a local dignitary paid for 2,000 of the town's poor to dine out, waited on by its leading figures. The intention was to celebrate the king's fifty years on the throne – and to distract public attention from an expensive, exhausting and politically oppressive war.[92] Five years later the pattern was repeated in a 'Grand National Jubilee' marking the Peace of Paris, after which the idea of jubilee as a patriotic celebration was established. At the end of the century, Queen Victoria's golden and diamond jubilees were magnificent and self-confident affairs of national pride and confidence in which special jubilee hymns celebrated all that was glorious about being British.[93]

The other jubilee celebration during the Blair premiership was a little less expected. Growing awareness of the ruinously high levels of debt that were being serviced by many low-income countries led in the 1990s to a range of Churches, aid agencies and trades union groups campaigning for the remission or abolition of payments. What began life as the 'Debt Crisis Network' became the 'Jubilee 2000' coalition, based on the words of Leviticus 25: 'Proclaim liberty throughout all the land unto all the inhabitants thereof: it shall be a jubile[e] unto you.'[94]

On 16 May 1998 some 70,000 campaigners formed a human chain around Birmingham city centre where the leaders of the G8 countries were at a summit meeting. The leaders themselves had been moved to a 'safer' location but the global media attention forced their hand and Tony Blair left the conference early to meet the Jubilee leaders. Subsequently he, his chancellor and a number of other world leaders pledged their support to the Jubilee campaign. Although the extent to which Jubilee demands have since been met is debatable, 'third world' debt has been established as, and remains, a major political issue.

This more politically subversive jubilee has an equally long if intermittent English history. Its radical economic implications recommended it to sectaries of the seventeenth century. It was later coloured with millenarian expectations, especially among Primitive Methodists, and used by radicals to denounce and prophesy against the political order. 'Freedom's Jubilee, July 14th' became a British Jacobin toast of the 1790s, commemorating Bastille Day. A banner recorded at a 'Peterloo' meeting in Halifax in 1819 read: 'We groan, being burdened, waiting to be delivered. But we rejoice in the hopes of Jubilee.'[95] Thomas Spence, a Newcastle-born radical who advocated common ownership of land, drew on the radical jubilee and even composed a jubilee hymn, to the tune of the national anthem, which was 'to be sung at the End of Oppression, or the Commencement of the political MILLENNIUM, when there shall be neither Lords nor Landlords, but God and Man will be all in all'. It was precisely for reasons such as these that loyalists seized on and refashioned King George's jubilee celebrations of 1809.

This dual usage of the jubilee epitomises the influence the Bible has had on our political history. On one hand, it has supported, sustained and justified the political order. The Bible helped create a national consciousness, of England in the seventh to tenth centuries, and of Britain in the eighteenth, a consciousness that remains today, albeit heavily submerged. It united and, in the process, excluded. It sanctified monarchs, proclaiming their divine right. It demanded deference and submission. It explained why political disobedience was a particularly wicked sin. It justified political repression and legitimised intolerance. It kept political order and maintained social peace.

On the other hand, it was the Bible that provided the most effective challenge to that order. It insisted on the inevitability and implacability of divine judgement on even the most powerful. It demanded that earthly rulers honour religious freedom. When put into the vernacular, especially through William Tyndale's masterly translation, it created a spiritual democracy that would one day undermine political authority. It insisted on fundamental human equality. It provided innumerable models for political subversion. It proclaimed freedom to debtors, liberty for prisoners and release for the oppressed. It rooted the idea of helping the poor, feeding the hungry and healing the sick in the life of God himself. It helped drag a nation into civil war and undermine the idea of the divine right of kings. It sanctified life on earth, and inspired many to fight for their and other people's freedom.

Throughout British political history the Bible has been both a hierarchical book and a levelling book, a royal book and a Jacobin book, a text for royalists and a text for radicals. The two jubilee moments around the year 2000 show how, even in the pluralised politics of our age, biblical language and logic can still speak to millions, shaping our political landscape, on the one hand helping to generate public order and stability and, on the other, the moral energy always needed for political change.

Postscript

In 2007 Nicholas Lash, formerly Norris-Hulse Professor of Divinity at Cambridge University, wrote an article entitled 'Where Does *The God Delusion* Come From?'.[1] The essay sought, first, to examine some of the book's chief weaknesses[2] and second 'to address the question of what it is about the climate of the times that enables so ill-informed and badly argued a tirade to be widely welcomed by many apparently well-educated people'. Lash offered a number of subtle and persuasive reasons, such as 'the illusion, unique to the English-speaking world, that there is some single set of procedures which uniquely qualify as "scientific"', but omitted the single, most obvious explanation: when the book was published.[3]

Richard Dawkins' *The God Delusion* hit the shelves in October 2006. That was six years into the Republican presidency of George W. Bush, an evangelical Christian who allegedly claimed that God wanted him to be President[4] and who had come to power by drawing heavily on the support of the so-called 'Christian Right'. It was six years into the Second Palestinian Intifada, in which several thousand people were killed. It was five years after the attacks on the Twin Towers and the Pentagon by Islamic extremists. It was three years into an enormously divisive and bloody invasion of Iraq, British participation in which was largely determined by the convictions of another publicly Christian leader. It was a year after a series of attacks on the London transport system by Islamic extremists, which killed fifty-six people. It was also a year or so after the nuclear programme of the Islamic Republic of Iran had first become a serious international concern, and a year or so after the Islamist group Hamas had unexpectedly won the Palestinian elections. All in all, it was not an auspicious moment for religion, let alone the interface of religion and politics.

This convergence of events helps explain the popularity of *The God*

Delusion. It helps explain the general nervousness that there is in Britain about the relationship between religion and politics. And it also helps to account for the crudity of anti-religious arguments of which *The God Delusion* was only the most prominent example. Early on in his book on John Locke's religious politics, Jeremy Waldron characterises such arguments thus: 'Secular theorists often assume that they know what a religious argument is like: they present it as a crude prescription from God, backed up with threat of hellfire, derived from general or particular revelation, and they contrast it with the elegant simplicity of a philosophical argument by Rawls (say) or Dworkin.'[5]

Waldron goes on to remark that 'those who have bothered to make themselves familiar with existing religious-based arguments in modern political theory know that this is mostly a travesty.' You have to go back about 350 years in English history to come across the 'because the Bible says so' argument being used anywhere near the heart of the nation's politics, and even then it was commonly deployed with far greater sophistication and nuance than modern polemicists would have us believe. It was, after all, during this most biblical of political crises that we know as the English Civil Wars, that the most coherent case for democracy the country had yet seen was presented. Three centuries on, Bible-thumping is not a serious danger for British politics, in spite of the American spectres so often conjured by reasonable, secular commentators. If, as the last chapter argued, we are witnessing a gradual reinvigoration of Christian politics in Britain, it seems unlikely that we need fear politicians citing chapter and verse in the chamber in the expectation that opponents will fall into theological line.

Nor is there much need to fear that introducing biblically informed reflection into political discourse will invariably grant one particular party or policy divine authority, loading it with a metaphysical weight that no politics can bear. Again this fear is associated with America, in particular with the way in which some of the faithful there think biblical Christianity is incompatible with a vote for the Democratic Party. This situation has changed significantly over recent years, however.[6] Even the smallest measure of intelligent theological reflection shows that God does not vote Tory, or Labour, or Republican, or Democrat.

And of historical reflection: for if one fact is incontrovertible from a history of the English political Bible, it is that scripture has been used on both sides of most arguments. What history shows, with repetitive clarity, is that Bible and theology can and have been used to defend more or less every conceivable political position, from the supremacy of the monarch to his subservience to the Church; from the divine right of kings to their equality with their subjects; from slavery to abolitionism; from political authoritarianism to political radicalism; from a return to Christendom to a surge forward to collectivism. As outlined in the introduction, there are ways of explaining and navigating this complexity. Moreover, just because the Bible has been used to justify two mutually contradictory positions it does not mean it has been used equally well in both instances. One of the reasons Locke dwelt so heavily on scripture in his *First Treatise* is that he thought Robert Filmer had done it so badly.

Nevertheless the point stands. The real threat to Christian politics does not lie in any alleged bullishness or tendency to adopt a single, immutable, inflexible position. Obdurate, wild-eyed, bibliolatrous fanatics striding through the corridors of power – as opposed to on the fringes of society where they rub shoulders with similarly consumed secular militants – are simply a thing of the past. The real threat to Christian politics lies not in its tendency to fixate on a particular position but its inability to do so. As the poet Edmund Waller remarked when the nation was tumbling towards civil war, the danger is that the Bible can be made to prove just about anything.[7]

This, then, is the greatest challenge that history poses to Christian politics. It is to develop a coherent theological basis for politics or, more directly, to avoid simply adopting the ideas of the moment and baptising them with scripture. In particular, it is to listen to voices from the periphery. It is noteworthy how many important and, eventually, mainstream ideas in English theo-political history began on the margins – whether it was Wyclif and Tyndale insisting that the Bible was for all; the Marian exiles developing arguments for political resistance; seventeenth-century sectaries arguing for democracy and the redistribution of wealth; seventeenth-century Baptists arguing for radical toleration; eighteenth-century Quakers arguing for the abolition of slavery; nineteenth-century radical Christians fighting against the apparently immutable laws of political economy; or Victorian Christian Socialists contending that the kingdom of God was now as well as in the future. Perhaps this should not surprise us. The centre-piece of the Christian story is of God himself living among the broken and lost of an occupied and humiliated people. Christianity invites us to see life from underneath. Beside this challenge to Christian politics, the one most often levelled by secularists – 'don't Bible-bash when you are talking to those who don't share your beliefs' – hardly seems like a challenge at all.

If this is the main challenge that the history of the English political Bible presents to Christian politics, the challenge to secularists is no less acute. Every indication is that the religious influence in politics around the world will grow in the twenty-first century, even in the atypically irreligious Europe.[8] The once confident secularisation thesis is in tatters.[9] Analysis seems to show that societies do not necessarily become more secular with modernity (although that does not mean that some won't) but that they become more plural, able to afford a wider range of beliefs and commitments.[10] This, combined with historically high levels of migration, means that as the century progresses it will become increasingly difficult to be sure that those with whom I share my physical space and political infrastructure also share my values, my 'moral compass'. In such circumstances, it is incumbent on all of us to be willing to explain why we hold the social and political commitments that we do – why we *value* what we do – rather than simply to assume that we are all ideologically the same under the skin. This presents secularists with two challenges in particular.

First, it is incumbent on them and their fellow travellers to recognise that they too have a 'worldview', a set of beliefs and commitments that may be more or less rational but is certainly not rational *simpliciter*. Their social and political stance will be 'underdetermined' by the available evidence, like everyone else's. Whether it is relating to obvious moral issues like abortion, euthanasia, reproductive technology and war, or less obvious but no less moral ones like citizenship, healthcare, welfare reform and transport policy, secularists adopt a 'faith' position that they should, like everyone else, endeavour to justify at the bar of public opinion. As the philosopher Michael Sandel, who delivered the BBC Reith lectures in 2009, has argued, 'it's not possible to decide these big questions of policy, law, justice and rights without presupposing some account of the good life or of the goods at stake in particular social practices . . . It's not as if . . . we have available a safe, risk-free, neutral alternative.'[11]

All public engagement is, in a sense, faith-based engagement in as far as it is premised on conceptions of the good that are not necessarily shared or provable. One does not have to look back very far in European or American history to find examples of intelligent, educated people making rational and, to their mind, irrefutable arguments for the sterilisation of the 'feeble-minded'. Such arguments are horrendous to most Westerners today, and yet their proximity to us reminds us that social and political values can differ enormously within relatively homogeneous societies in relatively short spaces of time depending on our moral and metaphysical preconceptions, and that 'science' and 'reason' cannot settle matters in the way that some secularists claim.[12] If we are to hope to reach any resolution or, less ambitiously, some satisfactory modus vivendi in our politics, we all need to be prepared, as it were, to show our moral workings. To quote Jeremy Waldron again, writing with reference to Locke and equality:

> If we don't get to the bottom of these issues, if we shy away from the foundations of equality because we are afraid of offending somebody or of requiring others to go somewhere in their thoughts and deliberations where they would rather not go, then we risk making our egalitarian political order more shallow and less articulate than it ought to be.[13]

The second (and related) challenge to secularists is not to chase back into their ideological ghettos those political figures who do indeed go public about their inner motivations, especially if those motivations are religious. Just as everyone has a worldview, everyone engages in public affairs for private and personal reasons. Those reasons may be more or less public-spirited – according to British public opinion they have been less rather than more public-spirited of late – but they are no less personal for that. It is a fallacy to believe that the only legitimate motivation for public service is some kind of universal, disinterested commitment to the public good. Everyone engages from a particular position, in a particular way, with particular objectives. Our responsibility is to be willing to listen to and even learn from those positions, motivations and objectives with which we disagree.

Secularists do not have an entirely admirable record of doing this, often preferring to exclude awkward religious commitments from public debate rather than listen to them.[14] This is a mistake, not only because it betrays the values of a liberal society, but also because it is counter-productive. There is good historical evidence to suggest that attempts to silence religious voices in public debate and confine them to the private sphere in fact drives them underground and radicalises them.[15] If, as demographer Eric Kaufman has recently argued, fertility data suggest that irrespective of where one goes in the world the religious outbreed the irreligious (and the conservative religious outbreed the liberal religious), it will do little good for secularists to demand that everyone must think like them before being admitted to public debate. The challenge to secularists is to allow those opinions that they don't like to take a seat at the table, provided they participate in debate in an amenable and constructive way, rather than simply banishing them from negotiations altogether.[16] Reviewing a series of books that have changed the world[17] in *New Statesman* magazine in 2006, philosopher John Gray concluded: 'the return of religion as a pivotal factor in politics and war is one of the defining features of the age, and it is time Paine, Marx and other secular prophets were gently shelved in the stacks ... the books that have most formed the past, and which are sure also to shape the future, are the central texts of the world religions.'[18] In such circumstances it is incumbent on all to know something about them and the history of their use.

All this comprises a serious but entirely negative argument for recognising and engaging with biblically informed political arguments in public debate, for not dismissing every such argument as Bible-bashing and every such politician as a fundamentalist. But the challenge to engage with such thinking is more positive than that, than simply wearily acknowledging that we're going to have to deal with such thinking in the future, so I suppose we better get used to it.

On a superficial level, there is a positive argument for deploying the Bible rhetorically in debate, as long as it is done with care and attention. As many politicians instinctively recognise, such usage can lend political speechmaking a weight that it often desperately needs. Writing of Churchill's religion, Paul Addison concluded that the great man 'belonged to an era of secularised religion in which the doctrines of liberalism, socialism and imperialism were all bathed in the afterglow of a Christian sunset. Now the afterglow has gone: and political discourse has shrunk into a narrow, stultifying recital of economic indicators, enlivened by occasional outbreaks of xenophobia.'[19] There is much truth and many implications in this, as savvy politicians recognise. Barack Obama, one of the savviest of recent years, remarked in his book, *The Audacity of Hope*, with specific reference to the Democratic Party, that 'in reaction to religious over-reach, we equate tolerance with secularism, and forfeit the moral language that would help infuse our policies with a larger meaning.'[20] One of the reasons for his success was his willingness and ability to infuse his politics with that 'larger meaning', much of it drawn from the Christian tradition.

But the positive argument for engaging with biblically informed political thought goes beyond using beautiful or weighty language. Put at its most provocative, it is that some of the things we cherish politically may be difficult, perhaps even unsustainable, if we move outside a Christian framework. This is an obviously contentious statement, so demands a little unpacking.

Writing about Malcolm Muggeridge's book *The Thirties* in April 1940, George Orwell commented, 'Brotherhood implies a common father. Therefore it is often argued that men can never develop the sense of a community unless they believe in God.'[21] Unbeliever that he was, he naturally disagreed that such faith was necessary. Instead, he argued that the sense of brotherhood could also be achieved by our 'dim' awareness that 'man is not an individual, [but] only a cell in an everlasting body . . . some organism, stretching into the future and the past, within which they feel themselves to be immortal.' That body is naturally limited to 'fragmentary communities – nation, race, creed, class', but, Orwell argued, 'a very slight increase of consciousness, and their [i.e. human being's] sense of loyalty could be transferred to humanity itself, which is not an abstraction.'

This is a hopeful and inspiring idea. Indeed, it is precisely the idea that has inspired the great modern tradition of humanist thought.

We do not need God, revelation, the Bible or the Christian tradition in order to ground fundamental moral and political ideas, such as human 'brotherhood' or equality. Careful and reasonable reflection on the facts of our existence is sufficient.

It is not without its problems, however. First, Orwell was more aware than many of his contemporaries of the horrors of Soviet communism. He must, therefore, have also been alert to the dangers of a statement like 'man is not an individual, [but] only a cell in an everlasting body.' Seventy years later, after the books have been fully opened on communism and the socialist project to which Orwell committed himself has largely disintegrated, talk of man being 'only a cell in an everlasting body' is deeply problematic.

Second, Orwell's ability to talk about the sense of belonging to 'some organism, stretching into the future and the past' was, as he intimates, clearly informed by the English culture that he loved and celebrated. However, he seems to have been unaware of the extent to which it depended on the on-going maintenance of, and respect for, certain specific structures within that culture, such as crown, empire, parliament and Church, and consequently of its fragility. A motivating sense of belonging did not simply float free in the air, but was anchored to specific people, places and institutions. Seventy years on, the sense that individuals naturally feel they belong to some national, cultural body, stretching into the future and the past, the sense on which Orwell depended in order to generate a sense of brotherhood, is massively diminished.[22]

Third, and most problematically, the 'very slight increase of consciousness' that Orwell claims is necessary for transferring a 'sense of [fragmentary] loyalty' to 'humanity itself' seems to be a sleight of hand. Is it really 'very slight'? If so, why has humanity so singularly failed to make it? Why, in an age of international communications and travel, do the global rich seem so indifferent to the cause of the global poor? Why are so many millions seemingly oblivious to the environmental damage they are inflicting on millions more? Ignorance can no longer be a valid excuse. Perhaps it is because the shift from group to universal loyalty is not 'slight' as Orwell imagined, and instead demands compelling reason and considerable moral energy. All in all, one cannot escape the nagging feeling that

Orwell's vision, so fundamental to humanist thinking is, in fact, a castle in the air – a beautiful, inspiring castle no doubt, but an airborne one nonetheless.

In contrast to such challenges, there appears to be a growing awareness of the debt owed by some apparently self-evident and much valued contemporary moral and political commitments to the Christian framework from which they emerged. Three examples will suffice. Jeremy Waldron's book on John Locke's biblical politics does not simply argue that Locke's politics was irreducibly Christian. It goes further to suggest, tentatively, that the ideas for which Locke fought are unsustainable outside the framework he used to develop them. 'I actually don't think it is clear that we – now – *can* shape and defend an adequate conception of basic human equality apart from some religious foundation,' Waldron wrote.[23] This is the kind of claim that leaves humanists reaching for their moral indignation but Waldron's is no ill-informed rant. Locke, he observes, was faced with the need to articulate a defence of equality that went all the way down, as it were. There could be no assumption of mutually agreed premises, no self-evident truths, no complacent references to 'a very slight increase of consciousness'. If Locke was to defend equality against Filmer he would need to do so from first principles, and this he did by drawing on biblically rooted ideas. Is it really possible, Waldron wonders, to do the same today, without the same resources?

A second example may be drawn from human rights rather than equality. Nicholas Wolterstorff, Noah Porter Professor Emeritus of Philosophical Theology at Yale University, explored the basis for human rights in his 2008 book, *Justice: Rights and Wrongs*.[24] Asking 'Is a secular grounding of human rights possible?' he answers in the negative. Inalienable and equitable rights, he argues, were simply not possible within the accepted moral framework of the ancient world, and that even the modern, Kantian approach, grounded in our rational capacities, is fatally flawed. 'If we insist that the capacity for rational agency gives worth to all and only those who stand to the capacity in the relation to actually possessing it, then it is not *human* rights that are grounded but the rights of those who possess the capacity.'[25] Rather, it was 'the incursion of Scripture into the thought world of late antiquity that made possible the rights culture that we are all familiar with'.²⁶ Some may question whether this 'rights culture' is as desirable as is often assumed but that criticism is beyond Wolterstorff's point. It is, he contends, only the uniquely Christian idea that 'God loves equally and permanently each and every creature who bears the *imago dei*' that provides a sufficient grounding for human rights.²⁷ In the same way as a secure defence of equality may only be possible by digging down to religious foundations, so might human rights demand a similar theological excavation.

A final example can be located in the idea of toleration. To most modern Westerners, religion is the very antithesis of tolerance, a belief for which they can cite many persuasive historical examples. But those examples also make the opposing argument. Just as Locke was forced to defend political equality because he was faced with those who argued against it, so post-Reformation Christians were forced, by innumerable examples of intolerance and its effect on society, to develop a robust defence of toleration. That defence was based on principles concerning the legitimacy and proper extent of *adiaphora*, 'things indifferent', the acceptable boundary between temporal and spiritual jurisdictions, and the appropriate function of law in adjudicating between different scriptural interpretations. And all these principles were rooted ultimately, and sometimes explicitly, in biblical teaching. This is not to claim that toleration is not possible beyond biblical bounds. That is obviously not the case. It is, however, to suggest that toleration was hard won and remains a far from self-evident virtue. The confusion and consternation that dog current debates about toleration, reflect a little of our historical amnesia concerning its origins.

This is not the place to discuss the merits of these three arguments, each of which demands close examination, although it is worth noting that such ideas are not limited to the pens of Christian philosophers.²⁸ Nor does it constitute a call for the kind of 'Bible-says-so' politics that has been absent from mainstream political debate for 350 years. Rather it is simply to recognise that all politics rests on wider 'myths', that 'economy and politics . . . must have ground beneath themselves,' and that in Britain that ground has been biblical from the very earliest days. It would be a brave or perhaps a complacent person to suggest that we can change plots without the structure we have erected on this one being undermined.

Select Bibliography

What follows is an abbreviated list of the key primary and secondary sources consulted for *Freedom and Order*. Details of other sources may be found in the endnotes.

Primary Sources

Anon., *Sermons, or Homilies, Appointed to be read in Churches* (London: Prayer Book and Homily Society, 1833)

Augustine of Hippo, *The City of God against the Pagans*, ed. R.W. Dyson (Cambridge University Press, 1998)

Bede, *Ecclesiastical History of the English People* (Penguin Books, 1955; rev. 1968)

Chalmers, Thomas, *On Political Economy in Connexion with the Moral State and Moral Prospects of Society* (Glasgow, 1832)

Church of England, *Christianity and Industrial Problems: Being the Report of the Archbishops' Fifth Committee of Inquiry* (London: SPCK, 1918)

—— *Faith in the City: A Call for Action by Church and Nation* (London: Church House Publishing, 1985)

Churchill, Winston S., *Blood, Toil, Tears and Sweat: Winston Churchill's Famous Speeches*, ed. David Cannadine (London: Cassell, 1989)

Clarkson, Thomas, *The History of the Rise, Progress, and Accomplishment of the Abolition of the African Slave-Trade by the British Parliament* (London: Longman, Rees, and Orme, 1808)

Cromwell, Oliver, *The Writings and Speeches of Oliver Cromwell*, 4 vols., ed. W.C. Abbot (Cambridge, Mass., 1937–47)

Douglas, D.C. and Greenaway, G.W., eds., *English Historical Documents, Vol. 2: 1042–1189* (Eyre and Spottiswoode, 1953)

Douglas, David C. and Williams, C.H., eds., *English Historical Document, Vol. 5, 1485–1558*, (Eyre and Spottiswoode, 1996)

Equiano, Olaudah, *The Interesting Narrative and Other Writings*, ed. V. Caretta (Penguin, 2003)

Filmer, Robert, *Patriarcha and Other Writings*, ed. J.P. Sommerville (Cambridge, 1991)

Gardiner, Stephen, *Obedience in Church and State: Three Political Tracts by Stephen Gardiner*, trans. and ed. Pierre Janelle (Cambridge: Cambridge University Press, 1930)

Gisborne, Thomas, *The Principles of Moral Philosophy* (London, 1789)

Goodman, Christopher, *How Superior Powers Ought to be Obeyed of their Subjects* (1558)

Harris, Raymund, *Scriptural Researches on the Licitness of the Slave Trade, Shewing its Conformity with the Principles of Natural and Revealed Religion, Delineated in the Sacred Writings of the Word of God* (London: John Stockdale, 1788)

Headlam, S.D., *Christian Socialism: A Lecture* (Fabian Society, 1907)

Hobbes, Thomas, *Leviathan* (Oxford World's Classics, 1998)

Hooker, Richard, *Of the Laws of Ecclesiastical Polity*, ed. Arthur Stephen McGrade (Cambridge University Press, 1989)

Hughes, H.P., *Ethical Christianity. A Series of Sermons* (1892)

John of Salisbury, *John of Salisbury: Policraticus*, ed. Cary Nederman (Cambridge, 1990)

Keynes, Simon and Lapidge, Michael, eds., *Alfred the Great: Asser's Life of King Alfred and Other Contemporary Sources* (Penguin, 1984)

Locke, John, *The Reasonableness of Christianity*, ed. I.T. Ramsey (Stanford University Press, 1958)

——*Two Treatises of Government* and *A Letter Concerning Toleration*, ed. Ian Shapiro (Yale University Press, 2003)

Luther, Martin, *Luther's Works: Vol. 44–45, The Christian in Society I, II*, ed. Walther Brandt (Philadelphia: Fortress Press, 1962–66)

Malthus, Thomas Robert, *An Essay on the Principle of Population* (Oxford World's Classics, 1999)

Maurice, F.D., *The Life of Frederick Denison Maurice: Chiefly Told in his own Letters* (2nd edn, 1884)

—— *To Build Christ's Kingdom: F.D. Maurice and his Writings*, ed. Jeremy Morris (Norwich: Canterbury Press, 2007)

O'Donovan, Oliver and O'Donovan, Joan Lockwood, *From Irenaeus to Grotius: A Sourcebook in Christian Political Thought* (Cambridge: Eerdmans, 1999)

Paget, F.E., *Milford Malvoisin; or, Pews and Pewholders* (London, 1842)

—— *The Warden of Berkingholt; or, Rich and Poor* (Oxford, 1843)

Paine, Thomas, *The Rights of Man* (Penguin Books, 1985)

Paley, William, *Natural Theology* (Oxford World's Classics, 2008)

Pollard, A.F., ed., *Records of the English Bible: The Documents Relating to the Translation and Publication of the Bible in English, 1525–1611* (Oxford University Press, 1911)

Ponet, John, *John Ponet (1516?–1556), Advocate of Limited Monarchy*, ed. Winthrop Hudson (Chicago, 1942)

Sharp, Granville, *An Essay on Slavery, Proving from Scripture its Inconsistency with Humanity and Religion* (London, 1776)

Stephens, John Rayner, *The Political Pulpit. Sermons, Feb.–Aug. 1839* (London, 1839)

Tawney, R.H., *The Acquisitive Society* (Bell, 1921)

—— *Religion and Rise of Capitalism: A Historical Study* (John Murray, 1926)

—— *Equality* (George Allen & Unwin, 1931)

Temple, William, *The Kingdom of God: A Course of Four Lectures Delivered at Cambridge during the Lent Term* (Macmillan, 1912)

—— *Christianity and Social Order* (Penguin, 1942)

Thatcher, Margaret, '"I Believe": A Speech on Christianity and Politics at St Lawrence Jewry', 31 Mar. 1978

—— 'Speech to General Assembly of the Church of Scotland', 21 May 1988

Tindal, Mathew, *Christianity as Old as Creation* (London, 1730)

Toland, John, *Christianity not Mysterious* (London, 1702)

Tyndale, William, *The Obedience of a Christian Man*, ed. David Daniell (Penguin, 2000)

Whitelock, Dorothy, ed., *English Historical Documents, Vol. 1: 500–1042*, (Eyre and Spottiswoode, 1955; 2nd edn 1996)

Wilberforce, Robert and Samuel, eds., *The Life of William Wilberforce*, 5 vols. (London: John Murray, 1838)

Wilberforce, William, *A Letter on the Abolitions of the Slave Trade* (London, 1807)

Winstanley, Gerrard, *The New Law of Righteousness* (London, 1649)

Wootton, David, ed., *Divine Right and Democracy: An Anthology of Political Writing in Stuart England* (Harmondsworth: Penguin, 1986)

Select Bibliography

Secondary Sources

Allen, Peter R., 'F.D. Maurice and J.M. Ludlow: A Reassessment of the Leaders of Christian Socialism', *Victorian Studies*, vol. 11, no. 4, June 1968, pp. 461–82

Atherstone, Andrew, *The Houses of Parliament: Cradle of Democracy* (DayOne Publications, 2010)

Baggini, Julian, 'The Rise, Fall and Rise Again of Secularism', *Public Policy Research*, vol. 12, issue 4, Jan.–Mar. 2006

Baldwin, John. W., 'Master Stephen Langton, Future Archbishop of Canterbury: The Paris Schools and Magna Carta', *English Historical Review*, vol. CXXIII, no. 503, pp. 812–46

Barclay, John M.G., '"Am I not a Man and a Brother?" The Bible and the British Anti-Slavery Campaign', *Expository Times*, 2007, 119, 3–14

Bartlett, Robert, *England under the Norman and Angevin Kings, 1075–1225* (Oxford: Clarendon Press, 1999)

Beales, Derek and Best, Geoffrey, eds., *History, Society and the Churches: Essays in Honour of Owen Chadwick* (Cambridge: Cambridge University Press, 1985)

Bebbington, David, *The Nonconformist Conscience: Chapel and Politics, 1870–1914* (London: Allen & Unwin, 1982)

—— *Evangelicalism in Modern Britain: A History from the 1730s to the 1980s* (Routledge, 1988)

—— *William Ewart Gladstone: Faith and Politics in Victorian Britain* (Grand Rapids, Mich.: W.B. Eerdmans, 1993)

—— *The Mind of Gladstone: Religion, Homer, and Politics* (Oxford: Oxford University Press, 2004)

Beer, Anna, *Milton: Poet, Pamphleteer, Patriot* (New York, N.Y.: Bloomsbury, 2008)

Bentley, Michael, ed., *Public and Private Doctrine: Essays in British History Presented to Maurice Cowling* (Cambridge, 1993)

Bentley, Michael and Stevenson, John, eds., *High and Low Politics in Modern Britain: Ten Studies* (Oxford: Clarendon, 1983)

Bevir, Mark, 'The Labour Church Movement, 1891–1902', *Journal of British Studies*, 38, Apr. 1999, pp. 217–45

—— 'New Labour: A Study in Ideology', *British Journal of Politics and International Relations*, vol. 2, no. 3, 2000, pp. 277–301

Bickley, Paul, *The Bible and Political Speech Making: A Case Study* (M.Litt. Thesis, University of St Andrews, 2009)

Select Bibliography

Bowman, Glen, 'Elizabethan Catholics and Romans 13: A Chapter in the History of Political Polemic', *Journal of Church and State*, Summer 2005, pp. 531-44

Bradley, Ian, *The Politics of Godliness: Evangelicals in Parliament, 1784–1832* (unpublished D.Phil. dissertation, Oxford, 1974)

Bradley, James E., 'The Anglican Pulpit, the Social Order, and the Resurgence of Toryism during the American Revolution', *Albion: A Quarterly Journal Concerned with British Studies*, vol. 21, no. 3, Autumn 1989, pp. 361–88

—— *Religion, Revolution and English Radicalism: Non-conformity in Eighteenth-Century Politics and Society* (Cambridge: Cambridge University Press, 1990)

Bradstock, Andrew, *Radical Religion in Cromwell's England : A Concise History from the English Civil War to the End of the Commonwealth* (London: I.B. Tauris, 2010)

Brown, Callum, *Religion and Society in Twentieth-Century Britain* (Harlow: Pearson Longman, 2006)

Brown, Malcolm and Ballard, Paul, *The Church and Economic Life: A Documentary Study: 1945 to the Present* (Peterborough: Epworth Press, 2006)

Campbell, James, ed., *The Anglo-Saxons* (London: Penguin, 1991)

Canning, Joseph, *A History of Medieval Political Thought* (Routledge, 1996)

Carr, Wesley, 'This Intimate Ritual: The Coronation Service', *Political Theology* 4.1, 2002, pp. 11–24

Chadwick, Owen, *The Victorian Church, Vols. 1&2* (Adam and Charles Black, 1966)

Chandler, Andrew, 'The Church of England and the Obliteration Bombing of Germany in the Second World War', *English Historical Review*, vol. 108, no. 429, Oct. 1993, pp. 920–46

Chase, Malcolm, 'From Millennium to Anniversary: The Concept of Jubilee in Late Eighteenth- and Nineteenth-Century England', *Past & Present*, no. 129, Nov. 1990, pp. 132–47

Chernaik, Warren, 'Biblical Republicanism', *Prose Studies*, vol. 23, no. l, Apr. 2000, pp. 147–60

Clark, Henry, *The Church under Thatcher* (SPCK, 1993)

Coffey, John, 'Puritanism and Liberty Revisited: The Case for Toleration in the English Revolution', *Historical Journal*, vol. 41, no. 4, Dec. 1998, pp. 961–85

Select Bibliography

—— 'The Impact of Apocalypticism during the Puritan Revolutions', *Perichoresis*, vol. 4.2, 2006, pp. 117–47

—— 'The Abolition of the Slave Trade: Christian Conscience and Political Action', *Cambridge Papers*, vol. 15, no. 2, June 2006

—— 'Evangelicals, Slavery and the Slave Trade: From Whitefield to Wilberforce', *ANVIL*, vol. 24, no. 2, 2007, pp. 97–120

Colley, Linda, *Britons: Forging the Nation, 1707–1837* (London: Yale University Press, 1992)

Collins, Jeffrey R., *The Allegiance of Thomas Hobbes* (Oxford: Oxford University Press, 2005)

Cubitt, Catherine, *Anglo-Saxon Church Councils, c.650–c.850* (London: Leicester University Press, 1995)

Daniell, David, *The Bible in English: Its History and Influence* (London: Yale University Press, 2003)

Duffy, Eamon, *Saints and Sinners: A History of the Popes* (Yale University Press, 1997)

Dunn, John, *The Political Thought of John Locke* (Cambridge, 1969)

Elazar, Daniel J., 'The Political Theory of Covenant: Biblical Origins and Modern Developments', *Publius*, vol. 10, no. 4, Autumn 1980, pp. 3–30

Ferguson, Niall, *Empire: How Britain Made the Modern World* (Allen Lane, 2003)

Furniss, Tom, 'Reading the Geneva Bible: Notes Toward An English Revolution?', *Prose Studies*, 31: 1, 1–21

Greaves, Richard L., 'Radicals, Rights, and Revolution: British Nonconformity and Roots of the American Experience', *Church History*, vol. 61, no. 2, June 1992, pp. 151–68

Hastings, Adrian, *A History of English Christianity, 1920–2000* (London: SCM Press, 2001)

Hennessy, Peter, 'Religion and the Writing of Contemporary History', the Digby Stuart Lecture, 2008

Hill, Christopher, *The English Bible and the Seventeenth-Century Revolution* (Allen Lane, 1993)

Hilton, Boyd, *The Age of Atonement: The Influence of Evangelicalism on Social and Economic Thought, 1785–1865* (Oxford: Clarendon Press, 1988)

Hobson, Theo, *Milton's Vision: The Birth of Christian Liberty* (London: Continuum, 2008)

Select Bibliography

Holden, Andrew, *Makers and Manners: Politics and Morality in Postwar Britain* (London: Politico's, 2004)

Hole, Robert, *Pulpits, Politics and Public Order in England, 1760–1832* (Cambridge: Cambridge University Press, 1989)

Holman, Bob, *Keir Hardie: Labour's Greatest Hero?* (Lion, 2010)

Holt, J.C., *Magna Carta* (Cambridge: Cambridge University Press, 1992)

Houlbrooke, Ralph, ed., *James VI and I: Ideas, Authority, and Government* (Ashgate, 2006)

Howse, E.M., *Saints in Politics: The 'Clapham Sect' and the Growth of Freedom* (University of Toronto Press, 1952)

Hudson, Anne, *The Premature Reformation: Wycliffite Texts and Lollard History* (Oxford: Clarendon Press, 1988)

Johnson, Dale A., 'Between Evangelicalism and a Social Gospel: The Case of Joseph Rayner Stephens', *Church History*, vol. 42, no. 2, June 1973, pp. 229–42

Jones, Paul Dafydd, 'Jesus Christ and the Transformation of English Society: The "Subversive Conservatism" of Frederick Denison Maurice', *Harvard Theological Review*, vol. 96, no. 2, Apr. 2003, pp. 205–28

Kenny, Anthony, *Wyclif* (Oxford, 1985)

Kent, John, *William Temple: Church, State, and Society in Britain, 1880–1950* (Cambridge: Cambridge University Press, 1992)

Lash, Nicholas, 'Where Does *The God Delusion* Come From?', *New Blackfriars*, vol. 88, issue 1017, Sept. 2007, pp. 507–21.

Leach, Robert, 'Christian Socialism: The Historical and Contemporary Significance of Christian Socialism within the Labour Party', Political Studies Association Annual Conference, 2002

Lyon, Eileen Groth, *Politicians in the Pulpit: Christian Radicalism in Britain from the Fall of the Bastille to the Disintegration of Chartism* (Ashgate, 1999)

MacCulloch, Diarmaid, *Tudor Church Militant: Edward VI and the Protestant Reformation* (London: Allen Lane, 1999)

—— *Reformation: Europe's House Divided, 1490–1700* (Allen Lane, 2003)

Mandler, Peter, 'Tories and Paupers: Christian Political Economy and the Making of the New Poor Law', *Historical Journal*, vol. 33, no. 1, Mar. 1990, pp. 81–103

McEachern, Claire and Shuger, Deborah, eds., *Religion and Culture in Renaissance England* (Cambridge: Cambridge University Press, 1997)

Select Bibliography

Morrill, John, ed., *Oliver Cromwell and the English Revolution* (Harlow: Longman, 1990)

Nederman, Cary J., 'A Duty to Kill: John of Salisbury's Theory of Tyrannicide', *Review of Politics*, vol. 50, no. 3, Summer 1988, pp. 365–89

Nelson, Eric, *The Hebrew Republic* (Harvard University Press, 2010)

Norman, Edward, *The Victorian Christian Socialists* (Cambridge: Cambridge University Press, 1987)

Packer, Ian, 'Religion and the New Liberalism: The Rowntree Family, Quakerism, and Social Reform', *Journal of British Studies*, vol. 42, no. 2, Apr. 2003, pp. 236–57

Parker, Kim, *The Biblical Politics of John Locke* (Wilfrid Laurier University Press, 2004)

Peck, Linda Levy, ed., *The Mental World of the Jacobean Court* (Cambridge: Cambridge University Press, 1991)

Pratt, David, *The Political Thought of King Alfred the Great* (Cambridge Studies in Medieval Life and Thought: Fourth Series, 2007)

Prochaska, Frank, *Christianity and Social Service in Modern Britain: The Disinherited Spirit* (Cambridge: Cambridge University Press, 2006)

Ranson, Guy H., 'The Kingdom of God as the Design of Society: An Important Aspect of F.D. Maurice's Theology', *Church History*, vol. 30, no. 4, Dec. 1961, pp. 458–72

Raven, James, 'The Abolition of the English State Lotteries', *Historical Journal*, vol. 34, no. 2, June 1991, pp. 371–89

Rex, Richard, 'The Crisis of Obedience: God's Word and Henry's Reformation', *Historical Journal*, vol. 39, no. 4, December 1996, pp. 863–94

Ryrie, Alec, *The Age of Reformation: The Tudor and Stewart Realms, 1485–1603* (Harlow: Longman, 2009)

Secor, Philip Bruce, *Richard Hooker: Prophet of Anglicanism* (Burnes and Oates, 1999)

Sherlock, Maeve, *The Influence of Religion on the British Campaign against the Slave Trade: An Exploration of its Biblical and Theological Roots up to 1807* (M.Phil. Thesis, Durham University)

Skinner, Quentin, *The Foundations of Modern Political Thought, Vol. 2* (Cambridge: Cambridge University Press, 1978)

Skinner, S.A., *Tractarians and the 'Condition of England': The Social and Political Thought of the Oxford Movement* (Oxford: Clarendon Press, 2000)

Smith, David J., '*Faith in the City* and Mrs Thatcher', *Policy Studies*, 11 (2), 1990

Smith, Graeme, 'Margaret Thatcher's Christian Faith: A Case Study in Political Theology', *Journal of Religious Ethics*, vol. 35.2, 2007, pp. 233–57

Sommerville, Johann, ed., *King James VI and I: Political Writings* (Cambridge University Press, 1995)

—— *Royalists and Patriots: Politics and Ideology in England, 1603–1640* (London: Longman, 1999)

Sorell, Tom and Foisneau, Luc, eds., *Leviathan after 350 Years* (Oxford: Clarendon Press, 2004)

Spurr, John, *The Post-Reformation: Religion, Politics and Society in Britain, 1603–1714* (Longman, 2006)

Stanley, Brian, '"Commerce and Christianity": Providence Theory, the Missionary Movement, and the Imperialism of Free Trade, 1842–1860', *Historical Journal*, vol. 26, no. 1, Mar. 1983, pp. 71–94

—— *The Bible and the Flag: Protestant Missions and British Imperialism in the Nineteenth and Twentieth Centuries* (Apollos, 1990)

Stewart, M.A., ed., *English Philosophy in the Age of Locke* (Oxford: Clarendon Press, 2000)

Tomkins, Stephen, *William Wilberforce* (Lion, 2007)

—— *The Clapham Sect* (Lion, 2010)

Torrance Kirby, W.J., ed., *Richard Hooker and the English Reformation* (Kluwar Academic Publishers, 2003)

Trinterud, L.J., 'A Reappraisal of William Tyndale's Debt to Martin Luther', *Church History*, vol. 31, no. 1, Mar. 1962, pp. 24–45

Turnbull, Richard, *Shaftesbury: The Great Reformer* (Lion, 2010)

Underdown, David, *Fire From Heaven: Life in an English Town in the Seventeenth Century* (London: HarperCollins, 1992)

Waldron, Jeremy, *God, Locke and Equality: Christian Foundations in Locke's Political Thought* (Cambridge: Cambridge University Press, 2002)

—— 'Response to Critics', *Review of Politics*, vol. 67, no. 3, Summer 2005, pp. 495–513

Walsh, Cheryl, 'The Incarnation and the Christian Socialist Conscience in the Victorian Church of England', *Journal of British Studies*, vol. 34, no. 3, Victorian Subjects, July 1995, pp. 351–74

Waterman, A.M.C., 'The Ideological Alliance of Political Economy and Christian Theology, 1798–1833', *Journal of Ecclesiastical History*, vol. 34, no. 2, Apr. 1983, pp. 231–44

Select Bibliography

Watts, Michael, *The Dissenters: Volume II: The Expansion of Evangelical Nonconformity* (Oxford: Clarendon Press, 1995)

Williamson, Philip, 'Christian Conservatives and the Totalitarian Challenge, 1933–40', *English Historical Review*, vol. 115, no. 462, June 2000), pp. 607–42

Winter, J.M., 'R.H. Tawney's Early Political Thought', *Past & Present*, no. 47, May 1970, pp. 71–96

Wolffe, John, ed., *Evangelical Faith and Public Zeal: Evangelicals and Society in Britain, 1780–1980* (London: SPCK, 1995)

Wollenberg, Bruce, *Christian Social Thought in Great Britain Between the Wars* (London: University Press of America, 1997)

Wollman, David H., 'The Biblical Justification for Resistance to Authority in Ponet's and Goodman's Polemics', *Sixteenth Century Journal*, vol. 13, no. 4, Winter 1982, pp. 29–41

Woolhouse, Roger, *John Locke* (Cambridge: Cambridge University Press, 2007)

Worden, Blair, 'Providence and Politics in Cromwellian England', *Past & Present*, no. 109, Nov. 1985, pp. 55–99

—— *The English Civil Wars, 1640–1660* (London: Weidenfeld & Nicolson, 2009)

Worley, Matthew, ed., *The Foundations of the British Labour Party: Identities, Cultures and Perspectives, 1900–1939* (Ashgate, 2009)

Yates, Nigel, *Eighteenth-Century Britain: Religion and Politics 1714–1815* (Harlow: Pearson/Longman, 2007)

Yeo, Eileen, 'Christianity in Chartist Struggle, 1838–1842', *Past & Present*, no. 91, May 1981, pp. 109–39

Endnotes

Introduction

1. He then added, improbably, 'it is important that religion should not be allowed to hijack this cultural resource.' See www.kingjamesbibletrust.org

2. The King James Bible Trust was set up to co-ordinate the celebrations of the 400th anniversary of the publication of the King James Version.

3. The fact that many of these statements also appear in the Geneva Bible and, before it, Tyndale's translations of the 1520s and 1530s is indicative of the bizarre bibliolatry that the King James Version provokes among English speakers.

4. For a general overview see Paul Cavill and Heather Ward, *The Christian Tradition in English Literature: Poetry, Plays, and Shorter Prose* (Zondervan, 2007). For a helpful website see www.crossref-it.info

5. Matthew 22:21. All direct biblical quotations are taken from the King James Version unless otherwise stated.

6. Wesley Carr, 'This Intimate Ritual: The Coronation Service', *Political Theology*, 4.1, 2002, pp. 11–24.

7. 'I was glad when they said unto me, We will go into the House of the Lord.'

8. Those 'other things' famously include to maintain 'the Protestant Reformed Religion established by law . . . [and] the settlement of the Church of England'.

9. 'Behold, O God our shield, and look upon the face of thine anointed.'

10. See 1 Kings 1:38–40.

11. Quoted in Eileen Groth Lyon, *Politicians in the Pulpit: Christian Radicalism in Britain from the Fall of the Bastille to the Disintegration of Chartism* (Ashgate, 1999), p. 9.

12. For useful introductions to the Old Testament see Bernhard Anderson, *The Living World of the Old Testament* (Longman, 1958; 4th edn 1993), Walter Brueggemann, *An Introduction to the Old Testament: The Canon and Christian Imagination* (Westminster/John Knox Press, 2004) and, more generally, *The Oxford Bible Commentary*, ed. John Barton and

John Muddiman (Oxford, 2001). The Old Testament books, according to the Protestant categorisation, comprise the Torah or Pentateuch (Genesis, Exodus, Leviticus, Numbers and Deuteronomy), the historical books (Joshua, Judges, Ruth, 1 and 2 Samuel, 1 and 2 Kings, 1 and 2 Chronicles, Ezra, Nehemiah and Esther), the books of poetry and wisdom (Job, Psalms, Proverbs, Ecclesiastes and Song of Solomon), and the books of the prophets (Isaiah, Jeremiah, Lamentations, Ezekiel, Daniel, Hosea, Joel, Amos, Obadiah, Jonah, Micah, Nahum, Habakkuk, Zephaniah, Haggai, Zechariah and Malachi).

13. See Genesis 12:1–5, 15:1–21, 17:1–8.

14. See Genesis 32:28–32.

15. See 1 Samuel 8, a chapter that would have enormous significance for English political thought.

16. See 2 Samuel 11.

17. The story is recorded in 1 and 2 Maccabees in the Apocrypha. The Apocrypha (meaning 'hidden') comprises those books about which there was some doubt concerning their authenticity when the Old Testament canon was being finalised in the fifth century and to which the Protestant Reformers accorded a secondary status. The books that were included in the King James Translation were: 1 Esdras, 2 Esdras, Tobit, Judith, the rest of the Book of Esther (Esther 10:4–16:24), Wisdom of Solomon, the Wisdom of Jesus the son of Sirach (Ecclesiasticus), Baruch, the Song of the Three Holy Children, the History of Susanna, Bel and the Dragon, the Prayer of Manasses, 1 Maccabees and 2 Maccabees.

18. Their early status as slaves is supported by the other popular name used of them, Hebrews, which is well attested in extra-biblical sources and seems to be a social rather than an ethnic or religious category, meaning people who were uprooted and on the edge of society, 'people of little account except for their nuisance value'. See Diarmaid MacCulloch, *A History of Christianity* (Allen Lane, 2009), p. 53.

1. 'Whether you will or not, you will have him as a judge'

1. Dorothy Whitelock, ed., *English Historical Documents, Vol. 1: 500–1042* (Eyre and Spottiswoode, 1955; 2nd edn 1996), no. 31, p. 396.

2. For the biblical precedent see 1 Corinthians 5:9–13, Matthew 18:15–17, Hebrews 13:4.

3. See Exodus 20:10, Deuteronomy 5:12–15.

4. Whitelock, *English Historical Documents, Vol. 1*, no. 32, p. 398.

5. 'If anyone is liable to the death penalty and he reaches a church, he is to retain his life and to compensate as the law directs him.' See Numbers 35:6–34.

6. Whitelock, *English Historical Documents, Vol. 1*, no. 33, pp. 407–16.

7. Patrick Wormald, in James Campbell, ed., *The Anglo-Saxons* (London: Penguin, 1991), p. 155.

8. Asser's *Life of King Alfred*, chap. 76, in Simon Keynes and Michael Lapidge, eds., *Alfred the Great: Asser's Life of King Alfred and Other Contemporary Sources* (Penguin, 1984), p. 91.

9. ibid., p. 75.

10. Prose Preface to Translation of Gregory's *Pastoral Care* in Keynes and Lapidge, *Alfred the Great*, p. 126.

11. David Pratt, *The Political Thought of King Alfred the Great* (Cambridge Studies in Medieval Life and Thought: Fourth Series, 2007), chap. 11.

12. Such as Exodus 23:1–2: 'Thou shalt not raise a false report: put not thine hand with the wicked to be an unrighteous witness. Thou shalt not follow a multitude to do evil; neither shalt thou speak in a cause to decline after many to wrest judgment,' and Exodus 23:6: 'Thou shalt not wrest the judgment of thy poor in his cause.'

13. Matthew 5:17.

14. Acts 15:29.

15. Deuteronomy 34:7.

16. Acts 1:15.

17. Patrick Wormald, *The Making of English Law: King Alfred to the Twelfth Century: Vol. 1: Legislation and its Limits* (Oxford, Blackwell Publishers, 1999), p. 417.

18. No Mercian law code exists from Offa's kingship and it is possible that Alfred is referring to the canons of a legatine council that were issued in 786, which the Mercians undertook to obey.

19. David Daniell, *The Bible in English: Its History and Influence* (London: Yale University Press, 2003), p. 45.

20. Quoted in Joseph Canning, *A History of Medieval Political Thought* (Routledge, 1996), p. 8.

21. Judith Herrin, *Byzantium: The Surprising Life of a Medieval Empire* (Allen Lane, 2007) p. 25.

22. Augustine of Hippo, *The City of God against the Pagans*, ed. R.W. Dyson (Cambridge University Press, 1998).

23. John 21:15–19.

24. 'Letter to Emperor Anastasius', in Oliver O'Donovan and Joan Lockwood O'Donovan, eds. *From Irenaeus to Grotius: A Sourcebook in Christian Political Thought* (Eerdmans, 1999) p. 179.

25. Whitelock, *English Historical Documents, Vol. 1*, no. 193, pp. 842–4.

26. Bede, *Ecclesiastical History of the English People* (Penguin Books, 1955; rev. 1968), II.14.

27. Bede, *Life of St Cuthbert*, in. D.H. Farmer, ed., *The Age of Bede* (Penguin Books, 1965; rev. 1983), chap. 3, pp. 46–7.

28. Barbara Yorke, *The Conversion of Britain: Religion, Politics and Society in Britain c.600–800* (Pearson Education, 2006) p. 243.

29. Whitelock, *English Historical Documents, Vol. 1*, no. 32, pp. 399.

30. Frank Stenton, *Anglo-Saxon England* (Oxford, 1943; 3rd edn 1971), pp. 153–7; Whitelock, *English Historical Documents, Vol. 1*, no. 40, p. 431.

31. Bede, *Ecclesiastical History*, III.2.

32. The Staffordshire Hoard: Discovery and Initial Assessment (www.staffordshirehoard.org.uk).

33. Patrick Wormald, 'Bede, Beowulf and the Conversion of the Anglo-Saxon Aristocracy', in Robert T. Farrell, ed., *Bede and Anglo-Saxon England: Papers in Honour of the 1300th Anniversary of the Birth of Bede* (London, 1978), pp. 32–95.

34. Quoted in Timothy Powell, 'The "Three Orders" of Society in Anglo-Saxon England', in *Anglo-Saxon England 23* (Cambridge University Press, 1994), pp. 103–32. Powell observes that 'this ought not to be viewed in monolithic terms as bad Christians (ignoring canon law and the teachings of the early Fathers of the church) [versus] good Christians . . . What we see is a conflict between two ideas of Christianity, one defined by reference to canon law and the early Fathers, the other defined by reference to service to the king as God's deputy on earth. Both points of view in their own terms are Christian, being marked by allegiance to a Christian God.'

35. See the Anglo-Saxon poem, *Judith*, for an example of such re-working.

36. See Catherine Cubitt, *Anglo-Saxon Church Councils, c.650–c.850* (Leicester University Press, 1995) pp. 158–83.

37. Quoted ibid., p. 166.

38. Bede, *Ecclesiastical History*, II.14.

39. ibid., III.24.

40. Whitelock, *English Historical Documents, Vol. 1*, no. 186, pp. 832–3.

41. ibid., no. 177, p. 816.

42. ibid., no. 193, pp. 842–4. For some of the many reference to God's judgement of all in the New Testament see John 5:16–30; Acts 17:31; Romans 2:16; 1 Corinthians 4:4–5; 2 Timothy 4:1; Hebrews 10:30; Hebrews 12:23; James 4:12; 1 Peter 1:17; 1 Peter 4:5; Revelation 6:10, 18:8, 18:20, 20:13.

43. Quoted in Canning, *History*, p. 49.

44. Whitelock, *English Historical Documents, Vol. 1*, no. 193, pp. 842–4.

45. Deuteronomy 17:18–20.

46. Whitelock, *English Historical Documents, Vol. 1*, no. 44, pp. 442–7. Dated to 1008.

47. ibid., no. 33, pp. 407–16.

48. ibid., no. 33, p. 408.

49. ibid., no. 44, pp. 442–7.

50. See Numbers 35:6–34.

51. Whitelock, *English Historical Documents, Vol. 1*, no. 32, pp. 398–407.

52. ibid., no. 44, pp. 444–7.

53. ibid., no. 44, pp. 441–7.

54. 'Then the King will say to those on his right, "Come, you who are blessed by my Father; take your inheritance, the kingdom prepared for you since the creation of the world."'

55. Whitelock, *English Historical Documents, Vol. 1*, no. 177, pp. 816–22. The reference is to Matthew 25:34–40.

56. Bede, *Ecclesiastical History*, III.6.

57. Whitelock, *English Historical Documents, Vol. 1*, no. 45, p. 447.

58. ibid., no. 177, pp. 816–22.

59. The reference is to 1 Corinthians 6:19.

60. Whitelock, *English Historical Documents, Vol. 1*, no. 40, p. 431.

61. ibid., no. 239, pp. 923–8. The reference is to Romans 13:4.

62. 'The dress, the way of wearing the hair, the luxurious habits of the princes and people . . . your trimming of beard and hair, in which you have wished to resemble the pagans . . . Are you not menaced by terror of them whose fashion you wish to follow?' *English Historical Documents, Vol. 1*, no. 193, pp. 842–4.

63. The reference is to John 10:1–18.

64. Whitelock, *English Historical Documents, Vol. 1*, no. 239, p. 925.

65. Canning, *History*, p. 19.

66. Gildas, *The Ruin of Britain*, ed. John Morris (Phillimore, 1978).

67. See Wulfstan's 'Sermon of the Wolf to the English' in Whitelock, *English Historical Documents, Vol. 1*, no. 240, p. 933.

68. Bede, *Ecclesiastical History*, V.24.

69. ibid., Preface.

70. ibid., I.1.

71. Alan Thacker, 'Bede and History', in *Cambridge Companion to Bede* (Cambridge University Press, 2010), p. 173.

72. See J. McClure, 'Bede's Old Testament Kings', in Patrick Wormald et al., eds., *Ideal and Reality in Frankish and Anglo-Saxon Society* (Oxford, 1983), pp.76–98.

73. John Burrow, *A History of Histories: Epics, Chronicles, Romances and Inquiries from Herodotus and Thucydides to the Twentieth Century* (Allen Lane, 2007), p. 215.

74. Arian Christians followed the teachings of the late third- to early fourth-century Egyptian Christian, Arius, whose understanding of Christ's relationship to God the Father was deemed to be heretical.

75. See Adrian Hastings, *The Construction of Nationhood: Ethnicity, Religion and Nationalism* (Cambridge, 1997).

76. The reference is to Amos 8:10.

77. Whitelock, *English Historical Documents, Vol. 1*, no. 44, pp. 442–7.

78. ibid., no. 41, pp. 434–6.

79. Bede, *Ecclesiastical History*, III.8.

80. ibid., II.2.

81. Whitelock, *English Historical Documents, Vol. 1*, no. 31, p. 396.

82. ibid., no. 240, pp. 928–35.

2. 'No traitor to the king but a priest of God'

1. Whitelock, *English Historical Documents, Vol. 1*, no. 53, p. 476.

2. Canning, *History*, p. 92.

3. ibid., p. 88.

4. D.C. Douglas and G.W. Greenaway, eds., *English Historical Documents, Vol. 2: 1042–1189* (Eyre and Spottiswoode, 1953), no. 101, p. 693.

Endnotes

5. Quoted in Frank Barlow, *Thomas Becket* (Phoenix, 1986), p. 63.
6. Quoted ibid., p. 235.
7. Cary Nederman, ed., *John of Salisbury: Policraticus* (Cambridge, 1990), p. xv.
8. ibid., IV.1, p. 28.
9. ibid., IV.2, pp. 30–31.
10. ibid., VIII.17, p. 191.
11. ibid., IV.4, pp. 35–6.
12. James 4:6; 1 Peter 5:5.
13. Luke 14:11.
14. Psalm 132:12.
15. Nederman, *Policraticus*, IV.11, pp. 56–7.
16. Quentin Taylor, 'John of Salisbury, the Policraticus, and Political Thought', *Humanitas*, 19 (2006), pp. 133–57.
17. Nederman, *Policraticus*, IV.1, p. 28. The reference is to Romans 13:2.
18. ibid., VIII.18, p. 201.
19. ibid., VIII.20, p. 207.
20. ibid., VIII.17, p. 191.
21. ibid., VIII.21, p. 210.
22. ibid., VIII.8.21, pp. 210–14.
23. John Baldwin, 'Master Stephen Langton, Future Archbishop of Canterbury: The Paris Schools and Magna Carta', *English Historical Review*, vol. CXXIII, no. 503, p. 813.
24. Quoted ibid., p. 815.
25. A translation from the Latin Vulgate ('erue eos qui ducuntur ad mortem') which captures better the sense in which Langton meant it than does the King James ('Deliver them that are led to death').
26. Quoted ibid., p. 818.
27. ibid., p. 820.
28. ibid., p. 824.
29. It should be noted that this account of events derives from Roger of Wendover's Chronicle which has come under some historical suspicion. See J.C. Holt, *Magna Carta* (Cambridge: Cambridge University Press, 1992), pp. 224–6 for further details.
30. Holt, *Magna Carta*, p. 420.
31. See ibid., Appendix 6.
32. ibid., p. 281.

Endnotes

33. See ibid., pp. 1–2, for more details of which chapters from which (re-) issues of Magna Carta remain law.

34. Jean Froissart, *Chronicles*, trans. Geoffrey Brereton (Penguin, 2004), p. 212.

35. The judgement is Walsingham's. *Chronica Maiora*, p. 162.

36. See Anthony Kenny, *Wyclif* (Oxford, 1985), p. 47.

37. Quoted ibid., p. 92.

38. Quoted ibid., p. 49.

39. See ibid, pp. 58–67.

40. Quoted ibid., p. 63.

41. Quoted ibid.

42. Quoted ibid., p. 65.

43. Daniell, *Bible*, p. 66.

44. ibid., p. 75.

45. Anne Hudson, The *Premature Reformation: Wycliffite Texts and Lollard History* (Oxford: Clarendon Press, 1988), p. 367.

46. Hebrews 4:.12.

3. 'The authority of princes may not be resisted'

1. The story is told in David Daniell, *William Tyndale: A Biography* (Yale University Press, 1994), pp. 209–17.

2. It is worth noting that some Luther scholars believe that Luther had not made his significant intellectual breakthrough until after 1517 and only did so as a result of the ensuing controversy. I am grateful to Graham Tomlin for alerting me to the difference of opinion in the community of Luther scholars.

3. A note on terms: the term 'Protestant' was first coined to describe those German states and cities which in 1529 issued a *protestatio*, a legal plea, for religious toleration. It is somewhat anachronistic for England until around 1550. Before then, the terms most commonly used were 'Lutheran', meaning those who followed Luther's teachings, or 'evangelical', meaning those whose teachings were based on the *evangel* or gospel, and was generally preferred by those of whom it is used. To avoid changing terms midway and to avoid confusion with the later and more familiar use of the terms 'Lutheran', meaning belonging to the Church established in Martin Luther's name, and 'evangelical', meaning,

in effect, a spiritual descendant of the eighteenth-century evangelical awakening, I have used Protestant (as a noun) in this chapter. I have, however, retained 'evangelical' as an adjective.

4. See Diarmaid MacCulloch, *Reformation: Europe's House Divided, 1490–1700* (Allen Lane, 2003), pp. 158–62.

5. Quoted ibid., p. 160.

6. Martin Luther, *Luther's Works, Vol. 45, Temporal Authority: To What Extent it Should be Obeyed* , ed. Walther Brandt (Philadelphia, 1962), pp. 75–129. On Luther's political thought generally see Quentin Skinner, *The Foundations of Modern Political Thought, Vol. 2* (Cambridge: Cambridge University Press, 1978), pp. 3–19.

7. Erasmus, *Paraclesis*, Preface to Greek New Testament, quoted in Daniell, *Tyndale*, p. 67.

8. Quoted in Daniell, *Bible*, p. 142.

9. *A copy of the letters, wherin the most redouted & mighty prince our souerayne lorde kyng Henry the eyght . . . made answere unto a certayne letter of Martyn Luther* (London, 1526), quoted in David Scott Kastan, " 'The Noyse of the New Bible': Reform and Reaction in Henrician England" in *Religion and Culture in Renaissance England*, (eds.) Claire McEachern and Debora Shuger (Cambridge: Cambridge University Press, 1997), p. 62 .

10. Quoted in Daniell, *Bible*, p. 158.

11. William Tyndale, *The Obedience of a Christian Man*, ed. David Daniell (Penguin, 2000), p. 26.

12. 1 Peter 3:1–2: 'Lykewyse let the wyves be in subieccio to their husbades that eve they which beleve not the worde maye with out the worde be wonne by the conversacion of ye wyves: whill they beholde youre pure coversacion coupled with feare' (Tyndale's 1525 New Testament).

13. Ephesians 5:22–3: 'Wemen submit youre selves vnto youre awne husbandes as vnto the Lorde. For the husbande is the wyves heed even as Christ is the heed of the congregacion and the same is the saveoure of the body' (Tyndale's 1525 New Testament).

14. 1 Peter 2:13–14: 'Submit youre selves vnto all manner ordinaunce of man for the lordes sake whether it be vnto the kynge as vnto the chefe heed: other vnto rulars as vnto them that are sent of him for the punysshment of evyll doars: but for the laude of them that do well' (Tyndale's 1525 New Testament).

15. Tyndale, *Obedience*, p. 38. The reference is to Deuteronomy 32:35.

16. ibid., p. 59. The reference is to Ephesians 6 and Colossians 5.

17. ibid., p. 61. See Ephesians 5.

18. ibid., p. 62.

19. ibid.

20. ibid., p. 63.

21. ibid.

22. ibid., p. 181.

23. Quoted in Skinner, *Foundations*, p. 69.

24. Robert Barnes, 'Men's Constitutions', in Neelak Tjernagel, ed., *The Reformation Essays of Dr Barnes*, (London: Concordia Publishing House, 1963), p. 90.

25. John G. Nichols, ed., *Narratives of the Days of the Reformation* (Camden Society, 1859), pp. 52–6.

26. 'If brethren dwell together, and one of them die, and have no child . . . her husband's brother shall go in unto her, and take her to him to wife, and perform the duty of an husband's brother unto her' (Deut. 25:5–10). The issue is raised again in a prominent discussion in the New Testament, Matthew 22:23–8.

27. Edward Foxe, *The True Difference between the Regal Power and the Ecclesiastical Power* (1534).

28. ibid.

29. ibid.

30. Stephen Gardiner, 'On True Obedience', in O'Donovan and O'Donovan, *From Irenaeus to Grotius,* pp. 648–9.

31. Quoted ibid.

32. Stephen Gardiner, *Obedience in Church and State: Three Political Tracts by Stephen Gardiner*, trans. and ed. Pierre Janelle (Cambridge: Cambridge University Press, 1930), p. 95.

33. *The King's Book, or, A Necessary Doctrine and Erudition for any Christian Man*, ed. T.A. Lacey (London, 1932), quoted in Richard Rex, 'The Crisis of Obedience: God's Word and Henry's Reformation', *Historical Journal*, 39, 4, 1996, p. 892.

34. Quoted in Daniell, *Bible*, p. 180.

35. James Gairdner, ed., *Letters and Papers, Foreign and Domestic, of the Reign of Henry VIII* (London: Longman, Green, Longman, & Roberts, 1862–1932), vol. 9 (1535), no. 226, p. 75.

36. Quoted in Rex, 'The Crisis of Obedience', p. 893.

37. A.F. Pollard, *Records of the English Bible: The Documents Relating to the Translation and Publication of the Bible in English, 1525–1611* (OUP, 1911), p. 215.

38. Isaiah 55:11: 'So shall my word be that goeth forth out of my mouth: it shall not return unto me void'; Acts 13:22: 'I have found David the son of Jesse, a man after mine own heart.'

39. 'I exhort, therefore, that first of all, supplications, prayers, intercessions and giving of thanks, be made for all men – for kings and for all that are in authority; that we may lead a quiet and peaceable life in all godliness and honesty.'

40. Quoted in Kastan, 'The Noyse of the New Bible', p. 60.

41. *Tudor Royal Proclamations. Vol. 1: The Early Tudors (1485–1553)*, ed. Paul L. Hughes and James F. Larkin (Yale University Press, 1964) p. 297.

42. Quoted in Kastan, 'The Noyse of the New Bible', p. 61.

43. Diarmaid MacCulloch, *Tudor Church Militant: Edward VI and the Protestant Reformation* (Allen Lane, 1999), pp.20–29.

44. Jehoshaphat was a godly king of Judah in the mid-ninth century BC (see 1 Kgs 22). Jehu was his son who ordered Jezebel to be killed (see 2 Kgs 9).

45. MacCulloch, *Tudor Church Militant*, p. 140.

46. *Sermons, or Homilies, Appointed to be read in Churches* (London: Prayer Book and Homily Society, 1833), Sermon 10, pp. 72–80.

4. 'God at this point gives the sword into the people's hand'

1. Skinner, *Foundations*, p. 196.

2. John Ponet, *A Short Treatise of Politic Power* (1556), reprinted in *John Ponet (1516?–1556), Advocate of Limited Monarchy*, ed. Winthrop Hudson (Chicago, 1942). For Ponet's political thought in general see Skinner, *Foundations*, pp. 217–41.

3. See Brian Tierney, *Religion, Law and the Growth of Constitutional Thought, 1150–1650* (Cambridge, 2008).

4. Christopher Goodman, *How Superior Powers Ought to be Obeyed of their Subjects and wherein they may lawfully by God's word be Disobeyed and Resisted* (Geneva, 1558). See Skinner, *Foundations*, pp. 217–41.

5. Preface, *Geneva Bible*.

6. Tom Furniss, 'Reading the Geneva Bible: Notes Toward An English Revolution?', *Prose Studies*, 31: 1, pp. 1–21.

7. ibid., p. 15.

8. *Sermons, or Homilies*, Sermon 33, pp. 384–419.

9. See O'Donovan and O'Donovan, *From Irenaeus to Grotius*, pp. 685–94.

10. Quoted in Skinner, *Foundations*, p. 237.

11. Daniel Elazar, 'The Political Theory of Covenant: Biblical Origins and Modern Developments', *Publius*, vol. 10, no. 4, Autumn 1980, pp. 3–30.

12. The Scottish Confession of Faith, chap. 24: Of the Civil Magistrate.

13. Another note on terms: Puritan, like the other Elizabethan term 'Precisian', was deployed primarily as a term of abuse. Puritans were more likely to think of themselves as 'the godly' or 'the elect'. I have used the terms interchangeably throughout this and the following chapter.

14. Quoted in Daniell, *Bible*, p. 365.

15. Robert Parsons, *A Brief Discourse Containing Certain Reasons Why Catholics Refuse to go to Church* (1580).

16. John Bridges, *The Supremacie of Christian Princes* (1573).

17. Richard Hooker, *Of the Laws of Ecclesiastical Polity*, ed. Arthur McGrade (Cambridge, 1989).

18. ibid., p. xiii.

19. ibid., I.16.8. See also Philip Bruce Secor, *Richard Hooker: Prophet of Anglicanism* (Burnes and Oates, 1999), chap. 15.

20. Hooker, *Laws*, II.7.7.

21. ibid., VIII.2.1.

22. ibid., VIII.9.3.

23. John Locke, *Second Treatise on Government*, II.5, in *Two Treatises of Government* and *A Letter Concerning Toleration*, ed. Ian Shapiro (Yale, 2003), p. 101.

5. 'A people set at liberty'

1. Quoted in Skinner, *Foundations*, p. 326.

2. ibid., p. 321.

3. George Buchanan, *The Right of the Kingdom in Scotland* (Edinburgh, 1579), pp. 32–3, 58, 62, quoted in Skinner, *Foundations*, p. 342.

4. Quoted in Johann Sommerville, *Royalists and Patriots: Politics and Ideology in England, 1603–1640* (London: Longman, 1999), p. 20.

5. Exodus 20:12.

6. Sommerville, *Royalists*, p. 51.

7.   Sir Robert Heath, quoted ibid., p. 158.

8.   James I, *Basilikon Doron* (Edinburgh, 1599), in *King James VI and I: Political Writings*, ed. Johann Sommerville (Cambridge University Press, 1995), pp. 1–61.

9.   James I, *The True Law of Free Monarchies* (Edinburgh, 1598) in *King James VI and I*, pp. 62–84.

10. William Barlow, *Summe and Substance of the Conference* (1604), quoted in Pollard, *Records*, pp. 46–7.

11. Richard Bancroft, *Rules to be observed in the Translation of the Bible* (1604), quoted in Pollard, *Records*, pp. 53–5.

12. Daniell, *Bible*, p. 446.

13. ibid., p. 451.

14. David Underdown, *Fire From Heaven: Life in an English Town in the Seventeenth Century* (HarperCollins, 1992), p. 5.

15. ibid., p. 148.

16. ibid., p. 223.

17. See Christopher Hill, *The English Bible and the Seventeenth-Century Revolution* (Allen Lane, 1993).

18. ibid., p. 325.

19. ibid., p. 329.

20. ibid., p. 113.

21. I am grateful to Andrew Bradstock for his advice on this section and, in particular, for allowing me to see an advance copy of his book *Radical Religion in Cromwell's England : A Concise History from the English Civil War to the End of the Commonwealth* (London: I.B. Tauris, 2010).

22. Quoted in John Spurr, *The Post-Reformation: Religion, Politics and Society in Britain, 1603–1714* (Longman, 2006), p. 101.

23. See Nicholas McDowell, *The English Radical Imagination: Culture, Religion, and Revolution, 1630–1660* (Oxford, 2003). I am grateful to John Coffey for bringing this point and this book to my attention.

24. Gerrard Winstanley, *The New Law of Righteousness* (London, 1649).

25. Gerard Winstanley, *The Fire in the Bush* (London: 1650), quoted in Bradstock, *Radical Religion*.

26. ibid.

27. As Christopher Hill has remarked, 'the Levellers were never a united, disciplined party or movement, as historians find to their cost when they try to define their doctrines with any precision.'

28. Quoted in Bradstock, *Radical Religion*.

29. Quoted ibid.

30. *Agreement of the People*, in *Divine Right and Democracy: An Anthology of Political Writing in Stuart England*, ed. David Wootton (Harmondsworth: Penguin, 1986), pp. 283–5.

31. *The Putney Debates*, in *Divine Right and Democracy*, pp. 285–317.

32. Quoted in Spurr, *Post-Reformation*, p. 107.

33. W.C. Abbot, *The Writings and Speeches of Oliver Cromwell*, 4 vols. (Cambridge, Mass., 1937–47), IV, pp. 272, 277–8, 965, quoted in John Morrill, ed., *Oliver Cromwell and the English Revolution* (Longman, 1990) p. 204.

34. Abbott, *Cromwell*, IV, pp. 271–2, quoted in Morrill, *Oliver Cromwell*, p. 211.

35. Socinianism refers to anti-Trinitarian beliefs, so named after Socinus, the Latinised name for Lelio Sozini and Fausto Paolo Sozzini, a sixteenth-century Italian uncle and nephew who first popularised the ideas in Europe. It lay some way beyond the bounds of Christian orthodoxy and was thus deemed dangerous and intolerable.

36. J.C. Davis, 'Cromwell's Religion', in Morrill, *Oliver Cromwell*, p. 189.

37. Abbott, *Cromwell*, III, p. 459, quoted in Morrill, *Oliver Cromwell*, pp. 193–4.

38. Anthony Fletcher, 'Oliver Cromwell and the Godly Nation', in Morrill, *Oliver Cromwell*, p. 233.

39. *Complete Prose Works of John Milton*, ed. Don M. Wolfe (OUP, 1953–82), vol. I, p. 650.

40. ibid., IV.344.

41. ibid., VII.456.

42. ibid., IV.378.

43. In which Jesus tells his disciples, 'Ye know that the princes of the Gentiles exercise dominion over them, and they that are great exercise authority upon them. But it shall not be so among you.'

44. Milton, *Complete Prose Works*, II.236.

45. ibid., II.340.

46. ibid., II.345.

47. ibid., II.596.

48. ibid., II.451.

49. ibid., I.795.

50. ibid., I.788.
51. ibid., VI.212.
52. ibid., IV.611.
53. ibid., IV.680.
54. ibid., VII.9–95.
55. Thomas Hobbes, *Leviathan* (Oxford World's Classics, 1998), p. 7.
56. ibid., pp.82–3.
57. ibid., p. 83.
58. ibid., p. 222.
59. ibid.
60. ibid.
61. ibid., p. 217.
62. The term comes from Job 41: 'Upon earth there is not his like, who is made without fear. He beholdeth all high things: he is a king over all the children of pride' (vv. 33–4). It is no accident that the three other references to Leviathan in the Bible, Psalm 74:14, Psalm 104:26 and Isaiah 27:1, all assert God's supremacy over him, most obviously the first: 'Thou brakest the heads of leviathan in pieces, and gavest him to be meat to the people inhabiting the wilderness.'
63. Hobbes, *Leviathan*, p. 218.
64. ibid., p. 291.
65. ibid., p. 248.
66. ibid., p. 272.
67. ibid., p. 297.
68. ibid., p. 257.
69. ibid., p. 252.
70. ibid., p. 253.
71. ibid., p. 257.
72. ibid., pp. 258–9.
73. ibid., p. 259.
74. Noel Malcolm, '*Leviathan*, the Pentateuch, and the Origins of Modern Biblical Criticism', in Tom Sorell and Luc Foisneau, eds., *Leviathan after 350 Years* (Clarendon Press, 2004), p. 255.
75. Quoted in Spurr, *Post-Reformation*, p. 131.
76. Quoted in Hill, *English Bible*, p. 232.
77. Not, however, millenarianism itself which remained a subject of fascination for many.

78. Coffey, 'The Impact of Apocalypticism during the Puritan Revolutions', *Perichoresis*, vol. 4.2, 2006, p. 131.

79. Hill, *English Bible*, p. 243.

80. Coffey, 'Impact of Apocalypticism', p. 135.

81. Matthew 10:28–9: 'And fear not them which kill the body, but are not able to kill the soul: but rather fear him which is able to destroy both soul and body in hell. Are not two sparrows sold for a farthing? and one of them shall not fall on the ground without your Father.'

82. *The Works of Richard Sibbes, D.D.*, ed. A.B. Grosart, 7 vols. (Edinburgh, 1857–64), vol. 5, p. 35; quoted in Blair Worden, 'Providence and Politics in Cromwellian England', *Past & Present*, no. 109 (Nov. 1985), p. 60.

6. 'Under our vines we'll sit and sing'

1. Hill, *English Bible* , p. 419.

2. *The Diary of John Evelyn*, ed. E.S. de Beer, 6 vols. (Oxford, 1955), vol. 5, pp. 177–8, quoted in Julian Hoppit, *A Land of Liberty?: England 1689–1727* (Oxford, 2000) p. 218.

3. It expired in 1668 but was made permanent in 1670.

4. Although, curiously, at least two editions were printed with the Geneva notes.

5. By taking communion according to the Anglican rite once a year.

6. Linda Colley, *Britons: Forging the Nation, 1707–1837* (Yale University Press, 1992), p. 54.

7. See Ruth Smith, *Handel's Oratorios and Eighteenth-Century Thought* (Cambridge: Cambridge University Press, 1995).

8. Quoted in Colley, *Britons*, p. 76.

9. *First Tract on Government*, quoted in Roger Woolhouse, *John Locke* (Cambridge, 2007) p. 42.

10. *First Tract on Government*, quoted in Kim Parker, *The Biblical Politics of John Locke* (Wilfrid Laurier University Press, 2004) p. 12.

11. ibid., p. 13.

12. Quoted in Woolhouse, *Locke*, p. 63.

13. Quoted ibid.

14. *Essay Concerning Toleration*, quoted in Woolhouse, *Locke*, p. 85.

15. John Smyth, *The Mistery of Iniquity* (1612), p. 69, quoted in John Coffey, 'Puritanism and Liberty Revisited: The Case for Toleration in

the English Revolution', *Historical Journal*, vol. 41, no. 4, Dec. 1998, p. 964.

16. Leonard Busher, *Religion's Peace: or, a Plea for Liberty of Conscience* (1614), quoted in Coffey, 'Puritanism and Liberty', pp. 964–5.

17. J.R. McMichael and B. Taft, eds., *The Writings of William Walwyn* (Athens, GA, 1989), pp. 57–9, quoted in Coffey, 'Puritanism and Liberty', p. 970.

18. Richard Laurence, *The Antichristian Presbyter* (1646), quoted in Coffey, 'Puritanism and Liberty', p. 967.

19. Henry Robinson, *Certaine Briefe Observations* (1644), quoted in Coffey, 'Puritanism and Liberty', p. 972.

20. Roger Williams, *Bloudy Tenent*, quoted in Coffey, 'Puritanism and Liberty', p. 972.

21. Locke, *Toleration*, p. 219.
22. ibid.
23. ibid., p. 239.
24. ibid.
25. ibid., pp. 239–40.
26. ibid.
27. ibid., p. 218.
28. ibid.
29. ibid.
30. ibid., p. 233.
31. ibid., p. 220.
32. ibid., p. 226.
33. ibid., pp. 240–41.
34. ibid., p. 245.
35. ibid., p. 246.
36. ibid.
37. ibid., p. 233.
38. ibid., p. 251.
39. ibid., p. 243.
40. Eric Nelson makes a convincing if counter-intuitive argument that it was the model of Israel in the Old Testament that inspired toleration in seventeenth-century Europe, by blurring civil and religious domains, in a way that most Erastian thinkers seized upon, and then implying that only minimal religious legislation (i.e. relating to public order) was legitimate.

See Eric Nelson, *The Hebrew Republic* (Harvard University Press, 2010), especially pp. 88–137.

41. Robert Filmer, *Patriarcha and Other Writings*, ed. J.P. Sommerville (Cambridge, 1991), I.1, p. 2.

42. ibid., II.5, p. 19.

43. ibid., I.4, p. 7.

44. ibid., I.10, p. 11.

45. 'When the Jews asked our Blessed Saviour whether they should pay tribute, He did not first demand what the law of the land was, or whether there was any statute against it, nor inquired whether the tribute were given by consent of the people, nor advised them to stay their payment till they should grant it' Filmer, *Patriarcha*, III.3, p. 39.

46. Jeremy Waldron, *God, Locke and Equality: Christian Foundations in Locke's Political Thought* (Cambridge, 2002), p. 191.

47. Locke, *First Treatise*, #16.

48. ibid., #30.

49. ibid., #44.

50. ibid., #60.

51. ibid.

52. ibid., #29.

53. Including Leviticus 19:3: 'Ye shall fear every man his mother, and his father'; Deuteronomy 27:16: 'Cursed be he that setteth light by his father or his mother'; Proverbs 1:8: 'My son, hear the instruction of thy father, and forsake not the law of thy mother'; Isaiah 45:10: 'Woe unto him, that saith unto his father, What begettest thou? or to the woman, What hast thou brought forth?'; Ezekiel 22:7: 'In thee have they set light by father and mother'; Matthew 15:4: 'Honour thy father and mother: and, he that curseth father or mother, let him die the death!'; and Ephesians 6:1: 'Children, obey your parents,' of which Locke remarks typically, 'I do not remember, that I any where read, Children, obey your father' Locke, *First Treatise*, #61.

54. Locke, *First Treatise*, #15.

55. ibid., #55.

56. 'Thy desire shall be to thy husband, and he shall rule over thee.'

57. Locke, *First Treatise*, #47.

58. Locke, *Second Treatise*, #82.

59. ibid., #4.

60. ibid., #6.

61. John Locke, *The Reasonableness of Christianity*, ed. I.T. Ramsey (Stanford University Press, 1958), p. 76.

62. Locke's most noted modern interpreter, James Dunn, has observed that 'Jesus Christ (and Saint Paul) may not appear in person in the text of the Two Treatises but their presence can hardly be missed when we come upon the normative creaturely equality of all men in virtue of their shared species-membership' (Dunn, *Political Thought of John Locke* (Cambridge, 1969), p. 99). In his recent study of Locke's political thought, *God, Locke and Equality*, Jeremy Waldron emphasises the theological basis of Locke's work and goes as far as to say: 'I don't actually think it is clear that we – now – can shape and defend an adequate conception of basic human equality apart from some religious foundation' (p. 13).

63. Quoted in Robert Hole, *Pulpits, Politics and Public Order in England, 1760–1832* (Cambridge, 1989), p. 15.

64. John Locke, *An Essay Concerning Human Understanding* (Oxford World's Classics, 2008), p. 451.

65. Locke, *Reasonableness*, p. 25.

66. ibid., p. 32.

67. ibid., p. 61.

68. John Toland, *Christianity not Mysterious* (London, 1702), p. 6.

69. ibid., p. 46.

70. ibid., p. 37.

71. Mathew Tindal, *Christianity as Old as Creation* (London, 1730), pp. vi–viii.

72. ibid., p. 262.

7. 'The inestimable price of Christ's blood'

1. David Bebbington, *Evangelicalism in Modern Britain: A History from the 1730s to the 1980s* (Routledge, 1988).

2. ibid., p. 11.

3. ibid., p. 87.

4. Wesley to Thomas Rutherford, 28 Mar. 1768, quoted in Bebbington, *Evangelicalism*, p. 52.

5. This is not to claim that there were no instances of political involvement,

for example during the Seven Years War, but rather that the underlying principle was one of political detachment. I am grateful to David Bebbington for pointing this out to me.

6. Luke 12:13–14: 'And one of the company said unto him, Master, speak to my brother, that he divide the inheritance with me. And he said unto him, Man, who made me a judge or a divider over you?'

7. Matthew 22:21: 'They say unto him, Caesar's. Then saith he unto them, Render therefore unto Caesar the things which are Caesar's; and unto God the things that are God's.'

8. 2 Timothy 2:4.

9. John Newton, *Works of the Revd John Newton* (London, 1824) vol. VI, p. 594. It was, however, Newton who also helped persuade Wilberforce *not* to quit politics after his conversion. I am grateful to Steve Tomkins for reminding me of this fact.

10. John Newton, *Political Debate on Christian Principles: or, the Substance of a Correspondence between the Reverend John Newton and the Reverend David Williamson* (Edinburgh, 1793), quoted in Lyon, *Politicians*, p. 24.

11. J. Owen, *Memoir of the Rev. T. Jones, late of Creaton* (London, 1851), p. 160, quoted in Bebbington, *Evangelicalism*, p. 72.

12. *A Letter to Richard Hill, Esq. by a freeholder* (2nd edn, 1782), p. 30, quoted in Ian Bradley, *The Politics of Godliness: Evangelicals in Parliament, 1784–1832* (unpublished D.Phil. dissertation, Oxford, 1974), p. 72.

13. Quoted in Stephen Tomkins, *William Wilberforce* (Lion, 2007), p. 58.

14. Quoted in John Coffey, 'Evangelicals, Slavery and the Slave Trade: From Whitefield to Wilberforce', *Anvil*, vol. 24, no. 2, 2007, p. 98.

15. 'Whether it be lawful for Christians to buy slaves, and thereby encourage the nations from whom they are bought, to be at perpetual war with each other, I shall not take upon me to determine.' Quoted in Coffey, 'Evangelicals, Slavery and the Slave Trade', p. 98.

16. Quoted in Coffey, 'Evangelicals, Slavery and the Slave Trade', p. 99.

17. 'The sense of this Meeting that the Importing of Negroes from their native Country and Relations by Friends is not a commendable nor allowed practice which Answers and sense is approved and that practice [is] censured by this meeting . . .' Quoted in Maeve Sherlock, *The Influence of Religion on the British Campaign against the Slave Trade: An Exploration of its Biblical and Theological Roots up to 1807* (unpublished M.Phil. Thesis) p. 2.

18. Epistle from the 1763 London Yearly Meeting, quoted in Sherlock, *Influence*, p. 3.

19. Although this did not prevent him from using thumbscrews on some of his 'cargo'.

20. Olaudah Equiano, *The Interesting Narrative and Other Writings*, ed. V. Caretta (Penguin, 2003), pp. 1–34.

21. Quoted in John M.G. Barclay, '"Am I not a Man and a Brother?" The Bible and the British Anti-Slavery Campaign', *Expository Times*, 2007, vol. 119, no. 1, p. 12.

22. Abraham Booth, *Commerce in the Human Species, and the Enslaving of Innocent Persons, inimical to the Law of Moses and the Gospel of Christ* (London, 1792), p. 28, quoted in John Coffey, 'The Abolition of the Slave Trade', *Cambridge Papers*, vol. 15, no. 2, June 2006.

23. Ottabah Cugoano, *Thoughts and Sentiments on the Evil of Slavery* (London, 1787), p. 25, quoted in Coffey, 'Abolition'.

24. Equiano, *Interesting Narrative*, p. 339.

25. Raymund Harris, *Scriptural Researches on the Licitness of the Slave-Trade, Shewing its Conformity with the Principles of Natural and Revealed Religion, Delineated in the Sacred Writings of the Word of God* (London: John Stockdale, 1788).

26. ibid., p. 35.

27. ibid., p. 57.

28. 1 Timothy 6:1: 'Let as many servants as are under the yoke count their own masters worthy of all honour, that the name of God and his doctrine be not blasphemed.'

29. Philemon 10–11: 'I beseech thee for my son Onesimus, whom I have begotten in my bonds: Which in time past was to thee unprofitable, but now profitable to thee and to me.'

30. Harris, *Scriptural Researches*, p. 71.

31. Booth, *Commerce,* quoted in Coffey, 'Abolition'.

32. For example Exodus 21:16 ('He that stealeth a man, and selleth him, or if he be found in his hand, he shall surely be put to death') or Deuteronomy 24:7 ('If a man be found stealing any of his brethren of the children of Israel, and maketh merchandise of him, or selleth him; then that thief shall die; and thou shalt put evil away from among you'). Cugoano, *Thoughts and Sentiments*, quoted in Coffey, 'Abolition'.

33. 1 Timothy 1:9–10: 'the law is not made for a righteous man, but for the lawless and disobedient, for the ungodly and for sinners, for unholy and profane, for murderers of fathers and murderers of mothers, for manslayers, for whoremongers, for them that defile themselves with mankind, for menstealers, for liars, for perjured persons . . .'

34. Thomas Gisborne, *The Principles of Moral Philosophy* (London, 1789). I am grateful to Steve Tomkins for alerting me to these arguments.

35. Granville Sharp, *The Law of Retribution* (London, 1776), 4–6, quoted in Sherlock, *Influence*, p. 13.

36. Granville Sharp, *An Essay on Slavery, proving from Scripture its Inconsistency with Humanity and Religion* (London, 1776), pp. 31–2.

37. When, in June 1806, Charles James Fox moved a resolution in the Commons and Grenville in the Lords condemning the slave trade, at least one MP insisted that the trade was defensible on scriptural ground, quoting Leviticus to justify his contention. See Thomas Clarkson, *The History of the Rise, Progress, and Accomplishment of the Abolition of the African Slave-Trade by the British Parliament* (London: Longman, Rees, and Orme, 1808), vol. 2, p. 515, quoted in Sherlock, *Influence*, pp. 10–11.

38. David Brion Davis, *The Problem of Slavery in the Age of Revolution 1770–1823*, (Ithaca, N.Y: Cornell University Press, 1975), p. 549.

39. Quoted in Coffey, 'Evangelicals', p. 114.

40. Augustin Barruel, *Memoirs Illustrating the History of Jacobinism* (London, 1797), p. xxi, quoted in Lyon, *Politicians*, p. 44.

41. Anon., *Reflections, Moral, and Political, on the Murder of Louis XVI* (London, 1793), quoted in Lyon, *Politicians*, p. 19.

42. Thoms Biddulph, *Seasonable Hints to the Poor, on the Duties of Frugality, Piety, and Loyalty* (Bristol, 1797), p. 24, quoted in Lyon, *Politicians*, p. 19.

43. Quoted in Lyon, *Politicians*, p. 78.

44. ibid.

45. Quoted in Michael Watts, *The Dissenters: Volume II: The Expansion of Evangelical Nonconformity* (Oxford: Clarendon Press, 1995), p. 351.

46. Quoted ibid.

47. Quoted ibid., p. 356.

48. Andrew Fuller, *The Backslider* (1801), quoted in Watts, *Dissenters*, p. 357.

Endnotes

49. Hansard, 1819, xii, 135, quoted in Bradley, *Politics*, p. 225.

50. Henry Bathurst, *Christianity and Present Politics How Far Reconcilable* (London, 1818), pp. 33, 68, quoted in Bradley, *Politics*, p. 226.

51. It was this mentality that lay behind one of the most important theses – and debates – relating to the role of Christianity in British history, i.e. whether the evangelical (or Methodist) revival in the eighteenth century saved the nation from the violent revolutions that dominated European history. The argument (that it did) is most commonly associated with Elie Halévy's six-volume *History of the English People in the Nineteenth Century* (London: Benn, 1949–52) and provoked important responses from Edward Thompson, *The Making of the English Working Class* (London: Victor Gollancz,, 1963) and Eric Hobsbawm, *Labouring Men: Studies in the History of Labour* (Weidenfeld and Nicolson, 1964). Discussing the thesis Michael Watts concludes 'the growth of Evangelical Nonconformity in the first half of the nineteenth century did not prevent political upheaval, radical protest, or growing class conflict; but it did guarantee that most of that protest and conflict would be contained within constitutional limits, accompanied by a minimum of violence, and expressed for much of the time in the language of the Bible' (Watts, *Dissenters*, p. 377).

52. Although a third, London's Bishop Blomfield, later claimed he would have voted in favour if he had been able to attend the House. Owen Chadwick, *The Victorian Church, Part 1* (Adam and Charles Black, 1966), p. 25.

53. Quoted in Hole, *Pulpits*, p. 90.

54. Benjamin Rhodes, *A Discourse on Civil Government, and Religious Liberty* (London: J. Belcher, 1796), quoted in Hole, *Pulpits*, p. 114.

55. Henry Best, *The Christian Religion Briefly Defended against the Philosophers and Republicans of France* (London, 1793), p. 47, quoted in Lyon, *Politicians*, p. 16.

56. Charles Daubeny, *A Sermon Applicable to the Present Times* (Bath, 1793), p. 3, quoted in Lyon, *Politicians*, p. 17.

57. Thomas Robert Malthus, *An Essay on the Principle of Population* (Oxford World Classics, 1999), II.9, p. 13.

58. Malthus, *Essay*, (6th edn, 1826) II.9.

59. Malthus, *Essay*, V.6, p. 37.

60. William Paley, *Natural Theology* (Oxford World's Classics, 2008), p. 264.

61. Thomas Chalmers, *The Bridgewater Treatises on the Power, Wisdom and Goodness of God as Manifested in Creation, Treatise 1: The Adaptation of External Nature to the Moral and Intellectual Constitution of Man*, 2 vols. (London, 1833). Quoted in A.M.C. Waterman, 'The Ideological Alliance of Political Economy and Christian Theology, 1798–1833', *Journal of Ecclesiastical History*, vol. 34, no. 2, Apr. 1983, p. 237.

62. Malthus, *Essay*, XVIII.11, p. 146.

63. J.B. Sumner, *A Treatise on the Records of Creation with Particular Reference to the Jewish History, and the Consistency of the Principle of Population with the Wisdom and Goodness of the Deity* (London, 1816), ii, 143, quoted in Waterman, 'Ideological Alliance', p. 235.

64. Paley, *Natural Theology*, p. 263.

65. Malthus, *Essay*, XV. 6, p. 117.

66. Richard Whatley, *Introductory Lectures on Political Economy* (London, 1832), Lecture 4, pp. 93–6.

67. Goldwin Smith, *An Inaugural Lecture* (Oxford and London, 1859), quoted in Boyd Hilton, *The Age of Atonement: The Influence of Evangelicalism on Social and Economic Thought, 1785–1865* (Oxford: Clarendon Press, 1988), p. 54.

68. Hilton, *Atonement*, p. 8.

69. Adam Smith, *The Theory of Moral Sentiments*, (Penguin Classics, 2010), p. 187.

70. Thomas Chalmers, *On Political Economy in Connexion with the Moral State and Moral Prospects of Society* (Glasgow, 1832), pp. 411–25, quoted in Waterman, 'Ideological Alliance', pp. 241–2.

71. Thomas Spencer, *Objections to the New Poor Law Answered, Part II* (London, 1841), p. 3, quoted in Lyon, *Politicians*, p. 160.

72. Quoted in Hilton, *Atonement*, p. 99.

73. Acts 6:2.

74. E. Copleston, *A Second Letter to the Right Hon. Robert Peel, M.P. for the University of Oxford, on the Causes of the Increase in Pauperism and the Poor Laws* (Oxford, 1819), p. 17, quoted in Waterman, 'Ideological Alliance', p. 241.

75. Copleston, *Second Letter*, p. 22, quoted in Peter Mandler, 'Tories and Paupers: Christian Political Economy and the Making of the New Poor Law', *Historical Journal*, vol. 33, no. 1, Mar. 1990, pp. 81–103.

76. Copleston, *Second Letter*, pp. 21–2, quoted in Waterman, 'Ideological Alliance', p. 241.

77. Chalmers, *Bridgewater Treatises*, pp. 248–9.

78. Malthus, *Essay*, (6th edn, 1826) VIII,7.

79. Robert and Samuel Wilberforce, eds., *The Life of William Wilberforce* (London, 1838), III.298.

80. James Raven, 'The Abolition of the English State Lotteries', *Historical Journal*, vol. 34, no. 2, June 1991, pp. 371–89.

81. Quoted in Bradley, *Politics*, p. 117.

82. Quoted ibid., p. 116.

83. It is worth noting that many of these societies were not exclusively evangelical, often being supported, and sometimes run by, High churchmen who were equally concerned with the moral state of society. I am grateful to Steve Tomkins for pointing this out to me.

84. Quoted in Tomkins, *Wilberforce*, p. 220.

85. Quoted in Bradley, *Politics*, p. 119.

86. Bradley, *Politics*, p. 132.

87. Wilberforce, *Life of William Wilberforce*, II.436–7.

88. Hansard, 1831, viii, 421, quoted in Bradley, *Politics*, p. 227.

89. Wilberforce, *Life of William Wilberforce*, V.126.

8. *'Everything for time, and nothing for eternity'*

1. Quoted in Hilton, *Atonement*, p. 102.

2. Quoted ibid., p. 103.

3. J. Wellman Warner, *The Wesleyan Movement in the Industrial Revolution* (London: Longmans, 1930) p. 210, quoted in John Wolffe, ed., *Evangelical Faith and Public Zeal: Evangelicals and Society in Britain, 1780–1980* (London: SPCK, 1995) p. 31. Wesley himself practised what he preached.

4. Kathleen Heasman, *Evangelicals in Action: An Appraisal of their Social Work in the Victorian Era* (Geoffery Bliss, 1962), p. 14.

5. National Probation Service, *A Century of Cutting Crime* (Home Office, 2007).

6. Quoted in Frank Prochaska, *Christianity and Social Service in Modern Britain: The Disinherited Spirit* (Cambridge: Cambridge University Press, 2006), p. 24.

7. Quoted in Hole, *Pulpits*, p. 139.

8. Quoted in Lyon, *Politicians*, p. 20.

9. Quoted in Bradley, *Politics*, p. 221.

10. Hansard, 1829, xxi, 981, quoted in Bradley, *Politics*, p. 221.

11. Quoted in Richard Turnbull, *Shaftesbury: The Great Reformer* (Lion, 2010) p. 14.

12. Turnbull discusses the debate about when exactly Shaftesbury was converted. See *Shaftesbury*, pp. 21–39.

13. Quoted in Turnbull, *Shaftesbury*, p. 21; *Record*, 16 May 1839.

14. See Norman Cohn, *The Pursuit of the Millennium: Revolutionary Millenarians and Mystical Anarchists of the Middle Ages* (Paladin, 1970).

15. Quoted in Turnbull, *Shaftesbury*, p. 222.

16. Quoted ibid., p. 62.

17. Quoted ibid., p. 64.

18. Of which he remarked, 'I will not consent to give my support, however humble, towards the existence of exoteric and esoteric doctrines in the Church of England, to obscure the perspicuity of the Gospel by the philosophy of Paganism' (quoted in Turnbull, *Shaftesbury*, p. 103).

19. This had received a grant since its foundation in 1795 but in the mid-1840s Robert Peel sought to calm Irish anger by increasing the sum. It proved a hugely controversial move.

20. When the re-established English Roman Catholic hierarchy talked openly of a Catholic England restored to the orbit of Rome.

21. Quoted in Turnbull, *Shaftesbury*, p. 88.

22. Quoted ibid.

23. Concerning the failure of his Sweeps Bill in 1854 he remarked in his diary: 'Very sad and low about the loss of the Sweeps Bill – the prolonged sufferings, the terrible degradation, the licensed tyranny, the helpless subjection, the enormous mass of cruelty and crime on the part of parents and employers, are overwhelming', a comment typical of his humanitarian concerns (quoted in Turnbull, *Shaftesbury*, p. 162).

24. Quoted in Turnbull, *Shaftesbury*, p. 204.

25. Niall Ferguson, *Empire: How Britain Made the Modern World* (Allen Lane, 2003), p. 1.

26. Geneva Version, quoted in Ferguson, *Empire*, p. 5.

27. J.A. James, *The Attraction of the Cross: A Sermon* (London, 1819),

quoted in Brian Stanley, *The Bible and the Flag: Protestant Missions and British Imperialism in the Nineteenth and Twentieth Centuries* (Apollos, 1990), p. 62.

28. Psalm 2:8.
29. Revelation 11:15.
30. Quoted in Stanley, *Bible*, p. 68.
31. For Smith's story see Stanley, *Bible*, pp. 86–8.
32. Quoted in Bebbington, *Evangelicalism*, p. 133.
33. Charles Darwin, *Voyage of the Beagle* (London: Henry Colburn, 1839), p. 607.
34. ibid., pp. 493–4.
35. William Shaw, *The Story of my Mission in South-Eastern Africa* (London, 1860), pp. 137–8, quoted in Stanley, *Bible*, p. 95.
36. For example, 'neither fornicators, nor idolaters, nor adulterers, nor effeminate, nor abusers of themselves with mankind, nor thieves, nor covetous, nor drunkards, nor revilers, nor extortioners, shall inherit the kingdom of God' (1 Cor. 6:9–10).
37. A. Mayhew, *Christianity and the Government of India* (London, 1929) p. 22, quoted in Stanley, *Bible*, p. 99.
38. Quoted in Ferguson, *Empire*, p. 136.
39. Quoted ibid., p. 155.
40. Stanley, *Bible*, p. 49.
41. Watts, *Dissenters*, p. 526.
42. Hilton, *Atonement*, p. 246.
43. J.C. Buckmaster, *A Village Politician* (London: T. Fisher Unwin, 1897), pp. 39, 190, quoted in Eugenio F. Biagini, *Liberty, Retrenchment and Reform: Popular Liberalism in the Age of Gladstone, 1860–1880* (Cambridge: Cambridge University Press, 1992), pp. 32, 38.
44. In reference to which Gladstone remarked, 'I have no fear of Atheism in this House. Truth is the expression of the Divine mind; and however little our feeble vision may be able to discern the means by which God will provide for its preservation, we may leave the matter in His hands, and we may be quite sure that a firm and courageous application of every principle of justice and of equity is the best method we can adopt for the preservation and influence of truth.' See David Bebbington, *William Ewart Gladstone: Faith and Politics in Victorian Britain* (Grand Rapids, Mich.: W.B. Eerdmans, 1993), p. 194.

45. Quoted in David Bebbington, *The Nonconformist Conscience: Chapel and Politics, 1870–1914* (London: Allen & Unwin, 1982), p. 3.

46. Quoted ibid., p. 10.

47. Quoted ibid., p. 21.

48. Andrew Mearns, *The Bitter Cry of Outcast London* (London: London Congregational Union, 1883).

49. Quoted in Bebbington, *Nonconformist Conscience*, p. 158.

50. Quoted in Hole, *Pulpits*, p. 236.

51. Quoted in Bradley, *Politics*, p. 183.

52. *Christian Observer*, 23, 1824, 265.

53. Hansard, 1830, xxiii, 1298, quoted in Bradley, *Politics*, p. 252; reference to Micah 6:8.

54. Hansard, 3rd series, 1832, x, 392, quoted in Bradley, *Politics*, p. 258.

55. Hansard, 1832, ix, 901.

56. Quoted in Bradley, *Politics*, p. 259.

57. Quoted in Hilton, *Atonement*, p. 279.

58. Charles Gore, *Belief in God* (Murray, 1921), pp. 19–20.

59. Quoted in Bebbington, *Evangelicalism*, p. 194.

60. Quoted in Turnbull, *Shaftesbury*, p. 151.

61. Quoted in Prochaska, *Christianity*, p. 46.

62. The answer is near the town of Adullam. It was where King David, already anointed as the next King of Israel, sought refuge with his companions from the murderous Saul. The story is told in 1 Samuel 22 and is not as spectacularly obscure as virtually all modern readers will assume, coming from a seminal moment in Israel's history and giving rise to the term Adullamites, meaning a group of political outsiders plotting their comeback, especially after a recent defeat, and being used as a derisory name for a dissident faction within Victorian politics.

9. *'Jesus Christ was the first Chartist'*

1. Dissenters, despite being given the freedom to worship, were required to meet in unlocked buildings and to register their assemblies with the local bishop, archdeacon or justice of the peace, as well, of course, as paying tithes for services they didn't use.

2. Such as the 1719 Act for Quieting and Establishing Corporations (which provided that anyone elected to a town corporation, whose tenure was not

Endnotes

questioned six months thereafter, was freed from the need for any sacramental qualification) and the 1726 Indemnity Act (which allowed holders of corporate office to receive the sacrament according to Anglican rite *after* achieving office, rather than insisting they did so a year beforehand, as had been the case).

3. In fact, under the conditions of the Act of Toleration, they only had to subscribe to thirty-six of the Thirty-Nine Articles, being exempt from Articles 34, 35 and 36.

4. James Murray, *Eikon Basilike* (Newcastle, 1778), p. 29, quoted in James E. Bradley, *Religion, Revolution and English Radicalism: Non-conformity in Eighteenth-Century Politics and Society* (Cambridge: Cambridge University Press, 1990), pp. 152–3.

5. Caleb Evans, *A Reply to the Rev. Mr. Fletcher's Vindication of Mr. Wesley's Calm Address to Our American Colonies* (Bristol, 1776), p. 52, quoted in Bradley, *Religion*, p. 155.

6. James Murray, *The Fast. A Poem* (Newcastle upon Tyne: T. Robson and Co, 1778), p. 7, quoted in Bradley, *Religion*, p. 156.

7. George Walker, *The Doctrine of Providence*, in *Sermons*, 4:273–4 (London, 1790), quoted in Bradley, *Religion*, pp. 163–4.

8. See Richard Holmes, *Coleridge: Early Visions* (London: Hodder and Stoughton, 1989), pp. 94–8.

9. Richard Holmes, *Coleridge: Darker Reflections* (London: HarperCollins, 1998), p. 440.

10. James Pilkington, *The Doctrine of Equality of Rank and Condition examined and supported on the Authority of the New Testament, and on the Principles of Reason and Benevolence* (London, 1795), p. 8, quoted in Lyon, *Politicians*, p. 38.

11. Robert Hall, *Christianity Consistent with a Love of Freedom*, in Olinthus Gregory, ed., *The Works of Robert Hall* (London, 1832), III.51, quoted in Lyon, *Politicians*, p. 35.

12. Anon., *Remarks on a Sermon Lately Published by the Rev. John Clayton* (London, 1791), p. 12, quoted in Lyon, *Politicians*, p. 34.

13. Noah Hill, *A Remonstrance with Rev. Mr Clayton* (London, 1791), pp.35–41, quoted in Lyon, *Politicians*, p. 35.

14. Thomas Paine, *The Rights of Man* (Penguin Books, 1985), p. 66.

15. *Gorgon*, no. 29, 5 Dec. 1818, p. 230, quoted in Lyon, *Politicians*, p. 66.

16. Anon., *A Sermon for the Conversion of the Bishops to Christianity* (London, n.d.), pp. 6–7, quoted in Lyon, *Politicians*, p. 74.

17. i.e. 'blameless . . . vigilant, sober, of good behaviour . . . not greedy'. The advertisement can be seen in Lyon, *Politicians*, p. 91.

18. John Wade, *The Black Book; or Corruption Unmasked!*, 2 vols. (London, 1820), I.274, quoted in Hole, *Pulpits*, p. 232.

19. John Cartwright, *Commonwealth in Danger* (London, 1795), pp. lxxi–lxxiii; and *The Constitutional Defence of England* (London, 1796), p. 45, quoted in Hole, *Pulpits*, p. 147.

20. Roger Radical, *Why are we Poor?* (London, 1820), quoted in Lyon, *Politicians*, p. 75.

21. See Hole, *Pulpits*, chap. 15.

22. Anon., *Jesus Christ the Only Radical Reformer* (Manchester, 1838), quoted in Lyon, *Politicians*, p. 73.

23. Henry Bathurst, *Christianity and Present Politics* (London, 1818), pp. 66–9, quoted in Hole, *Pulpits*, p. 184.

24. Thomas Gisborne, *Plain Proof to the Poor that the Bible is the Word of God, with some advice suited to present times* (London, 1833), quoted in Lyon, *Politicians*, p. 87.

25. Vicesimus Knox, *Spirit of Despotism* (London, 1822), pp. 44–5, quoted in Hole, *Pulpits*, p. 224.

26. Respectively Luke 10:30–37, 16:19–31, Matthew 5:1–11 and Matthew 25:42–6.

27. Anon., *The Poor Man's Advocate, And People's Library*, No. 10 (24 Mar. 1832), p. 78, quoted in Lyon, *Politicians*, p. 142. The reference is to Matthew 18:2.

28. Cavie Richardson, *The Day Dream, or A Letter to King Richard, Containing a Vision of the trial of Mr Factory Longhours, at York Castle* (Leeds, 1832), p. 8, quoted in Lyon, *Politicians*, p. 140.

29. Samuel Roberts, *The Revd. Dr. Pye Smith and the New Poor Law* (London, 1839), p. 11, quoted in Lyon, *Politicians*, p. 187. The references are to Matthew 4:8–9 and Luke 4:5–7.

30. John Rayner Stephens, *The Political Pulpit. Sermons, Feb.–Aug. 1839* (London, 1839). The reference is to Genesis 9:1–17.

31. *Northern Star*, 16 Oct. 1838, quoted in Eileen Yeo, 'Christianity in Chartist Struggle, 1838–1842', *Past & Present*, no. 91, May 1981, p. 112.

Endnotes

32. See, for example, Leviticus 19:9–10, 23:22; Deuteronomy 14:28–9, 15:7–11, 24:20–21.

33. Stephens, *Political Pulpit*, p. 49. For example: Deuteronomy 19:14 reads: 'Thou shalt not remove thy neighbour's landmark, which they of old time have set in thine inheritance.' Deuteronomy 27:17 reads: 'Cursed be he that removeth his neighbour's landmark.' Proverbs 22:28 reads: 'Remove not the ancient landmark, which thy fathers have set.' Proverbs 23:10 reads: 'Remove not the old landmark; and enter not into the fields of the fatherless.' Job 24:2 reads: 'Some remove the landmarks; they violently take away flocks, and feed thereof.'

34. Stephens, *Political Pulpit*, p. 5.

35. *The West Riding Herald*, 18 Mar. 1837, quoted in Lyon, *Politicians*, p. 176.

36. Samuel Roberts, *Chartism! Its Cause and Cure* (Sheffield, 1839), p. 4, quoted in Lyon, *Politicians*, p. 187.

37. 'The people of the land have used oppression, and exercised robbery, and have vexed the poor and needy: yea, they have oppressed the stranger wrongfully. And I sought for a man among them, that should make up the hedge, and stand in the gap before me for the land, that I should not destroy it: but I found none.'

38. Stephens, *Political Pulpit*, p. 16, quoted in Lyon, *Politicians*, p. 183. See Ezekiel 37:1–14.

39. Stephens, *The Political Preacher* (London, 1839), pp. 12–13.

40. *Ashton Chronicle*, 29 Apr. 1848, quoted in Dale A. Johnson, 'Between Evangelicalism and a Social Gospel: The Case of Joseph Rayner Stephens', *Church History*, vol. 42, no. 2, June 1973, p. 237.

41. *Northern Star*, 17 Aug. 1839, quoted in Yeo, 'Christianity', p. 121.

42. Stephens, *Political Pulpit*, p. 63, quoted in Lyon, *Politicians*, p. 184.

43. Quoted in Henry Jephson, *The Platform: Its Rise and Progress* (London, 1892), pp. 215–16.

44. Stephens, *Political Pulpit*, p. 91, quoted in Lyon, *Politicians*, p. 186. Genesis 9:6 reads: 'Whoso sheddeth man's blood, by man shall his blood be shed: for in the image of God made he man.'

45. *Champion*, 10 Nov. 1849, quoted in Johnson, 'Between Evangelicalism', p. 237.

46. Stephens, *Political Pulpit*, p. 61, quoted in Johnson, 'Between Evangelicalism', p. 236.

47. ibid.

48. J.R. Stephens, *Political Pulpit*, pp. 12–13; Stephens, *Political Preacher*, p. 40, quoted in Johnson, 'Between Evangelicalism', p. 235.

49. Stephens, *Political Pulpit*, p. 22, quoted in Johnson, 'Between Evangelicalism', p. 239.

50. Quoted in Yeo, 'Christianity', p. 126.

51. Quoted in Lyon, *Politicians*, p. 193.

52. Henry Solly, *What Christianity Says to the Present Distress* (London, 1842), p. 33.

53. Quoted in Yeo, 'Christianity', p. 110.

54. *Northern Star*, 11 June 1842, quoted in Lyon, *Politicians*, p. 194.

55. Benjamin Parsons, *The Shaking of the Nations and Downfall of Tyranny* (London, 1848), quoted in Lyon, *Politicians*, p. 230.

56. *Northern Liberator*, 7 Sept. 1839, quoted in Yeo, 'Christianity', p. 109.

57. Luke 22:36 was often used on Chartist banners, alongside a text adapted from Lamentations 4:9: 'Better to die by the sword than to perish with hunger.' See Yeo, 'Christianity', p. 113.

58. *Bradford Observer*, 9 May 1839, quoted in Yeo, 'Christianity', p. 123.

59. See Yeo, 'Christianity', p. 122.

60. Proverbs 14:31.

61. Isaiah 3:15.

62. Mark 12;40; John 10;12.

63. 'We have mortgaged our lands, vineyards, and houses, that we might buy corn, because of the dearth . . .'

64. 'Six days shalt thou labour . . .'

65. '. . . ye have eaten up the vineyard; the spoil of the poor is in your houses. What mean ye that ye beat my people to pieces, and grind the faces of the poor? . . .'

66. 'Hear this, O ye that swallow up the needy . . .'

67. 'Jesus said unto him, If thou wilt be perfect, go and sell that thou hast, and give to the poor, and thou shalt have treasure in heaven: and come and follow me.'

68. 'Go to now, ye rich men, weep and howl for your miseries that shall come upon you. Your riches are corrupted, and your garments are motheaten. Your gold and silver is cankered; and the rust of them shall be a witness against you, and shall eat your flesh as it were fire. Ye have reaped treasure together for the last days. Behold, the hire of the labourers who have

reaped down your fields, which is of you kept back by fraud, crieth: and the cries of them which have reaped are entered into the ears of the Lord of sabaoth. Ye have lived in pleasure on the earth, and been wanton; ye have nourished your hearts as in a day of slaughter. Ye have condemned and killed the just; and he doth not resist you.'

69. *Blackburn Standard*, 7 Aug. 1839, quoted in Yeo, 'Christianity', p. 134.

70. *Sheffield Mercury*, 24 Aug. 1839, quoted in Lyon, *Politicians*, p. 213.

71. *Preston Observer*, 17 Aug. 1839, quoted in Yeo, 'Christianity', p. 130.

72. *Sheffield Iris*, 17 Sept. 1839, quoted in Yeo, 'Christianity', p. 136.

73. Quoted in Lyon, *Politicians*, p. 9.

74. Stephens, *Political Pulpit*.

10. 'He meant us to do secular work in His name'

1. Thus Raymond Chapman: 'Its first leaders, devout and compassionate men as they were, had little interest in schemes for social reform and could be charged with concern for ecclesiastic minutiae to the neglect of possible improvements in material conditions.' See *Faith and Revolt: Studies in the Literary Influence of the Oxford Movement* (London: Weidenfeld and Nicolson, 1970), p. 1.

2. J.H. Newman, *The Arians of the Fourth Century* (Rivington, 1833), pp. 276–8.

3. Frederick Oakeley, *Christ manifested to the Faithful through his Church. A sermon [on Col. 2.10]* (Oxford, 1839), p. 10.

4. J.H. Newman, *Parochial and Plain Sermons*, vol. 4, 157, quoted in S.A. Skinner, *Tractarians and the 'Condition of England': The Social and Political Thought of the Oxford Movement* (Oxford, 2000), p. 137.

5. E.B. Pusey, *The Royal Supremacy, not an arbitrary authority but limited by the laws of the church* (Oxford: Parker, 1850), p. 208.

6. Quoted in Skinner, *Tractarians*, p. 118.

7. Favoured texts included Isaiah 10:5; Isaiah 49:22–3; Isaiah 60:3–4, 10, 12, 19; Daniel 2:21: Daniel 4:25; Jeremiah 27:5–7; and Psalm 76:10.

8. Henry Wilberforce, *The Parochial System, An appeal to English Churchmen* (London, 1838), p. 3.

9. Frederick Oakeley, *Christians, the Salt of the Earth* (Oxford and London, 1838), quoted in Skinner, *Tractarians*, p. 113.

10. Skinner, *Tractarians*, p. 15.

11. In which the British government and Prussian king sanctioned a Protestant bishopric in Palestine, thereby angering High churchmen who disliked the high-handed manner of this otherwise unauthorised communion between Churches and were disappointed that so few Anglican bishops protested.

12. In which the Judicial Committee of the Privy Council found for the evangelical George Gorham and against Bishop Philpotts of Exeter, who had refused to institute him on the grounds that he believed only in conditional regeneration at baptism, thereby pronouncing on the doctrine of the Church.

13. Which moved the jurisdiction over wills and marriages from ecclesiastical to civil courts, thereby treating marriage as a contract rather than a sacrament.

14. Which came into force in 1871.

15. After a six-year battle: Bradlaugh had originally won Northampton in 1880 but had been denied his seat in the House of Commons for refusing to take the Oath of Allegiance.

16. E.B. Pusey, *Christianity without the Cross a Corruption of the Gospel of Christ* (Oxford and London, 1875), quoted in Skinner, *Tractarians*, p. 222.

17. F.E. Paget, *The Warden of Berkingholt; or, Rich and Poor* (Oxford, 1843), pp. 67–8.

18. E.B. Pusey, *Parochial Sermons* (Rivington, 1886), vol. 3, p. 145, quoted in Skinner, *Tractarians*, p. 195.

19. H.W. Wilberforce, *The Building of the House of God. A sermon* (Oxford and London, 1839), quoted in Skinner, *Tractarians*, p. 193.

20. Pusey, *Sermons*, quoted in Skinner, *Tractarians*, p. 270.

21. Bosanquet, 'The Age of Unbelief', quoted in Skinner, *Tractarians*, p. 241.

22. E.B. Pusey, *The Minor Prophets* (Oxford: James Parker, 1877), p. 78.

23. R.I. Wilberforce, *Charge to Clergy of East Riding* (1846), quoted in Skinner, *Tractarians*, p. 260.

24. Wilberforce, *East Riding*. Wilberforce published a 548-page tome exploring *The Doctrine of the Incarnation of our Lord Jesus Christ, in its relation to mankind and to the Church* (London, 1848).

25. G. Faber, *Oxford Apostles: A Character Study of the Oxford Movement* (Harmondsworth, 1954), quoted in Skinner, *Tractarians*, p. 262.

26. Thomas Mozley, 'Pews', *British Critic*, 32, 1842, quoted in Skinner, *Tractarians*, p. 169.

27. F.E. Paget, *Milford Malvoisin; or, Pews and Pewholders* (London, 1842) pp. 11, 213–14.

28. The text (minus caps) reads: 'For if there come unto your assembly a man with a gold ring, in goodly apparel, and there come in also a poor man in vile raiment; and ye have respect to him that weareth the gay clothing, and say unto him, Sit thou here in a good place; and say to the poor, Stand thou there, or sit here under my footstool: are ye not then partial in yourselves, and are become judges of evil thoughts? Hearken, my beloved brethren, hath not God chosen the poor of this world rich in faith, and heirs of the kingdom which he hath promised to them that love him? But ye have despised the poor. Do not rich men oppress you, and draw you before the judgment seats?'

29. *British Critic*, quoted in Skinner, *Tractarians*, p. 274.

30. Thomas Mozley, 'Armed Associations for the Protection of Life and Property', *British Critic*, 26, 1839, quoted in Skinner, *Tractarians*, p. 279.

31. F. Oakeley, *The Dignity and Claims of the Christian Poor: Two Sermons* (1840), quoted in Skinner, *Tractarians*, p. 284.

32. Oakeley, *Dignity and Claims*, quoted in Skinner, *Tractarians*, p. 285.

33. The text of the placards is reprinted in E.C. Mather, ed., *Chartism and Society: An Anthology of Documents* (New York: Holmes and Meier, 1980), pp. 283–4.

34. Edward Norman, *The Victorian Christian Socialists* (Cambridge: Cambridge University Press, 1987) p. 35.

35. Charles Kingsley, *Alton Locke: Tailor and Poet: An Autobiography* (Oxford: Oxford University Press, 1983), p. 383.

36. And was therefore disappointed to be seen latterly as the leader of the 'Broad Church' party.

37. *Politics for the People*, 28, pp. 59–60, quoted in Chadwick, *Victorian Church, Vol. 1*, pp. 352–3.

38. F.D. Maurice, *The Kingdom of Christ*, 3 Vols. (London, 1837–8), vol. 2, p. 321.

39. F.D. Maurice, *Reasons for Co-operation: A Lecture delivered at the Office for Promoting Working Men's Associations* (London: John W. Parker, 1851), p. 22.

40. F.D. Maurice, *The Life of Frederick Denison Maurice: Chiefly Told in his own Letters*, 2 Vols. (2nd edn, 1884), I.450–51.

41. F.D. Maurice, *The Doctrine of Sacrifice deduced from the Scriptures. A Series of Sermons* (Cambridge, 1854), pp. 193–4.

42. Indicatively, *Politics for the People* was attacked by the Chartist *Commonwealth* for its clerical tendencies and by the *Oxford Herald* for its democratic tendencies.

43. Letter to Ludlow, 24 Sept. 1852, Maurice, *Life*, II.136–8.

44. F.D. Maurice, *On the Right and Wrong Methods of Supporting Protestantism* (n.p., 1843), p. 10, quoted in K.S. Inglis, *Churches and the Working Classes in Victorian England* (London: Routledge & Paul, 1963), p. 264.

45. Maurice, *Reasons for Co-operation*, p. 23.

46. F.D. Maurice, 'Fraternity', in *Politics*, no.1, 6 May 1848, 3, quoted in Paul Dafydd Jones, 'Jesus Christ and the Transformation of English Society: The "Subversive Conservatism" of Frederick Denison Maurice', *Harvard Theological Review*, vol. 96, no. 2, Apr. 2003, p. 215.

47. The term was coined by an exasperated Ludlow in March 1850.

48. F.D. Maurice, 'An Address to the Clergy, By a Clergyman,' (George Bell, n.d.) p. 7, quoted in Jones, 'Jesus Christ', p. 224.

49. Letter to Ludlow, 24 Sept. 1852, Maurice, *Life*, II.136–8.

50. Maurice, *Reasons for Co-operation*, p. 15.

51. F.D. Maurice, 'A Dialogue Between A. and B., Two Clergymen, On the Doctrine of Circumstances as it Affects Priests and People', *Tracts on Christian Socialism*, no. 7, p . 11., quoted in Jones, 'Jesus Christ', p. 226.

52. F.D. Maurice, *Learning and Working: The Religion of Rome* (Macmillan, 1855), p. vii.

53. And it did: Shaftesbury once remarked of chimney sweeps, 'their guilt is our guilt; we incur it by conniving at it.' Hansard, 18 Feb. 1845, Col. 655, quoted in Turnbull, *Shaftesbury*, p. 212.

54. Charles Kingsley, 'The National Gallery, No. 1', *Politics for the People*, no. 1, 6 May 1848,5. See also 'The National Gallery, No. 2', *Politics for the People*, no. 3, 20 May 1848, 38–41, quoted in Jones, 'Jesus Christ', p. 213.

55. H.P. Hughes, *Ethical Christianity: A Series of Sermons* (1892), p. 18.

56. H.P. Hughes, *Social Christianity* (London: Hodder & Stoughton, 1890), p. 56.

57. H.P. Hughes, *Essential Christianity* (London: Isbister, 1894), p. 172.

58. Hughes, *Social Christianity*, p. 31.

59. H.P. Hughes, *Philanthropy of God* (London: Hodder & Stoughton, 1890), p. 275.

60. In which he was heavily involved; his West London Mission boasted temperance works, penny banks, clothing and provident clubs, a thrift society, soup kitchen, two Dispensaries for the sick, a Labour Bureau for the unemployed, a servants' registry, a crèche, university extension lectures and a Poor Man's Lawyers for free legal advice.

61. Hughes, *Ethical Christianity*, p. 29.

62. Hughes, *Social Christianity*, p. 3, p. viii

63. Hughes, *Philanthropy*, p. 242.

64. Hughes, *Social Christianity*, p. 15.

65. ibid., p. 141.

66. Hughes, *Essential Christianity*, p. 6.

67. Hughes, *Philanthropy*, p. 254.

68. B.F. Westcott, *Christian Aspects of Life* (London: Macmillan, 1897), p. 234.

69. B.F. Westcott, *Social Aspects of Christianity* (London: Macmillan, 1887), p. 86.

70. S.D. Headlam, *Christian Socialism: A Lecture* (Fabian Society, 1907).

71. S.D. Headlam, *The Sure Foundation. An Address given before the Guild of S. Matthew, at the Annual Meeting, 1883* (London: F. Verinder, 1883), p. 6.

72. S.D. Headlam, *The Meaning of the Mass* (London: S.C. Brown, Langham, 1905), p. 72.

73. Headlam, *Christian Socialism*, p. 2.

74. S.D. Headlam, *The Service of Humanity*, p. 11 .

75. Headlam, *Service*, p. 7.

76. Headlam, *Christian Socialism*, p. 7.

77. Headlam, *Service*, p. 58.

78. Headlam, *Sure Foundation*, p. 12.

79. Norman, *Victorian Christian Socialists*, p. 105.

80. Kenneth Morgan, *Keir Hardie: Radical and Socialist* (London: Weidenfield and Nicolson, 1984), p. 9; Bob Holman, *Keir Hardie: Labour's Greatest Hero?* (Lion, 2010).

81. Quoted in Holman, *Keir Hardie*, p. 87.

82. Quoted ibid., p. 199.

83. Quoted ibid.

84. J.K. Hardie, *From Serfdom to Socialism* (1907), p. 37.

85. ibid., p. 38.

86. ibid., p. 36.

87. Quoted in Holman, *Keir Hardie*, p. 85.

88. Thomas Hancock, *Christ and the People: Sermons* (Daldy, 1875), pp. 25–9.

89. Philip Wicksteed, 'What does the Labour Church Stand For?', *Labour Prophet Tracts*, Second Series, no. 1, 1896, p. 3, quoted in Mark Bevir, 'The Labour Church Movement, 1891–1902', *Journal of British Studies*, 38, Apr. 1999, pp. 217–45.

90. Sam Hobson, *Possibilities of the Labour Church* (Cardiff, 1893), pp. 4–5.

91. Quoted in Bevir, 'Labour Church', p. 227.

92. *Labour Prophet*, Jan. 1894, quoted in Bevir, 'Labour Church', p. 240.

93. See Chadwick, *Victorian Church*, II.285.

11. *'The role of the State in Christian Society is to encourage virtue, not to usurp it'*

1. Quoted in Callum Brown, *Religion and Society in Twentieth-Century Britain* (Harlow: Pearson Longman, 2006), p. 106.

2. Gwendolen Stephenson, *Edward Stuart Talbot, 1844–1934* (SPCK, 1936), p. 221.

3. Quoted in G.L. Prestige, *The Life of Charles Gore: A Great Englishman* (Heinemann, 1935), p. 370.

4. Quoted in Michael Burleigh, *Earthly Powers: Religion and Politics in Europe from the Enlightenment to the Great War* (London: HarperCollins, 2005), p. 442.

5. D.S. Cairns, ed., *The Army and Religion* (London: Macmillan, 1919), quoted in Robin Gill, *The Myth of the Empty Church* (London: SPCK, 1993).

6. See J.M. Winter, *Socialism and the Challenge of War: Ideas and Politics in Britain, 1912–1918* (London and Boston: Routledge and Kegan Paul, 1974), pp. 172–5.

7. Church of England, *Christianity and Industrial Problems: being the Report of the Archbishops' Fifth Committee of Inquiry* (SPCK: London, 1918), p. 104.

8. Hilaire Belloc, *The Servile State* (T.N. Foulis: London and Edinburgh, 1912). George Orwell, writing in April 1940, remarked of *The Servile State*: 'It must be about thirty years since Mr Hilaire Belloc . . . foretold with astonishing accuracy the things that are happening now . . . Unfortunately he had no remedy to offer. He could conceive nothing between slavery and a return to small-ownership, which is obviously not going to happen and in fact cannot happen.' See Peter Davidson, ed., *George Orwell: The Complete Works*, vol. 12, no. 604 (London: Secker and Warburg, 1998), pp. 121–7.

9. See Bruce Wollenberg, *Christian Social Thought in Great Britain Between the Wars* (London: University Press of America, 1997), p. 44.

10. R.H. Tawney, *The Acquisitive Society* (Bell, 1921); *Religion and Rise of Capitalism: A Historical Study* (John Murray, 1926); *Equality* (George Allen & Unwin, 1931).

11. R.H. Tawney, *R.H. Tawney's Commonplace Book*, ed. J.M. Winter (London: Cambridge University Press, 1972), quoted in W.H. Greenleaf, *The British Political Tradition, 4 Vols.* (London: Methuen, 1983–7), II.447.

12. Tawney, *Acquisitive Society*, pp. 33–4.

13. ibid., p. 157.

14. Quoted in Paul Addison, 'The Religion of Winston Churchill', in Michael Bentley, ed., *Public and Private Doctrine: Essays in British History Presented to Maurice Cowling* (Cambridge, 1993), p. 239.

15. William Temple, *The Kingdom of God: A Course of Four Lectures Delivered at Cambridge during the Lent Term* (Macmillan, 1912), p. 79.

16. ibid., p. 96.

17. Quoted in John Kent, *William Temple: Church, State, and Society in Britain, 1880–1950* (Cambridge: Cambridge University Press, 1992), p. 125.

18. Quoted ibid., p. 125.

19. These were that every child should find itself 'a member of a family housed with decency and dignity'; every child 'should have the opportunity of an education till years of maturity'; every citizen 'should be secure in possession of such income as will enable him to maintain a home and bring up children'; every citizen 'should have a voice in the conduct of the business or industry which is carried on by means of his labour'; every citizen 'should have sufficient daily [weekly and annual] leisure . . . to enable him to enjoy a full personal life'; and every citizen 'should have

assured liberty in the forms of freedom of worship, of speech, of assembly, and of association for special purposes'. This, according to Temple, was the basis of a Christian social order the aim of which was 'the fullest possible development of individual personality in the widest and deepest possible fellowship' (Temple, *Christianity and Social Order* (Penguin, 1942), pp. 96–7).

20. Correlli Barnett, *The Audit of War: The Illusion and Reality of Britain as a Great Nation* (London: Macmillan, 1986), p. 29.

21. Hugh Cecil, *Natural Instinct the Basis of Social Institutions* (London: Oxford University Press, 1926), p. 6, quoted in W.H. Greanleaf, *The British Political Tradition – Vol. 2: The ideological heritage* (Routledge, 1988), p. 290.

22. Winston S. Churchill, *Blood, Toil, Tears and Sweat: Winston Churchill's Famous Speeches*, ed. David Cannadine (London: Cassell, 1989), p. 282.

23. ibid., p. 334. The biblical reference is to Numbers 35.

24. To the House of Commons, 22 Jan. 1941.

25. Winston S. Churchill, *My Early Life: A Roving Commission* (Thornton Butterworth, 1930), p. 115.

26. John Colville, *The Fringes of Power: Downing Street Diaries, 1939–1945* (London: Hodder and Stoughton, 1985), p. 239.

27. Winston S. Churchill, *The World Crisis* (Thornton Butterworth, 1923), p. 38, quoted in Addison, 'Religion of Winston Churchill', p. 244.

28. Churchill, *Blood*, p. 314. He made similar references to Christian civilisation in his BBC Broadcast, 'The War of the Unknown Warriors', on 14 July 1940, and after the war when speaking in Fulton, Missouri, on 5 March 1946 (on 'The Sinews of Power') and in Zurich on 19 September 1946 (on 'the Tragedy of Europe').

29. *The Times*, 3 Dec. 1934, quoted in Philip Williamson, 'Christian Conservatives and the Totalitarian Challenge, 1933–40', *English Historical Review*, vol. 115, no. 462, June 2000, p. 617.

30. *New York Times*, 17 Aug. 1939, quoted in Williamson, 'Christian Conservatives', p. 617.

31. Quoted in Ian McLaine, *Ministry of Morale: Home Front Morale and the Ministry of Information in World War II* (London: Allen and Unwin, 1979), p. 151.

32. Quoted in Adrian Hastings, *A History of English Christianity, 1920–2000* (London: SCM Press, 2001), p. 348.

Endnotes

33. *Fortnightly Review*, cxlvi (1939), 638–43, quoted in Andrew Chandler, 'The Church of England and the Obliteration Bombing of Germany in the Second World War', *English Historical Review*, vol. 108, no. 429, Oct. 1993, p. 925.

34. *The Times*, 17 Apr. 1941, quoted in Chandler, 'Obliteration Bombing', p. 929.

35. Quoted in Chandler, 'Obliteration Bombing', p. 938.

36. Hansard, vol. cxxx, 739–46, 9 Feb. 1944, quoted in Chandler, 'Obliteration Bombing', p. 939.

37. Quoted in Keith Robbins, 'Britain, 1940 and "Christian Civilisation"', in Derek Beales and Geoffrey Best, eds., *History, Society and the Churches: Essays in Honour of Owen Chadwick* (Cambridge: Cambridge University Press, 1985), p. 286.

38. 'Notes on the Way', *Time and Tide*, 30 Mar. and 6 Apr. 1940, in *George Orwell: The Complete Works*, vol. 12, no. 604, pp. 121–7.

39. Coined, it should be noted, in specific contrast to the 'power state' of contemporary totalitarianism, rather than in direct anticipation, still less delineation, of the Beveridge plan. I am grateful to Malcolm Brown for this point and also for his helpful critical reading of this entire chapter.

40. The debate is oddly similar to the one about whether the English Reformation was a near inevitability, given the corrupt and much despised nature of later medieval Catholicism (as English historians used to insist), or whether it was a widely resented programme of change driven through by a small number of atypical but highly influential converts (as several contemporary English historians, most notably Eamon Duffy, have argued.) In the case of 1960s legislation, the evidence points in both directions. Some legislation was passed by the Anglican-flavoured Macmillan government rather than the secular-flavoured Wilson one; some measures, such as ending theatre censorship or decriminalising homosexual acts, had general public support, whereas others, in particular the suspension and abolition of capital punishment, did not.

41. *Rayden and Jackson on Divorce and Family Matters*, 18th edn.

42. Andrew Holden, *Makers and Manners: Politics and Morality in Postwar Britain* (London: Politico's, 2004), p. 27.

43. Matthew 19:8.

44. Genesis 9:6.

45. See Holden, *Makers*, pp. 210–15.

Endnotes

46. Quoted ibid., p. 211.

47. Quoted ibid., p. 152.

48. Church of England Moral Welfare Council, *The Problem of Homosexuality* (Church Information Board, London, 1952).

49. *Putting Asunder: A Divorce Law for Contemporary Society* (London: SPCK, 1966), pp. 10, 37. Its further recommendation that courts should enquire as to whether marriages had reached a point of irretrievable breakdown was dismissed as being too difficult and too paternalistic.

50. Interview for *Sunday Times*, 22 Feb. 1983. See also Hugo Young, *One of Us: A Biography of Margaret Thatcher* (London: Pan Books, 1993), pp. 420, 426.

51. Quoted in Graeme Smith, 'Margaret Thatcher's Christian Faith: A Case Study in Political Theology', *Journal of Religious Ethics*, vol. 35.2, 2007, p. 233.

52. Margaret Thatcher, *The Downing Street Years* (London: HarperCollins, 1993), p. 509.

53. Margaret Thatcher, 'Speech to Party Conference', 10 Oct. 1975.

54. Margaret Thatcher, *The Path to Power* (London: HarperCollins, 1995), pp. 305–6.

55. Margaret Thatcher, 'Scottish Party Conference', 1988; *Path to Power*, p. 554; 'Speech to Conservative Central Council', 1975.

56. Margaret Thatcher, 'Speech to General Assembly of the Church of Scotland', 21 May 1988.

57. Margaret Thatcher, '"I Believe": A Speech on Christianity and Politics at St Lawrence Jewry', 31 Mar. 1978.

58. ibid.

59. ibid.

60. *Catholic Herald*, 22 Dec. 1978.

61. Thatcher, 'St Lawrence Jewry'.

62. Thatcher, 'General Assembly'.

63. The anecdote is recounted in Humphrys' book *Devil's Advocate* (Arrow Books, 2000), pp. 261–2. It is probably worth noting that Humphrys' instincts for opening with the question, 'Prime Minister, what is the essence of Christianity?' – he had expected to trick her into 'mumbl[ing] something about morality or love' – were right. The imperative to choose plays a relatively small role in the Bible (and is more clearly pronounced in the Old Testament (e.g. Deut. 30:11–20)

than in the New) compared, for instance, to the imperative to love. Interestingly Humphrys was himself persuaded by her answer, going on to write: 'too late I realised exactly what she meant and, dammit, she was right. The whole point of Christianity is that you have a choice between doing good and doing evil. If you end up in Heaven, that's because you made the right choice; if you end up in Hell, it's your fault.' The entire incident is fascinating not simply for the light it sheds on Thatcher's Christianity but also for the light it sheds on popular conceptions of what Christianity is.

64. Luke 7:36–8: 'remember the woman with the alabaster jar of ointment' and Matthew 22:21: 'the things that are Caesar's'.

65. 2 Thessalonians 3:10: 'If a man will not work he shall not eat' and 1 Timothy 5.8: 'anyone who neglects to provide for his own house . . . is "worse than an infidel".'

66. 1 Timothy 6:10: 'it is not the creation of wealth that is wrong but love of money for its own sake.'

67. Leviticus 19:18: 'love our neighbour "as ourselves"'.

68. Exodus 20:17: 'the Tenth Commandment – Thou shalt not covet – recognises that making money and owning things could become selfish activities.'

69. 'Abundance rather than poverty has a legitimacy which derives from the very nature of Creation.'

70. 'When I survey the wondrous Cross' and 'I vow to thee my country'.

71. Thatcher 'was spitting blood' according to Denis Thatcher, quoted in Monica Furlong, *C of E: The State It's In* (London: Hodder & Stoughton, 2000), p. 129.

72. Quoted in Andrew Partington, *Church and State: The Contribution of the Church of England Bishops to the House of Lords during the Thatcher Years* (Milton Keynes: Paternoster, 2006), p. 41.

73. In full and abridged versions.

74. Church of England, *Faith in the City: A Call for Action by Church and Nation* (London: Church House Publishing, 1985), 3.34. For an analysis see Charles Carter, 'Faith in the City, but not in the Government', *Policy Studies*, 6. 4, 1986.

75. *Faith in the City*, 3.16.

76. 'Doctrine is formulated, not in the abstract, but to settle questions already in dispute; theological commissions are set up, not to create systems, but

to respond to particular issues. So it has been in our own work,' the report contended. 'It would be highly misleading if we were to propose a "theology of the city" that claimed to be appropriate to such a wide variety of situations. An authentic theology can arise only as a response to each particular circumstance' (*Faith in the City*, 3.44).

77. Partington, *Church and State*, p. 248.
78. *Sunday Times*, 17 July 1994.
79. The one book so far published that purports to answer this question, John Burton's *We Don't do God: Blair's Religious Belief and its Consequences* (Continuum, 2009) fails to shed anything but the weakest light on the issue. Blair's own autobiography is similarly opaque.
80. 'Practising for Power', *Third Way* , Oct. 1993.
81. The ellipsis in the quotation above hides the suggestive phrase, 'where my political and personal beliefs coincide completely'.
82. Quoted in Burton, *We Don't do God*, p. xix.
83. Alastair Campbell, *The Blair Years: The Alastair Campbell Diaries* (London: Hutchinson, 2007), pp. 111–12.
84. The interview transcript can be found at http://news.bbc.co.uk/1/hi/uk_politics/4773874.stm
85. Rumsfeld's briefers apparently placed verses alongside apposite photographs, such as 'It is God's will that by doing good you should silence the ignorant talk of foolish men' (1 Pet. 2:15) beside Saddam Hussein; 'Their arrows are sharp, all their bows are strung; their horses' hoofs seem like flint, their chariot wheels are like a whirlwind' (Isa. 5:28) beside a photo of US soldiers at prayer; and 'Open the gates that the righteous nation may enter, the nation that keeps faith' (Isa. 26:2) alongside a picture of US tanks rolling into Baghdad underneath Saddam Hussein's Victory Arch (all quotes from New International Version). See Stephen Moss, 'Donald Rumsfeld said "Let there be Biblical quotes" – and it was so,' *Guardian*, 21 May 2009.
86. 'George W. Bush et le Code Ezéchiel', *Politique*, Sept. 2007: http://www2.unil.ch/unicom/allez_savoir/as39/pages/pdf/4_Gog_Magog.pdf
87. Julian Baggini, 'The Rise, Fall and Rise Again of Secularism', *Public Policy Review*, vol. 12, issue 4, Jan.–Mar. 2006, p. 202.
88. For Radical Orthodoxy see Simon Oliver, *Radical Orthodoxy: An Introduction* (London: Routledge, 2010); John Milbank and Simon Oliver, eds., *The Radical Orthodoxy Reader* (London: Routledge, 2009).

89. Chris Cook, 'Christian Tories Rewrite Party Doctrine', *Financial Times*, 12 Feb. 2010.

90. Mark Bevir, 'New Labour: A Study in Ideology', *British Journal of Politics and International Relations*, vol. 2, no. 3, 2000, pp. 277–301.

91. See Paul Bickley, *The Bible and Political Speech Making: A Case Study* (M.Litt. Thesis, University of St Andrews, 2009).

92. Malcolm Chase, 'From Millennium to Anniversary: The Concept of Jubilee in Late Eighteenth- and Nineteenth-Century England', *Past & Present*, no. 129, Nov. 1990), pp. 132–47.

93. For example, 'Empress and Queen – Whose Rule Extends', *Jubilee Hymns, 1887* (London: Society for the Propagation of the Gospel, 1887).

94. Leviticus 25:10.

95. Quoted in Chase, 'From Millennium to Anniversary', p. 138.

Postscript

1. Nicholas Lash, 'Where Does *The God Delusion* Come From?' New Blackfriars, vol. 88, issue 1017, Sept. 2007, pp. 507–21.

2. Among which Lash includes 'its ignorance of the grammar of "God" and of "belief in God"; the crudeness of its account of how texts are best read; its lack of interest in ethics'.

3. In Lash's defence he does at one point refer to Dawkins's 'preoccupation with contemporary American fundamentalism' (Lash, *God Delusion*, p. 513).

4. See Madeleine Albright, *The Mighty and the Almighty* (Macmillan, 2006), pp. 153–62. Albright adds a note that Bush's oft-quoted statement, 'I believe God wants me to be President,' was, according to Richard Land of the Southern Baptist Convention, incomplete. He actually said, 'I believe God wants me to be President, but if that doesn't happen, that's OK.'

5. Waldron, *Locke*, p. 20.

6. See Jim Wallis, *God's Politics: Why the American Right Gets it Wrong and the Left Doesn't Get It* (Lion Hudson, 2006), and *Seven Ways to Change the World: Reviving Faith and Politics* (Lion Hudson, 2008), and also the research from the Pew Forum on Religion and Public Life: www.pewforum.org

7. Edmund Waller, *Speech . . . Concerning Episcopacie* (1641), p. 6, quoted in Hill, *English Bible*, p. 227.

8. See Eric Kaufman, *Shall the Religious Inherit the Earth?* (Profile Books, 2010) pp. 158–209.

9. For a colourful obituary see Rodney Stark, 'Secularization, R.I.P.', *Sociology of Religion*, 60 (3), 1999, pp. 249–73.

10. See John Micklethwait and Adrian Wooldridge, *God is Back: How the Global Rise of Faith is Changing the World* (Allen Lane, 2009).

11. Interview with author; see www.theosthinktank,co.uk and also Michael Sandel, *Justice: What's the Right Thing to Do* (Penguin, 2009).

12. See Denis Sewell, *The Political Gene* (Picador, 2009); Denis R. Alexander and Ronald L. Numbers, eds., *Biology and Ideology – From Descartes to Dawkins* (Chicago University Press, 2010). An example of the idea that we need more rationality to settle such debates was given by Evan Harris, former MP for Oxford West and Abingdon, who asked Michael Sandel after one of his Reith Lectures, 'Shouldn't we be arguing that we should be bringing evidence into the moral arguments where appropriate, not bring[ing] morality in when it's already there on both sides?'

13. Waldron, *Locke*, p. 238.

14. A reasonably typical example of this was *Guardian* columnist Jackie Ashley's contribution to the heated debate on Catholic influence on 'life' issues in parliament: 'If any MP really thinks their personal religious views take precedence over everything else then they should leave the House of Commons. Their place is in church, mosque, synagogue or temple. Parliament is the place for compromises, for negotiations in a secular sphere under the general overhead light of the liberal tradition. So liberalism is privileged, is it? Yes. For without it, none of these religions . . . would have such an easy time. Cardinals, come to terms with the society we live in' (*Guardian*, 4 June 2007).

15. See Karen Armstrong, *The Battle for God: Fundamentalism in Judaism, Christianity and Islam* (HarperCollins, 2001).

16. On the nature of religious participation in public debate see Nigel Biggar and Linda Hogan, eds., *Religious Voices in Public Places* (Oxford: Oxford University Press, 2010).

17. Darwin's *Origin of Species*, Marx's *Das Kapital*, Plato's *Republic*, Paine's *Rights of Man* and the *Qur'an*.

18. 'Battle of the Books', *New Statesman*, 31 July 2006. http://www.newstatesman.com/200607310052 I am grateful to John Coffey for drawing my attention to this review.

19. Addison, 'Religion of Winston Churchill', p. 250.
20. Barack Obama, *The Audacity of Hope* (Canongate, 2007), p. 39.
21. *George Orwell: The Complete Works*, vol. 12, no. 604, pp. 121–7.
22. For an excoriating analysis of this see Phillip Blond, *Red Tory: How Left and Right have Broken Britain and How we can Fix It* (Faber, 2010).
23. Waldron, *Locke*, p. 13.
24. Nicholas Wolterstorff, *Justice: Rights and Wrongs* (Princeton University Press, 2008).
25. ibid., p. 333.
26. ibid., p. 136.
27. ibid., p. 352.
28. Thus, the secularist philosopher Jürgen Habermas remarked in an interview in 1999: 'Egalitarian universalism, from which sprang the ideas of freedom and social solidarity, of an autonomous conduct of life and emancipation, of the individual morality of conscience, human rights and democracy, is the direct heir of the Judaic ethic of justice and the Christian ethic of love. This legacy, substantially unchanged, has been the object of continual critical appropriation and reinterpretation. To this day, there is no alternative to it. And in light of the current challenges of a postnational constellation, we continue to draw on the substance of this heritage. Everything else is just idle postmodern talk.' See Jürgen Habermas, *Time of Transitions* (Polity Press, 2006), pp. 150–51.

Index

Numerals in **bold** refer to illustrations